The Adventures of Ferdinand Count Fathom

by
Tobias Smollett

The Adventures of Ferdinand Count Fathom
by Tobias Smollett

Copyright © 2023

All Rights reserved.

No part of this publication may be reproduced, stored in a retrieval system, or transmitted in any form or by any means, electronic, mechanical, photocopying or Otherwise, without the written permission of the publisher.
The author/editor asserts the moral right to be identified as the author/editor of this work.

ISBN: 978-93-58018-88-2

Published by
DOUBLE 9 BOOKS
2/13-B, Ansari Road
Daryaganj, New Delhi – 110002
info@double9books.com
www.double9books.com
Tel. 011-40042856

This book is under public domain

ABOUT THE AUTHOR

Tobias Smollett was a Scottish novelist, poet, and journalist who was born in 1721 in Dalquhurn, Scotland. He studied medicine in Glasgow and worked as a surgeon's mate in the Royal Navy, an experience that inspired his writing in later years. Smollett's first published work was "The Regicide," a play that was staged in 1749. He went on to write a number of novels, including "The Adventures of Roderick Random" (1748), "The Adventures of Peregrine Pickle" (1751), and "The Expedition of Humphry Clinker" (1771), all of which were popular and influential in their time. In addition to his literary work, Smollett was a journalist and editor, and he wrote political and social commentary for a number of newspapers and magazines. He was also a translator, and he translated a number of works from French and Italian into English. Smollett was known for his satirical and humorous writing style, and his works often reflected his experiences in the military and his observations of society. He died in Italy in 1771 at the age of 50, leaving behind a legacy as one of the most significant writers of the 18th century.

CONTENTS

INTRODUCTION 13

PART I.
TO DOCTOR 18

CHAPTER ONE.
SOME SAGE OBSERVATIONS THAT NATURALLY
INTRODUCE OUR IMPORTANT HISTORY 22

CHAPTER TWO.
A SUPERFICIAL VIEW OF OUR HERO'S INFANCY 26

CHAPTER THREE.
HE IS INITIATED IN A MILITARY LIFE,
AND HAS THE GOOD FORTUNE TO ACQUIRE
A GENEROUS PATRON. 29

CHAPTER FOUR.
HIS MOTHER'S PROWESS AND DEATH; TOGETHER
WITH SOME INSTANCES OF HIS OWN SAGACITY 32

CHAPTER FIVE.
A BRIEF DETAIL OF HIS EDUCATION. 36

CHAPTER SIX.
HE MEDITATES SCHEMES OF IMPORTANCE 41

CHAPTER SEVEN.
ENGAGES IN PARTNERSHIP WITH A FEMALE
ASSOCIATE, IN ORDER TO PUT HIS TALENTS IN ACTION 45

CHAPTER EIGHT.
THEIR FIRST ATTEMPT; WITH A DIGRESSION
WHICH SOME READERS MAY THINK IMPERTINENT. 49

CHAPTER NINE.
    THE CONFEDERATES CHANGE THEIR BATTERY, AND ACHIEVE A REMARKABLE ADVENTURE. 53

CHAPTER TEN.
    THEY PROCEED TO LEVY CONTRIBUTIONS WITH GREAT SUCCESS, UNTIL OUR HERO SETS OUT WITH THE YOUNG COUNT FOR VIENNA, WHERE HE ENTERS INTO LEAGUE WITH ANOTHER ADVENTURER. 56

CHAPTER ELEVEN.
    FATHOM MAKES VARIOUS EFFORTS IN THE WORLD OF GALLANTRY. 60

CHAPTER TWELVE.
    HE EFFECTS A LODGMENT IN THE HOUSE OF A RICH JEWELLER. 63

CHAPTER THIRTEEN.
    HE IS EXPOSED TO A MOST PERILOUS INCIDENT IN THE COURSE OF HIS INTRIGUE WITH THE DAUGHTER. 67

CHAPTER FOURTEEN.
    HE IS REDUCED TO A DREADFUL DILEMMA, IN CONSEQUENCE OF AN ASSIGNATION WITH THE WIFE. 71

CHAPTER FIFTEEN.
    BUT AT LENGTH SUCCEEDS IN HIS ATTEMPT UPON BOTH. 74

CHAPTER SIXTEEN.
    HIS SUCCESS BEGETS A BLIND SECURITY, BY WHICH HE IS ONCE AGAIN WELL-NIGH ENTRAPPED IN HIS DULCINEA'S APARTMENT. 79

CHAPTER SEVENTEEN.
    THE STEP-DAME'S SUSPICIONS BEING AWAKENED, SHE LAYS A SNARE FOR OUR ADVENTURER, FROM WHICH HE IS DELIVERED BY THE INTERPOSITION OF HIS GOOD GENIUS. 84

CHAPTER EIGHTEEN.
    OUR HERO DEPARTS FROM VIENNA, AND QUITS THE DOMAIN OF VENUS FOR THE ROUGH FIELD OF MARS. 90

CHAPTER NINETEEN.
    HE PUTS HIMSELF UNDER THE GUIDANCE OF HIS ASSOCIATE, AND STUMBLES UPON THE FRENCH CAMP, WHERE HE FINISHES HIS MILITARY CAREER. 94

CHAPTER TWENTY.
    HE PREPARES A STRATAGEM BUT FINDS HIMSELF COUNTERMINED—PROCEEDS ON HIS JOURNEY, AND IS OVERTAKEN BY A TERRIBLE TEMPEST. 99

CHAPTER TWENTY-ONE.
    HE FALLS UPON SCYLLA, SEEKING TO AVOID CHARYBDIS. 104

CHAPTER TWENTY-TWO.
    HE ARRIVES AT PARIS, AND IS PLEASED WITH HIS RECEPTION. 108

CHAPTER TWENTY-THREE.
    ACQUITS HIMSELF WITH ADDRESS IN A NOCTURNAL RIOT. 112

CHAPTER TWENTY-FOUR.
    HE OVERLOOKS THE ADVANCES OF HIS FRIENDS, AND SMARTS SEVERELY FOR HIS NEGLECT. 119

CHAPTER TWENTY-FIVE.
    HE BEARS HIS FATE LIKE A PHILOSOPHER; AND CONTRACTS ACQUAINTANCE WITH A VERY REMARKABLE PERSONAGE. 126

CHAPTER TWENTY-SIX.
    THE HISTORY OF THE NOBLE CASTILIAN. 130

CHAPTER TWENTY-SEVEN.
A FLAGRANT INSTANCE OF FATHOM'S VIRTUE, IN THE MANNER OF HIS RETREAT TO ENGLAND. 145

CHAPTER TWENTY-EIGHT.
SOME ACCOUNT OF HIS FELLOW-TRAVELLERS. 149

CHAPTER TWENTY-NINE.
ANOTHER PROVIDENTIAL DELIVERANCE FROM THE EFFECTS OF THE SMUGGLER'S INGENIOUS CONJECTURE. 152

CHAPTER THIRTY.
THE SINGULAR MANNER OF FATHOM'S ATTACK AND TRIUMPH OVER THE VIRTUE OF THE FAIR ELENOR. 158

CHAPTER THIRTY-ONE.
HE BY ACCIDENT ENCOUNTERS HIS OLD FRIEND, WITH WHOM HE HOLDS A CONFERENCE, AND RENEWS A TREATY. 162

CHAPTER THIRTY-TWO.
HE APPEARS IN THE GREAT WORLD WITH UNIVERSAL APPLAUSE AND ADMIRATION. 167

CHAPTER THIRTY-THREE.
HE ATTRACTS THE ENVY AND ILL OFFICES OF THE MINOR KNIGHTS OF HIS OWN ORDER, OVER WHOM HE OBTAINS A COMPLETE VICTORY. 172

CHAPTER THIRTY-FOUR.
HE PERFORMS ANOTHER EXPLOIT, THAT CONVEYS A TRUE IDEA OF HIS GRATITUDE AND HONOUR. 177

CHAPTER THIRTY-FIVE.
HE REPAIRS TO BRISTOL SPRING, WHERE HE REIGNS PARAMOUNT DURING THE WHOLE SEASON. 185

CHAPTER THIRTY-SIX.
HE IS SMITTEN WITH THE CHARMS OF A FEMALE ADVENTURER, WHOSE ALLUREMENTS SUBJECT HIM TO A NEW VICISSITUDE OF FORTUNE. 188

CHAPTER THIRTY-SEVEN.
    FRESH CAUSE FOR EXERTING HIS EQUANIMITY
    AND FORTITUDE. 192

CHAPTER THIRTY-EIGHT.
    THE BITER IS BIT. 198

    BY TOBIAS SMOLLETT 202

PART II.

CHAPTER THIRTY-NINE.
    OUR ADVENTURER IS MADE ACQUAINTED
    WITH A NEW SCENE OF LIFE. 203

CHAPTER FORTY.
    HE CONTEMPLATES MAJESTY AND ITS
    SATELLITES IN ECLIPSE. 209

CHAPTER FORTY-ONE.
    ONE QUARREL IS COMPROMISED, AND
    ANOTHER DECIDED BY UNUSUAL ARMS. 213

CHAPTER FORTY-TWO.
    AN UNEXPECTED RENCONTRE, AND
    A HAPPY REVOLUTION IN THE AFFAIRS
    OF OUR ADVENTURER. 218

CHAPTER FORTY-THREE.
    FATHOM JUSTIFIES THE PROVERB,
    "WHAT'S BRED IN THE BONE WILL NEVER
    COME OUT OF THE FLESH." 223

CHAPTER FORTY-FOUR.
    ANECDOTES OF POVERTY, AND EXPERIMENTS
    FOR THE BENEFIT OF THOSE WHOM IT
    MAY CONCERN. 226

CHAPTER FORTY-FIVE.
    RENALDO'S DISTRESS DEEPENS, AND
    FATHOM'S PLOT THICKENS. 232

CHAPTER FORTY-SIX.
OUR ADVENTURER BECOMES ABSOLUTE IN HIS POWER OVER THE PASSIONS OF HIS FRIEND, AND EFFECTS ONE HALF OF HIS AIM. 237

CHAPTER FORTY-SEVEN.
THE ART OF BORROWING FURTHER EXPLAINED, AND AN ACCOUNT OF A STRANGE PHENOMENON. 247

CHAPTER FORTY-EIGHT.
COUNT FATHOM UNMASKS HIS BATTERY; IS REPULSED; AND VARIES HIS OPERATIONS WITHOUT EFFECT. 254

CHAPTER FORTY-NINE.
MONIMIA'S HONOUR IS PROTECTED BY THE INTERPOSITION OF HEAVEN. 259

CHAPTER FIFTY.
FATHOM SHIFTS THE SCENE, AND APPEARS IN A NEW CHARACTER. 266

CHAPTER FIFTY-ONE.
TRIUMPHS OVER A MEDICAL RIVAL. 273

CHAPTER FIFTY-TWO.
REPAIRS TO THE METROPOLIS, AND ENROLS HIMSELF AMONG THE SONS OF PAEAN. 280

CHAPTER FIFTY-THREE.
ACQUIRES EMPLOYMENT IN CONSEQUENCE OF A LUCKY MISCARRIAGE. 285

CHAPTER FIFTY-FOUR.
HIS ECLIPSE, AND GRADUAL DECLINATION. 290

CHAPTER FIFTY-FIVE.
AFTER DIVERS UNSUCCESSFUL EFFORTS, HE HAS RECOURSE TO THE MATRIMONIAL NOOSE. 295

CHAPTER FIFTY-SIX.
IN WHICH HIS FORTUNE IS EFFECTUALLY STRANGLED. 302

CHAPTER FIFTY-SEVEN.
FATHOM BEING SAFELY HOUSED, THE READER
IS ENTERTAINED WITH A RETROSPECT. 306

CHAPTER FIFTY-EIGHT.
RENALDO ABRIDGES THE PROCEEDINGS AT LAW,
AND APPROVES HIMSELF THE SON OF HIS FATHER. 311

CHAPTER FIFTY-NINE.
HE IS THE MESSENGER OF HAPPINESS TO
HIS SISTER, WHO REMOVES THE FILM WHICH
HAD LONG OBSTRUCTED HIS PENETRATION,
WITH REGARD TO COUNT FATHOM. 317

CHAPTER SIXTY.
HE RECOMPENSES THE ATTACHMENT OF
HIS FRIEND; AND RECEIVES A LETTER THAT
REDUCES HIM TO THE VERGE OF DEATH
AND DISTRACTION. 323

CHAPTER SIXTY-ONE.
RENALDO MEETS WITH A LIVING MONUMENT
OF JUSTICE, AND ENCOUNTERS A PERSONAGE
OF SOME NOTE IN THESE MEMOIRS. 331

CHAPTER SIXTY-TWO.
HIS RETURN TO ENGLAND, AND MIDNIGHT
PILGRIMAGE TO MONIMIA'S TOMB. 337

CHAPTER SIXTY-THREE.
HE RENEWS THE RITES OF SORROW,
AND IS ENTRANCED. 345

CHAPTER SIXTY-FOUR.
THE MYSTERY UNFOLDED—ANOTHER
RECOGNITION, WHICH, IT IS TO BE HOPED,
THE READER COULD NOT FORESEE... 352

CHAPTER SIXTY-FIVE.
A RETROSPECTIVE LINK, NECESSARY FOR
THE CONCATENATION OF THESE MEMOIRS. 360

CHAPTER SIXTY-SIX.
THE HISTORY DRAWS NEAR A PERIOD.. 367

CHAPTER SIXTY-SEVEN.
THE LONGEST AND THE LAST. 377

INTRODUCTION

The Adventures of Ferdinand Count Fathom, Smollett's third novel, was given to the world in 1753. Lady Mary Wortley Montagu, writing to her daughter, the Countess of Bute, over a year later [January 1st, 1755], remarked that "my friend Smollett . . . has certainly a talent for invention, though I think it flags a little in his last work." Lady Mary was both right and wrong. The inventive power which we commonly think of as Smollett's was the ability to work over his own experience into realistic fiction. Of this, Ferdinand Count Fathom shows comparatively little. It shows relatively little, too, of Smollett's vigorous personality, which in his earlier works was present to give life and interest to almost every chapter, were it to describe a street brawl, a ludicrous situation, a whimsical character, or with venomous prejudice to gibbet some enemy. This individuality—the peculiar spirit of the author which can be felt rather than described—is present in the dedication of Fathom to Doctor ———, who is no other than Smollett himself, and a candid revelation of his character, by the way, this dedication contains. It is present, too, in the opening chapters, which show, likewise, in the picture of Fathom's mother, something of the author's peculiar "talent for invention." Subsequently, however, there is no denying that the Smollett invention and the Smollett spirit both flag. And yet, in a way, Fathom displays more invention than any of the author's novels; it is based far less than any other on personal experience. Unfortunately such thoroughgoing invention was not suited to Smollett's genius. The result is, that while uninteresting as a novel of contemporary manners, Fathom has an interest of its own in that it reveals a new side of its author. We think of Smollett, generally, as a rambling storyteller, a rational, unromantic man of the world, who fills his pages with his own oddly-metamorphosed acquaintances and experiences. The Smollett of Count Fathom, on the contrary, is rather a forerunner of the romantic school, who has created a tolerably organic tale of adventure out of his own brain. Though this is notably less readable than the author's earlier works, still the wonder is that when the man is so far "off his beat," he should yet know so well how to meet the strange conditions which confront him. To one whose idea of Smollett's genius is formed entirely by Random and Pickle and Humphry Clinker, Ferdinand Count Fathom will offer many surprises.

The first of these is the comparative lifelessness of the book. True, here again are action and incident galore, but generally unaccompanied by that rough Georgian hurly-burly, common in Smollett, which is so interesting to contemplate from a comfortable distance, and which goes so far towards making his fiction seem real. Nor are the characters, for the most part, life-like enough to be interesting. There is an apparent exception, to be sure, in the hero's mother, already mentioned, the hardened camp-follower, whom we confidently expect to become vitalised after the savage fashion of Smollett's characters. But, alas! we have no chance to learn the lady's style of conversation, for the few words that come from her lips are but partially characteristic; we have only too little chance to learn her manners and customs. In the fourth chapter, while she is making sure with her dagger that all those on the field of battle whom she wishes to rifle are really dead, an officer of the hussars, who has been watching her lucrative progress, unfeelingly puts a brace of bullets into the lady's brain, just as she raises her hand to smite him to the heart. Perhaps it is as well that she is thus removed before our disappointment at the non-fulfilment of her promise becomes poignant. So far as we may judge from the other personages of Count Fathom, even this interesting Amazon would sooner or later have turned into a wooden figure, with a label giving the necessary information as to her character.

Such certainly is her son, Fathom, the hero of the book. Because he is placarded, "Shrewd villain of monstrous inhumanity," we are fain to accept him for what his creator intended; but seldom in word or deed is he a convincingly real villain. His friend and foil, the noble young Count de Melvil, is no more alive than he; and equally wooden are Joshua, the high-minded, saint-like Jew, and that tedious, foolish Don Diego. Neither is the heroine alive, the peerless Monimia, but then, in her case, want of vitality is not surprising; the presence of it would amaze us. If she were a woman throbbing with life, she would be different from Smollett's other heroines. The "second lady" of the melodrama, Mademoiselle de Melvil, though by no means vivified, is yet more real than her sister-in-law.

The fact that they are mostly inanimate figures is not the only surprise given us by the personages of Count Fathom. It is a surprise to find few of them strikingly whimsical; it is a surprise to find them in some cases far more distinctly conceived than any of the people in Roderick Random or Peregrine Pickle. In the second of these, we saw Smollett beginning to understand the use of incident to indicate consistent development of character. In Count Fathom, he seems fully to understand this principle of art, though he has not learned to apply it successfully. And so, in spite of an excellent conception, Fathom, as I have said, is unreal. After all his villainies, which he perpetrates without any apparent qualms of conscience, it is incredible that he should honestly repent of his crimes. We are much inclined to doubt when we read that "his vice and ambition was now quite mortified within him," the subsequent testimony of Matthew Bramble, Esq., in Humphry Clinker, to the contrary, notwithstanding. Yet Fathom up to this point is consistently drawn, and drawn for a purpose:—

to show that cold-blooded roguery, though successful for a while, will come to grief in the end. To heighten the effect of his scoundrel, Smollett develops parallel with him the virtuous Count de Melvil. The author's scheme of thus using one character as the foil of another, though not conspicuous for its originality, shows a decided advance in the theory of constructive technique. Only, as I have said, Smollett's execution is now defective.

"But," one will naturally ask, "if Fathom lacks the amusing, and not infrequently stimulating, hurly-burly of Smollett's former novels; if its characters, though well-conceived, are seldom divertingly fantastic and never thoroughly animate; what makes the book interesting?" The surprise will be greater than ever when the answer is given that, to a large extent, the plot makes Fathom interesting. Yes, Smollett, hitherto indifferent to structure, has here written a story in which the plot itself, often clumsy though it may be, engages a reader's attention. One actually wants to know whether the young Count is ever going to receive consolation for his sorrows and inflict justice on his basely ungrateful pensioner. And when, finally, all turns out as it should, one is amazed to find how many of the people in the book have helped towards the designed conclusion. Not all of them, indeed, nor all of the adventures, are indispensable, but it is manifest at the end that much, which, for the time, most readers think irrelevant—such as Don Diego's history—is, after all, essential.

It has already been said that in Count Fathom Smollett appears to some extent as a romanticist, and this is another fact which lends interest to the book. That he had a powerful imagination is not a surprise. Any one versed in Smollett has already seen it in the remarkable situations which he has put before us in his earlier works. These do not indicate, however, that Smollett possessed the imagination which could excite romantic interest; for in Roderick Random and in Peregrine Pickle, the wonderful situations serve chiefly to amuse. In Fathom, however, there are some designed to excite horror; and one, at least, is eminently successful. The hero's night in the wood between Bar-le-duc and Chalons was no doubt more blood-curdling to our eighteenth-century ancestors than it is to us, who have become acquainted with scores of similar situations in the small number of exciting romances which belong to literature, and in the greater number which do not. Still, even to-day, a reader, with his taste jaded by trashy novels, will be conscious of Smollett's power, and of several thrills, likewise, as he reads about Fathom's experience in the loft in which the beldame locks him to pass the night.

This situation is melodramatic rather than romantic, as the word is used technically in application to eighteenth and nineteenth-century literature. There is no little in Fathom, however, which is genuinely romantic in the latter sense. Such is the imprisonment of the Countess in the castle-tower, whence she waves her handkerchief to the young Count, her son and would-be rescuer.

And especially so is the scene in the church, when Renaldo (the very name is romantic) visits at midnight the supposed grave of his lady-love. While he was waiting for the sexton to open the door, his "soul . . . was wound up to the highest pitch of enthusiastic sorrow. The uncommon darkness, . . . the solemn silence, and lonely situation of the place, conspired with the occasion of his coming, and the dismal images of his fancy, to produce a real rapture of gloomy expectation, which the whole world could not have persuaded him to disappoint. The clock struck twelve, the owl screeched from the ruined battlement, the door was opened by the sexton, who, by the light of a glimmering taper, conducted the despairing lover to a dreary aisle, and stamped upon the ground with his foot, saying, 'Here the young lady lies interred.'"

We have here such an amount of the usual romantic machinery of the "grave-yard" school of poets—that school of which Professor W. L. Phelps calls Young, in his Night Thoughts, the most "conspicuous exemplar"—that one is at first inclined to think Smollett poking fun at it. The context, however, seems to prove that he was perfectly serious. It is interesting, then, as well as surprising, to find traces of the romantic spirit in his fiction over ten years before Walpole's Castle of Otranto. It is also interesting to find so much melodramatic feeling in him, because it makes stronger the connection between him and his nineteenth-century disciple, Dickens.

From all that I have said, it must not be thought that the usual Smollett is always, or almost always, absent from Count Fathom. I have spoken of the dedication and of the opening chapters as what we might expect from his pen. There are, besides, true Smollett strokes in the scenes in the prison from which Melvil rescues Fathom, and there is a good deal of the satirical Smollett fun in the description of Fathom's ups and downs, first as the petted beau, and then as the fashionable doctor. In chronicling the latter meteoric career, Smollett had already observed the peculiarity of his countrymen which Thackeray was fond of harping on in the next century—"the maxim which universally prevails among the English people . . . to overlook, . . . on their return to the metropolis, all the connexions they may have chanced to acquire during their residence at any of the medical wells. And this social disposition is so scrupulously maintained, that two persons who live in the most intimate correspondence at Bath or Tunbridge, shall, in four-and-twenty hours . . . meet in St. James's Park, without betraying the least token of recognition." And good, too, is the way in which, as Dr. Fathom goes rapidly down the social hill, he makes excuses for his declining splendour. His chariot was overturned "with a hideous crash" at such danger to himself, "that he did not believe he should ever hazard himself again in any sort of wheel carriage." He turned off his men for maids, because "men servants are generally impudent, lazy, debauched, or dishonest." To avoid the din of the street, he shifted his lodgings into a quiet, obscure court. And so forth and so on, in the true Smollett vein.

But, after all, such of the old sparks are struck only occasionally. Apart from its plot, which not a few nineteenth-century writers of detective-stories might have improved, The Adventures of Ferdinand Count Fathom is less interesting for itself than any other piece of fiction from Smollett's pen. For a student of Smollett, however, it is highly interesting as showing the author's romantic, melodramatic tendencies, and the growth of his constructive technique.

G. H. MAYNADIER

PART I.

TO DOCTOR ——

You and I, my good friend, have often deliberated on the difficulty of writing such a dedication as might gratify the self-complacency of a patron, without exposing the author to the ridicule or censure of the public; and I think we generally agreed that the task was altogether impracticable.—Indeed, this was one of the few subjects on which we have always thought in the same manner. For, notwithstanding that deference and regard which we mutually pay to each other, certain it is, we have often differed, according to the predominancy of those different passions, which frequently warp the opinion, and perplex the understanding of the most judicious.

In dedication, as in poetry, there is no medium; for, if any one of the human virtues be omitted in the enumeration of the patron's good qualities, the whole address is construed into an affront, and the writer has the mortification to find his praise prostituted to very little purpose.

On the other hand, should he yield to the transports of gratitude or affection, which is always apt to exaggerate, and produce no more than the genuine effusions of his heart, the world will make no allowance for the warmth of his passion, but ascribe the praise he bestows to interested views and sordid adulation.

Sometimes too, dazzled by the tinsel of a character which he has no opportunity to investigate, he pours forth the homage of his admiration upon some false Maecenas, whose future conduct gives the lie to his eulogium, and involves him in shame and confusion of face. Such was the fate of a late ingenious author [the Author of the "Seasons"], who was so often put to the blush for the undeserved incense he had offered in the heat of an enthusiastic disposition, misled by popular applause, that he had resolved to retract, in his last will, all the encomiums which he had thus prematurely bestowed, and stigmatise the unworthy by name—a laudable scheme of poetical justice, the execution of which was fatally prevented by untimely death.

Whatever may have been the fate of other dedicators, I, for my own part, sit down to write this address, without any apprehension of disgrace or disappointment; because I know you are too well convinced of my affection and sincerity to repine at what I shall say touching your character and conduct. And you will do me the justice to believe, that this public distinction is a testimony of my particular friendship and esteem.

Not that I am either insensible of your infirmities, or disposed to conceal them from the notice of mankind. There are certain foibles which can only be cured by shame and mortification; and whether or not yours be of that species, I shall have the comfort to think my best endeavours were used for your reformation.

Know then, I can despise your pride, while I honour your integrity, and applaud your taste, while I am shocked at your ostentation.—I have known you trifling, superficial, and obstinate in dispute; meanly jealous and awkwardly reserved; rash and haughty in your resentments; and coarse and lowly in your connexions. I have blushed at the weakness of your conversation, and trembled at the errors of your conduct—yet, as I own you possess certain good qualities, which overbalance these defects, and distinguish you on this occasion as a person for whom I have the most perfect attachment and esteem, you have no cause to complain of the indelicacy with which your faults are reprehended. And as they are chiefly the excesses of a sanguine disposition and looseness of thought, impatient of caution or control, you may, thus stimulated, watch over your own intemperance and infirmity with redoubled vigilance and consideration, and for the future profit by the severity of my reproof.

These, however, are not the only motives that induce me to trouble you with this public application. I must not only perform my duty to my friends, but also discharge the debt I owe to my own interest. We live in a censorious age; and an author cannot take too much precaution to anticipate the prejudice, misapprehension, and temerity of malice, ignorance, and presumption.

I therefore think it incumbent upon me to give some previous intimation of the plan which I have executed in the subsequent performance, that I may not be condemned upon partial evidence; and to whom can I with more propriety appeal in my explanation than to you, who are so well acquainted with all the sentiments and emotions of my breast?

A novel is a large diffused picture, comprehending the characters of life, disposed in different groups, and exhibited in various attitudes, for the purposes of an uniform plan, and general occurrence, to which every individual figure is subservient. But this plan cannot be executed with propriety, probability, or success, without a principal personage to attract the attention, unite the incidents, unwind the clue of the labyrinth, and at last close the scene, by virtue of his own importance.

Almost all the heroes of this kind, who have hitherto succeeded on the English stage, are characters of transcendent worth, conducted through the vicissitudes of fortune, to that goal of happiness, which ever ought to be the repose of extraordinary desert.—Yet the same principle by which we rejoice at the remuneration of merit, will teach us to relish the disgrace and discomfiture of vice, which is always an example of extensive use and influence, because it leaves a deep impression of terror upon the minds of those who were not confirmed in the pursuit of morality and virtue, and, while the balance wavers, enables the right scale to preponderate.

In the drama, which is a more limited field of invention, the chief personage is often the object of our detestation and abhorrence; and we are as well pleased to see the wicked schemes of a Richard blasted, and the perfidy of a Maskwell exposed, as to behold a Bevil happy, and an Edward victorious.

The impulses of fear, which is the most violent and interesting of all the passions, remain longer than any other upon the memory; and for one that is allured to virtue, by the contemplation of that peace and happiness which it bestows, a hundred are deterred from the practice of vice, by that infamy and punishment to which it is liable, from the laws and regulations of mankind.

Let me not, therefore, be condemned for having chosen my principal character from the purlieus of treachery and fraud, when I declare my purpose is to set him up as a beacon for the benefit of the unexperienced and unwary, who, from the perusal of these memoirs, may learn to avoid the manifold snares with which they are continually surrounded in the paths of life; while those who hesitate on the brink of iniquity may be terrified from plunging into that irremediable gulf, by surveying the deplorable fate of Ferdinand Count Fathom.

That the mind might not be fatigued, nor the imagination disgusted, by a succession of vicious objects, I have endeavoured to refresh the attention with occasional incidents of a different nature; and raised up a virtuous character, in opposition to the adventurer, with a view to amuse the fancy, engage the affection, and form a striking contrast which might heighten the expression, and give a relief to the moral of the whole.

If I have not succeeded in my endeavours to unfold the mysteries of fraud, to instruct the ignorant, and entertain the vacant; if I have failed in my attempts to subject folly to ridicule, and vice to indignation; to rouse the spirit of mirth, wake the soul of compassion, and touch the secret springs that move the heart; I have, at least, adorned virtue with honour and applause, branded iniquity with reproach and shame, and carefully avoided every hint or expression which could give umbrage to the most delicate reader—circumstances which (whatever may be my fate with the public) will with you always operate in favour of,

Dear sir, your very affectionate friend and servant,

THE AUTHOR.

CHAPTER ONE.
SOME SAGE OBSERVATIONS THAT NATURALLY INTRODUCE OUR IMPORTANT HISTORY.

Cardinal de Retz very judiciously observes, that all historians must of necessity be subject to mistakes, in explaining the motives of those actions they record, unless they derive their intelligence from the candid confession of the person whose character they represent; and that, of consequence, every man of importance ought to write his own memoirs, provided he has honesty enough to tell the truth, without suppressing any circumstance that may tend to the information of the reader. This, however, is a requisite that, I am afraid, would be very rarely found among the number of those who exhibit their own portraits to the public. Indeed, I will venture to say, that, how upright soever a man's intentions may be, he will, in the performance of such a task, be sometimes misled by his own phantasy, and represent objects, as they appeared to him, through the mists of prejudice and passion.

An unconcerned reader, when he peruses the history of two competitors, who lived two thousand years ago, or who perhaps never had existence, except in the imagination of the author, cannot help interesting himself in the dispute, and espousing one side of the contest, with all the zeal of a warm adherent. What wonder, then, that we should be heated in our own concerns, review our actions with the same self-approbation that they had formerly acquired, and recommend them to the world with all the enthusiasm of paternal affection?

Supposing this to be the case, it was lucky for the cause of historical truth, that so many pens have been drawn by writers, who could not be suspected of such partiality; and that many great personages, among the ancients as well as moderns, either would not or could not entertain the public with their own memoirs. From this want of inclination or capacity to write, in our hero himself, the undertaking is now left to me, of transmitting to posterity the remarkable adventures of FERDINAND COUNT FATHOM; and by the time the reader shall have glanced over the subsequent sheets, I doubt not but he will bless God that the adventurer was not his own historian.

This mirror of modern chivalry was none of those who owe their dignity to the circumstances of their birth, and are consecrated from the cradle for the purposes of greatness, merely because they are the accidental children of wealth. He was heir to no visible patrimony, unless we reckon a robust constitution, a tolerable appearance, and an uncommon capacity, as the advantages of inheritance. If the comparison obtains in this point of consideration, he was as much as any man indebted to his parent; and pity it was, that, in the sequel of his fortune, he never had an opportunity of manifesting his filial gratitude and regard. From this agreeable act of duty to his sire, and all those tendernesses that are reciprocally enjoyed betwixt the father and the son, he was unhappily excluded by a small circumstance; at which, however, he was never heard to repine. In short, had he been brought forth in the fabulous ages of the world, the nature of his origin might have turned to his account; he might, like other heroes of antiquity, have laid claim to divine extraction, without running the risk of being claimed by an earthly father. Not that his parents had any reason to disown or renounce their offspring, or that there was anything preternatural in the circumstances of his generation and birth; on the contrary, he was, from the beginning, a child of promising parts, and in due course of nature ushered into the world amidst a whole cloud of witnesses. But, that he was acknowledged by no mortal sire, solely proceeded from the uncertainty of his mother, whose affections were so dissipated among a number of admirers, that she could never pitch upon the person from whose loins our hero sprung.

Over and above this important doubt under which he was begotten, other particularities attended his birth, and seemed to mark him out as something uncommon among the sons of men. He was brought forth in a waggon, and might be said to be literally a native of two different countries; for, though he first saw the light in Holland, he was not born till after the carriage arrived in Flanders; so that, all these extraordinary circumstances considered, the task of determining to what government he naturally owed allegiance, would be at least as difficult as that of ascertaining the so much contested birthplace of Homer.

Certain it is, the Count's mother was an Englishwoman, who, after having been five times a widow in one campaign, was, in the last year of the renowned Marlborough's command, numbered among the baggage of the allied army, which she still accompanied, through pure benevolence of spirit, supplying the ranks with the refreshing streams of choice Geneva, and accommodating individuals with clean linen, as the emergency of their occasions required. Nor was her philanthropy altogether confined to such ministration; she abounded with "the milk of human kindness," which flowed plentifully among her fellow-creatures; and to every son of Mars who cultivated her favour, she liberally dispensed her smiles, in order to sweeten the toils and dangers of the field.

And here it will not be amiss to anticipate the remarks of the reader, who, in the chastity and excellency of his conception, may possibly exclaim, "Good Heaven! will these authors never reform their imaginations, and lift their ideas from the obscene objects of low life? Must the public be again disgusted with the grovelling adventures of a waggon? Will no writer of genius draw his pen in the vindication of taste, and entertain us with the agreeable characters, the dignified conversation, the poignant repartee, in short, the genteel comedy of the polite world?"

Have a little patience, gentle, delicate, sublime critic; you, I doubt not, are one of those consummate connoisseurs, who, in their purifications, let humour evaporate, while they endeavour to preserve decorum, and polish wit, until the edge of it is quite worn off. Or, perhaps, of that class, who, in the sapience of taste, are disgusted with those very flavours in the productions of their own country which have yielded infinite delectation to their faculties, when imported from another clime; and d—n an author in despite of all precedent and prescription;—who extol the writings of Petronius Arbiter, read with rapture the amorous sallies of Ovid's pen, and chuckle over the story of Lucian's ass; yet, if a modern author presumes to relate the progress of a simple intrigue, are shocked at the indecency and immorality of the scene;—who delight in following Guzman d'Alfarache, through all the mazes of squalid beggary; who with pleasure accompany Don Quixote and his squire, in the lowest paths of fortune; who are diverted with the adventures of Scarron's ragged troop of strollers, and highly entertained with the servile situations of Gil Blas; yet, when a character in humble life occasionally occurs in a performance of our own growth, exclaim, with an air of disgust, "Was ever anything so mean! sure, this writer must have been very conversant with the lowest scenes of life;"—who, when Swift or Pope represents a coxcomb in the act of swearing, scruple not to laugh at the ridiculous execrations; but, in a less reputed author, condemn the use of such profane expletives;—who eagerly explore the jakes of Rabelais, for amusement, and even extract humour from the dean's description of a lady's dressing-room; yet in a production of these days, unstamped with such venerable names, will stop their noses, with all the signs of loathing and abhorrence, at a bare mention of the china chamber-pot;—who applauded Catullus, Juvenal, Persius, and Lucan, for their spirit in lashing the greatest names of antiquity; yet, when a British satirist, of this generation, has courage enough to call in question the talents of a pseudo-patron in power, accuse him of insolence, rancour, and scurrility.

If such you be, courteous reader, I say again, have a little patience; for your entertainment we are about to write. Our hero shall, with all convenient despatch, be gradually sublimed into those splendid connexions of which you are enamoured; and God forbid, that, in the meantime, the nature of his extraction should turn to his prejudice in a land of freedom like this, where individuals are every day ennobled in consequence of their own qualifications, without the least retrospective regard to the rank or merit of their ancestors. Yes, refined reader, we are hastening to that goal of perfection, where satire dares not show her face; where nature is castigated, almost even to still life; where humour turns changeling, and slavers in an insipid grin; where wit is volatilised into a mere vapour; where decency, divested of all substance, hovers about like a fantastic shadow; where the salt of genius, escaping, leaves nothing but pure and simple phlegm; and the inoffensive pen for ever drops the mild manna of soul-sweetening praise.

CHAPTER TWO.
A SUPERFICIAL VIEW OF OUR HERO'S INFANCY.

Having thus bespoken the indulgence of our guests, let us now produce the particulars of our entertainment, and speedily conduct our adventurer through the stage of infancy, which seldom teems with interesting incidents.

As the occupations of his mother would not conveniently permit her to suckle this her firstborn at her own breast, and those happy ages were now no more, in which the charge of nursing a child might be left to the next goat or she-wolf, she resolved to improve upon the ordinances of nature, and foster him with a juice much more energetic than the milk of goat, wolf, or woman; this was no other than that delicious nectar, which, as we have already hinted, she so cordially distributed from a small cask that hung before her, depending from her shoulders by a leathern zone. Thus determined, ere he was yet twelve days old, she enclosed him in a canvas knapsack, which being adjusted to her neck, fell down upon her back, and balanced the cargo that rested on her bosom.

There are not wanting those who affirm, that, while her double charge was carried about in this situation, her keg was furnished with a long and slender flexible tube, which, when the child began to be clamorous, she conveyed into his mouth, and straight he stilled himself with sucking; but this we consider as an extravagant assertion of those who mix the marvellous in all their narrations, because we cannot conceive how the tender organs of an infant could digest such a fiery beverage, which never fails to discompose the constitutions of the most hardy and robust. We therefore conclude that the use of this potation was more restrained, and that it was with simple element diluted into a composition adapted to his taste and years. Be this as it will, he certainly was indulged in the use of it to such a degree as would have effectually obstructed his future fortune, had not he been happily cloyed with the repetition of the same fare, for which he conceived the utmost detestation and abhorrence, rejecting it with loathing and disgust, like those choice spirits, who, having been crammed with religion in their childhood, renounce it in their youth, among other absurd prejudices of education.

While he was thus dangled in a state of suspension, a German trooper was transiently smit with the charms of his mother, who listened to his honourable addresses, and once more received the silken bonds of matrimony; the ceremony having been performed as usual at the drum-head. The lady had no sooner taken possession of her new name, than she bestowed it upon her son, who was thenceforward distinguished by the appellation of Ferdinand de Fadom; nor was the husband offended at this presumption in his wife, which he not only considered as a proof of her affection and esteem, but also as a compliment, by which he might in time acquire the credit of being the real father of such a hopeful child.

Notwithstanding this new engagement with a foreigner, our hero's mother still exercised the virtues of her calling among the English troops, so much was she biassed by that laudable partiality, which, as Horace observes, the natale solum generally inspires. Indeed this inclination was enforced by another reason, that did not fail to influence her conduct in this particular; all her knowledge of the High Dutch language consisted in some words of traffic absolutely necessary for the practice of hex vocation, together with sundry oaths and terms of reproach, that kept her customers in awe; so that, except among her own countrymen, she could not indulge that propensity to conversation, for which she had been remarkable from her earliest years. Nor did this instance of her affection fail of turning to her account in the sequel. She was promoted to the office of cook to a regimental mess of officers; and, before the peace of Utrecht, was actually in possession of a suttling-tent, pitched for the accommodation of the gentlemen in the army.

Meanwhile, Ferdinand improved apace in the accomplishments of infancy; his beauty was conspicuous, and his vigour so uncommon, that he was with justice likened unto Hercules in the cradle. The friends of his father-in-law dandled him on their knees, while he played with their whiskers, and, before he was thirteen months old, taught him to suck brandy impregnated with gunpowder, through the touch-hole of a pistol. At the same time, he was caressed by divers serjeants of the British army, who severally and in secret contemplated his qualifications with a father's pride, excited by the artful declaration with which the mother had flattered each apart.

Soon as the war was (for her unhappily) concluded, she, as in duty bound, followed her husband into Bohemia; and his regiment being sent into garrison at Prague, she opened a cabaret in that city, which was frequented by a good many guests of the Scotch and Irish nations, who were devoted to the exercise of arms in the service of the Emperor. It was by this communication that the

English tongue became vernacular to young Ferdinand, who, without such opportunity, would have been a stranger to the language of his forefathers, in spite of all his mother's loquacity and elocution; though it must be owned, for the credit of her maternal care, that she let slip no occasion of making it familiar to his ear and conception; for, even at those intervals in which she could find no person to carry on the altercation, she used to hold forth in earnest soliloquies upon the subject of her own situation, giving vent to many opprobrious invectives against her husband's country, between which and Old England she drew many odious comparisons; and prayed, without ceasing, that Europe might speedily be involved in a general war, so as that she might have some chance of re-enjoying the pleasures and emoluments of a Flanders campaign.

CHAPTER THREE.
HE IS INITIATED IN A MILITARY LIFE, AND HAS THE GOOD FORTUNE TO ACQUIRE A GENEROUS PATRON.

While she wearied Heaven with these petitions, the flame of war broke out betwixt the houses of Ottoman and Austria, and the Emperor sent forth an army into Hungary, under the auspices of the renowned Prince Eugene. On account of this expedition, the mother of our hero gave up housekeeping, and cheerfully followed her customers and husband into the field; having first provided herself with store of those commodities in which she had formerly merchandised. Although the hope of profit might in some measure affect her determination, one of the chief motives for her visiting the frontiers of Turkey, was the desire of initiating her son in the rudiments of his education, which she now thought high time to inculcate, he being, at this period, in the sixth year of his age; he was accordingly conducted to the camp, which she considered as the most consummate school of life, and proposed for the scene of his instruction; and in this academy he had not continued many weeks, when he was an eye-witness of that famous victory, which, with sixty thousand men, the Imperial general obtained over an army of one hundred and fifty thousand Turks.

His father-in-law was engaged, and his mother would not be idle on this occasion. She was a perfect mistress of all the camp qualifications, and thought it a duty incumbent on her to contribute all that lay in her power towards distressing the enemy. With these sentiments she hovered about the skirts of the army, and the troops were no sooner employed in the pursuit, than she began to traverse the field of battle with a poignard and a bag, in order to consult her own interest, annoy the foe, and exercise her humanity at the same time. In short, she had, with amazing prowess, delivered some fifty or threescore disabled Mussulmen of the pain under which they groaned, and made a comfortable booty of the spoils of the slain, when her eyes were attracted by the rich attire of an Imperial officer, who lay bleeding on the plain, to all appearance in the agonies of death.

She could not in her heart refuse that favour to a friend and Christian she had so compassionately bestowed upon so many enemies and infidels, and therefore drew near with the sovereign remedy, which she had already administered with such success. As she approached this deplorable object of pity, her ears were surprised with an ejaculation in the English tongue, which he fervently pronounced, though with a weak and languid voice, recommending his soul to God, and his family to the protection of Heaven. Our Amazon's purpose was staggered by this providential incident; the sound of her native language, so unexpectedly heard, and so pathetically delivered, had a surprising effect upon her imagination; and the faculty of reflection did not forsake her in such emergency. Though she could not recollect the features of this unhappy officer, she concluded, from his appearance, that he was some person of distinction in the service, and foresaw greater advantage to herself in attempting to preserve his life, than she could possibly reap from the execution of her first resolve. "If," said she to herself, "I can find means of conveying him to his tent alive, he cannot but in conscience acknowledge my humanity with some considerable recompense; and, should he chance to survive his wounds, I have everything to expect from his gratitude and power."

Fraught with these prudential suggestions, she drew near the unfortunate stranger, and, in a softened accent of pity and condolence, questioned him concerning his name, condition, and the nature of his mischance, at the same time making a gentle tender of her service. Agreeably surprised to hear himself accosted in such a manner, by a person whose equipage seemed to promise far other designs, he thanked her in the most grateful terms for her humanity, with the appellation of kind countrywoman; gave her to understand that he was colonel of a regiment of horse; that he had fallen in consequence of a shot he received in his breast at the beginning of the action; and, finally, entreated her to procure some carriage on which he might be removed to his tent. Perceiving him faint and exhausted with loss of blood, she raised up his head, and treated him with that cordial which was her constant companion. At that instant, espying a small body of hussars returning to the camp with the plunder they had taken, she invoked their assistance, and they forthwith carried the officer to his own quarters, where his wound was dressed, and his preserver carefully tended him until his recovery was completed.

In return for these good offices, this gentleman, who was originally of Scotland, rewarded her for the present with great liberality, assured her of his influence in promoting her husband, and took upon himself the charge of young Ferdinand's education; the boy was immediately taken into his protection, and entered as a trooper in his own regiment; but his good intentions towards his father-in-law were frustrated by the death of the German, who, in a few days after this disposition, was shot in the trenches before Temiswaer.

This event, over and above the conjugal affliction with which it invaded the lady's quiet, would have involved her in infinite difficulty and distress, with regard to her temporal concerns, by leaving her unprotected in the midst of strangers, had not she been thus providentially supplied with an effectual patron in the colonel, who was known by the appellation of Count Melvil. He no sooner saw her, by the death of her husband, detached from all personal connexions with a military life, than he proposed that she should quit her occupation in the camp, and retire to his habitation in the city of Presburg, where she would be entertained in ease and plenty during the remaining part of her natural life. With all due acknowledgments of his generosity, she begged to be excused from embracing his proposal, alleging she was so much accustomed to her present way of life, and so much devoted to the service of the soldiery, that she should never be happy in retirement, while the troops of any prince in Christendom kept the field.

The Count, finding her determined to prosecute her scheme, repeated his promise of befriending her upon all occasions; and in the meantime admitted Ferdinand into the number of his domestics, resolving that he should be brought up in attendance upon his own son, who was a boy of the same age. He kept him, however, in his tent, until he should have an opportunity of revisiting his family in person; and, before that occasion offered, two whole years elapsed, during which the illustrious Prince Eugene gained the celebrated battle of Belgrade, and afterwards made himself master of that important frontier.

CHAPTER FOUR.
HIS MOTHER'S PROWESS AND DEATH; TOGETHER WITH SOME INSTANCES OF HIS OWN SAGACITY.

It would have been impossible for the mother of our adventurer, such as she hath been described, to sit quietly in her tent, while such an heroic scene was acting. She was no sooner apprised of the general's intention to attack the enemy, than she, as usual, packed up her moveables in a waggon, which she committed to the care of a peasant in the neighbourhood, and put herself in motion with the troops; big with the expectation of re-acting that part in which she had formerly acquitted herself so much to her advantage.—Nay, she by this time looked upon her own presence as a certain omen of success to the cause which she espoused; and, in their march to battle, actually encouraged the ranks with repeated declarations, importing, that she had been eye-witness of ten decisive engagements, in all of which her friends had been victorious, and imputing such uncommon good fortune to some supernatural quality inherent in her person.

Whether or not this confidence contributed to the fortune of the day, by inspiring the soldiers to an uncommon pitch of courage and resolution, I shall not pretend to determine. But, certain it is, the victory began from that quarter in which she had posted herself; and no corps in the army behaved with such intrepidity as that which was manifested by those who were favoured with her admonitions and example; for she not only exposed her person to the enemy's fire, with the indifference and deliberation of a veteran, but she is said to have achieved a very conspicuous exploit by the prowess of her single arm. The extremity of the line to which she had attached herself, being assaulted in flank by a body of the spahis, wheeled about, in order to sustain the charge, and received them with such a seasonable fire, as brought a great number of turbans to the ground; among those who fell, was one of the chiefs or agas, who had advanced before the rest, with a view to signalise his valour.

Our English Penthesilea no sooner saw this Turkish leader drop, than, struck with the magnificence of his own and horse's trappings, she sprung forward to seize them as her prize, and found the aga not dead, though in a good measure disabled by his misfortune, which was entirely owing to the weight of his horse, that, having been killed by a musket-ball, lay upon his leg, so that he could not disengage himself. Nevertheless, perceiving the virago approach with fell intent, he brandished his symitar, and tried to intimidate his assailant with a most horrible exclamation; but it was not the dismal yell of a dismounted cavalier, though enforced with a hideous ferocity of countenance, and the menacing gestures with which he waited her approach, that could intimidate such an undaunted she-campaigner; she saw him writhing in the agonies of a situation from which he could not move; and, running towards him with the nimbleness and intrepidity of a Camilla, described a semicircle in the progress of her assault, and attacking him on one side, plunged her well-tried dagger in his throat. The shades of death encompassed him, his life-blood issued at the wound, he fell prone upon the earth, he bit the dust, and having thrice invoked the name of Allah! straight expired.

While his destiny was thus fulfilled, his followers began to reel; they seemed dismayed at the fate of their chief, beheld their companions drop like the leaves in autumn, and suddenly halted in the midst of their career. The Imperialists, observing the confusion of the enemy, redoubled their fire; and, raising a dreadful shout, advanced in order to improve the advantage they had gained. The spahis durst not wait the shock of such an encounter; they wheeled to the right-about, and clapping spurs to their horses, fled in the utmost disorder. This was actually the circumstance that turned the scale of battle. The Austrians pursued their good fortune with uncommon impetuosity, and in a few minutes left the field clear for the mother of our hero, who was such an adept in the art of stripping, that in the twinkling of an eye the bodies of the aga and his Arabian lay naked to the skin. It would have been happy for her, had she been contented with these first-fruits, reaped from the fortune of the day, and retired with her spoils, which were not inconsiderable; but, intoxicated with the glory she had won, enticed by the glittering caparisons that lay scattered on the plain, and without doubt prompted by the secret instinct of her fate, she resolved to seize opportunity by the forelock, and once for all indemnify herself for the many fatigues, hazards, and sorrows she had undergone.

Thus determined, she reconnoitred the field, and practised her address so successfully, that in less than half an hour she was loaded with ermine and embroidery, and disposed to retreat with her burden, when her regards were solicited by a splendid bundle, which she descried at some distance lying on the ground. This was no other than an unhappy officer of hussars; who, after having the good fortune to take a Turkish standard, was desperately wounded in the thigh, and obliged to quit his horse; finding himself in such a helpless condition, he had wrapped his acquisition round his body, that whatever might happen, he and his glory should not be parted; and thus shrouded, among the dying and the dead, he had observed the progress of our heroine, who stalked about the field, like another Atropos, finishing, wherever she came, the work of death. He did not at all doubt, that he himself would be visited in the course of her peregrinations, and therefore provided for her reception, with a pistol ready cocked in his hand, while he lay perdue beneath his covert, in all appearance bereft of life. He was not deceived in his prognostic; she no sooner eyed the golden crescent than, inflamed with curiosity or cupidity, she directed thitherward her steps, and discerning the carcase of a man, from which, she thought, there would be a necessity for disengaging it, she lifted up her weapon, in order to make sure of her purchase; and in the very instant of discharging her blow, received a brace of bullets in her brain.

Thus ended the mortal pilgrimage of this modern Amazon; who, in point of courage, was not inferior to Semiramis, Tomyris, Zenobia, Thalestris, or any boasted heroine of ancient times. It cannot be supposed that this catastrophe made a very deep impression upon the mind of young Ferdinand, who had just then attained the ninth year of his age, and been for a considerable time weaned from her maternal caresses; especially as he felt no wants nor grievances in the family of the Count, who favoured him with a particular share of indulgence, because he perceived in him a spirit of docility, insinuation, and sagacity, far above his years. He did not, however, fail to lament the untimely fate of his mother, with such filial expressions of sorrow, as still more intimately recommended him to his patron; who, being himself a man of extraordinary benevolence, looked upon the boy as a prodigy of natural affection, and foresaw in his future services a fund of gratitude and attachment, that could not fail to render him a valuable acquisition to his family.

In his own country, he had often seen connexions of that sort, which having been planted in the infancy of the adherent, had grown up to a surprising pitch of fidelity and friendship, that no temptation could bias, and no danger dissolve. He therefore rejoiced in the hope of seeing his own son accommodated with such a faithful attendant, in the person of young Fathom, on whom he resolved to bestow the same education he had planned for the other, though conveyed in such a manner as should be suitable to the sphere in which he was ordained to move. In consequence of these determinations, our young adventurer led a very easy life, in quality of page to the Count, in whose tent he lay upon a pallet, close to his field-bed, and often diverted him with his childish prattle in the English tongue, which the more seldom his master had occasion to speak, he the more delighted to hear. In the exercise of his function, the boy was incredibly assiduous and alert; far from neglecting the little particulars of his duty, and embarking in the mischievous amusements of the children belonging to the camp, he was always diligent, sedate, agreeably officious and anticipating; and in the whole of his behaviour seemed to express the most vigilant sense of his patron's goodness and generosity; nay, to such a degree had these sentiments, in all appearance, operated upon his reflection, that one morning, while he supposed the Count asleep, he crept softly to his bedside, and gently kissing his hand, which happened to be uncovered, pronounced, in a low voice, a most fervent prayer in his behalf, beseeching Heaven to shower down blessings upon him, as the widow's friend and the orphan's father. This benediction was not lost upon the Count, who chanced to be awake, and heard it with admiration; but what riveted Ferdinand in his good graces, was a discovery that our youth made, while his master was upon duty in the trenches before Belgrade.

Two foot soldiers, standing sentry near the door of the tent, were captivated with the sight of some valuable moveables belonging to it; and supposing, in their great wisdom, that the city of Belgrade was too well fortified to be taken during that campaign, they came to a resolution of withdrawing themselves from the severe service of the trenches, by deserting to the enemy, after they should have rifled Count Melvil's tent of the furniture by which they were so powerfully allured. The particulars of this plan were concerted in the French language, which, they imagined, would screen them from all risk of being detected, in case they should be overheard, though, as there was no living creature in sight, they had no reason to believe that any person was privy to their conversation. Nevertheless, they were mistaken in both these conjectures. The conference reached the ears of Fathom, who was at the other end of the tent, and had perceived the eager looks with which they considered some parts of the furniture. He had penetration enough to suspect their desire, and, alarmed by that suspicion, listened attentively to their discourse; which, from a slender knowledge in the French tongue, he had the good fortune partly to understand.

This important piece of intelligence he communicated to the Count at his return, and measures were immediately taken to defeat the design, and make an example of the authors, who being permitted to load themselves with the booty, were apprehended in their retreat, and punished with death according to their demerits.

CHAPTER FIVE.
A BRIEF DETAIL OF HIS EDUCATION.

Nothing could have more seasonably happened to confirm the good opinion which the colonel entertained of Ferdinand's principles. His intentions towards the boy grew every day more and more warm; and, immediately after the peace of Passarowitz, he retired to his own house at Presburg, and presented young Fathom to his lady, not only as the son of a person to whom he owed his life, but also as a lad who merited his peculiar protection and regard by his own personal virtue. The Countess, who was an Hungarian, received him with great kindness and affability, and her son was ravished with the prospect of enjoying such a companion. In short, fortune seemed to have provided for him an asylum, in which he might be safely trained up, and suitably prepared for more important scenes of life than any of his ancestors had ever known.

He was not, in all respects, entertained on the footing of his young master; yet he shared in all his education and amusements, as one whom the old gentleman was fully determined to qualify for the station of an officer in the service; and, if he did not eat with the Count, he was every day regaled with choice bits from his table; holding, as it were, a middle place between the rank of a relation and favourite domestic. Although his patron maintained a tutor in the house, to superintend the conduct of his heir, he committed the charge of his learning to the instructions of a public school; where he imagined the boy would imbibe a laudable spirit of emulation among his fellows, which could not fail of turning out to the advantage of his education. Ferdinand was entered in the same academy; and the two lads proceeded equally in the paths of erudition; a mutual friendship and intimacy soon ensued, and, notwithstanding the levity and caprice commonly discernible in the behaviour of such boys, very few or rather no quarrels happened in the course of their communication. Yet their dispositions were altogether different, and their talents unlike. Nay, this dissimilarity was the very bond of their union; because it prevented that jealousy and rivalship which often interrupts the harmony of two warm contemporaries.

The young Count made extraordinary progress in the exercises of the school, though he seemed to take very little pains in the cultivation of his studies; and became a perfect hero in all the athletic diversions of his fellow-scholars; but, at the same time, exhibited such a bashful appearance and uncouth address, that his mother despaired of ever seeing him improved into any degree of polite behaviour. On the other hand, Fathom, who was in point of learning a mere dunce, became, even in his childhood, remarkable among the ladies for his genteel deportment and vivacity; they admired the proficiency he made under the directions of his dancing-master, the air with which he performed his obeisance at his entrance and exit; and were charmed with the agreeable assurance and lively sallies of his conversation; while they expressed the utmost concern and disgust at the boorish demeanour of his companion, whose extorted bows resembled the pawings of a mule, who hung his head in silence like a detected sheep-stealer, who sat in company under the most awkward expressions of constraint, and whose discourse never exceeded the simple monosyllables of negation and assent.

In vain did all the females of the family propose to him young Fathom, as a pattern and reproach. He remained unaltered by all their efforts and expostulations, and allowed our adventurer to enjoy the triumph of his praise, while he himself was conscious of his own superiority in those qualifications which seemed of more real importance than the mere exteriors and forms of life. His present ambition was not to make a figure at his father's table, but to eclipse his rivals at school, and to acquire an influence and authority among these confederates. Nevertheless, Fathom might possibly have fallen under his displeasure or contempt, had not that pliant genius found means to retain his friendship by seasonable compliances and submission; for the sole study, or at least the chief aim of Ferdinand, was to make himself necessary and agreeable to those on whom his dependence was placed. His talent was in this particular suited to his inclination; he seemed to have inherited it from his mother's womb; and, without all doubt, would have raised upon it a most admirable superstructure of fortune and applause, had not it been inseparably yoked with a most insidious principle of self-love, that grew up with him from the cradle, and left no room in his heart for the least particle of social virtue. This last, however, he knew so well how to counterfeit, by means of a large share of ductility and dissimulation, that, surely, he was calculated by nature to dupe even the most cautious, and gratify his appetites, by levying contributions on all mankind.

So little are the common instructors of youth qualified to judge the capacities of those who are under their tutelage and care, that Fathom, by dint of his insinuating arts, made shift to pass upon the schoolmaster as a lad of quick parts, in despite of a natural inaptitude to retain his lessons, which all his industry could never overcome. In order to remedy, or rather to cloak this defect in his understanding, he had always recourse to the friendship of the young Count, who freely permitted him to transcribe his exercises, until a small accident happened, which had well-nigh put a stop to these instances of his generosity.—The adventure, inconsiderable as it is, we shall record, as the first overt act of Ferdinand's true character, as well as an illustration of the opinion we have advanced touching the blind and injudicious decisions of a right pedagogue.

Among other tasks imposed by the pedant upon the form to which our two companions belonged, they were one evening ordered to translate a chapter of Caesar's Commentaries. Accordingly the young Count went to work, and performed the undertaking with great elegance and despatch. Fathom, having spent the night in more effeminate amusements, was next morning so much hurried for want of time, that in his transcription he neglected to insert a few variations from the text, these being the terms on which he was allowed to use it; so that it was verbatim a copy of the original. As those exercises were always delivered in a heap, subscribed with the several names of the boys to whom they belonged, the schoolmaster chanced to peruse the version of Ferdinand, before he looked into any of the rest, and could not help bestowing upon it particular marks of approbation. The next that fell under his examination was that of the young Count, when he immediately perceived the sameness, and, far from imputing it to the true cause, upbraided him with having copied the exercise of our adventurer, and insisted upon chastising him upon the spot for his want of application.

Had not the young gentleman thought his honour was concerned, he would have submitted to the punishment without murmuring; but he inherited, from his parents, the pride of two fierce nations, and, being overwhelmed with reproaches for that which he imagined ought to have redounded to his glory, he could not brook the indignity, and boldly affirmed, that he himself was the original, to whom Ferdinand was beholden for his performance. The schoolmaster, nettled to find himself mistaken in his judgment, resolved that the Count should have no cause to exult in the discovery he had made, and, like a true flogger, actually whipped him for having allowed Fathom to copy his exercise. Nay, in the hope of vindicating his own penetration, he took an opportunity of questioning Ferdinand in private concerning the circumstances of the translation, and our hero, perceiving his drift, gave him such artful and ambiguous answers, as persuaded him that the young Count had acted the part of a plagiary, and that the other had been restrained from doing himself justice, by the consideration of his own dependence.

This profound director did not fail, in honour of his own discernment, to whisper about the misrepresentation, as an instance of the young Count's insolence, and Fathom's humility and good sense. The story was circulated among the servants, especially the maids belonging to the family, whose favour our hero had acquired by his engaging behaviour; and at length it reached the ears of his patron, who, incensed at his son's presumption and inhospitality, called him to a severe account, when the young gentleman absolutely denied the truth of the allegation, and appealed to the evidence of Fathom himself. Our adventurer was accordingly summoned by the father, and encouraged to declare the truth, with an assurance of his constant protection; upon which Ferdinand very wisely fell upon his knees, and, while the tears gushed from his eyes, acquitted the young Count of the imputation, and expressed his apprehension, that the report had been spread by some of his enemies, who wanted to prejudice him in the opinion of his patron.

The old gentleman was not satisfied of his son's integrity by this declaration; being naturally of a generous disposition, highly prepossessed in favour of the poor orphan, and chagrined at the unpromising appearance of his heir, he suspected that Fathom was overawed by the fear of giving offence, and that, notwithstanding what he had said, the case really stood as it had been represented. In this persuasion, he earnestly exhorted his son to resist and combat with any impulse he might feel within himself, tending to selfishness, fraud, or imposition; to encourage every sentiment of candour and benevolence, and to behave with moderation and affability to all his fellow-creatures. He laid upon him strong injunctions, not without a mixture of threats, to consider Fathom as the object of his peculiar regard; to respect him as the son of the Count's preserver, as a Briton, a stranger, and, above all, an helpless orphan, to whom the rights of hospitality were doubly due.

Such admonitions were not lost upon the youth, who, under the rough husk of his personal exhibition, possessed a large share of generous sensibility. Without any formal professions to his father, he resolved to govern himself according to his remonstrances; and, far from conceiving the least spark of animosity against Fathom, he looked upon the poor boy as the innocent cause of his disgrace, and redoubled his kindness towards him, that his honour might never again be called in question, upon the same subject. Nothing is more liable to misconstruction than an act of uncommon generosity; one half of the world mistake the motive, from want of ideas to conceive an instance of beneficence that soars so high above the level of their own sentiments; and the rest suspect it of something sinister or selfish, from the suggestions of their own sordid and vicious inclinations. The young Count subjected himself to such misinterpretation, among those who observed the increased warmth of civility and complaisance in his behaviour to Ferdinand. They ascribed it to his desire of still profiting by our adventurer's superior talents, by which alone they supposed him enabled to maintain any degree of reputation at school; or to the fear of being convicted by him of some misdemeanour of which he knew himself guilty. These suspicions were not effaced by the conduct of Ferdinand, who, when examined on the subject, managed his answers in such a manner, as confirmed their conjectures, while he pretended to refute them, and at the same time acquired to himself credit for his extraordinary discretion and self-denial.

If he exhibited such a proof of sagacity in the twelfth year of his age, what might not be expected from his finesse in the maturity of his faculties and experience? Thus secured in the good graces of the whole family, he saw the days of his puerility glide along in the most agreeable elapse of caresses and amusement. He never fairly plunged into the stream of school-education, but, by floating on the surface, imbibed a small tincture of those different sciences which his master pretended to teach. In short, he resembled those vagrant swallows that skim along the level of some pool or river, without venturing to wet one feather in their wings, except in the accidental pursuit of an inconsiderable fly. Yet, though his capacity or inclination was unsuited for studies of this kind, he did not fail to manifest a perfect genius in the acquisition of other more profitable arts. Over and above the accomplishments of address, for which he hath been already celebrated, he excelled all his fellows in his dexterity at fives and billiards; was altogether unrivalled in his skill at draughts and backgammon; began, even at these years, to understand the moves and schemes of chess; and made himself a mere adept in the mystery of cards, which he learned in the course of his assiduities and attention to the females of the house.

CHAPTER SIX.
HE MEDITATES SCHEMES OF IMPORTANCE.

It was in these parties that he attracted the notice and friendship of his patron's daughter, a girl by two years older than himself, who was not insensible to his qualifications, and looked upon him with the most favourable eyes of prepossession. Whether or not he at this period of his life began to project plans for availing himself of her susceptibility, is uncertain; but, without all doubt, he cultivated her esteem with as obsequious and submissive attention as if he had already formed the design, which, in his advanced age, he attempted to put in execution.

Divers circumstances conspired to promote him in the favour of this young lady; the greenness of his years secured him from any appearance of fallacious aim; so that he was indulged in frequent opportunities of conversing with his young mistress, whose parents encouraged this communication, by which they hoped she would improve in speaking the language of her father. Such connexions naturally produce intimacy and friendship. Fathom's person was agreeable, his talents calculated for the meridian of those parties, and his manners so engaging, that there would have been no just subject for wonder, had he made an impression upon the tender unexperienced heart of Mademoiselle de Melvil, whose beauty was not so attractive as to extinguish his hope, in raising up a number of formidable rivals; though her expectations of fortune were such as commonly lend additional lustre to personal merit.

All these considerations were so many steps towards the success of Ferdinand's pretensions; and though he cannot be supposed to have perceived them at first, he in the sequel seemed perfectly well apprised of his advantages, and used them to the full extent of his faculties. Observing that she delighted in music, he betook himself to the study of that art, and, by dint of application and a tolerable ear, learned of himself to accompany her with a German flute, while she sung and played upon the harpsichord. The Count, seeing his inclination, and the progress he had made, resolved that his capacity should not be lost for want of cultivation; and accordingly provided him with a master, by whom he was instructed in the principles of the art, and soon became a proficient in playing upon the violin.

In the practice of these improvements and avocations, and in attendance upon his young master, whom he took care never to disoblige or neglect, he attained to the age of sixteen, without feeling the least abatement in the friendship and generosity of those upon whom he depended; but, on the contrary, receiving every day fresh marks of their bounty and regard. He had before this time been smit with the ambition of making a conquest of the young lady's heart, and foresaw manifold advantages to himself in becoming son-in-law to Count Melvil, who, he never doubted, would soon be reconciled to the match, if once it could be effectuated without his knowledge. Although he thought he had great reason to believe that Mademoiselle looked upon him with an eye of peculiar favour, his disposition was happily tempered with an ingredient of caution, that hindered him from acting with precipitation; and he had discerned in the young lady's deportment certain indications of loftiness and pride, which kept him in the utmost vigilance and circumspection; for he knew, that, by a premature declaration, he should run the risk of forfeiting all the advantages he had gained, and blasting those expectations that now blossomed so gaily in his heart.

Restricted by these reflections, he acted at a wary distance, and determined to proceed by the method of sap, and, summoning all his artifice and attractions to his aid, employed them under the insidious cover of profound respect, in order to undermine those bulwarks of haughtiness or discretion, which otherwise might have rendered his approaches to her impracticable. With a view to enhance the value of his company, and sound her sentiments at the same time, he became more reserved than usual, and seldomer engaged in her parties of music and cards; yet, in the midst of his reserve, he never failed in those demonstrations of reverence and regard, which he knew perfectly well how to express, but devised such excuses for his absence, as she could not help admitting. In consequence of this affected shyness, she more than once gently chid him for his neglect and indifference, observing, with an ironical air, that he was now too much of a man to be entertained with such effeminate diversions; but her reproofs were pronounced with too much ease and good-humour to be agreeable to our hero, who desired to see her ruffled and chagrined at his absence, and to hear himself rebuked with an angry affectation of disdain. This effort, therefore, he reinforced with the most captivating carriage he could assume, in those hours which he now so sparingly bestowed upon his mistress. He regaled her with all the entertaining stories he could learn or invent, particularly such as he thought would justify and recommend the levelling power of love, that knows no distinctions of fortune. He sung nothing but tender airs and passionate complaints, composed by desponding or despairing swains; and, to render his performances of this kind the more pathetic, interlarded them with some seasonable sighs, while the tears, which he had ever at command, stood collected in either eye.

It was impossible for her to overlook such studied emotions; she in a jocose manner taxed him with having lost his heart, rallied the excess of his passion, and in a merry strain undertook to be an advocate for his love. Her behaviour was still wide of his wish and expectation. He thought she would, in consequence of her discovery, have betrayed some interested symptom; that her face would have undergone some favourable suffusion; that her tongue would have faltered, her breast heaved, and her whole deportment betokened internal agitation and disorder, in which case, he meant to profit by the happy impression, and declare himself, before she could possibly recollect the dictates of her pride.—Baffled however in his endeavours, by the serenity of the young lady, which he still deemed equivocal, he had recourse to another experiment, by which he believed he should make a discovery of her sentiments beyond all possibility of doubt. One day, while he accompanied Mademoiselle in her exercise of music, he pretended all of a sudden to be taken ill, and counterfeited a swoon in her apartment. Surprised at this accident, she screamed aloud, but far from running to his assistance, with the transports and distraction of a lover, she ordered her maid, who was present, to support his head, and went in person to call for more help. He was accordingly removed to his own chamber, where, willing to be still more certified of her inclinations, he prolonged the farce, and lay groaning under the pretence of a severe fever.

The whole family was alarmed upon this occasion; for, as we have already observed, he was an universal favourite. He was immediately visited by the old Count and his lady, who expressed the utmost concern at his distemper, ordered him to be carefully attended, and sent for a physician without loss of time. The young gentleman would scarce stir from his bedside, where he ministered unto him with all the demonstrations of brotherly affection; and Miss exhorted him to keep up his spirits, with many expressions of unreserved sympathy and regard. Nevertheless, he saw nothing in her behaviour but what might be naturally expected from common friendship, and a compassionate disposition, and was very much mortified at his disappointment.

Whether the miscarriage actually affected his constitution, or the doctor happened to be mistaken in his diagnostics, we shall not pretend to determine; but the patient was certainly treated secundum artem, and all his complaints in a little time realised; for the physician, like a true graduate, had an eye to the apothecary in his prescriptions; and such was the concern and scrupulous care with which our hero was attended, that the orders of the faculty were performed with the utmost punctuality. He was blooded, vomited, purged, and blistered, in the usual forms (for the physicians of Hungary are generally as well skilled in the arts of their occupation as any other leeches under the sun), and swallowed a whole dispensary of bolusses, draughts, and apozems, by which means he became fairly delirious in three days, and so untractable, that he could be no longer managed according to rule; otherwise, in all likelihood, the world would never have enjoyed the benefit of these adventures. In short, his constitution, though unable to cope with two such formidable antagonists as the doctor and the disease he had conjured up, was no sooner rid of the one, than it easily got the better of the other; and though Ferdinand, after all, found his grand aim unaccomplished, his malady was productive of a consequence, which, though he had not foreseen it, he did not fail to convert to his own use and advantage.

CHAPTER SEVEN.
ENGAGES IN PARTNERSHIP WITH A FEMALE ASSOCIATE, IN ORDER TO PUT HIS TALENTS IN ACTION.

While he displayed his qualifications in order to entrap the heart of his young mistress, he had unwittingly enslaved the affections of her maid. This attendant was also a favourite of the young lady, and, though her senior by two or three good years at least, unquestionably her superior in point of personal beauty; she moreover possessed a good stock of cunning and discernment, and was furnished by nature with a very amorous complexion. These circumstances being premised, the reader will not be surprised to find her smitten by those uncommon qualifications which we have celebrated in young Fathom. She had in good sooth long sighed in secret, under the powerful influence of his charms, and practised upon him all those little arts, by which a woman strives to attract the admiration, and ensnare the heart of a man she loves; but all his faculties were employed upon the plan which he had already projected; that was the goal of his whole attention, to which all his measures tended; and whether or not he perceived the impression he had made upon Teresa, he never gave her the least reason to believe he was conscious of his victory, until he found himself baffled in his design upon the heart of her mistress.—She therefore persevered in her distant attempts to allure him, with the usual coquetries of dress and address, and, in the sweet hope of profiting by his susceptibility, made shift to suppress her feelings, and keep her passion within bounds, until his supposed danger alarmed her fears, and raised such a tumult within her breast, that she could no longer conceal her love, but gave a loose to her sorrow in the most immoderate expressions of anguish and affliction, and, while his delirium lasted, behaved with all the agitation of a despairing shepherdess.

Ferdinand was, or pretended to be, the last person in the family who understood the situation of her thoughts; when he perceived her passion, he entered into deliberation with himself, and tasked his reflection and foresight, in order to discover how best he might convert this conquest to his own advantage. Here, then, that we may neglect no opportunity of doing justice to our hero, it will be proper to observe, that, howsoever unapt his understanding might be to receive and retain the usual culture of the schools, he was naturally a genius self-taught, in point of sagacity and invention.—He dived into the characters of mankind, with a penetration peculiar to himself, and, had he been admitted as a pupil in any political academy, would have certainly become one of the ablest statesmen in Europe.

Having revolved all the probable consequences of such a connexion, he determined to prosecute an amour with the lady whose affection he had subdued; because he hoped to interest her as an auxiliary in his grand scheme upon Mademoiselle, which he did not as yet think proper to lay aside; for he was not more ambitious in the plan, than indefatigable in the prosecution of it. He knew it would be impossible to execute his aims upon the Count's daughter under the eye of Teresa, whose natural discernment would be whetted with jealousy, and who would watch his conduct, and thwart his progress with all the vigilance and spite of a slighted maiden. On the other hand, he did not doubt of being able to bring her over to his interest, by the influence he had already gained, or might afterwards acquire over her passions; in which case, she would effectually espouse his cause, and employ her good offices with her mistress in his behalf; besides, he was induced by another motive, which, though secondary, did not fail in this case to have an effect upon his determination. He looked upon Teresa with the eyes of appetite, which he longed to gratify; for he was not at all dead to the instigations of the flesh, though he had philosophy enough to resist them, when he thought they interfered with his interest. Here the case was quite different. His desire happened to be upon the side of his advantage, and therefore, resolving to indulge it, he no sooner found himself in a condition to manage such an adventure, than he began to make gradual advances in point of warmth and particular complacency to the love-sick maid.

He first of all thanked her, in the most grateful terms, for the concern she had manifested at his distemper, and the kind services he had received from her during the course of it; he treated her upon all occasions with unusual affability and regard, assiduously courted her acquaintance and conversation, and contracted an intimacy that in a little time produced a declaration of love. Although her heart was too much intendered to hold out against all the forms of assault, far from yielding at discretion, she stood upon honourable terms, with great obstinacy of punctilio, and, while she owned he was master of her inclinations, gave him to understand, with a peremptory and resolute air, that he should never make a conquest of her virtue; observing, that, if the passion he professed was genuine, he would not scruple to give such a proof of it as would at once convince her of his sincerity; and that he could have no just cause to refuse her that satisfaction, she being his equal in point of birth and situation; for, if he was the companion and favourite of the young Count, she was the friend and confidant of Mademoiselle.

He acknowledged the strength of her argument, and that her condescension was greater than his deserts, but objected against the proposal, as infinitely prejudicial to the fortunes of them both. He represented the state of dependence in which they mutually stood; their utter incapacity to support one another under the consequences of a precipitate match, clandestinely made, without the consent and concurrence of their patrons. He displayed, with great eloquence, all those gay expectations they had reason to entertain, from that eminent degree of favour which they had already secured in the family; and set forth, in the most alluring colours, those enchanting scenes of pleasure they might enjoy in each other, without that disagreeable consciousness of a nuptial chain, provided she would be his associate in the execution of a plan which he had projected for their reciprocal convenience.

Having thus inflamed her love of pleasure and curiosity, he, with great caution, hinted his design upon the young lady's fortune, and, perceiving her listening with the most greedy attention, and perfectly ripe for the conspiracy, he disclosed his intention at full length, assuring her, with the most solemn protestations of love and attachment, that, could he once make himself legal possessor of an estate which Mademoiselle inherited by the will of a deceased aunt, his dear Teresa should reap the happy fruits of his affluence, and wholly engross his time and attention.

Such a base declaration our hero would not have ventured to make, had he not implicitly believed the damsel was as great a latitudinarian as himself, in point of morals and principle; and been well assured, that, though he should be mistaken in her way of thinking, so far as to be threatened with a detection of his purpose, he would always have it in his power to refute her accusation as mere calumny, by the character he had hitherto maintained, and the circumspection of his future conduct.

He seldom or never erred in his observations on the human heart. Teresa, instead of disapproving, relished the plan in general, with demonstrations of singular satisfaction. She at once conceived all the advantageous consequences of such a scheme, and perceived in it only one flaw, which, however, she did not think incurable. This defect was no other than a sufficient bond of union, by which they might be effectually tied down to their mutual interest. She foresaw, that, in case Ferdinand should obtain possession of the prize, he might, with great ease, deny their contract, and disavow her claim of participation. She therefore demanded security, and proposed, as a preliminary of the agreement, that he should privately take her to wife, with a view to dispel all her apprehensions of his inconstancy or deceit, as such a previous engagement would be a check upon his behaviour, and keep him strictly to the letter of their contract.

He could not help subscribing to the righteousness of this proposal, which, nevertheless, he would have willingly waived, on the supposition that they could not possibly be joined in the bands of wedlock with such secrecy as the nature of the case absolutely required. This would have been a difficulty soon removed, had the scene of the transaction been laid in the metropolis of England, where passengers are plied in the streets by clergymen, who prostitute their characters and consciences for hire, in defiance of all decency and law; but in the kingdom of Hungary, ecclesiastics are more scrupulous in the exercise of their function, and the objection was, or supposed to be, altogether insurmountable; so that they were fain to have recourse to an expedient, with which, after some hesitation, our she-adventurer was satisfied. They joined hands in the sight of Heaven, which they called to witness, and to judge the sincerity of their vows, and engaged, in a voluntary oath, to confirm their union by the sanction of the church, whenever a convenient opportunity for so doing should occur.

The scruples of Teresa being thus removed, she admitted Ferdinand to the privileges of a husband, which he enjoyed in stolen interviews, and readily undertook to exert her whole power in promoting his suit with her young mistress, because she now considered his interest as inseparably connected with her own. Surely nothing could be more absurd or preposterous than the articles of this covenant, which she insisted upon with such inflexibility. How could she suppose that her pretended lover would be restrained by an oath, when the very occasion of incurring it was an intention to act in violation of all laws human and divine? and yet such ridiculous conjuration is commonly the cement of every conspiracy, how dark, how treacherous, how impious soever it may be: a certain sign that there are some remains of religion left in the human mind, even after every moral sentiment hath abandoned it; and that the most execrable ruffian finds means to quiet the suggestions of his conscience, by some reversionary hope of Heaven's forgiveness.

CHAPTER EIGHT.
THEIR FIRST ATTEMPT; WITH A DIGRESSION WHICH SOME READERS MAY THINK IMPERTINENT.

Be this as it will, our lovers, though real voluptuaries, amidst the first transports of their enjoyment did not neglect the great political aim of their conjunction. Teresa's bedchamber, to which our hero constantly repaired at midnight, was the scene of their deliberations, and there it was determined that the damsel, in order to avoid suspicion, should feign herself irritated at the indifference of Ferdinand, her passion for whom was by this time no secret in the family; and that, with a view to countenance this affectation, he should upon all occasions treat her with an air of loftiness and disdain.

So screened from all imputation of fraud, she was furnished by him with artful instructions how to sound the inclinations of her young mistress, how to recommend his person and qualifications by the sure methods of contradiction, comparisons, revilings, and reproach; how to watch the paroxysms of her disposition, inflame her passions, and improve, for his advantage, those moments of frailty from which no woman is exempted. In short, this consummate politician taught his agent to poison the young lady's mind with insidious conversation, tending to inspire her with the love of guilty pleasure, to debauch her sentiments, and confound her ideas of dignity and virtue. After all, the task is not difficult to lead the unpractised heart astray, by dint of those opportunities her seducer possessed. The seeds of insinuation seasonably sown upon the warm luxuriant soil of youth, could hardly fail of shooting up into such intemperate desires as he wanted to produce, especially when cultured and cherished in her unguarded hours, by that stimulating discourse which familiarity admits, and the looser passions, ingrafted in every breast, are apt to relish and excuse.

Fathom had previously reconnoitred the ground, and discovered some marks of inflammability in Mademoiselle's constitution; her beauty was not such as to engage her in those gaieties of amusement which could flatter her vanity and dissipate her ideas; and she was of an age when the little loves and young desires take possession of the fancy; he therefore concluded, that she had the more leisure to indulge these enticing images of pleasure that youth never fails to create, particularly in those who, like her, were addicted to solitude and study.

Teresa, full fraught with the wily injunctions of her confederate, took the field, and opened the campaign with such remarkable sourness in her aspect when Ferdinand appeared, that her young lady could not help taking notice of her affected chagrin, and asked the reason of such apparent alteration in her way of thinking. Prepared for this question, the other replied, in a manner calculated for giving Mademoiselle to understand, that, whatever impressions Ferdinand might have formerly made on her heart, they were now altogether effaced by the pride and insolence with which he had received her advances; and that her breast now glowed with all the revenge of a slighted lover.

To evince the sincerity of this declaration, she bitterly inveighed against him, and even affected to depreciate those talents, in which she knew his chief merit to consist; hoping, by these means, to interest Mademoiselle's candour in his defence. So far the train succeeded. That young lady's love for truth was offended at the calumnies that were vented against Ferdinand in his absence. She chid her woman for the rancour of her remarks, and undertook to refute the articles of his dispraise. Teresa supported her own assertions with great obstinacy, and a dispute ensued, in which her mistress was heated into some extravagant commendations of our adventurer.

His supposed enemy did not fail to make a report of her success, and to magnify every advantage they had gained; believing, in good earnest, that her lady's warmth was the effect of a real passion for the fortunate Mr. Fathom. But he himself viewed the adventure in a different light, and rightly imputed the violence of Mademoiselle's behaviour to the contradiction she had sustained from her maid, or to the fire of her natural generosity glowing in behalf of innocence traduced. Nevertheless, he was perfectly well pleased with the nature of the contest; because, in the course of such debates, he foresaw that he should become habitually her hero, and that, in time, she would actually believe those exaggerations of his merit, which she herself had feigned, for the honour of her own arguments.

This presage, founded upon that principle of self-respect, without which no individual exists, may certainly be justified by manifold occurrences in life. We ourselves have known a very pregnant example, which we shall relate, for the emolument of the reader. A certain needy author having found means to present a manuscript to one of those sons of fortune who are dignified with the appellation of patrons, instead of reaping that applause and advantage with which he had regaled his fancy, had the mortification to find his performance treated with infinite irreverence and contempt, and, in high dudgeon and disappointment, appealed to the judgment of another critic, who, he knew, had no veneration for the first.

This common consolation, to which all baffled authors have recourse, was productive of very happy consequences to our bard; for, though the opinions of both judges concerning the piece were altogether the same, the latter, either out of compassion to the appellant, or desire of rendering his rival ridiculous in the eye of taste, undertook to repair the misfortune, and in this manner executed the plan. In a meeting of literati, to which both these wits belonged, he who had espoused the poet's cause, having previously desired another member to bring his composition on the carpet, no sooner heard it mentioned, than he began to censure it with flagrant marks of scorn, and, with an ironical air, looking at its first condemner, observed, that he must be furiously infected with the rage of patronising, who could take such a deplorable performance into his protection. The sarcasm took effect.

The person against whom it was levelled, taking umbrage at his presumption, assumed an aspect of disdain, and replied with great animosity, that nothing was more easily supported than the character of a Zoilus, because no production was altogether free from blemishes; and any man might pronounce against any piece by the lump, without interesting his own discernment; but to perceive the beauties of a work, it was requisite to have learning, judgment, and taste; and therefore he did not wonder that the gentleman had overlooked a great many in the composition which he so contemptuously decried. A rejoinder succeeded this reply, and produced a long train of altercation, in which the gentleman, who had formerly treated the book with such disrespect, now professed himself its passionate admirer, and held forth in praise of it with great warmth and elocution.

Not contented with having exhibited this instance of regard, he next morning sent a message to the owner, importing, that he had but superficially glanced over the manuscript, and desiring the favour of perusing it a second time. Being indulged in this request, he recommended it in terms of rapture to all his friends and dependants, and, by dint of unwearied solicitation, procured a very ample subscription for the author.

But, to resume the thread of our story. Teresa's practices were not confined to simple defamation. Her reproaches were contrived so as to imply some intelligence in favour of the person she reviled. In exemplifying his pertness and arrogance, she repeated his witty repartee; on pretence of blaming his ferocity, she recounted proofs of his spirit and prowess; and, in explaining the source of his vanity, gave her mistress to understand, that a certain young lady of fashion was said to be enamoured of his person. Nor did this well-instructed understrapper omit those other parts of her cue which the principal judged necessary for the furtherance of his scheme. Her conversation became less guarded, and took a freer turn than usual; she seized all opportunities of introducing little amorous stories, the greatest part of which were invented for the purposes of warming her passions, and lowering the price of chastity in her esteem; for she represented all the young lady's contemporaries in point of age and situation, as so many sensualists, who, without scruple, indulged themselves in the stolen pleasures of youth.

Meanwhile, Ferdinand seconded these endeavours with his whole industry and address. He redoubled, if possible, his deference and respect, whetting his assiduity to the keenest edge of attention; and, in short, regulated his dress, conversation, and deportment, according to the fancy, turn, and prevailing humour of his young mistress. He, moreover, attempted to profit by her curiosity, which he knew to be truly feminine; and having culled from the library of his patron certain dangerous books, calculated to debauch the minds of young people, left them occasionally upon the table in his apartment, after having directed Teresa to pick them up, as if by accident, in his absence, and carry them off for the entertainment of Mademoiselle; nay, this crafty projector found means to furnish his associate with some mischievous preparations, which were mingled in her chocolate, tea, or coffee, as provocations to warm her constitution; yet all these machinations, ingenious as they were, failed, not only in fulfilling their aim, but even in shaking the foundations of her virtue or pride, which stood their assaults unmoved, like a strong tower built upon a rock, impregnable to all the tempestuous blasts of heaven.

Not but that the conspirators were more than once mistaken in the effects of their artifices, and disposed to applaud themselves on the progress they had made. When at any time she expressed a desire to examine those performances which were laid before her as snares to entrap her chastity, they attributed that, which was no other than curiosity, to a looseness of sentiment; and when she discovered no aversion to hear those anecdotes concerning the frailty of her neighbours, they imputed to abatement of chastity that satisfaction which was the result of self-congratulation on her own superior virtue.

So far did the treacherous accomplice of Fathom presume upon these misconstructions, that she at length divested her tongue of all restraint, and behaved in such a manner, that the young lady, confounded and incensed at her indecency and impudence, rebuked her with great severity, and commanded her to reform her discourse, on pain of being dismissed with disgrace from her service.

CHAPTER NINE.
THE CONFEDERATES CHANGE THEIR BATTERY, AND ACHIEVE A REMARKABLE ADVENTURE.

Thunderstruck at this disappointment, the confederates held a council, in order to deliberate upon the next measures that should be taken; and Ferdinand, for the present, despairing of accomplishing his grand aim, resolved to profit in another manner, by the conveniency of his situation. He represented to his helpmate, that it would be prudent for them to make hay while the sun shone, as their connexion might be sooner or later discovered, and an end put to all those opportunities which they now so happily enjoyed. All principles of morality had been already excluded from their former plan; consequently he found it an easy task to interest Teresa in any other scheme tending to their mutual advantage, howsoever wicked and perfidious it might be. He therefore persuaded her to be his auxiliary in defrauding Mademoiselle at play, and gave her suitable directions for that purpose; and even tutored her how to abuse the trust reposed in her, by embezzling the young lady's effects, without incurring the suspicion of dishonesty.

On the supposition that every servant in the house was not able to resist such temptation, the purse of her mistress, to which the maid had always access, was dropped in a passage which the domestics had occasion to frequent; and Fathom posted himself in a convenient place, in order to observe the effect of his stratagem. Here he was not disappointed in his conjecture. The first person who chanced to pass that way, was one of the chambermaids, with whom Teresa had lived for some time in a state of inveterate enmity, because the wench had failed in that homage and respect which was paid to her by the rest of the servants.

Ferdinand had, in his heart, espoused the quarrel of his associate, and longed for an occasion to deliver her from the malicious observance of such an antagonist. When he, therefore, saw her approach, his heart throbbed with joyful expectations; but, when she snatched up the purse, and thrust it in her bosom, with all the eagerness and confusion of one determined to appropriate the windfall to her own use, his transports were altogether unspeakable. He traced her to her own apartment, whither she immediately retreated with great trepidation, and then communicated the discovery to Teresa, together with instructions how to behave in the sequel.

In conformity with these lessons, she took the first opportunity of going to Mademoiselle, and demanding money for some necessary expense, that the loss might be known before the finder could have leisure to make any fresh conveyance of the prize; and, in the meantime, Ferdinand kept a strict eye upon the motions of the chambermaid. The young lady, having rummaged her pockets in vain, expressed some surprise at the loss of her purse; upon which her attendant gave indications of extreme amazement and concern. She said, it could not possibly be lost; entreated her to search her escritoir, while she herself ran about the room, prying into every corner, with all the symptoms of fear and distraction. Having made this unsuccessful inquiry, she pretended to shed a flood of tears, bewailing her own fate, in being near the person of any lady who met with such a misfortune, by which, she observed, her character might be called in question. She produced her own keys, and begged upon her knees, that her chamber and boxes might be searched without delay.

In a word, she demeaned herself so artfully upon this occasion, that her mistress, who never entertained the least doubt of her integrity, now looked upon her as a miracle of fidelity and attachment, and was at infinite pains to console her for the accident which had happened; protesting that, for her own part, the loss of the money should never affect her with a moment's uneasiness, if she could retrieve a certain medal which she had long kept in her purse, as a remembrance of her deceased aunt, from whom she received it in a present.

Fathom entered accidentally into the midst of this well-acted scene, and, perceiving the agitation of the maid, and the concern of the mistress, desired, in a respectful manner, to know the cause of their disorder. Before the young lady had time to make him acquainted with the circumstances of the case, his accomplice exclaimed, in an affected passion, "Mr. Fathom, my lady has lost her purse; and, as no persons in the family are so much about her as you and I, you must give me leave, in my own justification, to insist upon Mademoiselle's ordering the apartments of us both to be searched without loss of time. Here are my pockets and my keys, and you cannot scruple to give her the same satisfaction; for innocence has nothing to fear."

Miss Melvil reprimanded her sharply for her unmannerly zeal; and Ferdinand eyeing her with a look of disdain, "Madam," said he, "I approve of your proposal; but, before I undergo such mortification, I would advise Mademoiselle to subject the two chambermaids to such inquiry; as they also have access to the apartments, and are, I apprehend, as likely as you or I to behave in such a scandalous manner."

The young lady declared that she was too well satisfied of Teresa's honesty and Ferdinand's honour, to harbour the least suspicion of either, and that she would sooner die than disgrace them so far as to comply with the proposal the former had made; but as she saw no reason for exempting the inferior servants from that examination which Fathom advised, she would forthwith put it in execution. The chambermaids being accordingly summoned, she calmly asked if either of them had accidentally found the purse she had dropped? and both replying in the negative, she assumed an air of severity and determination, and demanding their keys, threatened to examine their trunks on the instant.

The guilty Abigail, who, though an Hungarian, was not inferior, in point of effrontery, to any one of the sisterhood in England, no sooner heard this menace, than she affected an air of affronted innocence, thanked God she had lived in many reputable families, and been trusted with untold gold, but was never before suspected of theft; that the other maid might do as she should think proper, and be mean-spirited enough to let her things be tumbled topsy-turvy and exposed; but, for her own part, if she should be used in that inhuman and disgraceful manner, she would not stay another hour in the house; and in conclusion said, that Mademoiselle had more reason to look sharp after those who enjoyed the greatest share of her favour, than believe their malicious insinuations against innocent people whom they were well known to hate and defame.

This declaration, implying an hint to the prejudice of Teresa, far from diverting Miss Melvil from her purpose, served only to enhance the character of the accused in her opinion, and to confirm her suspicion of the accuser, of whom she again demanded her keys, protesting that, should she prove refractory, the Count himself should take cognisance of the affair, whereas, if she would deal ingenuously, she should have no cause to repent of her confession. So saying, she desired our adventurer to take the trouble of calling up some of the men-servants; upon which the conscious criminal began to tremble, and, falling upon her knees, acknowledged her guilt, and implored the forgiveness of her young mistress.

Teresa, seizing this occasion to signalise her generosity, joined in the request, and the offender was pardoned, after having restored the purse, and promised in the sight of Heaven, that the devil should never again entice her to the commission of such a crime. This adventure fully answered all the purposes of our politician; it established the opinion of his fellow-labourer's virtue, beyond the power of accident or information to shake, and set up a false beacon to mislead the sentiments of Mademoiselle, in case she should for the future meet with the like misfortune.

CHAPTER TEN.
THEY PROCEED TO LEVY CONTRIBUTIONS WITH GREAT SUCCESS, UNTIL OUR HERO SETS OUT WITH THE YOUNG COUNT FOR VIENNA, WHERE HE ENTERS INTO LEAGUE WITH ANOTHER ADVENTURER.

Under this secure cover, Teresa levied contributions upon her mistress with great success. Some trinket was missing every day; the young lady's patience began to fail; the faithful attendant was overwhelmed with consternation, and, with the appearance of extreme chagrin, demanded her dismission, affirming that these things were certainly effected by some person in the family, with a view of murdering her precious reputation. Miss Melvil, not without difficulty, quieted her vexation with assurances of inviolable confidence and esteem, until a pair of diamond earrings vanished, when Teresa could no longer keep her affliction within bounds. Indeed, this was an event of more consequence than all the rest which had happened, for the jewels were valued at five hundred florins.

Mademoiselle was accordingly alarmed to such a degree, that she made her mother acquainted with her loss, and that good lady, who was an excellent economist, did not fail to give indications of extraordinary concern. She asked, if her daughter had reason to suspect any individual in the family, and if she was perfectly confident of her own woman's integrity? Upon which Mademoiselle, with many encomiums on the fidelity and attachment of Teresa, recounted the adventure of the chambermaid, who immediately underwent a strict inquiry, and was even committed to prison, on the strength of her former misdemeanour. Our adventurer's mate insisted upon undergoing the same trial with the rest of the domestics, and, as usual, comprehended Fathom in her insinuations; while he seconded the proposal, and privately counselled the old lady to introduce Teresa to the magistrate of the place. By these preconcerted recriminations, they escaped all suspicion of collusion. After a fruitless inquiry, the prisoner was discharged from her confinement, and turned out of the service of the Count, in whose private opinion the character of no person suffered so much, as that of his own son, whom he suspected of having embezzled the jewels, for the use of a certain inamorata, who, at that time, was said to have captivated his affections.

The old gentleman felt upon this occasion all that internal anguish which a man of honour may be supposed to suffer, on account of a son's degeneracy; and, without divulging his sentiments, or even hinting his suspicions to the youth himself, determined to detach him at once from such dangerous connexions, by sending him forthwith to Vienna, on pretence of finishing his exercises at the academy, and ushering him into acquaintance with the great world. Though he would not be thought by the young gentleman himself to harbour the least doubt of his morals, he did not scruple to unbosom himself on that subject to Ferdinand, whose sagacity and virtue he held in great veneration. This indulgent patron expressed himself in the most pathetic terms, on the untoward disposition of his son; he told Fathom, that he should accompany Renaldo (that was the youth's name) not only as a companion, but a preceptor and pattern; conjured him to assist his tutor in superintending his conduct, and to reinforce the governor's precepts by his own example; to inculcate upon him the most delicate punctilios of honour, and decoy him into extravagance, rather than leave the least illiberal sentiment in his heart.

Our crafty adventurer, with demonstrations of the utmost sensibility, acknowledged the great goodness of the Count in reposing such confidence in his integrity; which, as he observed, none but the worst of villains could abuse; and fervently wished that he might no longer exist, than he should continue to remember and resent the obligations he owed to his kind benefactor. While preparations were making for their departure, our hero held a council with his associate, whom he enriched with many sage instructions touching her future operations; he at the same time disburdened her of all or the greatest part of the spoils she had won, and after having received divers marks of bounty from the Count and his lady, together with a purse from his young mistress, he set out for Vienna, in the eighteenth year of his age, with Renaldo and his governor, who were provided with letters of recommendation to some of the Count's friends belonging to the Imperial court.

Such a favourable introduction could not fail of being advantageous to a youth of Ferdinand's specious accomplishments; for he was considered as the young Count's companion, admitted into his parties, and included in all the entertainments to which Renaldo was invited. He soon distinguished himself by his activity and address, in the course of those exercises that were taught at the academy of which he was pupil; his manners were so engaging as to attract the acquaintance of his fellow-students, and his conversation being sprightly and inoffensive, grew into very great request; in a word, he and the young Count formed a remarkable contrast, which, in the eye of the world, redounded to his advantage.

They were certainly, in all respects, the reverse of each other. Renaldo, under a total defect of exterior cultivation, possessed a most excellent understanding, with every virtue that dignifies the human heart; while the other, beneath a most agreeable outside, with an inaptitude and aversion to letters, concealed an amazing fund of villany and ingratitude. Hitherto his observation had been confined to a narrow sphere, and his reflections, though surprisingly just and acute, had not attained to that maturity which age and experience give; but now, his perceptions began to be more distinct, and extended to a thousand objects which had never before come under his cognisance.

He had formerly imagined, but was now fully persuaded, that the sons of men preyed upon one another, and such was the end and condition of their being. Among the principal figures of life, he observed few or no characters that did not bear a strong analogy to the savage tyrants of the wood. One resembled a tiger in fury and rapaciousness; a second prowled about like an hungry wolf, seeking whom he might devour; a third acted the part of a jackal, in beating the bush for game to his voracious employer; and the fourth imitated the wily fox, in practising a thousand crafty ambuscades for the destruction of the ignorant and unwary. This last was the department of life for which he found himself best qualified by nature and inclination; and he accordingly resolved that his talent should not rust in his possession. He was already pretty well versed in all the sciences of play; but he had every day occasion to see these arts carried to such a surprising pitch of finesse and dexterity, as discouraged him from building his schemes on that foundation.

He therefore determined to fascinate the judgment, rather than the eyes of his fellow-creatures, by a continual exercise of that gift of deceiving, with which he knew himself endued to an unrivalled degree; and to acquire unbounded influence with those who might be subservient to his interest, by an assiduous application to their prevailing passions. Not that play was altogether left out in the projection of his economy.— Though he engaged himself very little in the executive part of gaming, he had not been long in Vienna, when he entered into league with a genius of that kind, whom he distinguished among the pupils of the academy, and who indeed had taken up his habitation in that place with a view to pillage the provincials on their first arrival in town, before they could be armed with proper circumspection to preserve their money, or have time to dispose of it in any other shape.

Similar characters naturally attract each other, and people of our hero's principles are, of all others, the most apt to distinguish their own likeness wheresoever it occurs; because they always keep the faculty of discerning in full exertion. It was in consequence of this mutual alertness, that Ferdinand and the stranger, who was a native of Tyrol, perceived themselves reflected in the dispositions of each other, and immediately entered into an offensive and defensive alliance; our adventurer undertaking for the articles of intelligence, countenance, and counsel, and his associate charging himself with the risk of execution.

CHAPTER ELEVEN.
FATHOM MAKES VARIOUS EFFORTS IN THE WORLD OF GALLANTRY.

Thus connected, they began to hunt in couples; and Fathom, in order to profit by the alliance with a good grace, contrived a small scheme that succeeded to his wish. Renaldo being one night intoxicated in the course of a merry-making with his fellow-pupils, from which Fathom had purposely absented himself, was by the Tyrolese so artfully provoked to play, that he could not resist the temptation, but engaged at passdice with that fell adversary, who, in less than an hour, stripped him of a pretty round sum. Next day, when the young gentleman recovered the use of his reflection, he was sensibly chagrined at the folly and precipitation of his own conduct, an account of which he communicated in confidence to our hero, with demonstrations of infinite shame and concern.

Ferdinand, having moralised upon the subject with great sagacity, and sharply inveighed against the Tyrolese, for the unfair advantage he had taken, retired to his closet, and wrote the following billet, which was immediately sent to his ally:—

"The obligations I owe, and the attachments I feel, to the Count de Melvil, will not suffer me to be an idle spectator of the wrongs offered to his son, in the dishonourable use, I understand, you made last night of his unguarded hours. I therefore insist upon your making immediate restitution of the booty which you so unjustly got; otherwise I expect you will meet me upon the ramparts, near the bastion de la Port Neuve, to-morrow morning at daybreak, in order to justify, with your sword, the finesse you have practised upon the friend of FERDINAND DE FATHOM."

The gamester no sooner received this intimation, than, according to the plan which had been preconcerted betwixt the author and him, he went to the apartment of Renaldo, and presenting the sum of money which he had defrauded him of the preceding night, told him, with a stern countenance, that, though it was a just acquisition, he scorned to avail himself of his good fortune against any person who entertained the smallest doubt of his honour.

The young Count, surprised at this address, rejected his offer with disdain, and desired to know the meaning of such an unexpected declaration. Upon which, the other produced Ferdinand's billet, and threatened, in very high terms, to meet the stripling according to his invitation, and chastise him severely for his presumption. The consequence of this explanation is obvious. Renaldo, imputing the officiousness of Fathom to the zeal of his friendship, interposed in the quarrel, which was amicably compromised, not a little to the honour of our adventurer, who thus obtained an opportunity of displaying his courage and integrity, without the least hazard to his person; while, at the same time, his confederate recommended himself to the esteem of the young Count, by his spirited behaviour on this occasion; so that Renaldo being less shy of his company for the future, the Tyrolese had the fairer opportunities to prosecute his designs upon the young gentleman's purse.

It would be almost superfluous to say, that these were not neglected. The son of Count Melvil was not deficient in point of penetration; but his whole study was at that time engrossed by the care of his education, and he had sometimes recourse to play as an amusement by which he sought to unbend the severity of his attention. No wonder then that he fell a prey to an artful gamester, who had been regularly trained to the profession, and made it the sole study of his life; especially as the Hungarian was remarkable for a warmth of temper, which a knight of the post always knows how to manage for his own advantage.

In the course of these operations, Fathom was a very useful correspondent. He instructed the Tyrolese in the peculiarities of Renaldo's disposition, and made him acquainted with the proper seasons for profiting by his dexterity. Ferdinand, for example, who, by the authority derived to him from the injunctions of the old Count, sometimes took upon himself the office of an adviser, cunningly chose to counsel the son at those conjunctures when he knew him least able to bear such expostulation. Advice improperly administered generally acts in diametrical opposition to the purpose for which it is supposed to be given; at least this was the case with the young gentleman, who, inflamed by the reproof of such a tutor, used to obey the dictates of his resentment in an immediate repetition of that conduct which our adventurer had taken the liberty to disapprove; and the gamester was always at hand to minister unto his indignation. By these means he was disencumbered of divers considerable remittances, with which his father cheerfully supplied him, on the supposition that they were spent with taste and liberality, under the direction of our adventurer.

But Ferdinand's views were not confined to the narrow field of this alliance. He attempted divers enterprises in the world of gallantry, conscious of his own personal qualifications, and never doubting that he could insinuate himself into the good graces of some married lady about court, or lay an opulent dowager under contribution. But he met with an obstacle in his endeavours of this kind, which all his art was unable to surmount. This was no other than the obscurity of his birth, and the want of a title, without which no person in that country lays claim to the privileges of a gentleman. Had he foreseen this inconvenience he might have made shift to obviate the consequences, by obtaining permission to appear in the character of the Count's kinsman; though, in all probability, such an expedient would not have been extremely agreeable to the old gentleman, who was very tenacious of the honour of his family; nevertheless, his generosity might have been prevailed upon to indulge Fathom with such a pretext, in consideration of the youth's supposed attachment, and the obligations for which he deemed himself indebted to his deceased mother.

True it is, Ferdinand, upon his first arrival at Vienna, had been admitted into fashionable company, on the footing of Renaldo's companion, because nobody suspected the defect of his pedigree; and even after a report had been circulated to the prejudice of his extraction, by the industry of a lacquey who attended the young Count, there were not wanting many young people of distinction who still favoured him with their countenance and correspondence; but he was no longer invited to private families, in which only he could expect to profit by his address among the ladies, and had the mortification of finding himself frequently excepted from parties which were expressly calculated for the entertainment of the young Count. Luckily, his spirit was so pliant as to sustain these slights without being much dejected; instead of repining at the loss of that respect which had been paid to him at first, he endeavoured, with all his might, to preserve the little that still remained, and resolved to translate into a humbler sphere that gallantry which he had no longer opportunities of displaying in the world of rank and fashion.

CHAPTER TWELVE.
HE EFFECTS A LODGMENT IN THE HOUSE OF A RICH JEWELLER.

In consequence of this determination, he to the uttermost exerted his good-humour among the few friends of consequence his fortune had left, and even carried his complaisance so far as to become the humble servant of their pleasures, while he attempted to extend his acquaintance in an inferior path of life, where he thought his talents would shine more conspicuous than at the assemblies of the great, and conduce more effectually to the interest of all his designs. Nor did he find himself disappointed in that expectation, sanguine as it was. He soon found means to be introduced to the house of a wealthy bourgeois, where every individual was charmed with his easy air and extraordinary qualifications. He accommodated himself surprisingly to the humours of the whole family; smoked tobacco, swallowed wine, and discoursed of stones with the husband, who was a rich jeweller; sacrificed himself to the pride and loquacity of the wife; and played upon the violin, and sung alternately, for the amusement of his only daughter, a buxom lass, nearly of his own age, the fruit of a former marriage.

It was not long before Ferdinand had reason to congratulate himself on the footing he had gained in this society. He had expected to find, and in a little time actually discovered, that mutual jealousy and rancour which almost always subsist between a daughter and her step-dame, inflamed with all the virulence of female emulation; for the disparity in their ages served only to render them the more inveterate rivals in the desire of captivating the other sex. Our adventurer having deliberated upon the means of converting this animosity to his own advantage, saw no method for this purpose so feasible as that of making his approaches to the hearts of both, by ministering to each in private, food for their reciprocal envy and malevolence; because he well knew that no road lies so direct and open to a woman's heart as that of gratifying her passions of vanity and resentment.

When he had an opportunity of being particular with the mother, he expressed his concern for having unwittingly incurred the displeasure of Mademoiselle, which, he observed, was obvious in every circumstance of her behaviour towards him; protesting he was utterly innocent of all intention of offending her; and that he could not account for his disgrace any other way, than by supposing she took umbrage at the direction of his chief regards towards her mother-in-law, which, he owned, was altogether involuntary, being wholly influenced by that lady's superior charms and politeness.

Such a declaration was perfectly well calculated for the meridian of a dame like her, who with all the intoxications of unenlightened pride, and an increased appetite for pleasure, had begun to find herself neglected, and even to believe that her attractions were actually on the wane. She very graciously consoled our gallant for the mishap of which he complained, representing Wilhelmina (that was the daughter's name) as a pert, illiterate, envious baggage, of whose disgust he ought to make no consideration; then she recounted many instances of her own generosity to that young lady, with the returns of malice and ingratitude she had made; and, lastly, enumerated all the imperfections of her person, education, and behaviour; that he might see with what justice the gypsy pretended to vie with those who had been distinguished by the approbation and even gallantry of the best people in Vienna.

Having thus established himself her confidant and gossip, he knew his next step of promotion would necessarily be to the degree of her lover; and in that belief resolved to play the same game with Mademoiselle Wilhelmina, whose complexion was very much akin to that of her stepmother; indeed they resembled each other too much to live upon any terms of friendship or even decorum. Fathom, in order to enjoy a private conversation with the young lady, never failed to repeat his visit every afternoon, till at length he had the pleasure of finding her disengaged, the jeweller being occupied among his workmen, and his wife gone to assist at a lying-in.

Our adventurer and the daughter had already exchanged their vows, by the expressive language of the eyes; he had even declared himself in some tender ejaculations which had been softly whispered in her ear, when he could snatch an opportunity of venting them unperceived; nay, he had upon divers occasions gently squeezed her fair hand, on pretence of tuning her harpsichord, and been favoured with returns of the same cordial pressure; so that, instead of accosting her with the fearful hesitation and reserve of a timid swain, he told her, after the exercise of the doux-yeux, that he was come to confer with her upon a subject that nearly concerned her peace; and asked if she had not observed of late an evident abatement of friendship in her mother's behaviour to him, whom she had formerly treated with such marks of favour and respect. Mademoiselle would not pay so ill a compliment to her own discernment as to say she had not perceived the alteration; which, on the contrary, she owned was extremely palpable; nor was it difficult to divine the cause of such estranged looks. This remark was accompanied with an irresistible glance; she smiled enchanting, the colour deepened on her cheeks, her breast began to heave, and her whole frame underwent a most agreeable confusion.

Ferdinand was not a man to let such a favourable conjuncture pass unregarded. "Yes, charming Wilhelmina!" exclaimed the politician in an affected rapture, "the cause is as conspicuous as your attractions. She hath, in spite of all my circumspection, perceived that passion which it is not in my power to conceal, and in consequence of which I now declare myself your devoted adorer; or, conscious of your superior excellence, her jealousy hath taken the alarm, and, though stung with conjecture only, repines at the triumph of your perfections. How far this spirit of malignity may be inflamed to my prejudice, I know not. Perhaps, as this is the first, it may be also the last opportunity I shall have of avowing the dearest sentiments of my heart to the fair object that inspired them; in a word, I may be for ever excluded from your presence. Excuse me, then, divine creature! from the practice of those unnecessary forms, which I should take pride in observing, were I indulged with the ordinary privileges of an honourable lover; and, once for all, accept the homage of an heart overflowing with love and admiration. Yes, adorable Wilhelmina! I am dazzled with your supernatural beauty; your other accomplishments strike me with wonder and awe. I am enchanted by the graces of your deportment, ravished with the charms of your conversation; and there is a certain tenderness of benevolence in that endearing aspect, which, I trust, will not fail to melt with sympathy at the emotions of a faithful slave like me."

So saying, he threw himself upon his knees, and, seizing her plump hand, pressed it to his lips with all the violence of real transport. The nymph, whose passions nature had filled to the brim, could not hear such a rhapsody unmoved. Being an utter stranger to addresses of this kind, she understood every word of it in the literal acceptation; she believed implicitly in the truth of the encomiums he had bestowed, and thought it reasonable he should be rewarded for the justice he had done to her qualifications, which had hitherto been almost altogether overlooked. In short, her heart began to thaw, and her face to hang out the flag of capitulation; which was no sooner perceived by our hero, than he renewed his attack with redoubled fervour, pronouncing in a most vehement tone, "Light of my eyes, and empress of my soul! behold me prostrate at your feet, waiting with the most pious resignation, for that sentence from your lips, on which my future happiness or misery must altogether depend. Not with more reverence does the unhappy bashaw kiss the sultan's letter that contains his doom, than I will submit to your fatal determination. Speak then, angelic sweetness! for never, ah! never will I rise from this suppliant posture, until I am encouraged to live and hope. No! if you refuse to smile upon my passion, here shall I breathe the last sighs of a despairing lover; here shall this faithful sword do the last office to its unfortunate master, and shed the blood of the truest heart that ever felt the cruel pangs of disappointed love."

The young lady, well-nigh overcome by this effusion, which brought the tears into her eyes, "Enough, enough," cried she, interrupting him, "sure you men were created for the ruin of our sex."—"Ruin!" re-echoed Fathom, "talk not of ruin and Wilhelmina! let these terms be for ever parted, far as the east and west asunder! let ever smiling peace attend her steps, and love and joy still wanton in her train! Ruin, indeed, shall wait upon her enemies, if such there be, and those love-lorn wretches who pine with anguish under her disdain. Grant me, kind Heaven, a more propitious boon; direct her genial regards to one whose love is without example, and whose constancy is unparalleled. Bear witness to my constancy and faith, ye verdant hills, ye fertile plains, ye shady groves, ye purling streams; and if I prove untrue, ah! let me never find a solitary willow or a bubbling brook, by help of which I may be enabled to put a period to my wretched life."

Here this excellent actor began to sob most piteously, and the tender-hearted Wilhelmina, unable longer to withstand his moving tale, with a repetition of the interjection, ah! gently dropped into his arms. This was the beginning of a correspondence that soon rose to a very interesting pitch; and they forthwith concerted measures for carrying it on without the knowledge or suspicion of her mother-in-law. Nevertheless, the young lady, vanquished as she was, and unskilled in the ways of men, would not all at once yield at discretion; but insisted upon those terms, without which no woman's reputation can be secured. Our lover, far from seeking to evade the proposal, assented to it in terms of uncommon satisfaction, and promised to use his whole industry in finding a priest upon whose discretion they could rely; nay, he certainly resolved to comply with her request in good earnest, rather than forfeit the advantages which he foresaw in their union. His good fortune, however, exempted him from the necessity of taking such a step, which at best must have been disagreeable; for so many difficulties occurred in the inquiry which was set on foot, and so artfully did Fathom in the meantime manage the influence he had already gained over her heart, that, before her passion could obtain a legal gratification, she surrendered to his wish, without any other assurance, than his solemn profession of sincerity and truth, on which she reposed herself with the most implicit confidence and faith.

CHAPTER THIRTEEN.
HE IS EXPOSED TO A MOST PERILOUS INCIDENT IN THE COURSE OF HIS INTRIGUE WITH THE DAUGHTER.

He was rejoiced to find her so easily satisfied in such a momentous concern, for the principal aim of the intrigue was to make her necessary to his interested views, and even, if possible, an associate in the fraudulent plans he had projected upon her father; consequently he considered this relaxation in her virtue as an happy omen of his future success. All the obstacles to their mutual enjoyment being thus removed, our adventurer was by his mistress indulged with an assignation in her own chamber, which, though contiguous to that of her stepmother, was provided with a door that opened into a common staircase, to which he had access at all hours of the night.

He did not neglect the rendezvous, but, presenting himself at the appointed time, which was midnight, made the signal they had agreed upon, and was immediately admitted by Wilhelmina, who waited for hire with a lover's impatience. Fathom was not deficient in those expressions of rapture that are current on those occasions; but, on the contrary, became so loud in the transports of self-congratulation, that his voice reached the ears of the vigilant stepmother, who wakening the jeweller from his first nap, gave him to understand that some person was certainly in close conversation with his daughter; and exhorted him to rise forthwith, and vindicate the honour of his family.

The German, who was naturally of a phlegmatic habit, and never went to bed without a full dose of the creature, which added to his constitutional drowsiness, gave no ear to his wife's intimation, until she had repeated it thrice, and used other means to rouse him from the arms of slumber. Meanwhile Fathom and his inamorata overheard her information, and our hero would have made his retreat immediately, through the port by which he entered, had not his intention been overruled by the remonstrances of the young lady, who observed that the door was already fast bolted, and could not possibly be opened without creating a noise that would confirm the suspicion of her parents; and that over and above this objection he would, in sallying from that door, run the risk of being met by her father, who in all probability would present himself before it, in order to hinder our hero's escape. She therefore conveyed him softly into her closet, where she assured him he might remain with great tranquillity, in full confidence that she would take such measures as would effectually screen him from detection.

He was fain to depend upon her assurance, and accordingly ensconced himself behind her dressing-table; but he could not help sweating with apprehension, and praying fervently to God for his deliverance, when he heard the jeweller thundering at the door, and calling to his daughter for admittance. Wilhelmina, who was already undressed, and had purposely extinguished the light, pretended to be suddenly waked from her sleep, and starting up, exclaimed in a tone of surprise and affright, "Jesu, Maria! what is the matter?" — "Hussy!" replied the German in a terrible accent, "open the door this instant; there is a man in your bedchamber, and, by the lightning and thunder! I will wash away the stain he has cast upon my honour with the schellum's heart's-blood."

Not at all intimidated by this boisterous threat, she admitted him without hesitation, and, with a shrillness of voice peculiar to herself, began to hold forth upon her own innocence and his unjust suspicion, mingling in her harangue sundry oblique hints against her mother-in-law, importing, that some people were so viciously inclined by their own natures, that she did not wonder at their doubting the virtue of other people; but that these people despised the insinuations of such people, who ought to be more circumspect in their own conduct, lest they themselves should suffer reprisals from those people whom they had so maliciously slandered.

Having uttered these flowers of rhetoric, which were calculated for the hearing of her step-dame, who stood with a light at her husband's back, the young lady assumed an ironical air, and admonished her father to search every corner of her apartment. She even affected to assist his inquiry; with her own hands pulled out a parcel of small drawers, in which her trinkets were contained; desired him to look into her needlecase and thimble, and, seeing his examination fruitless, earnestly intreated him to rummage her closet also, saying, with a sneer, that, in all probability, the dishonourer would be found in that lurking-place. The manner in which she pretended to ridicule his apprehensions made an impression upon the jeweller, who was very well disposed to retreat into his own nest, when his wife, with a certain slyness in her countenance, besought him to comply with his daughter's request, and look into that same closet, by which means Wilhelmina's virtue would obtain a complete triumph.

Our adventurer, who overheard the conversation, was immediately seized with a palsy of fear. He trembled at every joint, the sweat trickled down his forehead, his teeth began to chatter, his hair to stand on end; and he, in his heart, bitterly cursed the daughter's petulance, the mother's malice, together with his own precipitation, by which he was involved in an adventure so pregnant with danger and disgrace. Indeed, the reader may easily conceive his disorder, when he heard the key turning in the lock, and the German swearing that he would make him food for the beasts of the field and the fowls of the air.

Fathom had come unprepared with weapons of defence, was naturally an economist of his person, and saw himself on the brink of forfeiting not only the promised harvest of his double intrigue, but also the reputation of a man of honour, upon which all his future hopes depended. His agony was therefore unspeakable, when the door flew open; and it was not till after a considerable pause of recollection, that he perceived the candle extinguished by the motion of the air produced from the German's sudden irruption. This accident, which disconcerted him so much as to put a full stop to his charge, was very favourable to our hero, who, summoning all his presence of mind, crept up into the chimney, while the jeweller stood at the door, waiting for his wife's return with another light; so that, when the closet was examined, there was nothing found to justify the report which the stepmother had made; and the father, after having made a slight apology to Wilhelmina for his intrusion, retired with his yoke-fellow into their own chamber.

The young lady, who little thought that her papa would have taken her at her word, was overwhelmed with confusion and dismay, when she saw him enter the closet; and, had her lover been discovered, would, in all probability, have been the loudest in his reproach, and, perhaps, have accused him of an intention to rob the house; but she was altogether astonished when she found he had made shift to elude the inquiry of her parents, because she could not conceive the possibility of his escaping by the window, which was in the third storey, at a prodigious distance from the ground; and how he should conceal himself in the apartment, was a mystery which she could by no means unfold. Before her father and mother retired, she lighted her lamp, on pretence of being afraid to be in the dark, after the perturbation of spirits she had undergone; and her room was no sooner evacuated of such troublesome visitants, than she secured the doors, and went in quest of her lover.

Accordingly, every corner of the closet underwent a new search, and she called upon his name with a soft voice, which she thought no other person would overhear. But Ferdinand did not think proper to gratify her impatience, because he could not judge of the predicament in which he stood by the evidence of all his senses, and would not relinquish his post, until he should be better certified that the coast was clear. Meanwhile, his Dulcinea, having performed her inquiry to no purpose, imagined there was something preternatural in the circumstance of his vanishing so unaccountably, and began to cross herself with great devotion. She returned to her chamber, fixed the lamp in the fireplace, and, throwing herself upon the bed, gave way to the suggestions of her superstition, which were reinforced by the silence that prevailed, and the gloomy glimmering of the light. She reflected upon the trespass she had already committed in her heart, and, in the conjectures of her fear, believed that her lover was no other than the devil himself, who had assumed the appearance of Fathom, in order to tempt and seduce her virtue.

While her imagination teemed with those horrible ideas, our adventurer, concluding, from the general stillness, that the jeweller and his wife were at last happily asleep, ventured to come forth from his hiding-place, and stood before his mistress all begrimed with soot. Wilhelmina, lifting up her eyes, and seeing this sable apparition, which she mistook for Satan in propria persona, instantly screamed, and began to repeat her pater-noster with an audible voice. Upon which Ferdinand, foreseeing that her parents would be again alarmed, would not stay to undeceive her and explain himself, but, unlocking the door with great expedition, ran downstairs, and luckily accomplished his escape. This was undoubtedly the wisest measure he could have taken; for he had not performed one half of his descent toward the street, when the German was at his daughter's bedside, demanding to know the cause of her exclamation. She then gave him an account of what she had seen, with all the exaggerations of her own fancy, and, after having weighed the circumstances of her story, he interpreted the apparition into a thief, who had found means to open the door that communicated with the stair; but, having been scared by Wilhelmina's shriek, had been obliged to retreat before he could execute his purpose.

Our hero's spirits were so wofully disturbed by this adventure, that, for a whole week, he felt no inclination to visit his inamorata, and was not without apprehension that the affair had terminated in an explanation very little to his advantage. He was, however, delivered from this disagreeable suspense, by an accidental meeting with the jeweller himself, who kindly chid him for his long absence, and entertained him in the street with an account of the alarm which his family had sustained, by a thief who broke into Wilhelmina's apartment. Glad to find his apprehension mistaken, he renewed his correspondence with the family, and, in a little time, found reason to console himself for the jeopardy and panic he had undergone.

CHAPTER FOURTEEN.
HE IS REDUCED TO A DREADFUL DILEMMA, IN CONSEQUENCE OF AN ASSIGNATION WITH THE WIFE.

Nor was his whole care and attention engrossed by the execution of this scheme upon the daughter. While he managed his concerns in that quarter with incredible ardour and application, he was not the less indefatigable in the prosecution of his design upon the mother-in-law, which he forwarded with all his art during those opportunities he enjoyed in the absence of Wilhelmina, who was frequently called away by the domestic duties of the house. The passions of the jeweller's wife were in such a state of exaltation, as exempted our hero from the repulses and fatigue attending a long siege.

We have already observed how cunningly he catered for the gratification of her ruling appetite, and have exhibited pregnant proofs of his ability in gaining upon the human heart; the reader will not therefore be surprised at the rapidity of his conquest over the affections of a lady whose complexion was perfectly amorous, and whose vanity laid her open to all the attempts of adulation. In a word, matters were quickly brought to such a mutual understanding, that, one evening, while they amused themselves at lansquenet, Fathom conjured her to give him the rendezvous next day at the house of any third person of her own sex, in whose discretion she could confide; and, after a few affected scruples on her side, which he well knew how to surmount, she complied with his request, and the circumstances of the appointment were settled accordingly. After this treaty, their satisfaction rose to such a warmth, and the conversation became so reciprocally endearing, that our gallant expressed his impatience of waiting so long for the accomplishment of his wishes, and, with the most eager transport, begged she would, if possible, curtail the term of his expectation, that his brain might not suffer by his standing so many tedious hours on the giddy verge of rapture.

The dame, who was naturally compassionate, sympathised with his condition, and, unable to resist his pathetic supplications, gave him to understand that his desire could not be granted, without subjecting them both to some hazard, but that she was disposed to run any risk in behalf of his happiness and peace. After this affectionate preamble, she told him that her husband was then engaged in a quarterly meeting of the jewellers, from whence he never failed to return quite overwhelmed with wine, tobacco, and the phlegm of his own constitution; so that he would fall fast asleep as soon as his head should touch the pillow, and she be at liberty to entertain the lover without interruption, provided he could find means to deceive the jealous vigilance of Wilhelmina, and conceal himself in some corner of the house, unsuspected and unperceived.

Our lover, remembering his adventure with the daughter, would have willingly dispensed with this expedient, and began to repent of the eagerness with which he had preferred his solicitation; but, seeing there was now no opportunity of retracting with honour, he affected to enter heartily into the conversation, and, after much canvassing, it was determined, that, while Wilhelmina was employed in the kitchen, the mother should conduct our adventurer to the outer door, where he should pay the compliment of parting, so as to be overheard by the young lady; but, in the meantime, glide softly into the jeweller's bedchamber, which was a place they imagined least liable to the effects of a daughter's prying disposition, and conceal himself in a large press or wardrobe, that stood in one corner of the apartment. The scene was immediately acted with great success, and our hero cooped up in his cage, where he waited so long, that his desires began to subside, and his imagination to aggravate the danger of his situation.

"Suppose," said he to himself, "this brutal German, instead of being stupefied with wine, should come home inflamed with brandy, to the use of which he is sometimes addicted, far from feeling any inclination to sleep, he will labour under the most fretful anxiety of watching; every irascible particle in his disposition will be exasperated; he will be offended with every object that may present itself to his view; and, if there is the least ingredient of jealousy in his temper, it will manifest itself in riot and rage. What if his frenzy should prompt him to search his wife's chamber for gallants? this would certainly be the first place to which he would direct his inquiry; or, granting this supposition chimerical, I may be seized with an irresistible inclination to cough, before he is oppressed with sleep; he may be waked by the noise I shall make in disengaging myself from this embarrassed situation; and, finally, I may find it impracticable to retire unseen or unheard, after everything else shall have succeeded to my wish."

These suggestions did not at all contribute to the quiet of our adventurer, who, having waited three whole hours in the most uncomfortable suspense, heard the jeweller brought into the room in that very condition which his fears had prognosticated. He had, it seems, quarrelled over his cups with another tradesman, and received a salutation on the forehead with a candlestick, which not only left an ignominious and painful mark upon his countenance, but even disordered his brain to a very dangerous degree of delirium; so that, instead of allowing himself quietly to be undressed and put to bed by his wife, he answered all her gentle admonitions and caresses with the most opprobrious invectives and obstreperous behaviour; and, though he did not tax her with infidelity to his bed, he virulently accused her of extravagance and want of economy; observed, her expensive way of living would bring him to a morsel of bread; and unfortunately recollecting the attempt of the supposed thief, started up from his chair, swearing by G—'s mother that he would forthwith arm himself with a brace of pistols, and search every apartment in the house. "That press," said he, with great vociferation, "may, for aught I know, be the receptacle of some ruffian."

So saying, he approached the ark in which Fathom was embarked, and exclaiming, "Come forth, Satan," applied his foot to the door of it, with such violence as threw him from the centre of gravity, and laid him sprawling on his back. This address made such an impression upon our adventurer, that he had well-nigh obeyed the summons, and burst from his concealment, in a desperate effort to escape, without being recognised by the intoxicated German; and indeed, had the application been repeated, he in all likelihood would have tried the experiment, for by this time his terrors had waxed too strong to be much longer suppressed. From this hazardous enterprise he was, however, exempted by a lucky accident that happened to his disturber, whose head chancing to pitch upon the corner of a chair in his fall, he was immediately lulled into a trance, during which the considerate lady, guessing the disorder of her gallant, and dreading further interruption, very prudently released him from his confinement, after she had put out the light, and in the dark conveyed him to the door, where he was comforted with the promise that she would punctually remember the rendezvous of next day.

She then invoked the assistance of the servants, who, being waked for the purpose, lifted up their master, and tumbled him into bed, while Ferdinand hied him home in an universal sweat, blessing himself from any future achievement of that sort in a house where he had been twice in such imminent danger of life and reputation. Nevertheless, he did not fail to honour the assignation, and avail himself of the disposition his mistress manifested to make him all the recompense in her power for the disappointment and chagrin which he had undergone.

CHAPTER FIFTEEN.
BUT AT LENGTH SUCCEEDS IN HIS ATTEMPT UPON BOTH.

Having thus gained a complete victory over the affections of these two ladies, he began to convert his good fortune to the purposes of that principle, from which his view was never, no, not for a moment, detached. In other words, he used them as ministers and purveyors to his avarice and fraud. As for the mother-in-law, she was of herself so liberal as to anticipate the wishes of any moderate adventurer, and presented him with sundry valuable jewels, as memorials of her esteem; nor was the daughter backward in such expressions of regard; she already considered his interest as her own, and took frequent opportunities of secreting for his benefit certain stray trinkets that she happened to pick up in her excursions within doors.

All these gratifications he received with demonstrations of infinite constraint and reluctance, and, in the midst of his rapacious extortion, acted so cunningly as to impose himself upon both for a miracle of disinterested integrity. Yet, not contented with what he thus could earn, and despairing of being able to steer the bark of his fortune for any length of time between two such dangerous quicksands, he resolved to profit by the occasion while it lasted, and strike some considerable stroke at once. A plan was formed in consequence of this determination, and, at an appointment with the mother in the house of their female friend, our adventurer appeared with an air of dejection, which he veiled with a thin cover of forced pleasantry, that his mistress might suppose he endeavoured to conceal some mortal chagrin that preyed upon his heart.

The stratagem succeeded to his wish. She observed his countenance between whiles overcast, took notice of the involuntary sighs he heaved; and, with the most tender expressions of sympathy, conjured him to make her acquainted with the cause of his affliction. Instead of gratifying her request immediately, he evaded her questions with a respectful reserve, implying, that his love would not suffer him to make her a partner in his sorrow; and this delicacy on his part whetted her impatience and concern to such a degree, that, rather than keep her in such an agony of doubt and apprehension, he was prevailed upon to tell her, that he had been, the preceding night, engaged with a company of his fellow-students, where he had made too free with the champagne, so that his caution forsook him, and he had been decoyed into play by a Tyrolese gamester, who stripped him of all his ready money, and obtained from him an obligation for two hundred florins, which he could not possibly pay without having recourse to his relation the Count de Melvil, who would have just cause to be incensed at his extravagance.

This information he concluded, by declaring that, cost what it would, he was resolved to make a candid confession of the truth, and throw himself entirely upon the generosity of his patron, who could inflict no other punishment than that of discarding him from his favour and protection,—a misfortune which, how grievous soever it might be, he should be able to sustain with fortitude, could he fall upon some method of satisfying the Tyrolese, who was very importunate and savage in his demand. His kind mistress no sooner found out the source of his inquietude, than she promised to dry it up, assuring him that next day, at the same hour, she would enable him to discharge the debt; so that he might set his heart at ease, and recollect that gaiety which was the soul of her enjoyment.

He expressed the utmost astonishment at this generous proffer, which, however, he declined, with an affected earnestness of refusal, protesting, that he should be extremely mortified, if he thought she looked upon him as one of those mercenary gallants who could make such a sordid use of a lady's affection. "No, madam," cried our politician in a pathetic strain, "whatever happens, I shall never part with that internal consolation, that conscious honour never fails to yield in the deepest scenes of solitary distress. The attachment I have the honour to profess for your amiable person, is not founded on such inglorious motives, but is the genuine result of that generous passion which none but the noble-minded feel, and the only circumstance of this misfortune that I dread to encounter, is the necessity of withdrawing myself for ever from the presence of her whose genial smiles could animate my soul against all the persecution of adverse fortune."

This declamation, accompanied with a profound sigh, served only to inflame her desire of extricating him from the difficulty in which he was involved. She exhausted all her eloquence in attempting to persuade him that his refusal was an outrage against her affection. He pretended to refute her arguments, and remained unshaken by all the power of her solicitations, until she had recourse to the most passionate remonstrances of love, and fell at his feet in the posture of a forlorn shepherdess. What he refused to her reason, he granted to her tears, because his heart was melted by her affliction, and next day condescended to accept of her money, out of pure regard to her happiness and peace.

Encouraged by the success of this achievement, he resolved to practise the same experiment upon Wilhelmina, in hope of extracting an equal share of profit from her simplicity and attachment, and, at their very next nocturnal rendezvous in her chamber, reacted the farce already rehearsed, with a small variation, which he thought necessary to stimulate the young lady in his behalf. He rightly concluded, that she was by no means mistress of such a considerable sum as he had already extorted from her mother, and therefore thought proper to represent himself in the most urgent predicament, that her apprehension, on his account, might be so alarmed as to engage her in some enterprise for his advantage, which otherwise she would never have dreamed of undertaking. With this view, after having described his own calamitous situation, in consequence of her pressing entreaties, which he affected to evade, he gave her to understand, that there was no person upon earth to whom he would have recourse in this emergency; for which reason he was determined to rid himself of all his cares at once, upon the friendly point of his own faithful sword.

Such a dreadful resolution could not fail to operate upon the tender passions of his Dulcinea; she was instantly seized with an agony of fear and distraction. Her grief manifested itself in a flood of tears, while she hung round his neck, conjuring him in the most melting terms, by their mutual love, in which they had been so happy, to lay aside that fatal determination, which would infallibly involve her in the same fate; for, she took Heaven to witness, that she would not one moment survive the knowledge of his death.

He was not deficient in expressions of reciprocal regard. He extolled her love and tenderness with a most extravagant eulogium, and seemed wrung with mortal anguish at the prospect of parting for ever from his lovely Wilhelmina; but his honour was a stern and rigid creditor, that could not be appeased, except with his blood; and all the boon she could obtain, by dint of the most woful supplication, was a promise to defer the execution of his baleful purpose for the space of four-and-twenty hours, during which she hoped Heaven would compassionate her sufferings, and inspire her with some contrivance for their mutual relief. Thus he yielded to her fervent request, rather with a view to calm the present transports of her sorrow, than with any expectation of seeing himself redeemed from his fate by her interposition; such at least were his professions when he took his leave, assuring her, that he would not quit his being before he should have devoted a few hours to another interview with the dear object of his love.

Having thus kindled the train, he did not doubt that the mine of his craft would take effect, and repaired to his own lodging, in full persuasion of seeing his aim accomplished, before the time fixed for their last assignation. His prognostic was next morning verified by the arrival of a messenger, who brought to him a small parcel, to which was cemented, with sealing wax, the following epistle:—

"JEWEL OF MY SOUL!—Scarce had you, last night, quitted my disconsolate arms, when I happily recollected that there was in my possession a gold chain, of value more than sufficient to answer the exigence of your present occasions. It was pledged to my grandfather for two hundred crowns by a knight of Malta, who soon after perished in a sea engagement with the enemies of our faith, so that it became the property of our house, and was bequeathed to me by the old gentleman, as a memorial of his particular affection. Upon whom can I more properly bestow it, than him who is already master of my heart! Receive it, therefore, from the bearer of this billet, and convert it, without scruple, to that use which shall be most conducive to your ease and satisfaction; nor seek, from a true romantic notion of honour, which I know you entertain, to excuse yourself from accepting this testimony of my affection. For I have already sworn before an image of our blessed Lady, that I will no longer own you as the sovereign of my heart, nor even indulge you with another interview, if you reject this mark of tenderness and concern from your ever faithful WILHELMINA."

The heart of our adventurer began to bound with joy when he surveyed the contents of this letter; and his eyes sparkled with transport at sight of the chain, which he immediately perceived to be worth twice the sum she had mentioned. Nevertheless, he would not avail himself, without further question, of her generosity; but, that same night, repairing to her apartment at the usual hour of meeting, he prostrated himself before her, and counterfeiting extreme agitation of spirit, begged, in the most urgent terms, not even unaccompanied with tears, that she would take back the present, which he tendered for her acceptance, and spare him the most insufferable mortification of thinking himself exposed to the imputation of being mercenary in his love. Such, he said, was the delicacy of his passion, that he could not possibly exist under the apprehension of incurring a censure so unworthy of his sentiments; and he would a thousand times sooner undergo the persecution of his rancorous creditor, than bear the thought of being in the smallest consideration lessened in her esteem; nay, so far did he carry his pretensions to punctilio, as to protest, that, should she refuse to quiet the scruples of his honour on this score, her unyielding beneficence would serve only to hasten the execution of his determined purpose, to withdraw himself at once from a life of vanity and misfortune.

The more pathetically he pleaded for her compliance, the more strenuously did she resist his remonstrances. She advanced all the arguments her reason, love, and terror could suggest, reminded him of her oath, from which he could not suppose she would recede, whatever the consequence might be; and in conclusion vowed to Heaven, with great solemnity and devotion, that she would not survive the news of his death. Thus the alternative she offered was either to retain the chain and be happy in her affection, or forfeit all title to her love, and die in the conviction of having brought his innocent mistress to an untimely grave.

His fortitude was not proof against this last consideration. "My savage honour," said he, "would enable me to endure the pangs of eternal separation in the confidence of being endowed with the power of ending these tortures by the energy of my own hand; but the prospect of Wilhelmina's death, and that too occasioned by my inflexibility, disarms my soul of all her resolution, swallows up the dictates of my jealous pride, and fills my bosom with such a gush of tenderness and sorrow, as overwhelms the whole economy of my purpose! Yes, enchanting creature! I sacrifice my glory to that irresistible reflection; and, rather than know myself the cruel instrument of robbing the world of such perfection, consent to retain the fatal testimony of your love."

So saying, he pocketed the chain, with an air of ineffable mortification, and was rewarded for his compliance with the most endearing caresses of his Dulcinea, who, amidst the tumults of her joy, ejaculated a thousand acknowledgments to Heaven for having blessed her with the affection of such a man, whose honour was unrivalled by anything but his love.

CHAPTER SIXTEEN.
HIS SUCCESS BEGETS A BLIND SECURITY, BY WHICH HE IS ONCE AGAIN WELL-NIGH ENTRAPPED IN HIS DULCINEA'S APARTMENT.

In this manner did the crafty Fathom turn to account those ingratiating qualifications he inherited from nature, and maintain, with incredible assiduity and circumspection, an amorous correspondence with two domestic rivals, who watched the conduct of each other with the most indefatigable virulence of envious suspicion, until an accident happened, which had well-nigh overturned the bark of his policy, and induced him to alter the course, that he might not be shipwrecked on the rocks that began to multiply in the prosecution of his present voyage.

The jeweller, who, as a German, wanted neither pride nor ostentation, never failed to celebrate the anniversary of his birth by an annual feast granted to his neighbours and friends; and on these occasions was accustomed to wear that chain which, though bequeathed to his daughter, he considered as an ornament appertaining to the family, whereof he himself was head. Accordingly, when the time of this festival revolved, he, as usual, ordered Wilhelmina to surrender it for the day. This injunction, the reader will perceive, our young lady was in no condition to obey; she had, however, foreseen the demand, and contrived a scheme of behaviour for the occasion, which she forthwith put in execution.

With an air of uncommon cheerfulness, purposely assumed, she retired to her closet, on pretence of complying with his desire, and, having employed a few minutes in rummaging her drawers and disordering her moveables, uttered a loud shriek, that brought her father instantly into the apartment, where he found his daughter tossing about her clothes and trinkets with violent demonstrations of disorder and affright, and heard her, in a lamentable strain, declare that she was robbed of her chain, and for ever undone. This was so far from being an agreeable intimation to the jeweller, that he was struck dumb with astonishment and vexation, and it was not till after a long pause that he pronounced the word Sacrament! with an emphasis denoting the most mortifying surprise.

Soon as that exclamation escaped from his lips, he flew to the escritoire as if instinctively, and, joining Wilhelmina in her occupation, tumbled its whole contents upon the floor in a trice.

While he was thus employed, in the most expressive silence, the wife of his bosom chanced to pass that way, and seeing them both occupied with such violence and trepidation, believed at first that they were certainly actuated by the spirit of frenzy; but, when she interposed, by asking, with great earnestness, the cause of such transports and distracted behaviour, and heard her husband reply, with an accent of despair, "The chain! the chain of my forefathers is no more!" she immediately justified his emotion, by undergoing the same alarm, and, without further hesitation, engaged herself in the search, beginning with a song, which might be compared to the hymn of battle among the Greeks, or rather more aptly to that which the Spartan females sung round the altar of Diana, surnamed Orthian; for it was attended with strange gesticulations, and, in the course of utterance, became so loud and shrill, that the guests, who were by this time partly assembled, being confounded at the clamour, rushed towards the place from whence it seemed to proceed, and found their landlord, with his wife and daughter, in the attitudes of distraction and despair.

When they understood the nature of the case, they condoled the family on their misfortune, and would have retired, on the supposition that it would defeat the mirthful intent of their meeting; but the jeweller, mustering up his whole temper and hospitality, entreated them to excuse his disorder, and favour him with their company, which, he observed, was now more than ever wanted, to dispel the melancholy ideas inspired by his loss. Notwithstanding this apology, and the efforts he made in the sequel to entertain his friends with jollity and good-humour, his heart was so linked to the chain, that he could not detach himself from the thoughts of it, which invaded him at short intervals in such qualms as effectually spoiled his appetite, and hindered his digestion.

He revolved within himself the circumstances of his disaster, and, in canvassing all the probable means by which the chain would be stolen, concluded that the deed must have been done by some person in the family, who, in consequence of having access to his daughter's chamber, had either found the drawer left open by her carelessness and neglect, or found means to obtain a false key, by some waxen impression; for the locks of the escritoire were safe and uninjured. His suspicion being thus confined within his own house, sometimes pitched upon his workmen, and sometimes upon his wife, who, he thought, was the more likely to practise such finesse, as she considered Wilhelmina in the light of a daughter-in-law, whose interest interfered with her own, and who had often harangued to him in private on the folly of leaving this very chain in the young lady's possession.

The more he considered this subject, he thought he saw the more reason to attribute the damage he had sustained to the machinations of his spouse, who, he did not doubt, was disposed to feather her own nest, at the expense of him and his heirs, and who, with the same honest intention, had already secreted, for her private use, those inconsiderable jewels which of late had at different times been missing. Aroused by these sentiments, he resolved to retaliate her own schemes, by contriving means to visit her cabinet in secret, and, if possible, to rob the robber of the spoils she had gathered to his prejudice, without coming to any explanation, which might end in domestic turmoils and eternal disquiet.

While the husband exercised his reflection in this manner, his innocent mate did not allow the powers of her imagination to rest in idleness and sloth. Her observations touching the loss of the chain were such as a suspicious woman, biassed by hatred and envy, would naturally make. To her it seemed highly improbable, that a thing of such value, so carefully deposited, should vanish without the connivance of its keeper, and without much expense of conjecture, divined the true manner in which it was conveyed. The sole difficulty that occurred in the researches of her sagacity, was to know the gallant who had been favoured with such a pledge of Wilhelmina's affection; for, as the reader will easily imagine, she never dreamed of viewing Ferdinand in that odious perspective. In order to satisfy her curiosity, discover this happy favourite, and be revenged on her petulant rival, she prevailed upon the jeweller to employ a scout, who should watch all night upon the stair, without the knowledge of any other person in the family, alleging, that in all likelihood, the housemaid gave private admittance to some lover who was the author of all the losses they had lately suffered, and that they might possibly detect him in his nocturnal adventures; and observing that it would be imprudent to intimate their design to Wilhelmina, lest, through the heedlessness and indiscretion of youth, she might chance to divulge the secret, so as to frustrate their aim.

A Swiss, in whose honesty the German could confide, being hired for this purpose, was posted in a dark corner of the staircase, within a few paces of the door, which he was directed to watch, and actually stood sentinel three nights, without perceiving the least object of suspicion; but, on the fourth, the evil stars of our adventurer conducted him to the spot, on his voyage to the apartment of his Dulcinea, with whom he had preconcerted the assignation. Having made the signal, which consisted of two gentle taps on her door, he was immediately admitted; and the Swiss no sooner saw him fairly housed, than he crept softly to the other door, that was left open for the purpose, and gave immediate intimation of what he had perceived. This intelligence, however, he could not convey so secretly, but the lovers, who were always vigilant upon these occasions, overheard a sort of commotion in the jeweller's chamber, the cause of which their apprehension was ingenious enough to comprehend.

We have formerly observed that our adventurer could not make his retreat by the door, without running a very great risk of being detected, and the expedient of the chimney he had no inclination to repeat; so that he found himself in a very uncomfortable dilemma, and was utterly abandoned by all his invention and address, when his mistress, in a whisper, desired him to begin a dialogue, aloud, in an apology, importing, that he had mistaken the door, and that his intention was to visit her father, touching a ring belonging to the young Count Melvil, which she knew Fathom had put into his hands, in order to be altered.

Ferdinand, seizing the hint, availed himself of it without delay, and, unbolting the door, pronounced in an audible voice, "Upon my honour, Mademoiselle, you wrong my intention, if you imagine I came hither with any disrespectful or dishonourable motive. I have business with your father, which cannot be delayed till to-morrow, without manifest prejudice to my friend and myself; therefore I took the liberty of visiting him at these untimely hours, and it has been my misfortune to mistake the door in the dark. I beg pardon for my involuntary intrusion, and again assure you, that nothing was farther from my thoughts than any design to violate that respect which I have always entertained for you and your father's family."

To this remonstrance, which was distinctly heard by the German and his wife, who by this time stood listening at the door, the young lady replied, in a shrill accent of displeasure, "Sir, I am bound to believe that all your actions are conducted by honour; but you must give me leave to tell you, that your mistake is a little extraordinary, and your visit, even to my father, at this time of the night, altogether unseasonable, if not mysterious. As for the interruption I have suffered in my repose, I impute it to my own forgetfulness, in leaving my door unlocked, and blame myself so severely for the omission, that I shall, to-morrow, put it out of my own power to be guilty of the like for the future, by ordering the passage to be nailed up; meanwhile, if you would persuade me of your well-meaning, you will instantly withdraw, lest my reputation should suffer by your continuance in my apartment."

"Madam," answered our hero, "I will not give you an opportunity to repeat the command, which I shall forthwith obey, after having entreated you once more to forgive the disturbance I have given." So saying, he gently opened the door, and, at sight of the German and his wife, who, he well knew, waited for his exit, started back, and gave tokens of confusion, which was partly real and partly affected. The jeweller, fully satisfied with Fathom's declaration to his daughter, received him with a complaisant look, and, in order to alleviate his concern, gave him to understand, that he already knew the reason of his being in that apartment, and desired to be informed of what had procured him the honour to see him at such a juncture.

"My dear friend," said our adventurer, pretending to recollect himself with difficulty, "I am utterly ashamed and confounded to be discovered in this situation; but, as you have overheard what passed between Mademoiselle and me, I know you will do justice to my intention, and forgive my mistake. After begging pardon for having intruded upon your family at these hours, I must now tell you that my cousin, Count Melvil, was some time ago so much misrepresented to his mother by certain malicious informers, who delight in sowing discord in private families, that she actually believed her son an extravagant spendthrift, who had not only consumed his remittances in the most riotous scenes of disorder, but also indulged a pernicious appetite for gaming, to such a degree, that he had lost all his clothes and jewels at play. In consequence of such false information, she expostulated with him in a severe letter, and desired he would transmit to her that ring which is in your custody, it being a family stone, for which she expressed an inestimable value. The young gentleman, in his answer to her reproof, endeavoured to vindicate himself from the aspersions which had been cast upon his character, and, with regard to the ring, told her it was at present in the hands of a jeweller, in order to be new set according to her own directions, and that, whenever it should be altered, he would send it home to her by some safe conveyance. This account the good lady took for an evasion, and upon that supposition has again written to him, in such a provoking style, that, although the letter arrived but half an hour ago, he is determined to despatch a courier before morning with the mischievous ring, for which, in compliance with the impetuosity of his temper, I have taken the freedom to disturb you at this unseasonable hour."

The German paid implicit faith to every circumstance of his story, which indeed could not well be supposed to be invented extempore; the ring was immediately restored, and our adventurer took his leave, congratulating himself upon his signal deliverance from the snare in which he had fallen.

CHAPTER SEVENTEEN.
THE STEP-DAME'S SUSPICIONS BEING AWAKENED, SHE LAYS A SNARE FOR OUR ADVENTURER, FROM WHICH HE IS DELIVERED BY THE INTERPOSITION OF HIS GOOD GENIUS.

Though the husband swallowed the bait without further inquiry, the penetration of the wife was not so easily deceived. That same dialogue in Wilhelmina's apartment, far from allaying, rather inflamed her suspicion; because, in the like emergency, she herself had once profited by the same, or nearly the same contrivance. Without communicating her doubts to the father, she resolved to double her attention to the daughter's future conduct, and keep such a strict eye over the behaviour of our gallant, that he should find it very difficult, if not impossible, to elude her observation. For this purpose she took into her pay an old maiden, of the right sour disposition, who lived in a house opposite to her own, and directed her to follow the young lady in all her outgoings, whenever she should receive from the window a certain signal, which the mother-in-law agreed to make for the occasion. It was not long before this scheme succeeded to her wish. The door of communication betwixt Wilhelmina's apartment and the staircase being nailed up by the jeweller's express order, our adventurer was altogether deprived of those opportunities he had hitherto enjoyed, and was not at all mortified to find himself so restricted in a correspondence which began to be tiresome and disagreeable. But the case was far otherwise with his Dulcinea, whose passion, the more it was thwarted, raged with greater violence, like a fire, that, from the attempts that are made to extinguish it, gathers greater force, and flames with double fury.

Upon the second day of her misfortune, she had written a very tender billet, lamenting her unhappiness in being deprived of those meetings which constituted the chief joy of her life, and entreating him to contrive some means of renewing the delicious commerce in an unsuspected place. This intimation she proposed to convey privately into the hand of her lover, during his next visit to the family; but both were so narrowly eyed by the mother, that she found the execution of her design impracticable; and next forenoon, on pretence of going to church, repaired to the house of a companion, who, being also her confidant, undertook to deliver the billet with her own hand.

The she-dragon employed by her mother, in obedience to the sign which was displayed from the window immediately put on her veil, and followed Wilhelmina at a distance, until she saw her fairly housed. She would not even then return from her excursion, but hovered about in sight of the door, with a view of making further observations. In less than five minutes after the young lady disappeared, the scout perceived her coming out, accompanied by her comrade, from whom she instantly parted, and bent her way towards the church in good earnest, while the other steered her course in another direction. The duenna, after a moment's suspense and consideration, divined the true cause of this short visit, and resolved to watch the motions of the confidant, whom she traced to the academy in which our hero lodged, and from which she saw her return, after the supposed message was delivered.

Fraught with this intelligence, the rancorous understrapper hied her home to the jeweller's wife, and made a faithful recital of what she had seen, communicating at the same time her own conjectures on that subject. Her employer was equally astonished and incensed at this information. She was seized with all that frenzy which takes possession of a slighted woman, when she finds herself supplanted by a detested rival; and, in the first transports of her indignation, devoted them as sacrifices to her vengeance. Nor was her surprise so much the effect of his dissimulation, as of his want of taste and discernment. She inveighed against him, not as the most treacherous lover, but as the most abject wretch, in courting the smiles of such an awkward dowdy, while he enjoyed the favours of a woman who had numbered princes in the train of her admirers. For the brilliancy of her attractions, such as they at present shone, she appealed to the decision of her minister, who consulted her own satisfaction and interest, by flattering the other's vanity and resentment; and so unaccountable did the depravity of our hero's judgment appear to this conceited dame, that she began to believe there was some mistake in the person, and to hope that Wilhelmina's gallant was not in reality her professed admirer, Mr. Fathom, but rather one of his fellow-lodgers, whose passion he favoured with his mediation and assistance.

On this notion, which nothing but mere vanity could have inspired, in opposition to so many more weighty presumptions, she took the resolution of bringing the affair to a fuller explanation, before she would concert any measures to the prejudice of our adventurer, and forthwith despatched her spy back to his lodgings, to solicit, on the part of Wilhelmina, an immediate answer to the letter he had received. This was an expedition with which the old maiden would have willingly dispensed, because it was founded upon an uncertainty, which might be attended with troublesome consequences; but, rather than be the means of retarding a negotiation so productive of that sort of mischief which is particularly agreeable to all of her tribe, she undertook to manage and effect the discovery, in full confidence of her own talents and experience.

With such a fund of self-sufficiency and instigation, she repaired to the academy on the instant, and inquiring for Mr. Fathom, was introduced to his apartment, where she found him in the very act of writing a billet to the jeweller's daughter. The artful agent having asked, with the mysterious air of an expert go-between, if he had not lately received a message from a certain young lady, and, being answered in the affirmative, gave him to understand, that she herself was a person favoured with the friendship and confidence of Wilhelmina, whom she had known from her cradle, and often dandled on her knee; then, in the genuine style of a prattling dry nurse, she launched out in encomiums on his Dulcinea's beauty and sweetness of temper, recounting many simple occurrences of her infancy and childhood; and, finally, desiring a more circumstantial answer to that which she had sent to him by her friend Catherina. In the course of her loquacity she had also, according to her instructions, hinted at the misfortune of the door; and, on the whole, performed her cue with such dexterity and discretion that our politician was actually overreached, and, having finished his epistle, committed it to her care, with many verbal expressions of eternal love and fidelity to his charming Wilhelmina.

The messenger, doubly rejoiced at her achievement, which not only recommended her ministry, but also gratified her malice, returned to her principal with great exultation, and, delivering the letter, the reader will easily conceive the transports of that lady when she read the contents of it in these words:—

"ANGELIC WILHELMINA!—To forget those ecstatic scenes we have enjoyed together, or even live without the continuation of that mutual bliss, were to quit all title to perception, and resign every hope of future happiness. No! my charmer, while my head retains the least spark of invention, and my heart glows with the resolution of a man, our correspondence shall not be cut off by the machinations of an envious stepmother, who never had attractions to inspire a generous passion; and, now that age and wrinkles have destroyed what little share of beauty she once possessed, endeavours, like the fiend in paradise, to blast those joys in others, from which she is herself eternally excluded. Doubt not, dear sovereign of my soul! that I will study, with all the eagerness of desiring love, how to frustrate her malicious intention, and renew those transporting moments, the remembrance of which now warms the breast of your ever constant FATHOM."

Had our hero murdered her father, or left her a disconsolate widow, by effecting the death of her dear husband, there might have been a possibility of her exerting the Christian virtues of resignation and forgiveness; but such a personal outrage as that contained in this epistle precluded all hope of pardon, and rendered penitence of no signification. His atrocious crime being now fully ascertained, this virago gave a loose to her resentment, which became so loud and tempestuous, that her informer shuddered at the storm she had raised, and began to repent of having communicated the intelligence which seemed to have such a violent effect upon hex brain.

She endeavoured, however, to allay the agitation, by flattering her fancy with the prospect of revenge, and gradually soothed her into a state of deliberate ire; during which she determined to take ample vengeance on the delinquent. In the zenith of her rage, she would have had immediate recourse to poison or steel, had she not been diverted from her mortal purpose by her counsellor, who represented the danger of engaging in such violent measures, and proposed a more secure scheme, in the execution of which she would see the perfidious wretch sufficiently punished, without any hazard to her own person or reputation. She advised her to inform the jeweller of Fathom's efforts to seduce her conjugal fidelity, and impart to him a plan, by which he would have it in his power to detect our adventurer in the very act of practising upon her virtue.

The lady relished her proposal, and actually resolved to make an assignation with Ferdinand, as usual, and give notice of the appointment to her husband, that he might personally discover the treachery of his pretended friend, and inflict upon him such chastisement as the German's brutal disposition should suggest, when inflamed by that species of provocation. Had this project been brought to bear, Ferdinand, in all likelihood, would have been disqualified from engaging in any future intrigue; but fate ordained that the design should be defeated, in order to reserve him for more important occasions.

Before the circumstances of the plan could be adjusted, it was his good fortune to meet his Dulcinea in the street, and, in the midst of their mutual condolence on the interruption they had suffered in their correspondence, he assured her, that he would never give his invention respite, until he should have verified the protestations contained in the letter he had delivered to her discreet agent. This allusion to a billet she had never received, did not fail to alarm her fears, and introduce a very mortifying explanation, in which he so accurately described the person of the messenger, that she forthwith comprehended the plot, and communicated to our hero her sentiments on that subject.

Though he expressed infinite anxiety and chagrin at this misfortune, which could not fail to raise new obstacles to their love, his heart was a stranger to the uneasiness he affected; and rather pleased with the occasion, which would furnish him with pretences to withdraw himself gradually from an intercourse by this time become equally cloying and unprofitable. Being well acquainted with the mother's temperament, he guessed the present situation of her thoughts, and concluding she would make the jeweller a party in her revenge, he resolved from that moment to discontinue his visits, and cautiously guard against any future interview with the lady whom he had rendered so implacable.

It was well for our adventurer that his good fortune so seasonably interposed; for that same day, in the afternoon, he was favoured with a billet from the jeweller's wife, couched in the same tender style she had formerly used, and importing an earnest desire of seeing him next day at the wonted rendezvous. Although his penetration was sufficient to perceive the drift of this message, or at least to discern the risk he should run in complying with her request, yet he was willing to be more fully certified of the truth of his suspicion, and wrote an answer to the billet, in which he assured her, that he would repair to the place of appointment with all the punctuality of an impatient lover. Nevertheless, instead of performing this promise, he, in the morning, took post in a public-house opposite to the place of assignation, in order to reconnoitre the ground, and about noon had the pleasure of seeing the German, wrapped in a cloak, enter the door of his wife's she-friend, though the appointment was fixed at five in the evening. Fathom blessed his good angel for having conducted him clear of this conspiracy, and kept his station with great tranquillity till the hour of meeting, when he beheld his enraged Thalestris take the same route, and enjoyed her disappointment with ineffable satisfaction.

Thus favoured with a pretext, he took his leave of her, in a letter, giving her to understand, that he was no stranger to the barbarous snare she had laid for him; and upbraiding her with having made such an ungrateful return for all his tenderness and attachment. She was not backward in conveying a reply to this expostulation, which seemed to have been dictated in all the distraction of a proud woman who sees her vengeance baffled, as well as her love disdained. Her letter was nothing but a succession of reproaches, menaces, and incoherent execrations. She taxed him with knavery, insensibility, and dissimulation; imprecated a thousand curses upon his head, and threatened not only to persecute his life with all the arts that hell and malice could inspire, but also to wound him in the person of her daughter-in-law, who should be enclosed for life in a convent, where she should have leisure to repent of those loose and disorderly practices which he had taught her to commit, and of which she could not pretend innocence, as they had it in their power to confront her with the evidence of her lover's own confession. Yet all this denunciation was qualified with an alternative, by which he was given to understand, that the gates of mercy were still open, and that penitence was capable of washing out the deepest stain of guilt.

Ferdinand read the whole remonstrance with great composure and moderation, and was content to incur the hazard of her hate, rather than put her to the trouble of making such an effort of generosity, as would induce her to forgive the heinous offence he had committed; nor did his apprehension for Wilhelmina in the least influence his behaviour on this occasion. So zealous was he for her spiritual concerns, that he would have been glad to hear she had actually taken the veil; but he knew such a step was not at all agreeable to her disposition, and that no violence would be offered to her inclinations on that score, unless her stepmother should communicate to the father that letter of Fathom's which she had intercepted, and by which the German would be convinced of his daughter's backsliding; but this measure, he rightly supposed, the wife would not venture to take, lest the husband, instead of taking her advice touching the young lady, should seek to compromise the affair, by offering her in marriage to her debaucher, a proffer which, if accepted, would overwhelm the mother with vexation and despair. He therefore chose to trust to the effects of lenient time, which he hoped would gradually weaken the resentment of this Penthesilea, and dissolve his connexion with the other parts of the family, from which he longed to be totally detached.

How well soever he might have succeeded in his attempts to shake off the yoke of the mother, who by her situation in life was restrained from prosecuting those measures her resentment had planned against his fortitude and indifference, he would have found greater difficulty than he had foreseen, in disengaging himself from the daughter, whose affections he had won under the most solemn professions of honour and fidelity, and who, now she was debarred of his company and conversation, and in danger of losing him for ever, had actually taken the resolution of disclosing the amour to her father, that he might interpose in behalf of her peace and reputation, and secure her happiness by the sanction of the church.

CHAPTER EIGHTEEN.
OUR HERO DEPARTS FROM VIENNA, AND QUITS THE DOMAIN OF VENUS FOR THE ROUGH FIELD OF MARS.

Luckily for our adventurer, before she adhered to this determination, the young Count de Melvil was summoned to Presburg by his father, who desired to see him, before he should take the field, in consequence of a rupture between the Emperor and the French King; and Fathom of course quitted Vienna, in order to attend his patron, after he and Renaldo had resided two whole years in that capital, where the former had made himself perfect in all the polite exercises, become master of the French tongue, and learned to speak the Italian with great facility; over and above those other accomplishments in which we have represented him as an inimitable original.

As for the young Count, his exteriors were so much improved by the company to which he had access, since his departure from his father's house, that his parents were equally surprised and overjoyed at the alteration. All that awkwardness and rusticity, which hung upon his deportment, was, like the rough coat of a diamond, polished away; the connexion and disposition of his limbs seemed to have been adjusted anew; his carriage was become easy, his air perfectly genteel, and his conversation gay and unrestrained. The merit of this reformation was in a great measure ascribed to the care and example of Mr. Fathom, who was received by the old Count and his lady with marks of singular friendship and esteem; nor was he overlooked by Mademoiselle, who still remained in a state of celibacy, and seemed to have resigned all hope of altering her condition; she expressed uncommon satisfaction at the return of her old favourite, and readmitted him into the same degree of familiarity with which he had been honoured before his departure.

The joy of Teresa was so excessive at his arrival, that she could scarce suppress her raptures, so as to conceal them from the notice of the family; and our hero, upon this occasion, performed the part of an exquisite actor, in dissembling those transports which his bosom never knew. So well had this pupil retained the lessons of her instructor, that, in the midst of those fraudulent appropriations, which she still continued to make, she had found means to support her interest and character with Mademoiselle, and even to acquire such influence in the family, that no other servant, male or female, could pretend to live under the same roof, without paying incessant homage to this artful waiting-woman, and yielding the most abject submission to her will.

The young gentlemen having tarried at Presburg about six weeks, during which a small field equipage was prepared for Renaldo, they repaired to the camp at Heilbron, under the auspices of Count Melvil, in whose regiment they carried arms as volunteers, with a view to merit promotion in the service by their own personal behaviour. Our adventurer would have willingly dispensed with this occasion of signalising himself, his talents being much better adapted to another sphere of life; nevertheless, he affected uncommon alacrity at the prospect of gathering laurels in the field, and subscribed to his fortune with a good grace; foreseeing, that even in a campaign, a man of his art and ingenuity might find means to consult his corporal safety, without any danger to his reputation. Accordingly, before he had lived full three weeks in camp, the damp situation, and sudden change in his way of life, had such a violent effect upon his constitution, that he was deprived of the use of all his limbs, and mourned, without ceasing, his hard fate, by which he found himself precluded from all opportunity of exerting his diligence, courage, and activity, in the character of a soldier, to which he now aspired.

Renaldo, who was actually enamoured of a martial life, and missed no occasion of distinguishing himself, consoled his companion with great cordiality, encouraged him with the hope of seeing his constitution familiarised to the inconveniences of a camp, and accommodated him with everything which he thought would alleviate the pain of his body, as well as the anxiety of his mind. The old Count, who sincerely sympathised with his affliction, would have persuaded him to retire into quarters, where he could be carefully nursed, and provided with everything necessary to a person in his condition; but such was his desire of glory, that he resisted his patron's importunities with great constancy, till at length, seeing the old gentleman obstinately determined to consult his health by removing him from the field, he gradually suffered himself to recover the use of his hands, made shift to sit up in his bed, and amuse himself with cards or backgammon, and, notwithstanding the feeble condition of his legs, ventured to ride out on horseback to visit the lines, though the Count and his son would never yield to his solicitations so far, as to let him accompany Renaldo in those excursions and reconnoitring parties, by which a volunteer inures himself to toil and peril, and acquires that knowledge in the operations of war, which qualifies him for a command in the service.

Notwithstanding this exemption from all duty, our adventurer managed matters so as to pass for a youth of infinite mettle, and even rendered his backwardness and timidity subservient to the support of that character, by expressing an impatience of lying inactive, and a desire of signalising his prowess, which even the disabled condition of his body could scarce restrain. He must be a man of very weak nerves and excessive irresolution, who can live in the midst of actual service, without imbibing some portion of military fortitude: danger becomes habitual, and loses a great part of its terror; and as fear is often caught by contagion, so is courage communicated among the individuals of an army. The hope of fame, desire of honours and preferment, envy, emulation, and the dread of disgrace, are motives which co-operate in suppressing that aversion to death or mutilation, which nature hath implanted in the human mind; and therefore it is not to be wondered at, if Fathom, who was naturally chicken-hearted, gained some advantages over his disposition before the end of the campaign, which happened to be neither perilous nor severe.

During the winter, while both armies remained in quarters, our adventurer attended his patron to Presburg, and, before the troops were in motion, Renaldo obtained a commission, in consequence of which he went into garrison at Philipsburg, whither he was followed by our hero, while the old Count's duty called him to the field in a different place. Ferdinand for some time had no reason to be dissatisfied with this disposition, by which he was at once delivered from the fatigues of a campaign, and the inspection of a severe censor, in the person of Count Melvil; and his satisfaction was still increased by an accidental meeting with the Tyrolese who had been his confederate at Vienna, and now chanced to serve in garrison on the same footing with himself. These two knights-errant renewed their former correspondence, and, as all soldiers are addicted to gaming, levied contributions upon all those officers who had money to lose, and temerity to play.

However, they had not long pursued this branch of traffic, when their success was interrupted by a very serious occurrence, that for the present entirely detached the gentlemen in the garrison from such amusements. The French troops invested Fort Kehl, situated on the Rhine, opposite to Strasburg; and the Imperialists, dreading that the next storm would fall upon Philipsburg, employed themselves with great diligence to put that important fortress in a proper posture of defence. If the suspension of play was displeasing to our hero, the expectation of being besieged was by no means more agreeable. He knew the excellence of the French engineers, the power of their artillery, and the perseverance of their general. He felt, by anticipation, the toils of hard duty upon the works, the horrors of night-alarms, cannonading, bombardment, sallies, and mines blown up; and deliberated with himself whether or not he should privately withdraw, and take refuge among the besiegers; but, when he reflected that such a step, besides the infamy that must attend it, would be like that of running upon Scylla, seeking to avoid Charybdis, as he would be exposed to more danger and inconvenience in the trenches than he could possibly undergo in the town, and after all run the risk of being taken and treated as a deserter; upon these considerations he resolved to submit himself to his destiny, and endeavoured to mitigate the rigour of his fate by those arts he had formerly practised with success. He accordingly found means to enjoy a very bad state of health during the whole siege, which lasted about six weeks after the trenches were opened; and then the garrison marched out by capitulation, with all the honours of war.

CHAPTER NINETEEN.
HE PUTS HIMSELF UNDER THE GUIDANCE OF HIS ASSOCIATE, AND STUMBLES UPON THE FRENCH CAMP, WHERE HE FINISHES HIS MILITARY CAREER.

Nothing else of moment was transacted during that campaign; and in the winter our adventurer, with the young Count, and his friend the Tyrolese, were disposed in quarters of cantonment, where Ferdinand made himself amends for the chagrin he had undergone, by the exercise of those talents in which he excelled. Not that he was satisfied with the sphere of life in which he acted; though he knew himself consummate in the art of play, he was not at all ambitious of a gamester's name; nor did he find himself disposed to hazard those discoveries and explanations to which heroes of that class are sometimes necessarily exposed. His aim was to dwell among the tents of civil life, undisturbed by quarrels and the din of war, and render mankind subservient to his interest, not by stratagems which irritate, but by that suppleness of insinuation, which could not fail to soothe the temper of those on whom he meant to prey.

He saw that all his expectations of Count Melvil's future favour were connected with his choice of a military life; and that his promotion in the service would, in a great measure, depend upon his personal behaviour in such emergencies as he did not at all wish to encounter. On the other hand, he confided so much in his own dexterity and address, that he never doubted of being able to rear a splendid fortune for himself, provided he could once obtain a fixed and firm foundation. He had in fancy often enjoyed a prospect of England, not only as his native country, to which, like a true citizen, he longed to be united; but also as the land of promise, flowing with milk and honey, and abounding with subjects on which he knew his talents would be properly exercised.

These reflections never occurred, without leaving a strong impression upon the mind of our adventurer, which influenced his deliberations in such a manner, as at length amounted to a perfect resolution of withdrawing himself privately from a service that teemed with disagreeable events, and of transporting himself into the country of his ancestors, which he considered as the Canaan of all able adventurers. But, previous to his appearance on that stage, he was desirous of visiting the metropolis of France, in which he hoped to improve himself in the knowledge of men and things, and acquire such intelligence as would qualify him to act a more important part upon the British scene. After having for some time indulged these prospects in secret, he determined to accommodate himself with the company and experience of the Tyrolese, whom, under the specious title of an associate, he knew he could convert into a very serviceable tool, in forwarding the execution of his own projects.

Accordingly, the inclination of this confederate was sounded by distant hints, and being found apt, our hero made him privy to his design of decamping without beat of drum; though, at the same time, he begged his advice touching the method of their departure, that he might retire with as much delicacy as the nature of such a step would permit. Divers consultations were held upon this subject, before they adhered to the resolution of making their escape from the army, after it should have taken the field in the spring; because, in that case, they would have frequent opportunities of going abroad on foraging parties, and, during one of these excursions, might retire in such a manner as to persuade their companions that they had fallen into the enemy's hands.

Agreeable to this determination, the camp was no sooner formed in Alsace than our associates began to make preparations for their march, and had already taken all the previous measures for their departure, when an accident happened, which our hero did not fail to convert to his own advantage. This was no other than the desertion of Renaldo's valet, who, in consequence of a gentle chastisement, which he had richly merited, thought proper to disappear, after having plundered his master's portmanteau, which he had forced open for the purpose. Ferdinand, who was the first person that discovered the theft, immediately comprehended the whole adventure, and, taking it for granted that the delinquent would never return, resolved to finish what the fugitive had imperfectly performed.

Being favoured with the unreserved confidence of the young Count, he instantly had recourse to his bureau, the locks of which he found means to burst open, and, examining a private drawer, contrived with great art to conceal Renaldo's jewels and cash, made himself master of the contents without hesitation; then cutting open his cloak-bag, and strewing the tent with his linen and clothes, began to raise his voice, and produce such a clamour as alarmed the whole neighbourhood, and brought a great many officers into the tent.

He on this, as on all other occasions, performed his cue to a miracle, expressing confusion and concern so naturally in his gestures and exclamation, that no man could possibly suspect his sincerity; nay, to such a degree of finesse did his cunning amount, that when his friend and patron entered, in consequence of an intimation he soon received of his loss, our adventurer exhibited undoubted signs of distraction and delirium, and, springing upon Renaldo with all the frantic fury of a bedlamite, "Villain," cried he, "restore the effects you have stole from your master, or you shall be immediately committed to the care of the prevot." However mortified M. de Melvil might be at his own misfortune, the condition of his friend seemed to touch him more nearly; he undervalued his own loss as a trifle that could be easily repaired; said everything which he thought would tend to soothe and compose the agitation of Ferdinand; and finally prevailed upon him to retire to rest. The calamity was wholly attributed to the deserter; and Renaldo, far from suspecting the true author, took occasion, from his behaviour on this emergency, to admire him as a mirror of integrity and attachment; in such an exquisite manner did he plan all his designs, that almost every instance of his fraud furnished matter of triumph to his reputation.

Having thus profitably exercised his genius, this subtle politician thought it high time to relinquish his military expectations, and securing all his valuable acquisitions about his own person, rode out with his understrapper, in the midst of fifty dragoons, who went in quest of forage. While the troopers were employed in making up their trusses, the two adventurers advanced towards the skirt of a wood, on pretence of reconnoitring, and the Tyrolese, who undertook to be our hero's guide, directing him to a path which leads towards Strasburg, they suddenly vanished from the eyes of their companions, who in a few minutes hearing the report of several pistols, which the confederates purposely fired, conjectured that they had fallen in with a party of French, by whom they were made prisoners of war.

The Tyrolese had overrated his own knowledge when he took upon himself the charge of conducting our hero; for upon their arrival at a certain place, where two roads crossed each other, he chanced to follow that which not only frustrated their intention, but even led them directly to the French camp; so that, in the twilight, they fell in upon one of the outguards before they were aware of their mistake.

Whatever confusion and perplexity they might undergo, when they heard themselves questioned by the sentinel on the advanced post, certain it is, they betrayed no symptoms of fear or disorder; but while Ferdinand endeavoured to recollect himself, his fellow-traveller, with the appearance of admirable intrepidity and presence of mind, told the soldier that he and his companion were two gentlemen of family, who had quitted the Austrian army, on account of having sustained some ill-usage, which they had no opportunity of resenting in any other way, and that they were come to offer their services to the French general, to whose quarters they desired to be immediately conveyed.

The sentinel, to whom such an instance of desertion was neither rare, nor indeed uncommon, directed them without scruple to the next post, where they found a serjeant's party, from which, at their request, they were transmitted to the officer of the grand guard, and by him next morning introduced to Count Coigny, who very politely received them as volunteers in the army of France. Though this translation was not at all to our hero's liking, he was forced to acquiesce in his fate, glad to find himself, on these terms, in possession of his effects, of which he would otherwise have been infallibly rifled.

This campaign, however, was the most disagreeable period of his whole life; because the manner in which he had entered into the service subjected him to the particular observation and notice of the French officers; so that he was obliged to be very alert in his duty, and summon all his fortitude to maintain the character he had assumed. What rendered his situation still more unpalatable, was the activity of both armies in the course of this season, during which, over and above sundry fatiguing marches and countermarches, he was personally engaged in the affair of Halleh, which was very obstinate; where, being in the skirts of the detachment, he was actually wounded in the face by the sword of an hussar; but this was, luckily for him, the last time he found himself under the necessity of exerting his military prowess, for a cessation of arms was proclaimed before he was cured of his wound, and peace concluded about the end of the campaign.

During his sojourn in the French camp, he assumed the character of a man of family, who being disgusted at some supercilious treatment he had met with in the German service, and at the same time ambitious of carrying arms under the banners of France, took the opportunity of retreating by stealth from his friends, accompanied only by one with whom he could intrust his intention. In this capacity he had managed his matters to such advantage, that many French officers of rank were very well disposed to contribute their interest in his behalf, had his inclination verged towards promotion in the army; but he thought proper to conceal his real design, under the specious pretext of longing to see the metropolis of France, that centre of pleasure and politeness, in which he proposed to spend some time for the improvement of his address and understanding. These were motives too laudable to be opposed by his new patrons, some of whom furnished him with letters of recommendation to certain noblemen of the first rank at the court of Versailles, for which place he and his companion set out from the banks of the Rhine, very well satisfied with the honourable dismission they had obtained from a life of inconvenience, danger, and alarm.

CHAPTER TWENTY.
HE PREPARES A STRATAGEM BUT FINDS HIMSELF COUNTERMINED—PROCEEDS ON HIS JOURNEY, AND IS OVERTAKEN BY A TERRIBLE TEMPEST.

In the course of this journey, Ferdinand, who was never deficient in his political capacity, held a secret conclave with his own thoughts, not only touching the plan of his own future conduct, but also concerning his associate, of whose fidelity and adherence he began to entertain such doubts as discouraged him from the prosecution of that design in which the Tyrolese had been at first included; for he had lately observed him practise the arts of his occupation among the French officers, with such rapacity and want of caution, as indicated a dangerous temerity of temper, as well as a furious rage of acquiring, which might be some time or other satiated upon his own friends. In other words, our adventurer was afraid that his accomplice would profit by his knowledge of the road and countries through which they travelled, and, after having made free with his most valuable effects, in consequence of the familiarity subsisting between them, leave him some morning without the ceremony of a formal adieu.

Aroused by this suspicion, he resolved to anticipate the supposed intention of the Tyrolese, by taking his own departure in the same abrupt manner; and this scheme he actually put in execution, upon their arrival in Bar-le-duc, where it was agreed they should spend a day to repose and refresh themselves from the fatigue of hard riding. Ferdinand, therefore, taking the advantage of his companion's absence—for the Tyrolese had walked abroad to view the town—found means to hire a peasant, who undertook to conduct him through a by-road as far as Chalons, and with his guide he accordingly set out on horseback, after having discharged the bill, left a blank paper sealed up in form of a letter, directed to his friend, and secured behind his own saddle a pair of leathern bags, in which his jewels and cash were usually contained. So eager was our hero to leave the Tyrolese at a considerable distance behind, that he rode all night at a round pace without halting, and next morning found himself at a village distant thirteen good leagues from any part of the route which he and his companion had at first resolved to pursue.

Here, thinking himself safely delivered from the cause of all his apprehension, he determined to lie incognito for a few days, so as that he might run no risk of an accidental meeting upon the road with the person whose company he had forsaken; and accordingly took possession of an apartment, in which he went to rest, desiring his guide to wake him when dinner should be ready. Having enjoyed a very comfortable refreshment of sleep, with his bags under his pillow, he was summoned, according to his direction, and ate a very hearty meal, with great tranquillity and internal satisfaction. In the afternoon he amused himself with happy presages and ideal prospects of his future fortune, and, in the midst of these imaginary banquets, was seized with an inclination of realising his bliss, and regaling his eyesight with the fruits of that success which had hitherto attended his endeavours. Thus inflamed, he opened the repository, and, O reader! what were his reflections, when, in lieu of Mademoiselle Melvil's earrings and necklace, the German's golden chain, divers jewels of considerable value, the spoils of sundry dupes, and about two hundred ducats in ready money, he found neither more nor less than a parcel of rusty nails, disposed in such a manner as to resemble in weight and bulk the moveables he had lost.

It is not to be supposed our adventurer made this discovery without emotion. If the eternal salvation of mankind could have been purchased for the tenth part of his treasure, he would have left the whole species in a state of reprobation, rather than redeem them at that price, unless he had seen in the bargain some evident advantage to his own concerns. One may, therefore, easily conceive with what milkiness of resignation he bore the loss of the whole, and saw himself reduced from such affluence to the necessity of depending upon about twenty ducats, and some loose silver, which he carried in his pocket, for his expense upon the road. However bitter this pill might be in swallowing, he so far mastered his mortification, as to digest it with a good grace. His own penetration at once pointed out the canal through which this misfortune had flowed upon him; he forthwith placed the calamity to the account of the Tyrolese, and never doubting that he had retired with the booty across the Rhine, into some place to which he knew Fathom would not follow his footsteps, he formed the melancholy resolution of pursuing with all despatch his journey to Paris, that he might, with all convenient expedition, indemnify himself for the discomfiture he had sustained.

With regard to his confederate, his conjecture was perfectly right; that adventurer, though infinitely inferior to our hero in point of genius and invention, had manifestly the advantage of him in the articles of age and experience; he was no stranger to Fathom's qualifications, the happy exertion of which he had often seen. He knew him to be an economist of the most frugal order, consequently concluded his finances were worthy of examination; and, upon the true principles of a sharper, eased him of the encumbrance, taking it for granted, that, in so doing, he only precluded Ferdinand from the power of acting the same tragedy upon him, should ever opportunity concur with his inclination. He had therefore concerted his measures with the dexterity of an experienced conveyancer, and, snatching the occasion, while our hero, travel-tainted, lay sunk in the arms of profound repose, he ripped up the seams of the leather depository, withdrew the contents, introduced the parcel of nails, which he had made up for the purpose, and then repaired the breach with great deliberation.

Had Fathom's good genius prompted him to examine his effects next morning, the Tyrolese, in all probability, would have maintained his acquisition by force of arms; for his personal courage was rather more determined than that of our adventurer, and he was conscious of his own ascendency in this particular; but his good fortune prevented such explanation. Immediately after dinner, he availed himself of his knowledge, and, betaking himself to a remote part of the town, set out in a post-chaise for Luneville, while our hero was meditating his own escape.

Fathom's conception was sufficient to comprehend the whole of this adventure, as soon as his chagrin would give his sagacity fair play; nor would he allow his resolution to sink under the trial; on the contrary, he departed from the village that same afternoon, under the auspices of his conductor, and found himself benighted in the midst of a forest, far from the habitations of men. The darkness of the night, the silence and solitude of the place, the indistinct images of the trees that appeared on every side, "stretching their extravagant arms athwart the gloom," conspired, with the dejection of spirits occasioned by his loss, to disturb his fancy, and raise strange phantoms in his imagination. Although he was not naturally superstitious, his mind began to be invaded with an awful horror, that gradually prevailed over all the consolations of reason and philosophy; nor was his heart free from the terrors of assassination. In order to dissipate these disagreeable reveries, he had recourse to the conversation of his guide, by whom he was entertained with the history of divers travellers who had been robbed and murdered by ruffians, whose retreat was in the recesses of that very wood.

In the midst of this communication, which did not at all tend to the elevation of our hero's spirits, the conductor made an excuse for dropping behind, while our traveller jogged on in expectation of being joined again by him in a few minutes. He was, however, disappointed in that hope; the sound of the other horse's feet by degrees grew more and more faint, and at last altogether died away. Alarmed at this circumstance, Fathom halted in the middle of the road, and listened with the most fearful attention; but his sense of hearing was saluted with nought but the dismal sighings of the trees, that seemed to foretell an approaching storm. Accordingly, the heavens contracted a more dreary aspect, the lightning began to gleam, and the thunder to roll, and the tempest, raising its voice to a tremendous roar, descended in a torrent of rain.

In this emergency, the fortitude of our hero was almost quite overcome. So many concurring circumstances of danger and distress might have appalled the most undaunted breast; what impression then must they have made upon the mind of Ferdinand, who was by no means a man to set fear at defiance! Indeed, he had well-nigh lost the use of his reflection, and was actually invaded to the skin, before he could recollect himself so far as to quit the road, and seek for shelter among the thickets that surrounded him. Having rode some furlongs into the forest, he took his station under a tuft of tall trees, that screened him from the storm, and in that situation called a council within himself, to deliberate upon his next excursion. He persuaded himself that his guide had deserted him for the present, in order to give intelligence of a traveller to some gang of robbers with whom he was connected; and that he must of necessity fall a prey to those banditti, unless he should have the good fortune to elude their search, and disentangle himself from the mazes of the wood.

Harrowed with these apprehensions, he resolved to commit himself to the mercy of the hurricane, as of two evils the least, and penetrate straightforwards through some devious opening, until he should be delivered from the forest. For this purpose he turned his horse's head in a line quite contrary to the direction of the high road which he had left, on the supposition that the robbers would pursue that track in quest of him, and that they would never dream of his deserting the highway, to traverse an unknown forest, amidst the darkness of such a boisterous night. After he had continued in this progress through a succession of groves, and bogs, and thorns, and brakes, by which not only his clothes, but also his skin suffered in a grievous manner, while every nerve quivered with eagerness and dismay, he at length reached an open plain, and pursuing his course, in full hope of arriving at some village, where his life would be safe, he descried a rush-light at a distance, which he looked upon as the star of his good fortune, and riding towards it at full speed, arrived at the door of a lone cottage, into which he was admitted by an old woman, who, understanding he was a bewildered traveller, received him with great hospitality.

When he learned from his hostess, that there was not another house within three leagues; that she could accommodate him with a tolerable bed, and his horse with lodging and oats, he thanked Heaven for his good fortune, in stumbling upon this homely habitation, and determined to pass the night under the protection of the old cottager, who gave him to understand, that her husband, who was a faggot-maker, had gone to the next town to dispose of his merchandise; and that, in all probability, he would not return till next morning, on account of the tempestuous night. Ferdinand sounded the beldame with a thousand artful interrogations, and she answered with such appearance of truth and simplicity, that he concluded his person was quite secure; and, after having been regaled with a dish of eggs and bacon, desired she would conduct him into the chamber where she proposed he should take his repose. He was accordingly ushered up by a sort of ladder into an apartment furnished with a standing-bed, and almost half filled with trusses of straw. He seemed extremely well pleased with his lodging, which in reality exceeded his expectation; and his kind landlady, cautioning him against letting the candle approach the combustibles, took her leave, and locked the door on the outside.

CHAPTER TWENTY-ONE.
HE FALLS UPON SCYLLA, SEEKING TO AVOID CHARYBDIS.

Fathom, whose own principles taught him to be suspicious, and ever upon his guard against the treachery of his fellow-creatures, could have dispensed with this instance of her care, in confining her guest to her chamber, and began to be seized with strange fancies, when he observed that there was no bolt on the inside of the door, by which he might secure himself from intrusion. In consequence of these suggestions, he proposed to take an accurate survey of every object in the apartment, and, in the course of his inquiry, had the mortification to find the dead body of a man, still warm, who had been lately stabbed, and concealed beneath several bundles of straw.

Such a discovery could not fail to fill the breast of our hero with unspeakable horror; for he concluded that he himself would undergo the same fate before morning, without the interposition of a miracle in his favour. In the first transports of his dread, he ran to the window, with a view to escape by that outlet, and found his flight effectually obstructed by divers strong bars of iron. Then his heart began to palpitate, his hair to bristle up, and his knees to totter; his thoughts teemed with presages of death and destruction; his conscience rose up in judgment against him, and he underwent a severe paroxysm of dismay and distraction. His spirits were agitated into a state of fermentation that produced a species of resolution akin to that which is inspired by brandy or other strong liquors, and, by an impulse that seemed supernatural, he was immediately hurried into measures for his own preservation.

What upon a less interesting occasion his imagination durst not propose, he now executed without scruple or remorse. He undressed the corpse that lay bleeding among the straw, and, conveying it to the bed in his arms, deposited it in the attitude of a person who sleeps at his ease; then he extinguished the light, took possession of the place from whence the body had been removed, and, holding a pistol ready cocked in each hand, waited for the sequel with that determined purpose which is often the immediate production of despair. About midnight he heard the sound of feet ascending the ladder; the door was softly opened; he saw the shadow of two men stalking towards the bed, a dark lanthorn being unshrouded, directed their aim to the supposed sleeper, and he that held it thrust a poniard to his heart; the force of the blow made a compression on the chest, and a sort of groan issued from the windpipe of the defunct; the stroke was repeated, without producing a repetition of the note, so that the assassins concluded the work was effectually done, and retired for the present with a design to return and rifle the deceased at their leisure.

Never had our hero spent a moment in such agony as he felt during this operation; the whole surface of his body was covered with a cold sweat, and his nerves were relaxed with an universal palsy. In short, he remained in a trance that, in all probability, contributed to his safety; for, had he retained the use of his senses, he might have been discovered by the transports of his fear. The first use he made of his retrieved recollection, was to perceive that the assassins had left the door open in their retreat; and he would have instantly availed himself of this their neglect, by sallying out upon them, at the hazard of his life, had he not been restrained by a conversation he overheard in the room below, importing, that the ruffians were going to set out upon another expedition, in hopes of finding more prey. They accordingly departed, after having laid strong injunctions upon the old woman to keep the door fast locked during their absence; and Ferdinand took his resolution without farther delay. So soon as, by his conjecture, the robbers were at a sufficient distance from the house, he rose from his lurking-place, moved softly towards the bed, and, rummaging the pockets of the deceased, found a purse well stored with ducats, of which, together with a silver watch and a diamond ring, he immediately possessed himself without scruple; then, descending with great care and circumspection into the lower apartment, stood before the old beldame, before she had the least intimation of his approach.

Accustomed as she was to the trade of blood, the hoary hag did not behold this apparition without giving signs of infinite terror and astonishment, believing it was no other than the spirit of her second guest, who had been murdered; she fell upon her knees and began to recommend herself to the protection of the saints, crossing herself with as much devotion as if she had been entitled to the particular care and attention of Heaven. Nor did her anxiety abate, when she was undeceived in this her supposition, and understood it was no phantom, but the real substance of the stranger, who, without staying to upbraid her with the enormity of her crimes, commanded her, on pain of immediate death, to produce his horse, to which being conducted, he set her upon the saddle without delay, and, mounting behind, invested her with the management of the reins, swearing, in a most peremptory tone, that the only chance she had for her life, was in directing him safely to the next town; and that, so soon as she should give him the least cause to doubt her fidelity in the performance of that task, he would on the instant act the part of her executioner.

This declaration had its effect upon the withered Hecate, who, with many supplications for mercy and forgiveness, promised to guide him in safety to a certain village at the distance of two leagues, where he might lodge in security, and be provided with a fresh horse, or other convenience, for pursuing his intended route. On these conditions he told her she might deserve his clemency; and they accordingly took their departure together, she being placed astride upon the saddle, holding the bridle in one hand and a switch in the other; and our adventurer sitting on the crupper, superintending her conduct, and keeping the muzzle of a pistol close at her ear. In this equipage they travelled across part of the same wood in which his guide had forsaken him; and it is not to be supposed that he passed his time in the most agreeable reverie, while he found himself involved in the labyrinth of those shades, which he considered as the haunts of robbery and assassination.

Common fear was a comfortable sensation to what he felt in this excursion. The first steps he had taken for his preservation were the effects of mere instinct, while his faculties were extinguished or suppressed by despair; but now, as his reflection began to recur, he was haunted by the most intolerable apprehensions. Every whisper of the wind through the thickets was swelled into the hoarse menaces of murder, the shaking of the boughs was construed into the brandishing of poniards, and every shadow of a tree became the apparition of a ruffian eager for blood. In short, at each of these occurrences he felt what was infinitely more tormenting than the stab of a real dagger; and at every fresh fillip of his fear, he acted as a remembrancer to his conductress, in a new volley of imprecations, importing, that her life was absolutely connected with his opinion of his own safety.

Human nature could not longer subsist under such complicated terror. At last he found himself clear of the forest, and was blessed with the distant view of an inhabited place. He then began to exercise his thoughts upon a new subject. He debated with himself, whether he should make a parade of his intrepidity and public spirit, by disclosing his achievement, and surrendering his guide to the penalty of the law; or leave the old hag and her accomplices to the remorse of their own consciences, and proceed quietly on his journey to Paris in undisturbed possession of the prize he had already obtained. This last step he determined to take, upon recollecting, that, in the course of his information, the story of the murdered stranger would infallibly attract the attention of justice, and, in that case, the effects he had borrowed from the defunct must be refunded for the benefit of those who had a right to the succession. This was an argument which our adventurer could not resist; he foresaw that he should be stripped of his acquisition, which he looked upon as the fair fruits of his valour and sagacity; and, moreover, be detained as an evidence against the robbers, to the manifest detriment of his affairs. Perhaps too he had motives of conscience, that dissuaded him from bearing witness against a set of people whose principles did not much differ from his own.

Influenced by such considerations, he yielded to the first importunity of the beldame, whom he dismissed at a very small distance from the village, after he had earnestly exhorted her to quit such an atrocious course of life, and atone for her past crimes, by sacrificing her associates to the demands of justice. She did not fail to vow a perfect reformation, and to prostrate herself before him for the favour she had found; then she betook herself to her habitation, with full purpose of advising her fellow-murderers to repair with all despatch to the village, and impeach our hero, who, wisely distrusting her professions, stayed no longer in the place than to hire a guide for the next stage, which brought him to the city of Chalons-sur-Marne.

CHAPTER TWENTY-TWO.
HE ARRIVES AT PARIS, AND IS PLEASED WITH HIS RECEPTION.

He was not so smitten with the delightful situation of this ancient town, but that he abandoned it as soon as he could procure a post-chaise, in which he arrived at Paris, without having been exposed to any other troublesome adventure upon the road. He took lodgings at a certain hotel in the Fauxbourg de St. Germain, which is the general rendezvous of all the strangers that resort to this capital; and now sincerely congratulated himself upon his happy escape from his Hungarian connexions, and from the snares of the banditti, as well as upon the spoils of the dead body, and his arrival at Paris, from whence there was such a short conveyance to England, whither he was attracted, by far other motives than that of filial veneration for his native soil.

He suppressed all his letters of recommendation, which he justly concluded would subject him to a tedious course of attendance upon the great, and lay him under the necessity of soliciting preferment in the army, than which nothing was farther from his inclination; and resolved to make his appearance in the character of a private gentleman, which would supply him with opportunities of examining the different scenes of life in such a gay metropolis, so as that he should be able to choose that sphere in which he could move the most effectually to his own advantage. He accordingly hired an occasional domestic, and under the denomination of Count Fathom, which he had retained since his elopement from Renaldo, repaired to dinner at an ordinary, to which he was directed as a reputable place, frequented by fashionable strangers of all nations.

He found this piece of information perfectly just; for he no sooner entered the apartment, than his ears were saluted with a strange confusion of sounds, among which he at once distinguished the High and Low Dutch, barbarous French, Italian, and English languages. He was rejoiced at this occasion of displaying his own qualifications, took his place at one of the three long tables, betwixt a Westphalian count and a Bolognian marquis, insinuated himself into the conversation with his usual address, and in less than half an hour, found means to accost a native of each different country in his own mother-tongue.

Such extensive knowledge did not pass unobserved. A French abbe, in a provincial dialect, complimented him upon his retaining that purity in pronunciation, which is not to be found in the speech of a Parisian. The Bolognian, mistaking him for a Tuscan, "Sir," said he, "I presume you are from Florence. I hope the illustrious house of Lorrain leaves you gentlemen of that famous city no room to regret the loss of your own princes." The castle of Versailles becoming the subject of conversation, Monsieur le Compte appealed to him, as to a native German, whether it was not inferior in point of magnificence to the chateau of Grubenhagen. The Dutch officer, addressing himself to Fathom, drank to the prosperity of Faderland, and asked if he had not once served in garrison at Shenkenschans; and an English knight swore, with great assurance, that he had frequently rambled with him at midnight among the hundreds of Drury.

To each person he replied in a polite, though mysterious manner, which did not fail to enhance their opinion of his good breeding and importance; and, long before the dessert appeared, he was by all the company supposed to be a personage of great consequence, who for some substantial reasons, found it convenient to keep himself incognito. This being the case, it is not to be doubted that particular civilities were poured upon him from all quarters. He perceived their sentiments, and encouraged them, by behaving with that sort of complaisance which seems to be the result of engaging condescension in a character of superior dignity and station. His affability was general but his chief attention limited to those gentlemen already mentioned, who chanced to sit nearest him at table; and he no sooner gave them to understand that he was an utter stranger in Paris, than they unanimously begged to have the honour of making him acquainted with the different curiosities peculiar to that metropolis.

He accepted of their hospitality, accompanied them to a coffee-house in the afternoon, from whence they repaired to the opera, and afterwards adjourned to a noted hotel, in order to spend the remaining part of the evening. It was here that our hero secured himself effectually in the footing he had gained in their good graces. He in a moment saw through all the characters of the party, and adapted himself to the humour of each individual, without descending from that elevation of behaviour which he perceived would operate among them in his behalf. With the Italian he discoursed on music, in the style of a connoisseur; and indeed had a better claim to that title than the generality of those upon whom it is usually conferred; for he understood the art in theory as well as in practice, and would have made no contemptible figure among the best performers of the age.

He harangued upon taste and genius to the abbe, who was a wit and critic, ex officio, or rather ex vestitu for a young pert Frenchman, the very moment he puts on the petit collet, or little band, looks upon himself as an inspired son of Apollo; and every one of the fraternity thinks it incumbent upon him to assert the divinity of his mission. In a word, the abbes are a set of people that bear a strong analogy to the templars in London. Fools of each fabric, sharpers of all sorts, and dunces of every degree, profess themselves of both orders. The templar is, generally speaking, a prig, so is the abbe: both are distinguished by an air of petulance and self-conceit, which holds a middle rank betwixt the insolence of a first-rate buck and the learned pride of a supercilious pedant. The abbe is supposed to be a younger brother in quest of preferment in the church—the Temple is considered as a receptacle or seminary for younger sons intended for the bar; but a great number of each profession turn aside into other paths of life, long before they reach these proposed goals. An abbe is often metamorphosed into a foot soldier; a templar sometimes sinks into an attorney's clerk. The galleys of France abound with abbes; and many templars may be found in our American plantations; not to mention those who have made a public exit nearer home. Yet I would not have it thought that my description includes every individual of those societies. Some of the greatest scholars, politicians, and wits, that ever Europe produced, have worn the habit of an abbe; and many of our most noble families in England derive their honours from those who have studied law in the Temple. The worthy sons of every community shall always be sacred from my censure and ridicule; and, while I laugh at the folly of particular members, I can still honour and revere the institution.

But let us return from this comparison, which some readers may think impertinent and unseasonable, and observe, that the Westphalian count, Dutch officer, and English knight, were not excepted from the particular regard and attention of our adventurer. He pledged the German in every bumper; flattered the Hollander with compliments upon the industry, wealth, and policy of the Seven United Provinces; but he reserved his chief battery for his own countryman, on the supposition that he was, in all respects, the best adapted for the purposes of a needy gamester. Him, therefore, he cultivated with extraordinary care and singular observance; for he soon perceived him to be a humourist, and, from that circumstance, derived an happy presage of his own success. The baronet's disposition seemed to be cast in the true English mould. He was sour, silent, and contemptuous; his very looks indicated a consciousness of superior wealth; and he never opened his mouth, except to make some dry, sarcastic, national reflection. Nor was his behaviour free from that air of suspicion which a man puts on when he believes himself in a crowd of pick-pockets, whom his caution and vigilance set at defiance. In a word, though his tongue was silent on the subject, his whole demeanour was continually saying, "You are all a pack of poor lousy rascals, who have a design upon my purse. 'Tis true, I could buy your whole generation, but I won't be bubbled, d'ye see; I am aware of your flattery, and upon my guard against all your knavish pranks; and I come into your company for my own amusement only."

Fathom having reconnoitred this peculiarity of temper, instead of treating him with that assiduous complaisance, which he received from the other gentlemen of the party, kept aloof from him in the conversation, with a remarkable shyness of distant civility, and seldom took notice of what he said, except with a view to contradict him, or retort some of his satirical observations. This he conceived to be the best method of acquiring his good opinion; because the Englishman would naturally conclude he was a person who could have no sinister views upon his fortune, else he would have chosen quite a different manner of deportment. Accordingly, the knight seemed to bite at the hook. He listened to Ferdinand with uncommon regard; he was even heard to commend his remarks, and at length drank to their better acquaintance.

CHAPTER TWENTY-THREE.
ACQUITS HIMSELF WITH ADDRESS IN A NOCTURNAL RIOT.

The Italian and the abbe were the first who began to grow whimsical under the influence of the burgundy; and, in the heat of their elevation, proposed that the company should amuse themselves during the remaining part of the night, at the house of an obliging dame, who maintained a troop of fair nymphs for the accommodation of the other sex. The proposal was approved by all, except the Hollander, whose economy the wine had not as yet invaded; and, while he retreated soberly to his own lodgings, the rest of the society adjourned in two coaches to the temple of love, where they were received by the venerable priestess, a personage turned of seventy, who seemed to exercise the functions of her calling, in despite of the most cruel ravages of time; for age had bent her into the form of a Turkish bow. Her head was agitated by the palsy, like the leaf of the poplar tree; her hair fell down in scanty parcels, as white as the driven snow; her face was not simply wrinkled, but ploughed into innumerable furrows; her jaws could not boast of one remaining tooth; one eye distilled a large quantity of rheum, by virtue of the fiery edge that surrounded it; the other was altogether extinguished, and she had lost her nose in the course of her ministration. The Delphic sibyl was but a type of this hoary matron, who, by her figure, might have been mistaken for the consort of Chaos, or mother of Time. Yet there was something meritorious in her appearance, as it denoted her an indefatigable minister to the pleasure of mankind, and as it formed an agreeable contrast with the beauty and youth of the fair damsels that wantoned in her train. It resembled those discords in music, which, properly disposed, contribute to the harmony of the whole piece; or those horrible giants, who, in the world of romance, used to guard the gates of the castle in which the enchanted damsel was confined.

This Urganda seemed to be aware of her own importance, and perfectly well acquainted with the human appetite; for she compelled the whole company to undergo her embrace. Then a lacquey, in magnificent livery, ushered them into a superb apartment, where they waited some minutes, without being favoured with the appearance of the ladies, to the manifest dissatisfaction of the abbe, who, sending for the gouvernante, reprimanded her severely for her want of politesse. The old lady, who was by no means a pattern of patience and submission, retorted his reproaches with great emphasis and vivacity. Her eloquence flowed altogether in the Covent Garden strain; and I question whether the celebrated Mother Douglas herself could have made such a figure in an extemporaneous altercation.

After having bestowed upon the abbe the epithets of saucy insignificant pimp, she put him in mind of the good offices which he had received at her hands; how she had supplied him with bed, board, and bedfellow, in his greatest necessity; sent him abroad with money in his pockets—and, in a word, cherished him in her bosom, when his own mother had abandoned him to distress. She then reviled him for presuming to affront her before strangers, and gave the company to understand, that the young ladies would wait upon them as soon as they could be confessed and receive absolution from a worthy cordelier, who was now employed in performing that charitable office. The gentlemen were satisfied with this remonstrance, which argued the old lady's pious concern for the souls that were under her care, and our adventurer proposed an accommodation betwixt her and the abbe, who was prevailed upon to ask her pardon, and received her blessing upon his knees.

This affair had not been long adjusted, when five damsels were introduced in a very gay dishabille, and our hero was complimented with the privilege of choosing his Amanda from the whole bevy. When he was provided, the others began to pair themselves, and, unhappily, the German count chanced to pitch upon the same nymph who had captivated the desires of the British knight. A dispute immediately ensued; for the Englishman made his addresses to the lady, without paying the least regard to the priority of the other's claim; and she, being pleased with his attachment, did not scruple to renounce his rival, who swore by the thunder, lightning, and sacrament, that he would not quit his pretensions for any prince in Christendom, much less for a little English cavalier, whom he had already honoured too much in condescending to be his companion.

The knight, provoked at this stately declaration, which was the immediate effect of anger and ebriety, eyed his antagonist with a most contemptuous aspect, and advised him to avoid such comparisons for the future. "We all know," said he, "the importance of a German count; I suppose your revenue amounts to three hundred rix-dollars; and you have a chateau that looks like the ruins of an English gaol. I will bind myself to lend you a thousand pounds upon a mortgage of your estate, (and a bad bargain I am sure I shall have,) if I do not, in less than two months, find a yeoman of Kent, who spends more in strong ale than the sum-total of your yearly income; and, were the truth known, I believe that lace upon your coat is no better than tinsel, and those fringed ruffles, with fine Holland sleeves, tacked to a shirt of brown canvas, so that, were you to undress yourself before the lady, you would only expose your own poverty and pride."

The count was so much enraged at these sarcastic observations, that his faculty of speech was overwhelmed by his resentment; though, in order to acquit himself of the Englishman's imputation, he forthwith pulled off his clothes with such fury, that his brocade waistcoat was tore from top to bottom. The knight, mistaking his meaning, considered this demeanour as a fair challenge, to try which was the better man in the exercise of boxing; and, on that supposition, began to strip in his turn, when he was undeceived by Fathom, who put the right interpretation upon the count's behaviour, and begged that the affair might be compromised. By this time the Westphalian recovered the use of his tongue, and with many threats and imprecations, desired they would take notice how falsely he had been aspersed, and do him justice in espousing his claim to the damsel in question.

Before the company had time or inclination to interest themselves in the quarrel, his opponent observed that no person who was not a mere German, would ever dream of forcing the inclinations of a pretty girl, whom the accidents of fortune had subjected to his power; that such compulsion was equivalent to the most cruel rape that could be committed; and that the lady's aversion was not at all surprising; for, to speak his own sentiments, were he a woman of pleasure, he would as soon grant favours to a Westphalian hog, as to the person of his antagonist. The German, enraged at this comparison, was quite abandoned by his patience and discretion. He called the knight an English clown, and, swearing he was the most untoward beast of a whole nation of mules, snatched up one of the candlesticks, which he launched at him with such force and violence, that it sung through the air, and, winging its flight into the ante-chamber, encountered the skull of his own valet, who with immediate prostration received the message of his master.

The knight, that he might not be behindhand with the Westphalian in point of courtesy, returned the compliment with the remaining chandelier, which also missed its mark, and, smiting a large mirror that was fixed behind them, emitted such a crash as one might expect to hear if a mine were sprung beneath a manufacture of glass. Both lights being thus extinguished, a furious combat ensued in the dark; the Italian scampered off with infinite agility, and, as he went downstairs, desired that nobody would interpose, because it was an affair of honour, which could not be made up. The ladies consulted their safety in flight; Count Fathom slyly retired to one corner of the room; while the abbe, having upon him the terrors of the commissaire, endeavoured to appease and part the combatants, and, in the attempt, sustained a random blow upon his nose, which sent him howling into the other chamber, where, finding his band besmeared with his own blood, he began to caper about the apartment, in a transport of rage and vexation.

Meanwhile, the old gentlewoman being alarmed with the noise of the battle, and apprehensive that it would end in murder, to the danger and discredit of herself and family, immediately mustered up her myrmidons, of whom she always retained a formidable band, and, putting herself at their head, lighted them to the scene of uproar. Ferdinand, who had hitherto observed a strict neutrality, no sooner perceived them approach, than he leaped in between the disputants, that he might be found acting in the character of a peacemaker; and, indeed, by this time, victory had declared for the baronet, who had treated his antagonist with a cross-buttock, which laid him almost breathless on the floor. The victor was prevailed upon, by the entreaties of Fathom, to quit the field of battle, and adjourn into another room, where, in less than half an hour, he received a billet from the count, defying him to single combat on the frontiers of Flanders, at an appointed time and place. The challenge was immediately accepted by the knight, who, being flushed with conquest, treated his adversary with great contempt.

But, next day, when the fumes of the burgundy were quite exhaled, and the adventure recurred to his remembrance and sober reflection, he waited upon our adventurer at his lodgings, and solicited his advice in such a manner, as gave him to understand that he looked upon what had happened as a drunken brawl, which ought to have no serious consequences. Fathom foreseeing that the affair might be managed for his own interest, professed himself of the baronet's opinion; and, without hesitation, undertook the office of a mediator, assuring his principal, that his honour should suffer no stain in the course of his negotiation.

Having received the Englishman's acknowledgments for this instance of friendship, he forthwith set out for the place of the German's habitation, and understanding he was still asleep, insisted upon his being immediately waked, and told, that a gentleman from the chevalier desired to see him, upon business of importance which could not be delayed. Accordingly, his valet-de-chambre, pressed by Fathom's importunities and remonstrances, ventured to go in and shake the count by the shoulder; when this furious Teutonian, still agitated by the fever of the preceding night, leaped out of bed in a frenzy, and seizing his sword that lay upon a table, would have severely punished the presumption of his servant, had not he been restrained by the entrance of Ferdinand, who, with a peremptory countenance, gave him to understand that the valet had acted at his immediate instigation; and that he was come, as the Englishman's friend, to concert with him proper measures for keeping the appointment they had made at their last meeting.

This message effectually calmed the German, who was not a little mortified to find himself so disagreeably disturbed. He could not help cursing the impatience of his antagonist, and even hinting that he would have acted more like a gentleman and good Christian, in expressing a desire of seeing the affair accommodated, as he knew himself to be the aggressor, consequently the first offender against the laws of politeness and good-fellowship. Fathom, finding him in a fit temper of mind, took the opportunity of assenting to the reasonableness of his observation. He ventured to condemn the impetuosity of the baronet, who, he perceived, was extremely nice and scrupulous in the punctilios of honour; and said it was a pity that two gentlemen should forfeit each other's friendship, much less expose their lives, for such a frivolous cause. "My dear count," cried the Westphalian, "I am charmed to find your sentiments so conformable to my own. In an honourable cause, I despise all danger; my courage, thank Heaven! has been manifested in many public engagements as well as in private rencounters; but, to break with my friend, whose eminent virtues I admire, and even to seek his life, on such a scandalous occasion, for a little insignificant w—-e, who, I suppose, took the advantage of our intoxication, to foment the quarrel: by Heaven! my conscience cannot digest it."

Having expressed himself to this purpose, he waited impatiently for the reply of Ferdinand, who, after a pause of deliberation, offered his services in the way of mediation; though, he observed, it was a matter of great delicacy, and the event altogether uncertain. "Nevertheless," added our adventurer, "I will strive to appease the knight, who, I hope, will be induced by my remonstrances to forget the unlucky accident, which hath so disagreeably interrupted your mutual friendship." The German thanked him for this proof of his regard, which yielded him more satisfaction on account of the chevalier than of himself. "For, by the tombs of my fathers," cried he, "I have so little concern for my personal safety, that, if my honour were interested, I durst oppose myself singly to the whole ban of the empire; and I am now ready, if the chevalier requires it, to give him the rendezvous in the forest of Senlis, either on horseback or on foot, where this contest may be terminated with the life of one or both of us."

Count Fathom, with a view to chastise the Westphalian for this rhodomontade, told him, with a mortifying air of indifference, that if they were both bent upon taking the field, he would save himself the trouble of interposing farther in the affair; and desired to know the hour at which it would suit him to take the air with the baronet. The other, not a little embarrassed by this question, said, with a faltering tongue, he should be proud to obey the chevalier's orders; but, at the same time, owned he should be much better pleased if our hero would execute the pacific proposal he had made. Fathom accordingly promised to exert himself for that purpose, and returned to the knight, with whom he assumed the merit of having tranquillised the rage of an incensed barbarian, who was now disposed to a reconciliation upon equal terms. The baronet overwhelmed him with caresses and compliments upon his friendship and address; the parties met that same forenoon, as if by accident, in Fathom's apartment, where they embraced each other cordially, exchanged apologies, and renewed their former correspondence.

Our adventurer thought he had good reason to congratulate himself upon the part he had acted in this pacification. He was treated by both with signal marks of particular affection and esteem. The count pressed him to accept, as a token of his attachment, a sword of very curious workmanship, which he had received in a present from a certain prince of the empire. The knight forced upon his finger a very splendid diamond ring, as a testimony of his gratitude and esteem. But there was still another person to be appeased, before the peace of the whole company could be established. This was no other than the abbe, from whom each of the reconciled friends received at dinner a billet couched in these words:—

> "I have the honour to lament the infinite chagrin and mortification that compels me to address myself in this manner to a person of your rank and eminence, whom I should do myself the pleasure of waiting upon in person, were I not prevented by the misfortune of my nose, which was last night most cruelly disarranged, by a violent contusion I had the honour to receive, in attempting to compose that unhappy fracas, at the house of Madame la Maquerelle; and what puts the finishing stroke to my mishap, is my being rendered incapable of keeping three or four assignations with ladies of fashion, by whom I have the honour to be particularly esteemed. The disfiguration of my nose, the pain I have undergone, with the discomposure of brain which it produced, I could bear as a philosopher; but the disappointment of the ladies, my glory will not permit me to overlook. And as you know the injury was sustained in your service, I have the pleasure to hope you will not refuse to grant such reparation as will be acceptable to a gentleman, who has the honour to be with inviolable attachment,—
>
> Sir, your most devoted slave,
> PEPIN CLOTHAIRE CHARLE HENRI LOOUIS
> BARNABE DE FUMIER."

This epistle was so equivocal, that the persons to whom it was addressed did not know whether or not they ought to interpret the contents into a challenge; when our hero observed, that the ambiguity of his expressions plainly proved there was a door left open for accommodation; and proposed that they should forthwith visit the writer at his own apartment. They accordingly followed his advice, and found the abbe in his morning gown and slippers, with three huge nightcaps on his head, and a crape hat-band tied over the middle of his face, by way of bandage to his nose. He received his visitors with the most ridiculous solemnity, being still a stranger to the purport of their errand; but soon as the Westphalian declared they were come in consequence of his billet, in order to ask pardon for the undesigned offence they had given, his features retrieved their natural vivacity, and he professed himself perfectly satisfied with their polite acknowledgment. Then they condoled him upon the evil plight of his nose, and seeing some marks upon his shirt, asked with seeming concern, if he had lost any blood in the fray? To this interrogation he replied, that he had still a sufficient quantity left for the occasions of his friends; and that he should deem it his greatest glory to expend the last drop of it in their service.

Matters being thus amicably adjusted, they prevailed upon him to unease his nose, which retained no signs of the outrage he had suffered; and the amusements of the day were concerted. It was in consequence of this plan, that, after the comedy, they were entertained at the count's lodgings, where quadrille was proposed by the abbe, as the most innocent pastime, and the proposal was immediately embraced by all present, and by none with more alacrity than by our adventurer, who, without putting forth a moiety of his skill, went home with twenty louis clear gain. Though, far from believing himself greatly superior to the rest of the party, in the artifices of play, he justly suspected that they had concealed their skill, with a view of stripping him on some other occasion; for he could not suppose that persons of their figure and character should be, in reality, such novices as they affected to appear.

CHAPTER TWENTY-FOUR.
HE OVERLOOKS THE ADVANCES OF HIS FRIENDS, AND SMARTS SEVERELY FOR HIS NEGLECT.

Steeled with this cautious maxim, he guarded himself from their united endeavours, in sundry subsequent attacks, by which his first conjecture was confirmed, and still came off conqueror, by virtue of his unparalleled finesse and discretion; till at length they seemed to despair of making him their prey, and the count began to drop some hints, importing a desire of seeing him more closely united to the views and interest of their triumvirate. But Ferdinand, who was altogether selfish, and quite solitary in his prospects, discouraged all those advances, being resolved to trade upon his own bottom only, and to avoid all such connexions with any person or society whatever; much more, with a set of raw adventurers whose talents he despised. With these sentiments, he still maintained the dignity and reserve of his first appearance among them, and rather enhanced than diminished that idea of importance which he had inspired at the beginning; because, besides his other qualifications, they gave him credit for the address with which he kept himself superior to their united designs.

While he thus enjoyed his pre-eminence, together with the fruits of his success at play, which he managed so discreetly as never to incur the reputation of an adventurer, he one day chanced to be at the ordinary, when the company was surprised by the entrance of such a figure as had never appeared before in that place. This was no other than a person habited in the exact uniform of an English jockey. His leathern cap, cut bob, fustian frock, flannel waistcoat, buff breeches, hunting-boots and whip, were sufficient of themselves to furnish out a phenomenon for the admiration of all Paris. But these peculiarities were rendered still more conspicuous by the behaviour of the man who owned them. When he crossed the threshold of the outward door, he produced such a sound from the smack of his whip, as equalled the explosion of an ordinary cohorn; and then broke forth into the halloo of a foxhunter, which he uttered with all its variations, in a strain of vociferation that seemed to astonish and confound the whole assembly, to whom he introduced himself and his spaniel, by exclaiming, in a tone something less melodious than the cry of mackerel or live cod, "By your leave, gentlevolks, I hope there's no offence, in an honest plain Englishman's coming with money in his pocket, to taste a bit of your Vrench frigasee and ragooze."

This declaration was made in such a wild, fantastical manner, that the greatest part of the company mistook him for some savage monster or maniac, and consulted their safety by starting up from table, and drawing their swords. The Englishman, seeing such a martial apparatus produced against him, recoiled two or three steps, saying, "Waunds! a believe the people are all bewitched. What, do they take me for a beast of prey? is there nobody here that knows Sir Stentor Stile, or can speak to me in my own lingo?" He had no sooner pronounced these words, than the baronet, with marks of infinite surprise, ran towards him, crying, "Good Heaven! Sir Stentor, who expected to meet with you in Paris?" Upon which, the other eyeing him very earnestly, "Odds heartlikins!" cried he, "my neighbour, Sir Giles Squirrel, as I am a living soul!" With these words he flew upon him like a tiger, kissed him from ear to ear, demolished his periwig, and disordered the whole economy of his dress, to the no small entertainment of the company.

Having well-nigh stifled his countryman with embraces, and besmeared himself with pulville from head to foot, he proceeded in this manner, "Mercy upon thee, knight, thou art so transmographied, and bedaubed, and bedizened, that thou mought rob thy own mother without fear of information. Look ye here now, I will be trussed, if the very bitch that was brought up in thy own bosom knows thee again. Hey, Sweetlips, here hussy, d—n the tuoad, dos't n't know thy old measter? Ey, ey, thou may'st smell till Christmas, I'll be bound to be hanged, knight, if the creature's nose an't foundered by the d——d stinking perfumes you have got among you."

These compliments being passed, the two knights sat down by one another, and Sir Stentor being asked by his neighbour, upon what errand he had crossed the sea, gave him to understand, that he had come to France, in consequence of a wager with Squire Snaffle, who had laid a thousand pounds, that he, Sir Stentor, would not travel to Paris by himself, and for a whole month appear every day at a certain hour in the public walks, without wearing any other dress than that in which he saw him. "The fellor has got no more stuff in his pate," continued this polite stranger, "than a jackass, to think I could not find my way hither thof I could not jabber your French lingo. Ecod! the people of this country are sharp enough to find out your meaning, when you want to spend anything among them; and, as for the matter of dress, bodikins! for a thousand pound, I would engage to live in the midst of them, and show myself without any clothes at all. Odds heart! a true-born Englishman needs not be ashamed to show his face, nor his backside neither, with the best Frenchman that ever trod the ground. Thof we Englishmen don't beplaister our doublets with gold and silver, I believe as how we have our pockets better lined than most of our neighbours; and for all my bit of a fustian frock, that cost me in all but forty shillings, I believe, between you and me, knight, I have more dust in my fob, than all those powdered sparks put together. But the worst of the matter is this; here is no solid belly-timber in this country. One can't have a slice of delicate sirloin, or nice buttock of beef, for love nor money. A pize upon them! I could get no eatables upon the ruoad, but what they called bully, which looks like the flesh of Pharaoh's lean kine stewed into rags and tatters; and then their peajohn, peajohn, rabbet them! One would think every old woman of this kingdom hatched pigeons from her own body."

It is not to be supposed that such an original sat unobserved. The French and other foreigners, who had never been in England, were struck dumb with amazement at the knight's appearance and deportment; while the English guests were overwhelmed with shame and confusion, and kept a most wary silence, for fear of being recognised by their countryman. As for our adventurer, he was inwardly transported with joy at sight of this curiosity. He considered him as a genuine, rich country booby, of the right English growth, fresh as imported; and his heart throbbed with rapture, when he heard Sir Stentor value himself upon the lining of his pockets. He foresaw, indeed, that the other knight would endeavour to reserve him for his own game; but he was too conscious of his own accomplishments to think he should find great difficulty in superseding the influence of Sir Giles.

Meanwhile, the new-comer was by his friend helped to some ragout, which pleased his palate so well, that he declared he should now make a hearty meal, for the first time since he had crossed the water; and, while his good-humour prevailed, he drank to every individual around the table. Ferdinand seized this opportunity of insinuating himself into his favour, by saying in English, he was glad to find there was anything in France that was agreeable to Sir Stentor. To this compliment the knight replied with an air of surprise: "Waunds! I find here's another countryman of mine in this here company. Sir, I am proud to see you with all my heart." So speaking, he thrust out his right hand across the table, and shook our hero by the fist, with such violence of civility, as proved very grievous to a French marquis, who, in helping himself to soup, was jostled in such a manner, as to overturn the dividing-spoon in his own bosom. The Englishman, seeing the mischief he had produced, cried, "No offence, I hope," in a tone of vociferation, which the marquis in all probability misconstrued; for he began to model his features into a very sublime and peremptory look, when Fathom interpreted the apology, and at the same time informed Sir Stentor, that although he himself had not the honour of being an Englishman, he had always entertained a most particular veneration for the country, and learned the language in consequence of that esteem.

"Blood!" answered the knight, "I think myself the more obliged to you for your kind opinion, than if you was my countryman in good earnest. For there be abundance of we English—no offence, Sir Giles—that seem to be ashamed of their own nation, and leave their homes to come and spend their fortunes abroad, among a parcel of—you understand me, sir—a word to the wise, as the saying is."—Here he was interrupted by an article of the second course, that seemed to give him great disturbance. This was a roasted leveret, very strong of the fumet, which happened to be placed directly under his nose. His sense of smelling was no sooner encountered by the effluvia of this delicious fare, than he started up from table, exclaiming, "Odd's my liver! here's a piece of carrion, that I would not offer to e'er a hound in my kennel; 'tis enough to make any Christian vomit both gut and gall;" and indeed by the wry faces he made while he ran to the door, his stomach seemed ready to justify this last assertion.

The abbe, who concluded, from these symptoms of disgust, that the leveret was not sufficiently stale, began to exhibit marks of discontent, and desired that it might be brought to the other end of the table for his examination. He accordingly hung over it with the most greedy appetite, feasting his nostrils with the steams of animal putrefaction; and at length declared that the morceau was passable, though he owned it would have been highly perfect, had it been kept another week. Nevertheless, mouths were not wanting to discuss it, insipid as it was; for in three minutes there was not a vestige to be seen of that which had offended the organs of Sir Stentor, who now resumed his place, and did justice to the dessert. But what he seemed to relish better than any other part of the entertainment, was the conversation of our adventurer, whom, after dinner, he begged to have the honour of treating with a dish of coffee, to the seeming mortification of his brother knight, over which Fathom exulted in his own heart.

In short, our hero, by his affability and engaging deportment, immediately gained possession of Sir Stentor's good graces, insomuch, that he desired to crack a bottle with him in the evening, and they repaired to an auberge, whither his fellow-knight accompanied him, not without manifest signs of reluctance. There the stranger gave a loose to jollity; though at first he d—-ed the burgundy as a poor thin liquor, that ran through him in a twinkling, and, instead of warming, cooled his heart and bowels. However, it insensibly seemed to give the lie to his imputation; for his spirits rose to a more elevated pitch of mirth and good-fellowship; he sung, or rather roared, the Early Horn, so as to alarm the whole neighbourhood, and began to slabber his companions with a most bear-like affection. Yet whatever haste he made to the goal of ebriety, he was distanced by his brother baronet, who from the beginning of the party had made little other use of his mouth than to receive the glass, and now sunk down upon the floor, in a state of temporary annihilation.

He was immediately carried to bed by the direction of Ferdinand, who now saw himself in a manner possessor of that mine to which he had made such eager and artful advances. That he might, therefore, carry on the approaches in the same cautious manner, he gradually shook off the trammels of sobriety, gave a loose to that spirit of freedom which good liquor commonly inspires, and, in the familiarity of drunkenness, owned himself head of a noble family of Poland, from which he had been obliged to absent himself on account of an affair of honour, not yet compromised.

Having made this confession, and laid strong injunctions of secrecy upon Sir Stentor, his countenance seemed to acquire from every succeeding glass a new symptom of intoxication. They renewed their embraces, swore eternal friendship from that day, and swallowed fresh bumpers, till both being in all appearance quite overpowered, they began to yawn in concert, and even nod in their chairs. The knight seemed to resent the attacks of slumber, as so many impertinent attempts to interrupt their entertainment; he cursed his own propensity to sleep, imputing it to the d—-ed French climate, and proposed to engage in some pastime that would keep them awake. "Odd's flesh!" cried the Briton, "when I'm at home, I defy all the devils in hell to fasten my eyelids together, if so be as I'm otherwise inclined. For there's mother and sister Nan, and brother Numps and I, continue to divert ourselves at all-fours, brag, cribbage, tetotum, husslecap, and chuck-varthing, and, thof I say it, that should n't say it, I won't turn my back to e'er a he in England, at any of these pastimes. And so, Count, if you are so disposed, I am your man, that is, in the way of friendship, at which of these you shall please to pitch upon."

To this proposal Fathom replied, he was quite ignorant of all the games he had mentioned; but, in order to amuse Sir Stentor, he would play with him at lansquenet, for a trifle, as he had laid it down for a maxim, to risk nothing considerable at play. "Waunds!" answered the knight, "I hope you don't think I come here in quest of money. Thank God! I have a good landed estate worth five thousand a year, and owe no man a halfpenny; and I question whether there be many counts in your nation—no offence, I hope—that can say a bolder word. As for your lambskin net, I know nothing of the matter; but I will toss up with you for a guinea, cross or pile, as the saying is; or, if there's such a thing in this country as a box and dice, I love to hear the bones rattle sometimes."

Fathom found some difficulty in concealing his joy at the mention of this last amusement, which had been one of his chief studies, and in which he had made such progress, that he could calculate all the chances with the utmost exactness and certainty. However, he made shift to contain himself within due bounds, and, with seeming indifference, consented to pass away an hour at hazard, provided the implements could be procured. Accordingly, the landlord was consulted, and their desire gratified; the dice were produced, and the table resounded with the effects of their mutual eagerness. Fortune, at first, declared for the Englishman, who was permitted by our adventurer to win twenty broad pieces; and he was so elated with his success, as to accompany every lucky throw with a loud burst of laughter, and other savage and simple manifestations of excessive joy, exclaiming, in a tone something less sweet than the bellowing of a bull, "Now for the main, Count,—odd! here they come—here are the seven black stars, i'faith. Come along, my yellow boys—odd's heart! I never liked the face of Lewis before."

Fathom drew happy presages from these boyish raptures, and, after having indulged them for some time, began to avail himself of his arithmetic, in consequence of which the knight was obliged to refund the greatest part of his winning. Then he altered his note, and became as intemperate in his chagrin, as he had been before immoderate in his mirth. He cursed himself and his whole generation, d—-ed his bad luck, stamped with his feet upon the floor, and challenged Ferdinand to double stakes. This was a very welcome proposal to our hero, who found Sir Stentor just such a subject as he had long desired to encounter with; the more the Englishman laid, the more he lost, and Fathom took care to inflame his passions, by certain well-timed sarcasms upon his want of judgment, till at length he became quite outrageous, swore the dice were false, and threw them out at the window; pulled off his periwig, and committed it to the flames, spoke with the most rancorous contempt of his adversary's skill, insisted upon his having stripped many a better man, for all he was a Count, and threatening that, before they parted, he should not only look like a Pole, but also smell like a pole-cat.

This was a spirit which our adventurer industriously kept up, observing that the English were dupes to all the world; and that, in point of genius and address, they were no more than noisy braggadocios. In short, another pair of dice was procured, the stakes were again raised, and, after several vicissitudes, fortune declared so much in favour of the knight, that Fathom lost all the money in his pocket, amounting to a pretty considerable sum. By this time he was warmed into uncommon eagerness and impatience; being equally piqued at the success and provoking exultations of his antagonist, whom he now invited to his lodgings, in order to decide the contest. Sir Stentor complied with this request; the dispute was renewed with various success, till, towards daylight, Ferdinand saw this noisy, raw, inexperienced simpleton, carry off all his ready cash, together with his jewels, and almost everything that was valuable about his person; and, to crown the whole, the victor at parting told him with a most intolerable sneer, that as soon as the Count should receive another remittance from Poland, he would give him his revenge.

CHAPTER TWENTY-FIVE.
HE BEARS HIS FATE LIKE A PHILOSOPHER; AND CONTRACTS ACQUAINTANCE WITH A VERY REMARKABLE PERSONAGE.

This was a proper subject for our hero to moralise upon; and accordingly it did not pass without his remarks; he found himself fairly foiled at his own weapons, reduced to indigence in a foreign land, and, what he chiefly regretted, robbed of all those gay expectations he had indulged from his own supposed excellence in the wiles of fraud; for, upon a little recollection, he plainly perceived he had fallen a sacrifice to the confederacy he had refused to join; and did not at all doubt that the dice were loaded for his destruction. But, instead of beating his head against the wall, tearing his hair, imprecating vain curses upon himself, or betraying other frantic symptoms of despair, he resolved to accommodate himself to his fate, and profit by the lesson he had so dearly bought.

With this intention, he immediately dismissed his valet, quitted his lodgings, retired to an obscure street on the other side of the river, and, covering one eye with a large patch of black silk, presented himself in quality of a musician to the director of the opera, who, upon hearing a trial of his skill, received him into the band without further question. While he continued in this situation, he not only improved his taste and execution in music, but likewise found frequent opportunities to extend his knowledge of mankind; for, besides the employment he exercised in public, he was often concerned in private concerts that were given in the hotels of noblemen; by which means he became more and more acquainted with the persons, manners, and characters of high life, which he contemplated with the most industrious attention, as a spectator, who, being altogether unconcerned in the performance, is at more liberty to observe and enjoy the particulars of the entertainment.

It was in one of those assemblies he had the pleasure of seeing his friend Sir Stentor, dressed in the most fashionable manner, and behaving with all the overstrained politesse of a native Frenchman. He was accompanied by his brother knight and the abbe; and this triumvirate, even in Fathom's hearing, gave a most ludicrous detail of the finesse they had practised upon the Polish Count, to their entertainer, who was ambassador from a certain court, and made himself extremely merry with the particulars of the relation. Indeed, they made shift to describe some of the circumstances in such a ridiculous light, that our adventurer himself, smarting as he was with the disgrace, could not help laughing in secret at the account. He afterwards made it his business to inquire into the characters of the two British knights, and understood they were notorious sharpers, who had come abroad for the good of their country, and now hunted in couple among a French pack, that dispersed themselves through the public ordinaries, walks, and spectacles, in order to make a prey of incautious strangers.

The pride of Ferdinand was piqued at this information; and he was even animated with the desire of making reprisals upon this fraternity, from which he ardently longed to retrieve his honour and effects. But the issue of his last adventure had reinforced his caution; and, for the present, he found means to suppress the dictates of his avarice and ambition; resolving to employ his whole penetration in reconnoitring the ground, before he should venture to take the field again. He therefore continued to act the part of a one-eyed fiddler, under the name of Fadini, and lived with incredible frugality, that he might save a purse for his future operations. In this manner had he proceeded for the space of ten months, during which he acquired a competent knowledge of the city of Paris, when his curiosity was attracted by certain peculiarities in the appearance of a man who lived in one of the upper apartments belonging to the house in which he himself had fixed his habitation.

This was a tall, thin, meagre figure, with a long black beard, an aquiline nose, a brown complexion, and a most piercing vivacity in his eyes. He seemed to be about the age of fifty, wore the Persian habit, and there was a remarkable severity in his aspect and demeanour. He and our adventurer had been fellow-lodgers for some time, and, according to the laudable custom in these days, had hitherto remained as much estranged to one another, as if they had lived on opposite sides of the globe; but of late the Persian seemed to regard our hero with particular attention; when they chanced to meet on the staircase, or elsewhere, he bowed to Ferdinand with great solemnity, and complimented him with the pas. He even proceeded, in the course of this communication, to open his mouth, and salute him with a good-morrow, and sometimes made the common remarks upon the weather. Fathom, who was naturally complaisant, did not discourage these advances. On the contrary, he behaved to him with marks of particular respect, and one day desired the favour of his company to breakfast.

This invitation the stranger declined with due acknowledgment, on pretence of being out of order; and, in the meantime, our adventurer bethought himself of questioning the landlord concerning his outlandish guest. His curiosity was rather inflamed than satisfied with the information he could obtain from this quarter; for all he learned was, that the Persian went by the name of Ali Beker, and that he had lived in the house for the space of four months, in a most solitary and parsimonious manner, without being visited by one living soul; that, for some time after his arrival, he had been often heard to groan dismally in the night, and even to exclaim in an unknown language, as if he had laboured under some grievous affliction; and though the first transports of his grief had subsided, it was easy to perceive he still indulged a deep-rooted melancholy; for the tears were frequently observed to trickle down his beard. The commissaire of the quarter had at first ordered this Oriental to be watched in his outgoings, according to the maxims of the French police; but his life was found so regular and inoffensive, that this precaution was soon set aside.

Any man of humane sentiments, from the knowledge of these particulars, would have been prompted to offer his services to the forlorn stranger; but as our hero was devoid of all these infirmities of human nature, it was necessary that other motives should produce the same effect. His curiosity, therefore, joined with the hopes of converting the confidence of Ali to his own emolument, effectually impelled him towards his acquaintance; and, in a little time, they began to relish the conversation of each other. For, as the reader may have already observed, Fathom possessed all the arts of insinuation, and had discernment enough to perceive an air of dignity in the Persian, which the humility of his circumstances could not conceal. He was, moreover, a man of good understanding, not without a tincture of letters, perfectly well bred, though in a ceremonious style, extremely moral in his discourse, and scrupulously nice in his notions of honour.

Our hero conformed himself in all respects to the other's opinions, and managed his discretion so as to pass upon him for a gentleman reduced by misfortunes to the exercise of an employment which was altogether unsuitable to his birth and quality. He made earnest and repeated tenders of his good offices to the stranger, and pressed him to make use of his purse with such cordial perseverance, that, at length, Ali's reserve was overcome, and he condescended to borrow of him a small sum, which in all probability, saved his life; for he had been driven to the utmost extremity of want before he would accept of this assistance.

Fathom, having gradually stole into his good graces, began to take notice of many piteous sighs that escaped him in the moments of their intercourse, and seemed to denote an heart fraught with woe; and, on pretence of administering consolation and counsel, begged leave to know the cause of his distress, observing, that his mind would be disburdened by such communication, and, perhaps, his grief alleviated by some means which they might jointly concert and execute in his behalf.

Ali, thus solicited, would often shake his head, with marks of extreme sorrow and despondence, and, while the tears gushed from his eyes, declared that his distress was beyond the power of any remedy but death, and that, by making our hero his confidant, he should only extend his unhappiness to a friend, without feeling the least remission of his own torture. Notwithstanding these repeated declarations, Ferdinand, who was well enough acquainted with the mind of man to know that such importunity is seldom or never disagreeable, redoubled his instances, together with his expressions of sympathy and esteem, until the stranger was prevailed upon to gratify his curiosity and benevolence. Having, therefore, secured the chamber door one night, while all the rest of the family were asleep, the unfortunate Ali disclosed himself in these words.

CHAPTER TWENTY-SIX.
THE HISTORY OF THE NOBLE CASTILIAN.

I should be ungrateful, as well as unwise, did I longer resist the desire you express to know the particulars of that destiny which hath driven me to this miserable disguise, and rendered me in all considerations the most wretched of men. I have felt your friendship, am confident of your honour, and though my misfortunes are such as can never be repaired, because I am utterly cut off from hope, which is the wretch's last comfort, yet I may, by your means, be enabled to bear them with some degree of fortitude and resignation.

Know then, my name is not Ali; neither am I of Persian extraction. I had once the honour to own myself a Castilian, and was, under the appellation of Don Diego de Zelos, respected as the head of one of the most ancient families of that kingdom. Judge, then, how severe that distress must be, which compels a Spaniard to renounce his country, his honours, and his name. My youth was not spent in inglorious ease, neither did it waste unheeded in the rolls of fame. Before I had attained the age of nineteen, I was twice wounded in battle. I once fortunately recovered the standard of the regiment to which I belonged, after it had been seized by the enemy; and, at another occasion, made shift to save the life of my colonel, when he lay at the mercy of an enraged barbarian.

He that thinks I recapitulate these particulars out of ostentation, does wrong to the unhappy Don Diego de Zelos, who, in having performed these little acts of gallantry, thinks he has done nothing, but simply approved himself worthy of being called a Castilian. I mean only to do justice to my own character, and to make you acquainted with one of the most remarkable incidents of my life. It was my fate, during my third campaign, to command a troop of horse in the regiment of Don Gonzales Orgullo, between whom and my father a family feud had long been maintained with great enmity; and that gentleman did not leave me without reason to believe he rejoiced at the opportunity of exercising his resentment upon his adversary's son; for he withheld from me that countenance which my fellow-officers enjoyed, and found means to subject me to divers mortifications, of which I was not at liberty to complain. These I bore in silence for some time, as part of my probation in the character of a soldier; resolved, nevertheless, to employ my interest at court for a removal into another corps, and to take some future opportunity of explaining my sentiments to Don Gonzales upon the injustice of his behaviour.

While I animated myself with these sentiments against the discouragements I underwent, and the hard duty to which I was daily exposed, it was our fate to be concerned in the battle of Saragossa, where our regiment was so severely handled by the English infantry, that it was forced to give ground with the loss of one half of its officers and men. Don Gonzales, who acted as brigadier in another wing, being informed of our fate, and dreading the disgrace of his corps, which had never turned back to the enemy, put spurs to his horse, and, riding across the field at full speed, rallied our broken squadrons, and led us back to the charge with such intrepidity of behaviour, as did not fail to inspire us all with uncommon courage and alacrity. For my own part, I thought myself doubly interested to distinguish my valour, not only on account of my own glory, but likewise on the supposition, that, as I was acting under the eye of Gonzales, my conduct would be narrowly observed.

I therefore exerted myself with unusual vigour, and as he began the attack with the remains of my troop, fought close by his side during the rest of the engagement. I even acquired his applause in the very heat of battle. When his hat was struck off, and his horse fell under him, I accommodated and remounted him upon my own, and, having seized for my own use another that belonged to a common trooper, attended this stern commander as before, and seconded him in all his repeated efforts; but it was impossible to withstand the numbers and impetuosity of the foe, and Don Gonzales having had the mortification to see his regiment cut in pieces, and the greatest part of the army routed, was fain to yield to the fortune of the day; yet he retired as became a man of honour and a Castilian; that is, he marched off with great deliberation in the rear of the Spanish troops, and frequently faced about to check the pursuit of the enemy. Indeed, this exercise of his courage had well-nigh cost him his life; for, in one of those wheelings, he was left almost alone, and a small party of the Portuguese horse had actually cut off our communication with the retreating forces of Spain.

In this dilemma, we had no other chance of saving our lives and liberty, than that of opening a passage sword in hand; and this was what Gonzales instantly resolved to attempt. We accordingly recommended our souls to God, and, charging the line abreast of one another, bore down all opposition, and were in a fair way of accomplishing our retreat without further danger; but the gallant Orgullo, in crossing a ditch, had the misfortune to be thrown from his horse, and was almost the same instant overtaken by one of the Portuguese dragoons, whose sword was already suspended over his head, as he lay half stunned with his fall; when I rode up, discharged a pistol in the ruffian's brain, and, seating my colonel on his horse, had the good fortune to conduct him to a place of safety.

Here he was provided with such accommodation as his case required; for he had been wounded in the battle, and dangerously bruised by his fall, and, when all the necessary steps were taken towards his recovery, I desired to know if he had any further commands for his service, being resolved to join the army without delay. I thought proper to communicate this question by message, because he had not spoke one word to me during our retreat, notwithstanding the good office he had received at my hands; a reserve which I attributed to his pride, and resented accordingly. He no sooner understood my intention, than he desired to see me in his apartment, and, as near as I can remember, spoke to this effect: —

"Were your father Don Alonzo alive, I should now, in consequence of your behaviour, banish every suggestion of resentment, and solicit his friendship with great sincerity. Yes, Don Diego, your virtue hath triumphed over that enmity I bore your house, and I upbraid myself with the ungenerous treatment you have suffered under my command. But it is not enough for me to withdraw that rigour which it was unjust to exercise, and would be wicked to maintain. I must likewise atone for the injuries you have sustained, and make some suitable acknowledgment for that life which I have twice to-day owed to your valour and generosity. Whatever interest I have at court shall be employed in your behalf; and I have other designs in your favour, which shall be disclosed in due season. Meanwhile, I desire you will still add one obligation to the debt which I have already incurred, and carry this billet in person to my Estifania, who, from the news of this fatal overthrow must be in despair upon my account."

So saying, he presented a letter, directed to his lady, which I received in a transport of joy, with expressions suitable to the occasion, and immediately set out for his country house, which happened to be about thirty leagues from the spot. This expedition was equally glorious and interesting; for my thoughts upon the road were engrossed by the hope of seeing Don Orgullo's daughter and heiress Antonia, who was reported to be a young lady of great beauty, and the most amiable accomplishments. However ridiculous it may seem for a man to conceive a passion for an object which he hath never beheld, certain it is, my sentiments were so much prepossessed by the fame of her qualifications, that I must have fallen a victim to her charms, had they been much less powerful than they were. Notwithstanding the fatigues I had undergone in the field, I closed not an eye until I arrived at the gate of Gonzales, being determined to precede the report of the battle, that Madame d'Orgullo might not be alarmed for the life of her husband.

I declared my errand, and was introduced into a saloon, where I had not waited above three minutes, when my colonel's lady appeared, and in great confusion received the letter, exclaiming, "Heaven grant that Don Gonzales be well!" In reading the contents, she underwent a variety of agitations; but, when she had perused the whole, her countenance regained its serenity, and, regarding me with an air of ineffable complacency, "Don Diego," said she, "while I lament the national calamity, in the defeat of our army, I at the same time feel the most sincere pleasure on seeing you upon this occasion, and, according to the directions of my dear lord, bid you heartily welcome to this house, as his preserver and friend. I was not unacquainted with your character before this last triumph of your virtue, and have often prayed to Heaven for some lucky determination of that fatal quarrel which raged so long between the family of Gonzales and your father's house. My prayers have been heard, the long-wished-for reconciliation is now effected, and I hope nothing will ever intervene to disturb this happy union."

To this polite and affectionate declaration, I made such a reply as became a young man, whose heart overflowed with joy and benevolence, and desired to know how soon her answer to my commander would be ready, that I might gratify his impatience with all possible despatch. After having thanked me for this fresh proof of my attachment, she begged I would retire into a chamber, and repose myself from the uncommon fatigues I must have undergone; but, finding I persisted in the resolution of returning to Don Gonzales, without allowing myself the least benefit of sleep, she left me engaged in conversation with an uncle of Don Gonzales, who lodged in the house, and gave orders that a collation should be prepared in another apartment, while she retired to her closet, and wrote a letter to her husband.

In less than an hour from my first arrival, I was introduced into a most elegant dining-room, where a magnificent entertainment was served up, and where we were joined by Donna Estifania, and her beautiful daughter the fair Antonia, who, advancing with the most amiable sweetness, thanked me in very warm expressions of acknowledgment, for the generosity of my conduct towards her father. I had been ravished with her first appearance, which far exceeded my imagination, and my faculties were so disordered by this address, that I answered her compliment with the most awkward confusion. But this disorder did not turn to my prejudice in the opinion of that lovely creature, who has often told me in the sequel, that she gave herself credit for that perplexity in my behaviour, and that I never appeared more worthy of her regard and affection than at that juncture, when my dress was discomposed, and my whole person disfigured by the toils and duty of the preceding day; for this very dishabille presented itself to her reflection as the immediate effect of that very merit by which I was entitled to her esteem.

Wretch that I am! to survive the loss of such an excellent woman, endeared to my remembrance by the most tender offices of wedlock, happily exercised for the space of five-and-twenty years! Forgive these tears; they are not the drops of weakness, but remorse. Not to trouble you with idle particulars, suffice it is to say, I was favoured with such marks of distinction by Madame d'Orgullo, that she thought it incumbent upon her to let me know she had not overacted her hospitality, and, while we sat at table, accosted me in these words: "You will not be surprised, Don Diego, at my expressions of regard, which I own are unusual from a Spanish lady to a young cavalier like you, when I communicate the contents of this letter from Don Gonzales." So saying, she put the billet into my hand, and I read these words, or words to this effect:—

"AMIABLE ESTIFANIA,—You will understand that I am as well as a person can possibly be who hath this day lived to see the army of his king defeated. If you would know the particulars of this unfortunate action, your curiosity will be gratified by the bearer, Don Diego de Zelos, to whose virtue and bravery I am twice indebted for my life. I therefore desire you will receive him with that respect and gratitude which you shall think due for such an obligation; and, in entertaining him, dismiss that reserve which often disgraces the Spanish hospitality. In a word, let your own virtue and beneficence conduct you upon this occasion, and let my Antonia's endeavours be joined with your own in doing honour to the preserver of her father! Adieu."

Such a testimonial could not fail of being very agreeable to a young soldier, who by this time had begun to indulge the transporting hope of being happy in the arms of the adorable Antonia. I professed myself extremely happy in having met with an opportunity of acquiring such a degree of my colonel's esteem, entertained them with a detail of his personal prowess in the battle, and answered all their questions with that moderation which every man ought to preserve in speaking of his own behaviour. Our repast being ended, I took my leave of the ladies, and at parting received a letter from Donna Estifania to her husband, together with a ring of great value, which she begged I would accept, as a token of her esteem. Thus loaded with honour and caresses, I set out on my return for the quarters of Don Gonzales, who could scarce credit his own eyes when I delivered his lady's billet; for he thought it impossible to perform such a journey in so short a time.

When he had glanced over the paper, "Don Diego," said he, "by your short stay one would imagine you had met with indifferent reception at my house. I hope Estifania has not been deficient in her duty?" I answered this question, by assuring him my entertainment had been so agreeable in all respects, that nothing but my duty to him could have induced me to give it up so soon. He then turned the conversation upon Antonia, and hinted his intention of giving her in marriage to a young cavalier, for whom he had a particular friendship. I was so much affected by this insinuation, which seemed at once to blast all my hopes of love and happiness, that the blood forsook my face; I was seized with an universal trepidation, and even obliged to retire, on pretence of being suddenly taken ill.

Though Gonzales seemed to impute this disorder to fatigue and want of rest, he in his heart ascribed it to the true cause; and, after having sounded my sentiments to his own satisfaction, blessed me with a declaration, importing, that I was the person upon whom he had pitched for a son-in-law. I will not trouble you with a repetition of what passed on this interesting occasion, but proceed to observe, that his intention in my favour was far from being disagreeable to his lady; and that, in a little time, I had the good fortune to espouse the charming Antonia, who submitted to the will of her father without reluctance.

Soon after this happy event, I was, by the influence of Don Gonzales, joined to my own interest, promoted to the command of a regiment, and served with honour during the remaining part of the war. After the treaty of Utrecht, I was employed in reducing the Catalans to their allegiance; and, in an action with those obstinate rebels had the misfortune to lose my father-in-law, who by that time was preferred to the rank of a major-general. The virtuous Estifania did not long survive this melancholy accident; and the loss of these indulgent parents made such a deep impression upon the tender heart of my Antonia, that I took the first opportunity of removing her from a place in which every object served to cherish her grief, to a pleasant villa near the city of Seville, which I purchased on account of its agreeable situation. That I might the more perfectly enjoy the possession of my amiable partner, who could no longer brook the thoughts of another separation, peace was no sooner re-established than I obtained leave to resign my commission, and I wholly devoted myself to the joys of a domestic life.

Heaven seemed to smile upon our union, by blessing us with a son, whom, however, it was pleased to recall in his infancy, to our unspeakable grief and mortification; but our mutual chagrin was afterwards alleviated by the birth of a daughter, who seemed born with every accomplishment to excite the love and admiration of mankind. Why did nature debase such a masterpiece with the mixture of an alloy, which hath involved herself and her whole family in perdition? But the ways of Providence are unsearchable. She hath paid the debt of her degeneracy; peace be with her soul! The honour of my family is vindicated; though by a sacrifice which hath robbed me of everything else that is valuable in life, and ruined my peace past all redemption. Yes, my friend, all the tortures that human tyranny can inflict would be ease, tranquillity, and delight, to the unspeakable pangs and horrors I have felt.

But, to return from this digression.—Serafina, which was the name of that little darling, as she grew up, not only disclosed all the natural graces of external beauty, but likewise manifested the most engaging sweetness of disposition, and a capacity for acquiring with ease all the accomplishments of her sex. It is impossible to convey any adequate idea of a parent's raptures in the contemplation of such a fair blossom. She was the only pledge of our love, she was presumptive heiress to a large fortune, and likely to be the sole representative of two noble Castilian families. She was the delight of all who saw her, and a theme of praise for every tongue. You are not to suppose that the education of such a child was neglected. Indeed, it wholly engrossed the attention of me and my Antonia, and her proficiency rewarded our care. Before she had attained the age of fifteen, she was mistress of every elegant qualification, natural and acquired. Her person was, by that time, the confessed pattern of beauty. Her voice was enchantingly sweet, and she touched the lute with the most ravishing dexterity. Heaven and earth! how did my breast dilate with joy at the thoughts of having given birth to such perfection! how did my heart gush with paternal fondness, whenever I beheld this ornament of my name! and what scenes of endearing transport have I enjoyed with my Antonia, in mutual congratulation upon our parental happiness!

Serafina, accomplished as she was, could not fail to make conquests among the Spanish cavaliers, who are famous for sensibility in love. Indeed, she never appeared without a numerous train of admirers; and though we had bred her up in that freedom of conversation and intercourse which holds a middle space between the French licence and Spanish restraint, she was now so much exposed to the addresses of promiscuous gallantry, that we found it necessary to retrench the liberty of our house, and behave to our male visitants with great reserve and circumspection, that our honour and peace might run no risk from the youth and inexperience of our daughter.

This caution produced overtures from a great many young gentlemen of rank and distinction, who courted my alliance, by demanding Serafina in marriage; and from the number I had actually selected one person, who was in all respects worthy the possession of such an inestimable prize. His name was Don Manuel de Mendoza. His birth was noble, and his character dignified with repeated acts of generosity and virtue. Yet, before I would signify to him my approbation of his suit, I resolved to inform myself whether or not the heart of Serafina was totally unengaged, and indifferent to any other object, that I might not lay a tyrannical restraint upon her inclinations. The result of my inquiry was a full conviction of her having hitherto been deaf to the voice of love; and this piece of information, together with my own sentiments in his favour, I communicated to Don Manuel, who heard these tidings with transports of gratitude and joy. He was immediately favoured with opportunities of acquiring the affection of my daughter, and his endeavours were at first received with such respectful civility, as might have been easily warmed into a mutual passion, had not the evil genius of our family interposed.

O my friend! how shall I describe the depravity of that unhappy virgin's sentiments! how recount the particulars of my own dishonour! I that am descended from a long line of illustrious Castilians, who never received an injury they did not revenge, but washed away every blemish in their fame with the blood of those who attempted to stain it! In that circumstance I have imitated the example of my glorious progenitors, and that consideration alone hath supported me against all the assaults of despair.

As I grudged no pains and expense in perfecting the education of Serafina, my doors were open to every person who made an extraordinary figure in the profession of those amusing sciences in which she delighted. The house of Don Diego de Zelos was a little academy for painting, poetry, and music; and Heaven decreed that it should fall a sacrifice to its regard for these fatal and delusive arts. Among other preceptors, it was her fate to be under the instruction of a cursed German, who, though his profession was drawing, understood the elements and theory of music, possessed a large fund of learning and taste, and was a person remarkable for his agreeable conversation. This traitor, who like you had lost one eye, I not only admitted into my house for the improvement of my daughter, but even distinguished with particular marks of confidence and favour, little thinking he had either inclination or capacity to debauch the sentiments of my child. I was rejoiced beyond measure to see with what alacrity she received his lessons, with what avidity she listened to his discourse, which was always equally moral, instructing, and entertaining.

Antonia seemed to vie with me in expressions of regard for this accomplished stranger, whom she could not help supposing to be a person of rank and family, reduced to his present situation by some unfortunate vicissitude of fate. I was disposed to concur with this opinion, and actually conjured him to make me his confidant, with such protestations as left him no room to doubt my honour and beneficence; but he still persisted in declaring himself the son of an obscure mechanic in Bohemia; an origin to which surely no man would pretend who had the least claim to nobility of birth. While I was thus undeceived in my conjecture touching his birth and quality, I was confirmed in an opinion of his integrity and moderation, and looked upon him as a man of honour, in despite of the lowness of his pedigree. Nevertheless, he was at bottom a most perfidious wretch, and all this modesty and self-denial were the effects of the most villanous dissimulation, a cloak under which he, unsuspected, robbed me of my honour and my peace.

Not to trouble you with particulars, the recital of which would tear my heart-strings with indignation and remorse, I shall only observe, that, by the power of his infernal insinuation, he fascinated the heart of Serafina, brought over Antonia herself to the interests of his passion, and at once detached them both from their duty and religion. Heaven and earth! how dangerous, how irresistible is the power of infatuation! While I remained in the midst of this blind security, waiting for the nuptials of my daughter, and indulging myself with the vain prospect of her approaching felicity, Antonia found means to protract the negotiations of the marriage, by representing that it would be a pity to deprive Serafina of the opportunity she then had of profiting by the German's instructions; and, upon that account, I prevailed upon Don Manuel to bridle the impatience of his love.

During this interval, as I one evening enjoyed the cool air in my own garden, I was accosted by an old duenna, who had been my nurse and lived in the family since the time of my childhood.—"My duty," said she, "will no longer permit me to wink in silence at the wrongs I see you daily suffer. Dismiss that German from your house without delay, if you respect the glory of your name, and the rights of our holy religion; the stranger is an abominable heretic; and, grant Heaven! he may not have already poisoned the minds of those you hold most dear." I had been extremely alarmed at the beginning of this address; but, finding the imputation limited to the article of religion, in which, thank God, I am no bigot, I recovered my serenity of disposition, thanked the old woman for her zeal, commended her piety, and encouraged her to persevere in making observations on such subjects as should concern my honour and my quiet.

We live in such a world of wickedness and fraud, that a man cannot be too vigilant in his own defence: had I employed such spies from the beginning, I should in all probability have been at this day in possession of every comfort that renders life agreeable. The duenna, thus authorised, employed her sagacity with such success, that I had reason to suspect the German of a design upon the heart of Serafina; but, as the presumptions did not amount to conviction, I contented myself with exiling him from my house, under the pretext of having discovered that he was an enemy to the Catholic church; and forthwith appointed a day for the celebration of my daughter's marriage with Don Manuel de Mendoza. I could easily perceive a cloud of melancholy overspread the faces of Serafina and her mother, when I declared these my resolutions; but, as they made no objection to what I proposed, I did not at that time enter into an explanation of the true motives that influenced my conduct. Both parties were probably afraid of such expostulation.

Meanwhile, preparations were made for the espousals of Serafina; and, notwithstanding the anxiety I had undergone, on account of her connexion with the German, I began to think that her duty, her glory, had triumphed over all such low-born considerations, if ever they had been entertained; because she, and even Antonia, seemed to expect the ceremony with resignation, though the features of both still retained evident marks of concern, which I willingly imputed to the mutual prospect of their separation. This, however, was but a faithless calm, that soon, ah! too soon, brought forth a tempest which hath wrecked my hopes.

Two days before the appointed union of Don Manuel and Serafina, I was informed by the duenna, that, while she accompanied Antonia's waiting-maid at church, she had seen her receive a billet from an old woman, who, kneeling at her side, had conveyed it in such a mysterious manner, as awakened the duenna's apprehensions about her young lady; she had therefore hastened home to communicate this piece of intelligence, that I might have an opportunity of examining the messenger before she could have time to deposit her trust. I could not help shivering with fearful presages upon this occasion, and even abhorring the person to whose duty and zeal I was beholden for the intelligence, even while I endeavoured to persuade myself that the inquiry would end in the detection of some paltry intrigue between the maid and her own gallant. I intercepted her in returning from church, and, commanding her to follow me to a convenient place, extorted from her, by dint of threats, the fatal letter, which I read to this effect:—

"The whole business of my life, O divine Serafina! will be to repay that affection I have been so happy as to engage. With what transport then shall I obey your summons, in performing that enterprise, which will rescue you from the bed of a detested rival, and put myself in full possession of a jewel which I value infinitely more than life! Yes, adorable creature! I have provided everything for our escape, and at midnight will attend you in your own apartment, from whence you shall be conveyed into a land of liberty and peace, where you will, unmolested, enjoy the purity of that religion you have espoused, and in full security bless the arms of your ever faithful, ORLANDO."

Were you a fond parent, a tender husband, and a noble Castilian, I should not need to mention the unutterable horrors that took possession of my bosom, when I perused this accursed letter, by which I learned the apostasy, disobedience, and degeneracy of my idolised Serafina, who had overthrown and destroyed the whole plan of felicity which I had erected, and blasted all the glories of my name; and when the wretched messenger, terrified by my menaces and agitation, confessed that Antonia herself was privy to the guilt of her daughter, whom she had solemnly betrothed to that vile German, in the sight of Heaven, and that by her connivance this plebeian intended, that very night, to bereave me of my child, I was for some moments stupefied with grief and amazement, that gave way to an ecstasy of rage, which had well-nigh terminated in despair and distraction.

I now tremble, and my head grows giddy with the remembrance of that dreadful occasion. Behold how the drops trickle down my forehead; this agony is a fierce and familiar visitant; I shall banish it anon. I summoned my pride, my resentment, to my assistance; these are the cordials that support me against all other reflections; those were the auxiliaries that enabled me, in the day of trial, to perform that sacrifice which my honour demanded, in a strain so loud as to drown the cries of nature, love, and compassion. Yes, they espoused that glory which humanity would have betrayed, and my revenge was noble, though unnatural.

My scheme was soon laid, my resolution soon taken; I privately confined the wretch who had been the industrious slave of this infamous conspiracy, that she might take no step to frustrate or interrupt the execution of my design. Then repairing to the house of an apothecary who was devoted to my service, communicated my intention, which he durst not condemn, and could not reveal, without breaking the oath of secrecy I had imposed; and he furnished me with two vials of poison for the dismal catastrophe I had planned. Thus provided, I, on pretence of sudden business at Seville, carefully avoided the dear, the wretched pair, whom I had devoted to death, that my heart might not relent, by means of those tender ideas which the sight of them would have infallibly inspired; and, when daylight vanished, took my station near that part of the house through which the villain must have entered on his hellish purpose. There I stood, in a state of horrid expectation, my soul ravaged with the different passions that assailed it, until the fatal moment arrived; when I perceived the traitor approach the window of a lower apartment, which led into that of Serafina, and gently lifting the casement, which was purposely left unsecured, insinuated half of his body into the house. Then rushing upon him, in a transport of fury, I plunged my sword into his heart, crying, "Villain! receive the reward of thy treachery and presumption."

The steel was so well aimed as to render a repetition of the stroke unnecessary; he uttered one groan, and fell breathless at my feet. Exulting with this first success of my revenge, I penetrated into the chamber where the robber of my peace was expected by the unhappy Serafina and her mother, who, seeing me enter with a most savage aspect, and a sword reeking with the vengeance I had taken, seemed almost petrified with fear. "Behold," said I, "the blood of that base plebeian, who made an attempt upon the honour of my house; your conspiracy against the unfortunate Don Diego de Zelos is now discovered; that presumptuous slave, the favoured Orlando, is now no more."

Scarce had I pronounced these words, when a loud scream was uttered by both the unhappy victims. "If Orlando is slain," cried the infatuated Serafina, "what have I to do with life? O my dear lord! my husband, and my lover! how are our promised joys at once cut off! here, strike, my father! complete your barbarous sacrifice! the spirit of the murdered Orlando still hovers for his wife." These frantic exclamations, in which she was joined by Antonia, kept up the fury of my resentment, which by meekness and submission might have been weakened and rendered ineffectual. "Yes, hapless wretches," I replied, "ye shall enjoy your wish: the honour of my name requires that both shall die; yet I will not mangle the breast of Antonia, on which I have so often reposed; I will not shed the blood of Zelos, nor disfigure the beauteous form of Serafina, on which I have so often gazed with wonder and unspeakable delight. Here is an elixir, to which I trust the consummation of my revenge."

So saying, I emptied the vials into separate cups, and, presenting one in each hand, the miserable, the fair offenders instantly received the destined draughts, which they drank without hesitation; then praying to heaven for the wretched Don Diego, sunk upon the same couch, and expired without a groan. O well-contrived beverage! O happy composition, by which all the miseries of life are so easily cured!

Such was the fate of Antonia and Serafina; these hands were the instruments that deprived them of life, these eyes beheld them the richest prize that death had ever won. Powers supreme! does Don Diego live to make this recapitulation? I have done my duty; but ah! I am haunted by the furies of remorse; I am tortured with the incessant stings of remembrance and regret; even now the images of my wife and daughter present themselves to my imagination. All the scenes of happiness I have enjoyed as a lover, husband, and parent, all the endearing hopes I have cherished, now pass in review before me, embittering the circumstances of my inexpressible woe; and I consider myself as a solitary outcast from all the comforts of society. But, enough of these unmanly complaints; the yearnings of nature are too importunate.

Having completed my vengeance, I retired into my closet, and, furnishing myself with some ready money and jewels of considerable value, went into the stable, saddled my favourite steed, which I instantly mounted, and, before the tumults of my breast subsided, found myself at the town of St. Lucar. There I learned from inquiry, that there was a Dutch bark in the harbour ready to sail; upon which I addressed myself to the master, who, for a suitable gratification, was prevailed upon to weigh anchor that same night; so that, embarking without delay, I soon bid eternal adieu to my native country. It was not from reason and reflection that I took these measures for my personal safety; but, in consequence of an involuntary instinct, that seems to operate in the animal machine, while the faculty of thinking is suspended.

To what a dreadful reckoning was I called, when reason resumed her function! You may believe me, my friend, when I assure you, that I should not have outlived those tragedies I acted, had I not been restrained from doing violence upon myself by certain considerations, which no man of honour ought to set aside. I could not bear the thought of falling ingloriously by the hand of an executioner, and entailing disgrace upon a family that knew no stain; and I was deterred from putting an end to my own misery, by the apprehension of posthumous censure, which would have represented me as a desponding wretch, utterly destitute of that patience, fortitude, and resignation, which are the characteristics of a true Castilian. I was also influenced by religious motives that suggested to me the necessity of living to atone, by my sufferings and sorrow, for the guilt I had incurred in complying with a savage punctilio, which is, I fear, displeasing in the sight of Heaven.

These were the reasons that opposed my entrance into that peaceful harbour which death presented to my view; and they were soon reinforced by another principle that sanctioned my determination to continue at the servile oar of life. In consequence of unfavourable winds, our vessel for some days made small progress in her voyage to Holland, and near the coast of Gallicia we were joined by an English ship from Vigo, the master of which gave us to understand, that before he set sail, a courier had arrived from Madrid at that place, with orders for the corregidore to prevent the escape of any native Spaniard by sea from any port within his district; and to use his utmost endeavours to apprehend the person of Don Diego de Zelos, who was suspected of treasonable practices against the state. Such an order, with a minute description of my person, was at the same time despatched to all the seaports and frontier places in Spain.

You may easily suppose how I, who was already overwhelmed with distress, could bear this aggravation of misfortune and disgrace: I, who had always maintained the reputation of loyalty, which was acquired at the hazard of my life, and the expense of my blood. To deal candidly, I must own, that this intelligence roused me from a lethargy of grief which had begun to overpower my faculties. I immediately imputed this dishonourable charge to the evil offices of some villain, who had basely taken the advantage of my deplorable situation, and I was inflamed, inspirited with the desire of vindicating my fame, and revenging the injury. Thus animated, I resolved to disguise myself effectually from the observation of those spies which every nation finds its account in employing in foreign countries; I purchased this habit from the Dutch navigator, in whose house I kept myself concealed, after our arrival at Amsterdam, until my beard was grown to a sufficient length to favour my design, and then appeared as a Persian dealer in jewels. As I could gain no satisfactory information touching myself in this country, had no purpose to pursue, and was extremely miserable among a people, who, being mercenary and unsocial, were very ill adapted to alleviate the horrors of my condition, I gratified my landlord for his important services, with the best part of my effects; and having, by his means, procured a certificate from the magistracy, repaired to Rotterdam, from whence I set out in a travelling carriage for Antwerp, on my way to this capital; hoping, with a succession of different objects, to mitigate the anguish of my mind, and by the most industrious inquiry, to learn such particulars of that false impeachment, as would enable me to take measures for my own justification, as well as for projecting a plan of revenge against the vile perfidious author.

This, I imagined, would be no difficult task, considering the friendship and intercourse subsisting between the Spanish and French nations, and the communicative disposition for which the Parisians are renowned; but I have found myself egregiously deceived in my expectation. The officers of police in this city are so inquisitive and vigilant that the most minute action of a stranger is scrutinised with great severity; and, although the inhabitants are very frank in discoursing on indifferent subjects, they are at the same time extremely cautious in avoiding all conversation that turns upon state occurrences and maxims of government. In a word, the peculiarity of my appearance subjects me so much to particular observation, that I have hitherto thought proper to devour my griefs in silence, and even to bear the want of almost every convenience, rather than hazard a premature discovery, by offering my jewels to sale.

In this emergency I have been so far fortunate as to become acquainted with you, whom I look upon as a man of honour and humanity. Indeed, I was at first sight prepossessed in your favour, for, notwithstanding the mistakes which men daily commit in judging from appearances, there is something in the physiognomy of a stranger from which one cannot help forming an opinion of his character and disposition. For once, my penetration hath not failed me; your behaviour justifies my decision; you have treated me with that sympathy and respect which none but the generous will pay to the unfortunate. I have trusted you accordingly. I have put my life, my honour, in your power; and I must beg leave to depend upon your friendship, for obtaining that satisfaction for which alone I seek to live. Your employment engages you in the gay world; you daily mingle with the societies of men; the domestics of the Spanish ambassador will not shun your acquaintance; you may frequent the coffee-houses to which they resort; and, in the course of these occasions, unsuspected inform yourself of that mysterious charge which lies heavy on the fame of the unfortunate Don Diego. I must likewise implore your assistance in converting my jewels into money, that I may breathe independent of man, until Heaven shall permit me to finish this weary pilgrimage of life.

CHAPTER TWENTY-SEVEN.
A FLAGRANT INSTANCE OF FATHOM'S VIRTUE, IN THE MANNER OF HIS RETREAT TO ENGLAND.

Fathom, who had lent an attentive ear to every circumstance of this disastrous story, no sooner heard it concluded, than, with an aspect of generous and cordial compassion, not even unattended with tears, he condoled the lamentable fate of Don Diego de Zelos, deplored the untimely death of the gentle Antonia and the fair Serafina, and undertook the interest of the wretched Castilian with such warmth of sympathising zeal, as drew a flood from his eyes, while he wrung his benefactor's hand in a transport of gratitude. Those were literally tears of joy, or at least of satisfaction, on both sides; as our hero wept with affection and attachment to the jewels that were to be committed to his care; but, far from discovering the true source of his tenderness, he affected to dissuade the Spaniard from parting with the diamonds, which he counselled him to reserve for a more pressing occasion; and, in the meantime, earnestly entreated him to depend upon his friendship for present relief.

This generous proffer served only to confirm Don Diego's resolution, which he forthwith executed, by putting into the hands of Ferdinand jewels to the value of a thousand crowns, and desiring him to detain for his own use any part of the sum they would raise. Our adventurer thanked him for the good opinion he entertained of his integrity, an opinion fully manifested in honouring him with such important confidence, and assured him he would transact his affairs with the utmost diligence, caution, and despatch. The evening being by this time almost consumed, these new allies retired separately to rest; though each passed the night without repose, in very different reflections, the Castilian being, as usual, agitated with the unceasing pangs of his unalterable misery, interspersed with gleaming hopes of revenge; and Fathom being kept awake with revolving plans for turning his fellow-lodger's credulity to his own advantage. From the nature of the Spaniard's situation, he might have appropriated the jewels to himself, and remained in Paris without fear of a prosecution, because the injured party had, by the above narrative, left his life and liberty at discretion.— But he did not think himself secure from the personal resentment of an enraged desperate Castilian; and therefore determined to withdraw himself privately into that country where he had all along proposed to fix the standard of his finesse, which fortune had now empowered him to exercise according to his wish.

Bent upon this retreat, he went abroad in the morning, on pretence of acting in the concerns of his friend Don Diego, and having hired a post-chaise to be ready at the dawning of next day, returned to his lodgings, where he cajoled the Spaniard with a feigned report of his negotiation; then, securing his most valuable effects about his person, arose with the cock, repaired to the place at which he had appointed to meet the postillion with the carriage, and set out for England without further delay, leaving the unhappy Zelos to the horrors of indigence, and the additional agony of this fresh disappointment. Yet he was not the only person affected by the abrupt departure of Fathom, which was hastened by the importunities, threats, and reproaches of his landlord's daughter, whom he had debauched under promise of marriage, and now left in the fourth month of her pregnancy.

Notwithstanding the dangerous adventure in which he had been formerly involved by travelling in the night, he did not think proper to make the usual halts on this journey, for sleep or refreshment, nor did he once quit the chaise till his arrival at Boulogne, which he reached in twenty hours after his departure from Paris. Here he thought he might safely indulge himself with a comfortable meal; accordingly he bespoke a poulard for dinner, and while that was preparing, went forth to view the city and harbour. When he beheld the white cliffs of Albion, his heart throbbed with all the joy of a beloved son, who, after a tedious and fatiguing voyage, reviews the chimneys of his father's house. He surveyed the neighbouring coast of England with fond and longing eyes, like another Moses, reconnoitring the land of Canaan from the top of Mount Pisgah; and to such a degree of impatience was he inflamed by the sight, that, instead of proceeding to Calais, he resolved to take his passage directly from Boulogne, even if he should hire a vessel for the purpose. With these sentiments, he inquired if there was any ship bound for England, and was so fortunate as to find the master of a small bark, who intended to weigh anchor for Deal that same evening at high water.

Transported with this information, he immediately agreed for his passage, sold the post-chaise to his landlord for thirty guineas, as a piece of furniture for which he could have no further use, purchased a portmanteau, together with some linen and wearing apparel, and, at the recommendation of his host, took into his service an extra postillion or helper, who had formerly worn the livery of a travelling marquis. This new domestic, whose name was Maurice, underwent, with great applause, the examination of our hero, who perceived in him a fund of sagacity and presence of mind, by which he was excellently qualified for being the valet of an adventurer. He was therefore accommodated with a second-hand suit and another shirt, and at once listed under the banners of Count Fathom, who spent the whole afternoon in giving him proper instructions for the regulation of his conduct.

Having settled these preliminaries to his own satisfaction, he and his baggage were embarked about six o'clock in the month of September, and it was not without emotion that he found himself benighted upon the great deep, of which, before the preceding day, he had never enjoyed even the most distant prospect. However, he was not a man to be afraid, where there was really no appearance of danger; and the agreeable presages of future fortune supported his spirits, amidst the disagreeable nausea which commonly attends landsmen at sea, until he was set ashore upon the beach at Deal, which he entered in good health about seven o'clock in the morning.

Like Caesar, however, he found some difficulty in landing, on account of the swelling surf, that tumbled about with such violence as had almost overset the cutter that carried him on shore; and, in his eagerness to jump upon the strand, his foot slipped from the side of the boat, so that he was thrown forwards in an horizontal direction, and his hands were the first parts of him that touched English ground. Upon this occasion, he, in imitation of Scipio's behaviour on the coast of Africa, hailed the omen, and, grasping a handful of the sand, was heard to exclaim, in the Italian language: "Ah, ah, Old England, I have thee fast."

As he walked up to the inn, followed by Maurice loaded with his portmanteau, he congratulated himself upon his happy voyage, and the peaceable possession of his spoil, and could not help snuffing up the British air with marks of infinite relish and satisfaction. His first care was to recompense himself for the want of sleep he had undergone, and, after he had sufficiently recruited himself with several hours of uninterrupted repose, he set out in a post-chaise for Canterbury, where he took a place in the London stage, which he was told would depart next morning, the coach being already full. On this very first day of his arrival, he perceived between the English and the people among whom he had hitherto lived, such essential difference in customs, appearance, and way of living, as inspired him with high notions of that British freedom, opulence, and convenience, on which he had often heard his mother expatiate. On the road, he feasted his eyesight with the verdant hills covered with flocks of sheep, the fruitful vales parcelled out into cultivated enclosures; the very cattle seemed to profit by the wealth of their masters, being large, sturdy, and sleek, and every peasant breathed the insolence of liberty and independence. In a word, he viewed the wide-extended plains of Kent with a lover's eye, and, his ambition becoming romantic, could not help fancying himself another conqueror of the isle.

He was not, however, long amused by these vain chimeras, which soon vanished before other reflections of more importance and solidity. His imagination, it must be owned, was at all times too chaste to admit those overweening hopes, which often mislead the mind of the projector. He had studied mankind with incredible diligence, and knew perfectly well how far he could depend on the passions and foibles of human nature. That he might now act consistent with his former sagacity, he resolved to pass himself upon his fellow-travellers for a French gentleman, equally a stranger to the language and country of England, in order to glean from their discourse such intelligence as might avail him in his future operations; and his lacquey was tutored accordingly.

CHAPTER TWENTY-EIGHT.
SOME ACCOUNT OF HIS FELLOW-TRAVELLERS.

Those who had taken places for the coach, understanding the sixth seat was engaged by a foreigner, determined to profit by his ignorance; and, with that politeness which is peculiar to this happy island, fixed themselves in the vehicle, in such a manner, before he had the least intimation of their design, that he found it barely practicable to insinuate himself sidelong between a corpulent quaker and a fat Wapping landlady, in which attitude he stuck fast, like a thin quarto between two voluminous dictionaries on a bookseller's shelf. And, as if the pain and inconvenience of such compression was not sufficient matter of chagrin, the greatest part of the company entertained themselves with laughing at his ludicrous station.

The jolly dame at his left hand observed, with a loud exclamation of mirth, that monsieur would be soon better acquainted with a buttock of English beef; and said, by that time they should arrive at their dining-place, he might be spitted without larding. "Yes, verily," replied Obadiah, who was a wag in his way, "but the swine's fat will be all on one side." — "So much the better for you," cried mine hostess, "for that side is all your own." The quaker was not so much disconcerted by the quickness of this repartee, but that he answered with great deliberation, "I thank thee for thy love, but will not profit by thy loss, especially as I like not the savour of these outlandish fowls; they are profane birds of passage, relished only by the children of vanity, like thee."

The plump gentlewoman took umbrage at this last expression, which she considered as a double reproach, and repeated the words, "Children of vanity!" with an emphasis of resentment. "I believe, if the truth were known," said she, "there's more vanity than midriff in that great belly of yours, for all your pretending to humility and religion. Sirrah! my corporation is made up of good, wholesome, English fat; but you are puffed up with the wind of vanity and delusion; and when it begins to gripe your entrails, you pretend to have a motion, and then get up and preach nonsense. Yet you'll take it upon you to call your betters children. Marry come up, Mr. Goosecap, I have got children that are as good men as you, or any hypocritical trembler in England."

A person who sat opposite to the quaker, hearing this remonstrance, which seemed pregnant with contention, interposed in the conversation with a conscious leer, and begged there might be no rupture between the spirit and the flesh. By this remonstrance he relieved Obadiah from the satire of this female orator, and brought the whole vengeance of her elocution upon his own head. "Flesh!" cried she, with all the ferocity of an enraged Thalestris; "none of your names, Mr. Yellowchaps. What! I warrant you have an antipathy to flesh, because you yourself are nothing but skin and bone. I suppose you are some poor starved journeyman tailor come from France, where you have been learning to cabbage, and have not seen a good meal of victuals these seven years. You have been living upon rye-bread and soup-maigre, and now you come over like a walking atomy with a rat's tail at your wig, and a tinsey jacket. And so, forsooth, you set up for a gentleman, and pretend to find fault with a sirloin of roast beef."

The gentleman heard this address with admirable patience, and when she had rung out her alarm, very coolly replied, "Anything but your stinking fish madam. Since when, I pray, have you travelled in stage-coaches, and left off your old profession of crying oysters in winter, and rotten mackerel in June? You was then known by the name of Kate Brawn, and in good repute among the ale-houses in Thames Street, till that unlucky amour with the master of a corn-vessel, in which he was unfortunately detected by his own spouse; but you seem to have risen by that fall; and I wish you joy of your present plight. Though, considering your education on Bear Quay, you can give but a sorry account of yourself."

The Amazon, though neither exhausted nor dismayed, was really confounded at the temper and assurance of this antagonist, who had gathered all these anecdotes from the fertility of his own invention; after a short pause, however, she poured forth a torrent of obloquy sufficient to overwhelm any person who had not been used to take up arms against such seas of trouble; and a dispute ensued, which would have not only disgraced the best orators on the Thames, but even have made a figure in the celebration of the Eleusinian mysteries, during which the Athenian matrons rallied one another from different waggons, with that freedom of altercation so happily preserved in this our age and country.

Such a redundancy of epithets, and variety of metaphors, tropes, and figures were uttered between these well-matched opponents, that an epic bard would have found his account in listening to the contest; which, in all probability, would not have been confined to words, had it not been interrupted for the sake of a young woman of an agreeable countenance and modest carriage; who, being shocked at some of their flowers of speech, and terrified by the menacing looks and gestures of the fiery-featured dame, began to scream aloud, and beg leave to quit the coach. Her perturbation put an end to the high debate. The sixth passenger, who had not opened his mouth, endeavoured to comfort her with assurances of protection; the quaker proposed a cessation of arms; the male disputant acquiesced in the proposal, assuring the company he had entered the lists for their entertainment only, without acquiring the least grudge or ill-will to the fat gentlewoman, whom he protested he had never seen before that day, and who, for aught he knew, was a person of credit and reputation. He then held forth his hand in token of amity, and asked pardon of the offended party, who was appeased by his submission; and, in testimony of her benevolence, presented to the other female, whom she had discomposed, an Hungary-water bottle filled with cherry-brandy, recommending it as a much more powerful remedy than the sal-volatile which the other held to her nose.

Peace being thus re-established, in a treaty comprehending Obadiah and all present, it will not be improper to give the reader some further information, touching the several characters assembled in this vehicle. The quaker was a London merchant, who had been at Deal superintending the repairs of a ship which had suffered by a storm in the Downs. The Wapping landlady was on her return from the same place, where she had attended the payment of a man-of-war, with sundry powers of attorney, granted by the sailors, who had lived upon credit at her house. Her competitor in fame was a dealer in wine, a smuggler of French lace, and a petty gamester just arrived from Paris, in the company of an English barber, who sat on his right hand, and the young woman was daughter of a country curate, in her way to London, where she was bound apprentice to a milliner.

Hitherto Fathom had sat in silent astonishment at the manners of his fellow-travellers, which far exceeded the notions he had preconceived of English plainness and rusticity. He found himself a monument of that disregard and contempt which a stranger never fails to meet with from the inhabitants of this island; and saw, with surprise, an agreeable young creature sit as solitary and unheeded as himself.

He was, indeed, allured by the roses of her complexion, and the innocence of her aspect, and began to repent of having pretended ignorance of the language, by which he was restrained from exercising his eloquence upon her heart; he resolved, however, to ingratiate himself, if possible, by the courtesy and politeness of dumb show, and for that purpose put his eyes in motion without farther delay.

CHAPTER TWENTY-NINE.
ANOTHER PROVIDENTIAL DELIVERANCE FROM THE EFFECTS OF THE SMUGGLER'S INGENIOUS CONJECTURE.

During these deliberations, the wine merchant, with a view to make a parade of his superior parts and breeding, as well as to pave the way for a match at backgammon, made a tender of his snuff-box to our adventurer, and asked, in bad French, how he travelled from Paris. This question produced a series of interrogations concerning the place of Ferdinand's abode in that city, and his business in England, so that he was fain to practise the science of defence, and answered with such ambiguity, as aroused the suspicion of the smuggler, who began to believe our hero had some very cogent reason for evading his curiosity; he immediately set his reflection at work, and, after various conjectures, fixed upon Fathom's being the Young Pretender. Big with this supposition, he eyed him with the most earnest attention, comparing his features with those of the Chevalier's portrait which he had seen in France, and though the faces were as unlike as any two human faces could be, found the resemblance so striking as to dispel all his doubts, and persuade him to introduce the stranger to some justice on the road; a step by which he would not only manifest his zeal for the Protestant succession, but also acquire the splendid reward proposed by parliament to any person who should apprehend that famous adventurer.

These ideas intoxicated the brain of this man to such a pitch of enthusiasm, that he actually believed himself in possession of the thirty thousand pounds, and amused his fancy with a variety of magnificent projects to be executed by means of that acquisition, until his reverie was interrupted by the halting of the coach at the inn where the passengers used to eat their breakfasts. Waked as he was from the dream of happiness, it had made such impression upon his mind, that, seeing Fathom rise up with an intention to alight, he took it for granted his design was to escape, and seizing him by the collar, called aloud for assistance in the King's name.

Our hero, whose sagacity and presence of mind very often supplied the place of courage, instead of being terrified at this assault, which might have disturbed the tranquillity of an ordinary villain, was so perfectly master of every circumstance of his own situation, as to know at once that the aggressor could not possibly have the least cause of complaint against him; and therefore, imputing this violence either to madness or mistake, very deliberately suffered himself to be made prisoner by the people of the house, who ran to the coach door in obedience to the summons of the wine merchant. The rest of the company were struck dumb with surprise and consternation at this sudden adventure; and the quaker, dreading some fell resistance on the side of the outlandish man, unpinned the other coach door in the twinkling of an eye, and trundled himself into the mud for safety. The others, seeing the temper and resignation of the prisoner, soon recovered their recollection, and began to inquire into the cause of his arrest, upon which, the captor, whose teeth chattered with terror and impatience, gave them to understand that he was a state criminal, and demanded their help in conveying him to justice.

Luckily for both parties, there happened to be at the inn a company of squires just returned from the death of a leash of hares, which they had ordered to be dressed for dinner, and among these gentlemen was one of the quorum, to whom the accuser had immediate recourse, marching before the captive, who walked very peaceably between the landlord and one of his waiters, and followed by a crowd of spectators, some of whom had secured the faithful Maurice, who in his behaviour closely imitated the deliberation of his master. In this order did the procession advance to the apartment in which the magistrate, with his fellows of the chase, sat smoking his morning pipe over a tankard of strong ale, and the smuggler being directed to the right person, "May it please your worship," said he, "I have brought this foreigner before you, on a violent suspicion of his being a proclaimed outlaw; and I desire, before these witnesses, that my title may be made good to the reward that shall become due upon his conviction."

"Friend," replied the justice, "I know nothing of you or your titles; but this I know, if you have any information to give in, you must come to my house when I am at home, and proceed in a lawful way, that is, d'ye mind me, if you swear as how this here person is an outlaw; then if so be as he has nothing to say to the contrary, my clerk shall make out a mittimus, and so to jail with him till next 'size." "But, sir," answered the impeacher, "this is a case that admits of no delay; the person I have apprehended is a prisoner of consequence to the state." "How, fellor!" cried the magistrate, interrupting him, "is there any person of more consequence than one of his Majesty's justices of the peace, who is besides a considerable member of the landed interest! D'ye know, sirrah, who you are talking to? If you don't go about your business, I believe I shall lay you by the heels."

The smuggler, fearing his prize would escape through the ignorance, pride, and obstinacy of this country justice, approached his worship, and in a whisper which was overheard by all the company, assured him he had indubitable reason to believe the foreigner was no other than the Pretender's eldest son. At mention of this formidable name, every individual of the audience started, with signs of terror and amazement. The justice dropped his pipe, recoiled upon his chair, and, looking most ridiculously aghast, exclaimed, "Seize him, in the name of God and his Majesty King George! Has he got no secret arms about him!"

Fathom being thus informed of the suspicion under which he stood, could not help smiling at the eagerness with which the spectators flew upon him, and suffered himself to be searched with great composure, well knowing they would find no moveables about his person, but such as upon examination would turn to his account; he therefore very calmly presented to the magistrate his purse, and a small box that contained his jewels, and in the French language desired they might be preserved from the hands of the mob. This request was interpreted by the accuser, who, at the same time, laid claim to the booty. The justice took charge of the deposit, and one of his neighbours having undertaken the office of clerk, he proceeded to the examination of the culprit, whose papers were by this time laid on the table before him. "Stranger," said he, "you stand charged with being son of the Pretender to these realms; what have you to say in your own defence?" Our hero assured him, in the French language, that he was falsely impeached, and demanded justice on the accuser, who, without the least reason, had made such a malicious attack upon the life and honour of an innocent gentleman.

The smuggler, instead of acting the part of a faithful interpreter, told his worship, that the prisoner's answer was no more than a simple denial, which every felon would make who had nothing else to plead in his own behalf, and that this alone was a strong presumption of his guilt, because, if he was not really the person they suspected him to be, the thing would speak for itself, for, if he was not the Young Pretender, who then was he? This argument had great weight with the justice, who, assuming a very important aspect, observed, "Very true, friend, if you are not the Pretender, in the name of God, who are you? One may see with half an eye that he is no better than a promiscuous fellow."

Ferdinand now began to repent of having pretended ignorance of the English language, as he found himself at the mercy of a rascal, who put a false gloss upon all his words, and addressed himself to the audience successively in French, High Dutch, Italian, and Hungarian Latin, desiring to know if any person present understood any of these tongues, that his answers might be honestly explained to the bench. But he might have accosted them in Chinese with the same success: there was not one person present tolerably versed in his mother-tongue, much less acquainted with any foreign language, except the wine merchant, who, incensed at this appeal, which he considered as an affront to his integrity, gave the judge to understand, that the delinquent, instead of speaking to the purpose, contumaciously insulted his authority in sundry foreign lingos, which he apprehended was an additional proof of his being the Chevalier's son, inasmuch as no person would take the pains to learn such a variety of gibberish, except with some sinister intent.

This annotation was not lost upon the squire, who was too jealous of the honour of his office to overlook such a flagrant instance of contempt. His eyes glistened, his cheeks were inflated with rage. "The case is plain," said he; "having nothing of signification to offer in his own favour, he grows refractory, and abuses the court in his base Roman Catholic jargon; but I'll let you know, for all you pretend to be a prince, you are no better than an outlawed vagrant, and I'll show you what a thing you are when you come in composition with an English justice, like me, who have more than once extinguished myself in the service of my country. As nothing else accrues, your purse, black box, and papers shall be sealed up before witnesses, and sent by express to one of his Majesty's secretaries of state; and, as for yourself, I will apply to the military at Canterbury, for a guard to conduct you to London."

This was a very unwelcome declaration to our adventurer, who was on the point of haranguing the justice and spectators in their own language, when he was relieved from the necessity of taking that step by the interposition of a young nobleman just arrived at the inn, who, being informed of this strange examination, entered the court, and, at first sight of the prisoner, assured the justice he was imposed upon; for that he himself had often seen the Young Pretender in Paris, and that there was no kind of resemblance between that adventurer and the person now before him. The accuser was not a little mortified at his lordship's affirmation, which met with all due regard from the bench, though the magistrate took notice, that, granting the prisoner was not the Young Chevalier himself, it was highly probable he was an emissary of that house, as he could give no satisfactory account of himself, and was possessed of things of such value as no honest man could expose to the accidents of the road.

Fathom, having thus found an interpreter, who signified to him, in the French tongue, the doubts of the justice, told his lordship, that he was a gentleman of a noble house in Germany, who, for certain reasons, had come abroad incognito, with a view to see the world; and that, although the letters they had seized would prove the truth of that assertion, he should be loth to expose his private concerns to the knowledge of strangers, if he could possibly be released without that mortification. The young nobleman explained his desire to the court; but, his own curiosity being interested, observed, at the same time, that the justice could not be said to have discharged the duties of his station, until he should have examined every circumstance relating to the prisoner. Upon which remonstrance, he was requested by the bench to peruse the papers, and accordingly communicated the substance of one letter to this effect:—

"MY DEAR SON,

Though I am far from approving the rash step you have taken in withdrawing yourself from your father's house, in order to avoid an engagement which would have been equally honourable and advantageous to your family, I cannot so far suppress my affection, as to bear the thought of your undergoing those hardships which, for your disobedience, you deserve to suffer. I have therefore, without the knowledge of your father, sent the bearer to attend you in your peregrinations; his fidelity you know hath been tried in a long course of service, and I have entrusted to his care, for your use, a purse of two hundred ducats, and a box of jewels to the value of twice that sum, which, though not sufficient to support an equipage suitable to your birth, will, at least for some time, preserve you from the importunities of want. When you are dutiful enough to explain your designs and situation, you may expect further indulgence from your tender and disconsolate mother,—

THE COUNTESS OF FATHOM."

This letter, which, as well as the others, our hero had forged for the purpose, effectually answered his intent, in throwing dust in the eyes and understanding of the spectators, who now regarded the prisoner with looks of respectful remorse, as a man of quality who had been falsely accused. His lordship, to make a parade of his own politeness and importance, assured the bench, he was no stranger to the family of the Fathoms, and, with a compliment, gave Ferdinand to understand he had formerly seen him at Versailles. There being no longer room for suspicion, the justice ordered our adventurer to be set at liberty, and even invited him to be seated, with an apology for the rude manner in which he had been treated, owing to the misinformation of the accuser, who was threatened with the stocks, for his malice and presumption.

But this was not the only triumph our hero obtained over the wine merchant. Maurice was no sooner unfettered, than, advancing into the middle of the room, "My lord," said he, addressing himself in French to his master's deliverer, "since you have been so generous as to protect a noble stranger from the danger of such a false accusation, I hope you will still lay an additional obligation upon the Count, by retorting the vengeance of the law upon his perfidious accuser, whom I know to be a trader in those articles of merchandise which are prohibited by the ordinances of this nation. I have seen him lately at Boulogne, and am perfectly well acquainted with some persons who have supplied him with French lace and embroidery; and, as a proof of what I allege, I desire you will order him and this barber, who is his understrapper, to be examined on the spot."

This charge, which was immediately explained to the bench, yielded extraordinary satisfaction to the spectators, one of whom, being an officer of the customs, forthwith began to exercise his function upon the unlucky perruquier, who, being stripped of his upper garments, and even of his shirt, appeared like the mummy of an Egyptian king, most curiously rolled up in bandages of rich figured gold shalloon, that covered the skirts of four embroidered waistcoats. The merchant, seeing his expectation so unhappily reversed, made an effort to retire with a most rueful aspect, but was prevented by the officer, who demanded the interposition of the civil power, that he might undergo the same examination to which the other had been subjected. He was accordingly rifled without loss of time, and the inquiry proved well worth the care of him who made it; for a considerable booty of the same sort of merchandise was found in his boots, breeches, hat, and between the buckram and lining of his surtout. Yet, not contented with this prize, the experienced spoiler proceeded to search his baggage, and, perceiving a false bottom in his portmanteau, detected beneath it a valuable accession to the plunder he had already obtained.

CHAPTER THIRTY.
THE SINGULAR MANNER OF FATHOM'S ATTACK AND TRIUMPH OVER THE VIRTUE OF THE FAIR ELENOR.

Proper cognisance being thus taken of these contraband effects, and the informer furnished with a certificate, by which he was entitled to a share of the seizure, the coachman summoned his passengers to the carriage; the purse and jewels were restored to Count Fathom, who thanked the justice, and his lordship in particular, for the candour and hospitality with which he had been treated, and resumed his place in the vehicle, amidst the congratulations of all his fellow-travellers, except the two forlorn smugglers, who, instead of re-embarking in the coach, thought proper to remain at the inn, with view to mitigate, if possible, the severity of their misfortune.

Among those who felicitated Fathom upon the issue of this adventure, the young maiden seemed to express the most sensible pleasure at that event. The artful language of his eyes had raised in her breast certain fluttering emotions, before she knew the value of her conquest; but now that his rank and condition were discovered, these transports were increased by the ideas of vanity and ambition, which are mingled with the first seeds of every female constitution. The belief of having captivated the heart of a man who could raise her to the rank and dignity of a countess, produced such agreeable sensations in her fancy, that her eyes shone with unusual lustre, and a continual smile played in dimples on her rosy cheeks; so that her attractions, though not powerful enough to engage the affection, were yet sufficient to inflame the desire of our adventurer, who very honestly marked her chastity for prey to his voluptuous passion. Had she been well seasoned with knowledge and experience, and completely armed with caution against the artifice and villany of man, her virtue might not have been able to withstand the engines of such an assailant, considering the dangerous opportunities to which she was necessarily exposed. How easy then must his victory have been over an innocent, unsuspecting country damsel, flushed with the warmth of youth, and an utter stranger to the ways of life!

While Obadiah, therefore, and his plump companion, were engaged in conversation, on the strange incidents which had passed, Fathom acted a very expressive pantomime with this fair buxom nymph, who comprehended his meaning with surprising facility, and was at so little pains to conceal the pleasure she took in this kind of intercourse, that several warm squeezes were interchanged between her and her lover, before they arrived at Rochester, where they proposed to dine. It was during this period, he learned from the answers she made to the inquisitive quaker, that her sole dependence was upon a relation, to whom she had a letter, and that she was a perfect stranger in the great city; circumstances on which he soon formed the project of her ruin.

Upon their arrival at the Black Bull, he for the first time found himself alone with his Amanda, whose name was Elenor, their fellow-travellers being elsewhere employed about their own concerns; and, unwilling to lose the precious opportunity, he began to act the part of a very importunate lover, which he conceived to be a proper sequel to the prelude which had been performed in the coach. The freedoms which she, out of pure simplicity and good-humour, permitted him to take with her hand, and even her rosy lips, encouraged him to practise other familiarities upon her fair bosom, which scandalised her virtue so much, that, in spite of the passion she had begun to indulge in his behalf, she rejected his advances with all the marks of anger and disdain; and he found it necessary to appease the storm he had raised, by the most respectful and submissive demeanour; resolving to change his operations, and carry on his attacks, so as to make her yield at discretion, without alarming her religion or pride. Accordingly, when the bill was called after dinner, he took particular notice of her behaviour, and, perceiving her pull out a large leathern purse that contained her money, reconnoitred the pocket in which it was deposited, and, while they sat close to each other in the carriage, conveyed it with admirable dexterity into an hole in the cushion. Whether the corpulent couple, who sat opposite to these lovers, had entered into an amorous engagement at the inn, or were severally induced by other motives, is uncertain; but sure it is, both left the coach on that part of the road which lies nearest to Gravesend, and bade adieu to the other pair, on pretence of having urgent business at that place.

Ferdinand, not a little pleased at their departure, renewed his most pathetic expressions of love, and sung several French songs on that tender subject, which seemed to thrill to the soul of his beauteous Helen. While the driver halted at Dartford to water his horses, she was smit with the appearance of some cheesecakes, which were presented by the landlady of the house, and having bargained for two or three, put her hand in her pocket, in order to pay for her purchase; but what was her astonishment, when, after having rummaged her equipage, she understood her whole fortune was lost! This mishap was, by a loud shriek, announced to our hero, who affected infinite amazement and concern; and no sooner learned the cause of her affliction, than he presented her with his own purse, from which he, in emphatic dumb show, begged she would indemnify herself for the damage she had sustained. Although this kind proffer was some alleviation of her misfortunes, she did not fail to pour forth a most piteous lamentation, importing that she had not only lost all her money, amounting to five pounds, but also her letter of recommendation, upon which she had altogether relied for present employment.

The vehicle was minutely searched from top to bottom, by herself and our adventurer, assisted by Maurice and the coachman, who, finding their inquiry ineffectual, did not scruple to declare his suspicion of the two fat turtles who had deserted the coach in such an abrupt manner. In a word, he rendered this conjecture so plausible, by wresting the circumstances of their behaviour and retreat, that poor Elenor implicitly believed they were the thieves by whom she had suffered; and was prevailed upon to accept the proffered assistance of the generous Count, who, seeing her very much disordered by this mischance, insisted upon her drinking a large glass of canary, to quiet the perturbation of her spirits. This is a season, which of all others is most propitious to the attempts of an artful lover; and justifies the metaphorical maxim of fishing in troubled waters. There is an affinity and short transition betwixt all the violent passions that agitate the human mind. They are all false perspectives, which, though they magnify, yet perplex and render indistinct every object which they represent. And flattery is never so successfully administered, as to those who know they stand in need of friendship, assent, and approbation.

The cordial she swallowed, far from calming, increased the disturbance of her thoughts, and produced an intoxication; during which, she talked in an incoherent strain, laughed and wept by turns, and acted other extravagances, which are known to be symptoms of the hysterical affection. Fathom, though an utter stranger to the sentiments of honour, pity, and remorse, would not perpetrate his vicious purpose, though favoured by the delirium his villany had entailed upon this unfortunate young maiden; because his appetite demanded a more perfect sacrifice than that which she could yield in her present deplorable situation, when her will must have been altogether unconcerned in his success. Determined, therefore, to make a conquest of her virtue, before he would take possession of her person, he mimicked that compassion and benevolence which his heart had never felt, and, when the coach arrived at London, not only discharged what she owed for her place, but likewise procured for her an apartment in the house to which he himself had been directed for lodgings, and even hired a nurse to attend her during a severe fever, which was the consequence of her disappointment and despondence. Indeed, she was supplied with all necessaries by the generosity of this noble Count, who, for the interest of his passion, and the honour of his name, was resolved to extend his charity to the last farthing of her own money, which he had been wise enough to secure for this purpose.

Her youth soon got the better of her distemper, and when she understood her obligations to the Count, who did not fail to attend her in person with great tenderness, her heart, which had been before prepossessed in his favour, now glowed with all the warmth of gratitude, esteem, and affection. She knew herself in a strange place, destitute of all resource but in his generosity. She loved his person, she was dazzled by his rank; and he knew so well how to improve the opportunities and advantages he derived from her unhappy situation, that he gradually proceeded in sapping from one degree of intimacy to another, until all the bulwarks of her chastity were undermined, and she submitted to his desire; not with the reluctance of a vanquished people, but with all the transports of a joyful city, that opens its gates to receive a darling prince returned from conquest. For by this time he had artfully concentred and kindled up all the inflammable ingredients of her constitution; and she now looked back upon the virtuous principles of her education, as upon a disagreeable and tedious dream, from which she had waked to the fruition of never-fading joy.

CHAPTER THIRTY-ONE.
HE BY ACCIDENT ENCOUNTERS HIS OLD FRIEND, WITH WHOM HE HOLDS A CONFERENCE, AND RENEWS A TREATY.

Our hero, having thus provided himself with a proper subject for his hours of dalliance, thought it was now high time to study the ground which he had pitched upon for the scene of his exploits, and with that view made several excursions to different parts of the town, where there was aught of entertainment or instruction to be found. Yet he always, on these occasions, appeared in an obscure ordinary dress, in order to avoid singularity, and never went twice to the same coffee-house, that his person might not be afterwards known, in case he should shine forth to the public in a superior sphere. On his return from one of those expeditions, while he was passing through Ludgate, his eyes were suddenly encountered by the apparition of his old friend the Tyrolese, who, perceiving himself fairly caught in the toil, made a virtue of necessity, and, running up to our adventurer with an aspect of eagerness and joy, clasped him in his arms, as some dear friend, whom he had casually found after a most tedious and disagreeable separation.

Fathom, whose genius never failed him in such emergencies, far from receiving these advances with the threats and reproaches which the other had deserved at his hands, returned the salute with equal warmth, and was really overjoyed at meeting with a person who might one way or other make amends for the perfidy of his former conduct. The Tyrolese, whose name was Ratchcali, pleased with his reception, proposed they should adjourn to the next tavern, in which they had no sooner taken possession of an apartment, than he addressed himself to his old companion in these words: —

"Mr. Fathom, by your frank and obliging manner of treating a man who hath done you wrong, I am more and more confirmed in my opinion of your sagacity, which I have often considered with admiration; I will not therefore attempt to make an apology for my conduct at our last parting; but only assure you that this meeting may turn out to our mutual advantage, if we now re-enter into an unreserved union, the ties of which we will soon find it our interest and inclination to preserve. For my own part, as my judgment is ripened by experience, so are my sentiments changed since our last association. I have seen many a rich harvest lost, for want of a fellow-labourer in the vineyard; and I have more than once fallen a sacrifice to a combination, which I could have resisted with the help of one able auxiliary. Indeed, I might prove what I allege by mathematical demonstration; and I believe nobody will pretend to deny, that two heads are better than one, in all cases that require discernment and deliberation."

Ferdinand could not help owning the sanity of his observations, and forthwith acquiesced in his proposal of the new alliance; desiring to know the character in which he acted on the English stage, and the scheme he would offer for their mutual emolument. At the same time he resolved within himself to keep such a strict eye over his future actions, as would frustrate any design he might hereafter harbour, of repeating the prank he had so successfully played upon him, in their journey from the banks of the Rhine.

"Having quitted you at Bar-le-duc," resumed the Tyrolese, "I travelled without ceasing, until I arrived at Frankfort upon the Maine, where I assumed the character of a French chevalier, and struck some masterly strokes, which you yourself would not have deemed unworthy of your invention; and my success was the more agreeable, as my operations were chiefly carried on against the enemies of our religion. But my prosperity was not of long duration. Seeing they could not foil me at my own weapons, they formed a damned conspiracy, by which I not only lost all the fruits of my industry, but likewise ran the most imminent hazard of my life. I had ordered some of those jewels which I had borrowed of my good friend Fathom to be new set in a fashionable taste, and soon after had an opportunity to sell one of these, at a great advantage, to one of the fraternity, who offered an extraordinary price for the stone, on purpose to effect my ruin. In less than four-and-twenty hours after this bargain, I was arrested by the officers of justice upon the oath of the purchaser, who undertook to prove me guilty of a fraud, in selling a Saxon pebble for a real diamond; and this accusation was actually true; for the change had been artfully put upon me by the jeweller, who was himself engaged in the conspiracy.

"Had my conscience been clear of any other impeachment, perhaps I should have rested my cause upon the equity and protection of the law; but I foresaw that the trial would introduce an inquiry, to which I was not at all ambitious of submitting, and therefore was fain to compromise the affair, at the price of almost my whole fortune. Yet this accommodation was not made so secretly, but that my character was blasted, and my credit overthrown; so that I was fain to relinquish my occasional equipage, and hire myself as journeyman to a lapidary, an employment which I had exercised in my youth. In this obscure station, I laboured with great assiduity, until I made myself perfect in the knowledge of stones, as well as in the different methods of setting them off to the best advantage; and having, by dint of industry and address, got possession of a small parcel, set out for this kingdom, in which I happily arrived about four months ago; and surely England is the paradise of artists of our profession.

"One would imagine that nature had created the inhabitants for the support and enjoyment of adventurers like you and me. Not that these islanders open the arms of hospitality to all foreigners without distinction. On the contrary, they inherit from their fathers an unreasonable prejudice against all nations under the sun; and when an Englishman happens to quarrel with a stranger, the first term of reproach he uses is the name of his antagonist's country, characterised by some opprobrious epithet, such as a chattering Frenchman, an Italian ape, a German hog, and a beastly Dutchman; nay, their national prepossession is maintained even against those people with whom they are united under the same laws and government; for nothing is more common than to hear them exclaim against their fellow-subjects, in the expressions of a beggarly Scot, and an impudent Irish bog-trotter. Yet this very prejudice will never fail to turn to the account of every stranger possessed of ordinary talents; for he will always find opportunities of conversing with them in coffee-houses and places of public resort, in spite of their professed reserve, which, by the bye, is so extraordinary, that I know some people who have lived twenty years in the same house without exchanging one word with their next-door neighbours; yet, provided he can talk sensibly, and preserve the deportment of a sober gentleman, in those occasional conversations, his behaviour will be the more remarkably pleasing, as it will agreeably disappoint the expectation of the person who had entertained notions to his prejudice. When a foreigner has once crossed this bar, which perpetually occurs, he sails without further difficulty into the harbour of an Englishman's goodwill; for the pique is neither personal nor rancorous, but rather contemptuous and national; so that, while he despises a people in the lump, an individual of that very community may be one of his chief favourites.

"The English are in general upright and honest, therefore unsuspecting and credulous. They are too much engrossed with their own business to pry into the conduct of their neighbours, and too indifferent, in point of disposition, to interest themselves in what they conceive to be foreign to their own concerns. They are wealthy and mercantile, of consequence liberal and adventurous, and so well disposed to take a man's own word for his importance, that they suffer themselves to be preyed upon by such a bungling set of impostors, as would starve for lack of address in any other country under the sun. This being a true sketch of the British character, so far as I have been able to observe and learn, you will easily comprehend the profits that may be extracted from it, by virtue of those arts by which you so eminently excel;—the great, the unbounded prospect lies before me! Indeed, I look upon this opulent kingdom as a wide and fertile common, on which we adventurers may range for prey, without let or molestation. For so jealous are the natives of their liberties, that they will not bear the restraint of necessary police, and an able artist may enrich himself with their spoils, without running any risk of attracting the magistrate, or incurring the least penalty of the law.

"In a word, this metropolis is a vast masquerade, in which a man of stratagem may wear a thousand different disguises, without danger of detection. There is a variety of shapes in which we the knights of industry make our appearance in London. One glides into a nobleman's house in the capacity of a valet-de-chambre, and in a few months leads the whole family by the nose. Another exhibits himself to the public, as an empiric or operator for the teeth; and by dint of assurance and affidavits, bearing testimony to wonderful cures that never were performed, whirls himself into his chariot, and lays the town under contribution. A third professes the composition of music, as well as the performance, and by means of a few capriciosos on the violin, properly introduced, wriggles himself into the management of private and public concerts. And a fourth breaks forth at once in all the splendour of a gay equipage, under the title and denomination of a foreign count. Not to mention those inferior projectors, who assume the characters of dancers, fencing-masters, and French ushers, or, by renouncing their religion, seek to obtain a provision for life.

"Either of these parts will turn to the account of an able actor; and, as you are equally qualified for all, you may choose that which is most suitable to your own inclination. Though, in my opinion, you was designed by nature to shine in the great world, which, after all, is the most ample field for men of genius; because the game is deeper, and people of fashion being, for the most part, more ignorant, indolent, vain, and capricious, than their inferiors, are of consequence more easily deceived; besides, their morals sit generally so loose about them, that, when a gentleman of our fraternity is discovered in the exercise of his profession, their contempt of his skill is the only disgrace he incurs."

Our hero was so well pleased with this picture, that he longed to peruse the original, and, before these two friends parted, they settled all the operations of the campaign. Ratchcali, that same evening, hired magnificent lodgings for Count Fathom, in the court end of the town, and furnished his wardrobe and liveries from the spoils of Monmouth Street; he likewise enlisted another footman and valet-de-chambre into his service, and sent to the apartments divers large trunks, supposed to be filled with the baggage of this foreign nobleman, though, in reality, they contained little else than common lumber.

Next day, our adventurer took possession of his new habitation, after having left to his friend and associate the task of dismissing the unfortunate Elenor, who was so shocked at the unexpected message, that she fainted away; and when she recovered the use of her senses so well as to reflect upon her forlorn condition, she was seized with the most violent transports of grief and dismay, by which her brain was disordered to such a degree, that she grew furious and distracted, and was, by the advice and assistance of the Tyrolese, conveyed into the hospital of Bethlem; where we shall leave her for the present, happily bereft of her reason.

CHAPTER THIRTY-TWO.
HE APPEARS IN THE GREAT WORLD WITH UNIVERSAL APPLAUSE AND ADMIRATION.

Meanwhile, Fathom and his engine were busied in completing his equipage, so that in a few days he had procured a very gay chariot, adorned with painting, gilding, and a coat of arms, according to his own fancy and direction. The first use he made of this vehicle was that of visiting the young nobleman from whom he had received such important civilities on the road, in consequence of an invitation at parting, by which he learned his title and the place of his abode in London.

His lordship was not only pleased, but proud to see such a stranger at his gate, and entertained him with excess of complaisance and hospitality; insomuch that, by his means, our hero soon became acquainted with the whole circle of polite company, by whom he was caressed for his insinuating manners and agreeable conversation. He had thought proper to tell the nobleman, at their first interview in town, that his reasons for concealing his knowledge of the English tongue were now removed, and that he would no longer deny himself the pleasure of speaking a language which had been always music to his ear. He had also thanked his lordship for his generous interposition at the inn, which was an instance of that generosity and true politeness which are engrossed by the English people, who leave nought to other nations but the mere shadow of these virtues.

A testimony like this, from the mouth of such a noble stranger, won the heart of the peer, who professed a friendship for him on the spot, and undertook to see justice done to his lacquey, who in a short time was gratified with a share of the seizure which had been made upon his information, amounting to fifty or sixty pounds.

Ferdinand put not forth the whole strength of his accomplishments at once, but contrived to spring a new mine of qualification every day, to the surprise and admiration of all his acquaintance. He was gifted with a sort of elocution, much more specious than solid, and spoke on every subject that occurred in conversation with that familiarity and ease, which, one would think, could only be acquired by long study and application. This plausibility and confidence are faculties really inherited from nature, and effectually serve the possessor, in lieu of that learning which is not to be obtained without infinite toil and perseverance. The most superficial tincture of the arts and sciences in such a juggler, is sufficient to dazzle the understanding of half mankind; and, if managed with circumspection, will enable him even to spend his life among the literati, without once forfeiting the character of a connoisseur.

Our hero was perfectly master of this legerdemain, which he carried to such a pitch of assurance, as to declare, in the midst of a mathematical assembly, that he intended to gratify the public with a full confutation of Sir Isaac Newton's philosophy, to the nature of which he was as much a stranger as the most savage Hottentot in Africa. His pretensions to profound and universal knowledge were supported not only by this kind of presumption, but also by the facility with which he spoke so many different languages, and the shrewd remarks he had made in the course of his travels and observation.

Among politicians, he settled the balance of power upon a certain footing, by dint of ingenious schemes, which he had contrived for the welfare of Europe. With officers, he reformed the art of war, with improvements which had occurred to his reflection while he was engaged in a military life. He sometimes held forth upon painting, like a member of the Dilettanti club. The theory of music was a theme upon which he seemed to expatiate with particular pleasure. In the provinces of love and gallantry, he was a perfect Oroondates. He possessed a most agreeable manner of telling entertaining stories, of which he had a large collection; he sung with great melody and taste, and played upon the violin with surprising execution. To these qualifications let us add his affability and pliant disposition, and then the reader will not wonder that he was looked upon as the pattern of human perfection, and his acquaintance courted accordingly.

While he thus captivated the favour and affection of the English nobility, he did not neglect to take other measures in behalf of the partnership to which he had subscribed. The adventure with the two squires at Paris had weakened his appetite for play, which was not at all restored by the observations he had made in London, where the art of gaming is reduced into a regular system, and its professors so laudably devoted to the discharge of their functions, as to observe the most temperate regimen, lest their invention should be impaired by the fatigue of watching or exercise, and their ideas disturbed by the fumes of indigestion. No Indian Brachman could live more abstemious than two of the pack, who hunted in couple, and kennelled in the upper apartments of the hotel in which our adventurer lived. They abstained from animal food with the abhorrence of Pythagoreans, their drink was a pure simple element, they were vomited once a week, took physic or a glyster every third day, spent the forenoon in algebraical calculations, and slept from four o'clock till midnight, that they might then take the field with that cool serenity which is the effect of refreshment and repose.

These were terms upon which our hero would not risk his fortune; he was too much addicted to pleasure to forego every other enjoyment but that of amassing; and did not so much depend upon his dexterity in play as upon his talent of insinuation, which, by this time, had succeeded so far beyond his expectation, that he began to indulge the hope of enslaving the heart of some rich heiress, whose fortune would at once raise him above all dependence. Indeed, no man ever set out with a fairer prospect on such an expedition; for he had found means to render himself so agreeable to the fair sex, that, like the boxes of the playhouse, during the representation of a new performance, his company was often bespoke for a series of weeks; and no lady, whether widow, wife, or maiden, ever mentioned his name, without some epithet of esteem or affection; such as the dear Count! the charming Man! the Nonpareil, or the Angel!

While he thus shone in the zenith of admiration, it is not to be doubted, that he could have melted some wealthy dowager or opulent ward; but, being an enemy to all precipitate engagements, he resolved to act with great care and deliberation in an affair of such importance, especially as he did not find himself hurried by the importunities of want; for, since his arrival in England, he had rather increased than exhausted his finances, by methods equally certain and secure. In a word, he, with the assistance of Ratchcali, carried on a traffic, which yielded great profits, without subjecting the trader to the least loss or inconvenience. Fathom, for example, wore upon his finger a large brilliant, which he played to such advantage one night, at a certain nobleman's house, where he was prevailed upon to entertain the company with a solo on the violin, that everybody present took notice of its uncommon lustre, and it was handed about for the perusal of every individual. The water and the workmanship were universally admired; and one among the rest having expressed a desire of knowing the value of such a jewel, the Count seized that opportunity of entertaining them with a learned disquisition into the nature of stones; this introduced the history of the diamond in question, which he said had been purchased of an Indian trader of Fort St. George, at an under price; so that the present proprietor could afford to sell it at a very reasonable rate; and concluded with telling the company, that, for his own part, he had been importuned to wear it by the jeweller, who imagined it would have a better chance for attracting a purchaser on his finger, than while it remained in his own custody.

This declaration was no sooner made, than a certain lady of quality bespoke the refuse of the jewel, and desired Ferdinand to send the owner next day to her house, where he accordingly waited upon her ladyship with the ring, for which he received one hundred and fifty guineas, two-thirds of the sum being clear gain, and equally divided betwixt the associates. Nor was this bargain such as reflected dishonour upon the lady's taste, or could be productive of ill consequences to the merchant; for the method of estimating diamonds is altogether arbitrary; and Ratchcali, who was an exquisite lapidary, had set it in such a manner as would have imposed upon any ordinary jeweller. By these means of introduction, the Tyrolese soon monopolised the custom of a great many noble families, upon which he levied large contributions, without incurring the least suspicion of deceit. He every day, out of pure esteem and gratitude for the honour of their commands, entertained them with the sight of some new trinket, which he was never permitted to carry home unsold; and from the profits of each job, a tax was raised for the benefit of our adventurer.

Yet his indultos were not confined to the article of jewels, which constituted only one part of his revenue. By the industry of his understrapper, he procured a number of old crazy fiddles, which were thrown aside as lumber; upon which he counterfeited the Cremona mark, and otherwise cooked them up with great dexterity; so that, when he had occasion to regale the lovers of music, he would send for one of these vamped instruments, and extract from it such tones as quite ravished the hearers; among whom there was always some conceited pretender, who spoke in raptures of the violin, and gave our hero an opportunity of launching out in its praise, and declaring it was the best Cremona he had ever touched. This encomium never failed to inflame the desires of the audience, to some one of whom he was generous enough to part with it at prime cost—that is, for twenty or thirty guineas clear profit; for he was often able to oblige his friends in this manner, because, being an eminent connoisseur, his countenance was solicited by all the musicians, who wanted to dispose of such moveables.

Nor did he neglect the other resources of a skilful virtuoso. Every auction afforded some picture, in which, though it had been overlooked by the ignorance of the times, he recognised the style of a great master, and made a merit of recommending it to some noble friend. This commerce he likewise extended to medals, bronzes, busts, intaglios, and old china, and kept divers artificers continually employed in making antiques for the English nobility. Thus he went on with such rapidity of success in all his endeavours, that he himself was astonished at the infatuation he had produced. Nothing was so wretched among the productions of art, that he could not impose upon the world as a capital performance; and so fascinated were the eyes of his admirers, he could easily have persuaded them that a barber's bason was an Etrurian patera, and the cover of a copper pot no other than the shield of Ancus Martius. In short, it was become so fashionable to consult the Count in everything relating to taste and politeness, that not a plan was drawn, not even a house furnished, without his advice and approbation; nay, to such a degree did his reputation in these matters excel, that a particular pattern of paper-hangings was known by the name of Fathom; and his hall was every morning crowded with upholsterers, and other tradesmen, who came, by order of their employers, to learn his choice, and take his directions.

The character and influence he thus acquired, he took care to maintain with the utmost assiduity and circumspection. He never failed to appear the chief personage at all public diversions and private assemblies, not only in conversation and dress, but also in the article of dancing, in which he outstripped all his fellows, as far as in every other genteel accomplishment.

CHAPTER THIRTY-THREE.
HE ATTRACTS THE ENVY AND ILL OFFICES OF THE MINOR KNIGHTS OF HIS OWN ORDER, OVER WHOM HE OBTAINS A COMPLETE VICTORY.

Such a pre-eminence could not be enjoyed without exciting the malevolence of envy and detraction, in the propagation of which none were so industrious as the brethren of his own order, who had, like him, made a descent upon this island, and could not, without repining, see the whole harvest in the hands of one man, who, with equal art and discretion, avoided all intercourse with their society. In vain they strove to discover his pedigree, and detect the particular circumstances of his life and conversation; all their inquiries were baffled by the obscurity of his origin, and that solitary scheme which he had adopted in the beginning of his career. The whole fruit of their investigation amounted to no more than a certainty that there was no family of any consideration in Europe known by the denomination of Fathom; and this discovery they did not fail to divulge for the benefit of our adventurer, who had by this time taken such firm root in the favour of the great, as to set all those little arts at defiance; and when the report reached his ear, actually made his friends merry with the conjectures which had been circulated at his expense.

His adversaries, finding themselves disappointed in this effort, held a consultation to devise other measures against him, and came to a resolution of ending him by the sword, or rather of expelling him from the kingdom by the fear of death, which they hoped he had not courage enough to resist, because his deportment had always been remarkably mild and pacific. It was upon this supposition that they left to the determination of the dice the choice of the person who should execute their plan; and the lot falling upon a Swiss, who, from the station of a foot soldier in the Dutch service, out of which he had been drummed for theft, had erected himself into the rank of a self-created chevalier, this hero fortified himself with a double dose of brandy, and betook himself to a certain noted coffee-house, with an intent to affront Count Fathom in public.

He was lucky enough to find our adventurer sitting at a table in conversation with some persons of the first rank; upon which he seated himself in the next box, and after having intruded himself into their discourse, which happened to turn upon the politics of some German courts, "Count," said he to Ferdinand, in a very abrupt and disagreeable manner of address, "I was last night in company with some gentlemen, among whom a dispute happened about the place of your nativity; pray, what country are you of?" "Sir," answered the other, with great politeness, "I at present have the honour to be of England." "Oho!" replied the chevalier, "I ask your pardon, that is to say, you are incog; some people may find it convenient to keep themselves in that situation." "True," said the Count, "but some people are too well known to enjoy that privilege." The Swiss being a little disconcerted at this repartee, which extracted a smile from the audience, after some pause, observed, that persons of a certain class had good reason to drop the remembrance of what they have been; but a good citizen will not forget his country, or former condition. "And a bad citizen," said Fathom, "cannot, if he would, provided he has met with his deserts; a sharper may as well forget the shape of a die, or a discarded soldier the sound of a drum."

As the chevalier's character and story were not unknown, this application raised an universal laugh at his expense, which provoked him to such a degree, that, starting up, he swore Fathom could not have mentioned any object in nature that he himself resembled so much as a drum, which was exactly typified by his emptiness and sound, with this difference, however, that a drum was never noisy till beaten, whereas the Count would never be quiet, until he should have undergone the same discipline. So saying, he laid his hand upon his sword with a menacing look, and walked out as if in expectation of being followed by our adventurer, who suffered himself to be detained by the company, and very calmly took notice, that his antagonist would not be ill pleased at their interposition. Perhaps he would not have comported himself with such ease and deliberation, had not he made such remarks upon the disposition of the chevalier, as convinced him of his own safety. He had perceived a perplexity and perturbation in the countenance of the Swiss, when he first entered the coffee-room; his blunt and precipitate way of accosting him seemed to denote confusion and compulsion; and, in the midst of his ferocity, this accurate observer discerned the trepidation of fear. By the help of these signs, his sagacity soon comprehended the nature of his schemes, and prepared accordingly for a formal defiance.

His conjecture was verified next morning by a visit from the chevalier, who, taking it for granted that Fathom would not face an adversary in the field, because he had not followed him from the coffee-house, went to his lodgings with great confidence, and demanded to see the Count upon an affair that would admit of no delay. Maurice, according to his instructions, told him that his master was gone out, but desired he would have the goodness to repose himself in the parlour, till the Count's return, which he expected every moment. Ferdinand, who had taken post in a proper place for observation, seeing his antagonist fairly admitted, took the same road, and appearing before him, wrapped up in a long Spanish cloak, desired to know what had procured him the honour of such an early visit. The Swiss, raising his voice to conceal his agitation, explained his errand, in demanding reparation for the injury his honour had sustained the preceding day, in that odious allusion to a scandalous report which had been raised by the malice of his enemies; and insisted, in a very imperious style, upon his attending him forthwith to the nursery in Hyde Park. "Have a little patience," said our adventurer with great composure, "and I will do myself the pleasure to wait upon you in a few moments."

With these words, he rang the bell, and, calling for a bason of water, laid aside his cloak, and displayed himself in his shirt, with a sword in his right hand, which was all over besmeared with recent blood, as if he had just come from the slaughter of a foe. This phenomenon made such an impression upon the astonished chevalier, already discomposed by the resolute behaviour of the Count, that he became jaundiced with terror and dismay, and, while his teeth chattered in his head, told our hero he had hoped, from his known politeness, to have found him ready to acknowledge an injury which might have been the effect of anger or misapprehension, in which case the affair might have been compromised to their mutual satisfaction, without proceeding to those extremities which, among men of honour, are always accounted the last resource. To this representation Ferdinand answered, that the affair had been of the chevalier's own seeking, inasmuch as he had intruded himself into his company, and treated him with the most insolent and unprovoked abuse, which plainly flowed from a premeditated design against his honour and reputation; he, therefore, far from being disposed to own himself in the wrong, would not even accept of a public acknowledgment from him, the aggressor, whom he looked upon as an infamous sharper, and was resolved to chastise accordingly.

Here the conversation was interrupted by the arrival of a person who was brought to the door in a chair, and conducted into another apartment, from which a message was brought to the Count, importing, that the stranger desired to speak with him upon business of the last importance. Fathom having chid the servant for admitting people without his order, desired the Swiss to excuse him for a minute longer, and went in to the next room, from whence the following dialogue was overheard by this challenger:—"Count," said the stranger, "you are not ignorant of my pretensions to the heart of that young lady, at whose house I met you yesterday; therefore you cannot be surprised when I declare myself displeased with your visits and behaviour to my mistress, and demand that you will instantly promise to drop the correspondence." "Else what follows?" answered Ferdinand, with a cool and temperate voice. "My resentment and immediate defiance," replied the other; "for the only alternative I propose is, to forego your design upon that lady, or to decide our pretension by the sword."

Our hero, having expressed a regard for this visitant as the son of a gentleman whom he honoured, was at the pains to represent the unreasonableness of his demand, and the folly of his presumption; and earnestly exhorted him to put the issue of his cause upon a more safe and equitable footing. But this admonition, instead of appeasing the wrath, seemed to inflame the resentment of the opponent, who swore he would not leave him until he should have accomplished the purport of his errand. In vain our adventurer requested half an hour for the despatch of some urgent business, in which he was engaged with a gentleman in the other parlour. This impetuous rival rejected all the terms he could propose, and even challenged him to decide the controversy upon the spot; an expedient to which the other having assented with reluctance, the door was secured, the swords unsheathed, and a hot engagement ensued, to the inexpressible pleasure of the Swiss, who did not doubt that he himself would be screened from all danger by the event of this rencontre. Nevertheless, his hope was disappointed in the defeat of the stranger, who was quickly disarmed, in consequence of a wound through the sword-arm; upon which occasion Fathom was heard to say, that, in consideration of his youth and family, he had spared his life; but he would not act with the same tenderness towards any other antagonist. He then bound up the limb he had disabled, conducted the vanquished party to his chair, rejoined the chevalier with a serene countenance, and, asking pardon for having detained him so long, proposed they should instantly set out in a hackney-coach for the place of appointment.

The stratagem thus conducted, had all the success the inventor could desire. The fear of the Swiss had risen almost to an ecstasy before the Count quitted the room; but after this sham battle, which had been preconcerted betwixt our adventurer and his friend Ratchcali, the chevalier's terrors were unspeakable. He considered Fathom as a devil incarnate, and went into the coach as a malefactor bound for Tyburn. He would have gladly compounded for the loss of a leg or arm, and entertained some transient gleams of hope, that he should escape for half a dozen flesh-wounds, which he would have willingly received as the price of his presumption; but these hopes were banished by the remembrance of that dreadful declaration which he had heard the Count make, after having overcome his last adversary; and he continued under the power of the most unsupportable panic, until the carriage halted at Hyde Park Corner, where he crawled forth in a most piteous and lamentable condition; so that, when they reached the spot, he was scarce able to stand.

Here he made an effort to speak, and propose an accommodation upon a new plan, by which he promised to leave his cause to the arbitrement of those gentlemen who were present at the rupture, and to ask pardon of the Count, provided he should be found guilty of a trespass upon good manners; but this proposal would not satisfy the implacable Ferdinand, who, perceiving the agony of the Swiss, resolved to make the most of the adventure, and giving him to understand he was not a man to be trifled with, desired him to draw without further preamble. Thus compelled, the unfortunate gamester pulled off his coat, and, putting himself in a posture, to use the words of Nym, "winked, and held out his cold iron."

Our adventurer, far from making a gentle use of the advantages he possessed, fiercely attacked him, while he was incapable of making resistance, and, aiming at a fleshy part, ran him through the arm and outside of the shoulder at the very first pass. The chevalier, already stupefied with the horror of expectation, no sooner felt his adversary's point in his body than he fell to the ground, and, concluding he was no longer a man for this world, began to cross himself with great devotion; while Fathom walked home deliberately, and in his way sent a couple of chairmen to the assistance of the wounded knight.

This achievement, which could not be concealed from the knowledge of the public, not only furnished the character of Fathom with fresh wreaths of admiration and applause, but likewise effectually secured him from any future attempts of his enemies, to whom the Swiss, for his own sake, had communicated such terrible ideas of his valour, as overawed the whole community.

CHAPTER THIRTY-FOUR.
HE PERFORMS ANOTHER EXPLOIT, THAT CONVEYS A TRUE IDEA OF HIS GRATITUDE AND HONOUR.

It was not long after this celebrated victory, that he was invited to spend part of the summer at the house of a country gentleman, who lived about one hundred miles from London, possessed of a very opulent fortune, the greatest part of which was expended in acts of old English hospitality. He had met with our hero by accident at the table of a certain great man, and was so struck with his manner and conversation, as to desire his acquaintance, and cultivate his friendship; and he thought himself extremely happy in having prevailed upon him to pass a few weeks in his family.

Fathom, among his other observations, perceived that there was a domestic uneasiness, occasioned by a very beautiful young creature about the age of fifteen, who resided in the house under the title of the gentleman's niece, though she was in reality his natural daughter, born before his marriage. This circumstance was not unknown to his lady, by whose express approbation he had bestowed particular attention upon the education of the child, whom we shall distinguish by the name of Celinda. Their liberality in this particular had not been misapplied; for she not only gave marks of uncommon capacity, but, as she grew up, became more and more amiable in her person, and was now returned from the boarding school, possessed of every accomplishment that could be acquired by one of her age and opportunities. These qualifications, which endeared her to every other person, excited the jealousy and displeasure of her supposed aunt, who could not bear to see her own children eclipsed by this illegitimate daughter, whom she therefore discountenanced upon all occasions, and exposed to such mortifications as would in all appearance drive her from her father's house. This persecuting spirit was very disagreeable to the husband, who loved Celinda with a truly paternal affection, and produced abundance of family disquiet; but being a man of a peaceable and yielding disposition, he could not long maintain the resolution he had taken in her favour, and therefore he ceased opposing the malevolence of his wife.

In this unfortunate predicament stood the fair bastard, at the arrival of our adventurer, who, being allured by her charms, apprised of her situation at the same time, took the generous resolution to undermine her innocence, that he might banquet his vicious appetite with the spoils of her beauty. Perhaps such a brutal design might not have entered his imagination, if he had not observed, in the disposition of this hapless maiden, certain peculiarities from which he derived the most confident presages of success. Besides a total want of experience, that left her open and unguarded against the attacks of the other sex, she discovered a remarkable spirit of credulity and superstitious fear, which had been cherished by the conversation of her school-fellows. She was particularly fond of music, in which she had made some progress; but so delicate was the texture of her nerves, that one day, while Fathom entertained the company with a favourite air, she actually swooned with pleasure.

Such sensibility, our projector well knew, must be diffused through all the passions of her heart; he congratulated himself upon the sure ascendency he had gained over her in this particular; and forthwith began to execute the plan he had erected for her destruction. That he might the more effectually deceive the vigilance of her father's wife, he threw such a dash of affectation in his complaisance towards Celinda, as could not escape the notice of that prying matron, though it was not palpable enough to disoblige the young lady herself, who could not so well distinguish between overstrained courtesy and real good breeding. This behaviour screened him from the suspicion of the family, who considered it as an effort of politeness, to cover his indifference and disgust for the daughter of his friend, who had by this time given some reason to believe she looked upon him with the eyes of affection; so that the opportunities he enjoyed of conversing with her in private, were less liable to intrusion or inquiry. Indeed, from what I have already observed, touching the sentiments of her stepdame, that lady, far from taking measures for thwarting our hero's design, would have rejoiced at the execution of it, and, had she been informed of his intent, might have fallen upon some method to facilitate the enterprise; but, as he solely depended upon his own talents, he never dreamed of soliciting such an auxiliary.

Under cover of instructing and accomplishing her in the exercise of music, he could not want occasions for promoting his aim; when, after having soothed her sense of hearing, even to a degree of ravishment, so as to extort from her an exclamation, importing, that he was surely something supernatural! he never failed to whisper some insidious compliment or tale of love, exquisitely suited to the emotions of her soul. Thus was her heart insensibly subdued; though more than half his work was still undone; for, at all times, she disclosed such purity of sentiment, such inviolable attachment to religion and virtue, and seemed so averse to all sorts of inflammatory discourse, that he durst not presume upon the footing he had gained in her affection, to explain the baseness of his desire; he therefore applied to another of her passions, that proved the bane of her virtue. This was her timidity, which at first being constitutional, was afterwards increased by the circumstances of her education, and now aggravated by the artful conversation of Fathom, which he chequered with dismal stories of omens, portents, prophecies, and apparitions, delivered upon such unquestionable testimony, and with such marks of conviction, as captivated the belief of the devoted Celinda, and filled her imagination with unceasing terrors.

In vain she strove to dispel those frightful ideas, and avoid such topics of discourse for the future. The more she endeavoured to banish them, the more troublesome they became; and such was her infatuation, that as her terrors increased, her thirst after that sort of knowledge was augmented. Many sleepless nights did she pass amidst those horrors of fancy, starting at every noise, and sweating with dreary apprehension, yet ashamed to own her fears, or solicit the comfort of a bedfellow, lest she should incur the ridicule and censure of her father's wife; and what rendered this disposition the more irksome, was the solitary situation of her chamber, that stood at the end of a long gallery scarce within hearing of any other inhabited part of the house.

All these circumstances had been duly weighed by our projector, who, having prepared Celinda for his purpose, stole at midnight from his apartment, which was in another storey, and approaching her door, there uttered a piteous groan; then softly retired to his bed, in full confidence of seeing next day the effect of this operation. Nor did his arrow miss the mark. Poor Celinda's countenance gave such indications of melancholy and dismay, that he could not omit asking the cause of her disquiet, and she, at his earnest request, was prevailed upon to communicate the dreadful salutation of the preceding night, which she considered as an omen of death to some person of the family, in all probability to herself, as the groan seemed to issue from one corner of her own apartment. Our adventurer argued against this supposition, as contradictory to the common observation of those supernatural warnings which are not usually imparted to the person who is doomed to die, but to some faithful friend, or trusty servant, particularly interested in the event. He therefore supposed, that the groans foreboded the death of my lady, who seemed to be in a drooping state of health, and were, by her genius, conveyed to the organs of Celinda, who was the chief sufferer by her jealous and barbarous disposition; he likewise expressed an earnest desire to be an ear-witness of such solemn communication, and, alleging that it was highly improper for a young lady of her delicate feelings to expose herself alone to such another dismal visitation, begged he might be allowed to watch all night in her chamber, in order to defend her from the shocking impressions of fear.

Though no person ever stood more in need of a companion or guard, and her heart throbbed with transports of dismay at the prospect of night, she rejected his proposal with due acknowledgment, and resolved to trust solely to the protection of Heaven. Not that she thought her innocence or reputation could suffer by her compliance with his request; for, hitherto, her heart was a stranger to those young desires which haunt the fancy, and warm the breast of youth; so that, being ignorant of her danger, she saw not the necessity of avoiding temptation; but she refused to admit a man into her bedchamber, merely because it was a step altogether opposite to the forms and decorum of life. Nevertheless, far from being discouraged by this repulse, he knew her fears would multiply and reduce that reluctance, which, in order to weaken, he had recourse to another piece of machinery, that operated powerfully in behalf of his design.

Some years ago, a twelve-stringed instrument was contrived by a very ingenious musician, by whom it was aptly entitled the "Harp of Aeolus," because, being properly applied to a stream of air, it produces a wild irregular variety of harmonious sounds, that seem to be the effect of enchantment, and wonderfully dispose the mind for the most romantic situations. Fathom, who was really a virtuoso in music, had brought one of those new-fashioned guitars into the country, and as the effect of it was still unknown in the family, he that night converted it to the purposes of his amour, by fixing it in the casement of a window belonging to the gallery, exposed to the west wind, which then blew in a gentle breeze. The strings no sooner felt the impression of the balmy zephyr, than they began to pour forth a stream of melody more ravishingly delightful than the song of Philomel, the warbling brook, and all the concert of the wood. The soft and tender notes of peace and love were swelled up with the most delicate and insensible transition into a loud hymn of triumph and exultation, joined by the deep-toned organ, and a full choir of voices, which gradually decayed upon the ear, until it died away in distant sound, as if a flight of angels had raised the song in their ascent to heaven. Yet the chords hardly ceased to vibrate after the expiration of this overture, which ushered in a composition in the same pathetic style; and this again was succeeded by a third, almost without pause or intermission, as if the artist's hand had been indefatigable, and the theme never to be exhausted.

His heart must be quite callous, and his ear lost to all distinction, who could hear such harmony without emotion; how deeply, then, must it have affected the delicate Celinda, whose sensations, naturally acute, were whetted to a most painful keenness by her apprehension; who could have no previous idea of such entertainment, and was credulous enough to believe the most improbable tale of superstition! She was overwhelmed with awful terror, and, never doubting that the sounds were more than mortal, recommended herself to the care of Providence in a succession of pious ejaculations.

Our adventurer, having allowed some time for the effect of this contrivance, repaired to her chamber door, and, in a whisper, conveyed through the keyhole, asked if she was awake, begged pardon for such an unseasonable visit, and desired to know her opinion of the strange music which he then heard. In spite of her notions of decency, she was glad of his intrusion, and, being in no condition to observe punctilios, slipped on a wrapper, opened the door, and, with a faltering voice, owned herself frightened almost to distraction. He pretended to console her with reflections, importing, that she was in the hands of a benevolent Being, who would not impose upon his creatures any task which they could not bear; he insisted upon her returning to bed, and assured her he would not stir from her chamber till day. Thus comforted, she betook herself again to rest, while he sat down in an elbow-chair at some distance from the bedside, and, in a soft voice, began the conversation with her on the subject of those visitations from above, which, though undertaken on pretence of dissipating her fear and anxiety, was, in reality, calculated for the purpose of augmenting both.

"That sweet air," said he, "seems designed for soothing the bodily anguish of some saint in his last moments. Hark! how it rises into a more sprightly and elevated strain, as if it were an inspiriting invitation to the realms of bliss! Sure, he is now absolved from all the misery of this life! That full and glorious concert of voices and celestial harps betoken his reception among the heavenly choir, who now waft his soul to paradisian joys! This is altogether great, solemn, and amazing! The clock strikes one, the symphony hath ceased!"

This was actually the case; for he had ordered Maurice to remove the instrument at that hour, lest the sound of it should become too familiar, and excite the curiosity of some undaunted domestic, who might frustrate his scheme by discovering the apparatus. As for poor Celinda, her fancy was, by his music and discourse, worked up to the highest pitch of enthusiastic terrors; the whole bed shook with her trepidation, the awful silence that succeeded the supernatural music threw an additional damp upon her spirits, and the artful Fathom affecting to snore at the same time, she could no longer contain her horror, but called upon his name with a fearful accent, and, having owned her present situation insupportable, entreated him to draw near her bedside, that he might be within touch on any emergency.

This was a welcome request to our adventurer, who, asking pardon for his drowsiness, and taking his station on the side of her bed, exhorted her to compose herself; then locking her hand fast in his own, was again seized with such an inclination to sleep, that he gradually sunk down by her side, and seemed to enjoy his repose in that attitude. Meanwhile, his tender-hearted mistress, that he might not suffer in his health by his humanity and complaisance, covered him with the counterpane as he slept, and suffered him to take his rest without interruption, till he thought proper to start up suddenly with an exclamation of, "Heaven watch over us!" and then asked, with symptoms of astonishment, if she had heard nothing. Such an abrupt address upon such an occasion, did not fail to amaze and affright the gentle Celinda, who, unable to speak, sprung towards her treacherous protector; and he, catching her in his arms, bade her fear nothing, for he would, at the expense of his life, defend her from all danger.

Having thus, by tampering with her weakness, conquered the first and chief obstacles to his design, he, with great art and perseverance, improved the intercourse to such a degree of intimacy, as could not but be productive of all the consequences which he had foreseen. The groans and music were occasionally repeated, so as to alarm the whole family, and inspire a thousand various conjectures. He failed not to continue his nocturnal visits and ghastly discourse, until his attendance became so necessary to this unhappy maiden, that she durst not stay in her own chamber without his company, nor even sleep, except in contact with her betrayer.

Such a commerce between two such persons of a different sex could not possibly be long carried on, without degenerating from the Platonic system of sentimental love. In her paroxysms of dismay, he did not forget to breathe the soft inspirations of his passion, to which she listened with more pleasure, as they diverted the gloomy ideas of her fear; and by this time his extraordinary accomplishments had made a conquest of her heart. What therefore could be a more interesting transition than that from the most uneasy to the most agreeable sensation of the human breast?

This being the case, the reader will not wonder that a consummate traitor, like Fathom, should triumph over the virtue of an artless, innocent young creature, whose passions he had entirely under his command. The gradations towards vice are almost imperceptible, and an experienced seducer can strew them with such enticing and agreeable flowers, as will lead the young sinner on insensibly, even to the most profligate stages of guilt. All therefore that can be done by virtue, unassisted with experience, is to avoid every trial with such a formidable foe, by declining and discouraging the first advances towards a particular correspondence with perfidious man, howsoever agreeable it may seem to be. For here is no security but in conscious weakness.

Fathom, though possessed of the spoils of poor Celinda's honour, did not enjoy his success with tranquillity. Reflection and remorse often invaded her in the midst of their guilty pleasures, and embittered all those moments they had dedicated to mutual bliss. For the seeds of virtue are seldom destroyed at once. Even amidst the rank productions of vice, they regerminate to a sort of imperfect vegetation, like some scattered hyacinths shooting up among the weeds of a ruined garden, that testify the former culture and amenity of the soil. She sighed at the sad remembrance of that virgin dignity which she had lost; she wept at the prospect of that disgrace, mortification, and misery she should undergo, when abandoned by this transient lover, and severely reproached him for the arts he had used to shipwreck her innocence and peace.

Such expostulations are extremely unseasonable, when addressed to a man well-nigh sated with the effects of his conquest. They act like strong blasts of wind applied to embers almost extinguished, which, instead of reviving the flame, scatter and destroy every remaining particle of fire. Our adventurer, in the midst of his peculiarities, had inconstancy in common with the rest of his sex. More than half cloyed with the possession of Celinda, he could not fail to be disgusted with her upbraidings; and had she not been the daughter of a gentleman whose friendship he did not think it his interest to forfeit, he would have dropped this correspondence, without reluctance or hesitation. But, as he had measures to keep with a family of such consequence, he constrained his inclinations, so far as to counterfeit those raptures he no longer felt, and found means to appease those intervening tumults of her grief.

Foreseeing, however, that it would not be always in his power to console her on these terms, he resolved, if possible, to divide her affection, which now glowed upon him too intensely; and, with that view, whenever she complained of the vapours or dejection, he prescribed, and even insisted upon her swallowing certain cordials of the most palatable composition, without which he never travelled; and these produced such agreeable reveries and flow of spirits, that she gradually became enamoured of intoxication; while he encouraged the pernicious passion, by expressing the most extravagant applause and admiration at the wild irregular sallies it produced. Without having first made this diversion, he would have found it impracticable to leave the house with tranquillity; but, when this bewitching philtre grew into an habit, her attachment to Ferdinand was insensibly dissolved; she began to bear his neglect with indifference, and, sequestering herself from the rest of the family, used to solicit this new ally for consolation.

Having thus put the finishing stroke to the daughter's ruin, he took leave of the father, with many acknowledgments and expressions of gratitude for his hospitality and friendship, and, riding across the country to Bristol, took up his habitation near the hot well, where he stayed during the remaining part of the season. As for the miserable Celinda, she became more and more addicted to the vices in which she had been initiated by his superlative perfidy and craft, until she was quite abandoned by decency and caution. Her father's heart was torn with anguish, while his wife rejoiced in her fall; at length her ideas were quite debased by her infirmity; she grew every day more and more sensual and degenerate, and contracted an intimacy with one of the footmen, who was kind enough to take her to wife, in hope of obtaining a good settlement from his master; but, being disappointed in his aim, he conducted her to London, where he made shift to insinuate himself into another service, leaving her to the use, and partly the advantage, of her own person, which was still uncommonly attractive.

CHAPTER THIRTY-FIVE.
HE REPAIRS TO BRISTOL SPRING, WHERE HE REIGNS PARAMOUNT DURING THE WHOLE SEASON.

We shall therefore leave her in this comfortable situation, and return to our adventurer, whose appearance at Bristol was considered as a happy omen by the proprietor of the hot well, and all the people who live by the resort of company to that celebrated spring. Nor were they deceived in their prognostic. Fathom, as usual, formed the nucleus or kernel of the beau monde; and the season soon became so crowded, that many people of fashion were obliged to quit the place for want of lodging. Ferdinand was the soul that animated the whole society. He not only invented parties of pleasure, but also, by his personal talents, rendered them more agreeable. In a word, he regulated their diversions, and the master of the ceremonies never would allow the ball to be begun till the Count was seated.

Having thus made himself the object of admiration and esteem, his advice was an oracle, to which they had recourse in all doubtful cases of punctilio or dispute, or even of medicine; for among his other accomplishments, his discourse on that subject was so plausible, and well adapted to the understanding of his hearers, that any person who had not actually studied the medical art would have believed he was inspired by the spirit of Aesculapius. What contributed to the aggrandisement of his character in this branch of knowledge, was a victory he obtained over an old physician, who plied at the well, and had one day unfortunately begun to harangue in the pump-room upon the nature of the Bristol water. In the course of this lecture he undertook to account for the warmth of the fluid; and his ideas being perplexed with a great deal of reading, which he had not been able to digest, his disquisition was so indistinct, and his expression so obscure and unentertaining, that our hero seized the opportunity of displaying his own erudition, by venturing to contradict some circumstances of the doctor's hypothesis, and substituting a theory of his own, which, as he had invented it for the purpose, was equally amusing and chimerical.

He alleged, that fire was the sole vivifying principle that pervaded all nature; that, as the heat of the sun concocted the juice of vegetables, and ripened those fruits that grow upon the surface of this globe, there was likewise an immense store of central fire reserved within the bowels of the earth, not only for the generation of gems, fossils, and all the purposes of the mineral world, but likewise for cherishing and keeping alive those plants which would otherwise perish by the winter's cold. The existence of such a fire he proved from the nature of all those volcanoes, which in almost every corner of the earth are continually vomiting up either flames or smoke. "These," said he, "are the great vents appointed by nature for the discharge of that rarefied air and combustible matter, which, if confined, would burst the globe asunder; but, besides the larger outlets, there are some small chimneys through which part of the heat transpires; a vapour of that sort, I conceive, must pass through the bed or channel of this spring, the waters of which, accordingly retain a moderate warmth."

This account, which totally overthrew the other's doctrine, was so extremely agreeable to the audience, that the testy doctor lost his temper, and gave them to understand, without preamble, that he must be a person wholly ignorant of natural philosophy, who could invent such a ridiculous system, and they involved in worse than an Egyptian fog, that could not at once discern its weakness and absurdity. This declaration introduced a dispute, which was unanimously determined in favour of our adventurer. On all such occasions the stream of prejudice runs against the physician, even though his antagonist has nothing to recommend himself to the favour of the spectators; and this decision depends upon divers considerations. In the first place, there is a continual war carried on against the learned professions, by all those who, conscious of their own ignorance, seek to level the reputation of their superiors with their own. Secondly, in all disputes upon physic that happen betwixt a person who really understands the art, and an illiterate pretender, the arguments of the first will seem obscure and unintelligible to those who are unacquainted with the previous systems on which they are built; while the other's theory, derived from common notions, and superficial observation, will be more agreeable, because better adapted to the comprehension of the hearers. Thirdly, the judgment of the multitude is apt to be biassed by that surprise which is the effect of seeing an artist foiled at his own weapons, by one who engages him only for amusement.

Fathom, besides these advantages, was blessed with a flow of language, an elegant address, a polite and self-denying style of argumentation, together with a temper not to be ruffled; so that the victory could not long waver between him and the physician, to whom he was infinitely superior in every acquisition but that of solid learning, of which the judges had no idea. This contest was not only glorious but profitable to our adventurer, who grew into such request in his medical capacity, that the poor doctor was utterly deserted by his patients, and Fathom's advice solicited by every valetudinarian in the place; nor did he forfeit the character he thus acquired by any miscarriages in his practice. Being but little conversant with the materia medica, the circle of his prescriptions was very small; his chief study was to avoid all drugs of rough operation and uncertain effect, and to administer such only as should be agreeable to the palate, without doing violence to the constitution. Such a physician could not but be agreeable to people of all dispositions; and, as most of the patients were in some shape hypochondriac, the power of imagination, co-operating with his remedies, often effected a cure.

On the whole, it became the fashion to consult the Count in all distempers, and his reputation would have had its run, though the death of every patient had given the lie to his pretensions. But empty fame was not the sole fruit of his success. Though no person would presume to affront this noble graduate with a fee, they did not fail to manifest their gratitude by some more valuable present. Every day some superb piece of china, curious snuffbox, or jewel, was pressed upon him; so that, at the end of the season, he could almost have furnished a toyshop with the acknowledgments he had received. Not only his avarice, but his pleasure, was gratified in the course of his medical administration. He enjoyed free access, egress, and regress with all the females at the well, and no matron scrupled to put her daughter under his care and direction. These opportunities could not be lost upon a man of his intriguing genius; though he conducted his amours with such discretion, that, during the whole season, no lady's character suffered on his account, yet he was highly fortunate in his addresses, and we may venture to affirm, that the reproach of barrenness was more than once removed by the vigour of his endeavours.

CHAPTER THIRTY-SIX.
HE IS SMITTEN WITH THE CHARMS OF A FEMALE ADVENTURER, WHOSE ALLUREMENTS SUBJECT HIM TO A NEW VICISSITUDE OF FORTUNE.

Among those who were distinguished by his gallantry was the young wife of an old citizen of London, who had granted her permission to reside at the hot well for the benefit of her health, under the eye and inspection of his own sister, who was a maiden of fifty years. The pupil, whose name was Mrs. Trapwell, though low in stature, was finely shaped, her countenance engaging, though her complexion was brown, her hair in colour rivalled the raven's back, and her eyes emulated the lustre of the diamond. Fathom had been struck with her first appearance; but found it impracticable to elude the vigilance of her duenna, so as to make a declaration of his flame; until she herself, guessing the situation of his thoughts, and not displeased with the discovery, thought proper to furnish him with the opportunity he wanted, by counterfeiting an indisposition, for the cure of which she knew his advice would be implored. This was the beginning of an acquaintance, which was soon improved to his wish; and so well did she manage her attractions, as in some measure to fix the inconstancy of his disposition; for, at the end of the season, his passion was not sated; and they concerted the means of continuing their commerce, even after their return to London.

This intercourse effectually answered the purpose of the husband, who had been decoyed into matrimony by the cunning of his spouse, whom he had privately kept as a concubine before marriage. Conscious of her own precarious situation, she had resolved to impose upon the infirmities of Trapwell, and, feigning herself pregnant, gave him to understand she could no longer conceal her condition from the knowledge of her brother, who was an officer in the army, and of such violent passions, that, should he once discover her backsliding, he would undoubtedly wipe away the stains of his family dishonour with her own blood, as well as that of her keeper. The citizen, to prevent such a catastrophe, took her to wife; but soon after perceiving the trick which had been played upon him, set his invention at work, and at length contrived a scheme which he thought would enable him, not only to retrieve his liberty, but also indemnify himself for the mortification he had undergone.

Far from creating any domestic disturbance, by upbraiding her with her finesse, he seemed perfectly well pleased with his acquisition; and, as he knew her void of any principle, and extremely addicted to pleasure, he chose proper occasions to insinuate, that she might gratify her own inclination, and at the same time turn her beauty to good account. She joyfully listened to these remonstrances, and, in consequence of their mutual agreement, she repaired to Bristol Spring, on pretence of an ill state of health, accompanied by her sister-in-law, whom they did not think proper to intrust with the real motive of her journey. Fathom's person was agreeable, and his finances supposed to be in flourishing order; therefore, she selected him from the herd of gallants, as a proper sacrifice to the powers which she adored; and, on her arrival in London, made her husband acquainted with the importance of her conquest.

Trapwell overwhelmed her with caresses and praise for her discreet and dutiful conduct, and faithfully promised that she should pocket in her own privy purse one-half of the spoils that should be gathered from her gallant, whom she therefore undertook to betray, after he had swore, in the most solemn manner, that his intention was not to bring the affair to a public trial, which would redound to his own disgrace, but to extort a round sum of money from the Count, by way of composition. Confiding in this protestation, she in a few days gave him intelligence of an assignation she had made with our adventurer, at a certain bagnio near Covent Garden; upon which he secured the assistance of a particular friend and his own journeyman, with whom, and a constable, he repaired to the place of rendezvous, where he waited in an adjoining room, according to the directions of his virtuous spouse, until she made the preconcerted signal of hemming three times aloud, when he and his associates rushed into the chamber and surprised our hero in bed with his inamorata.

The lady on this occasion acted her part to a miracle; she screamed at their approach; and, after an exclamation of "Ruined and undone!" fainted away in the arms of her spouse, who had by this time seized her by the shoulders, and begun to upbraid her with her infidelity and guilt. As for Fathom, his affliction was unutterable, when he found himself discovered in that situation, and made prisoner by the two assistants, who had pinioned him in such a manner, that he could not stir, much less accomplish an escape. All his ingenuity and presence of mind seemed to forsake him in this emergency. The horrors of an English jury overspread his imagination; for he at once perceived that the toil into which he had fallen was laid for the purpose; consequently he took it for granted that there would be no deficiency in point of evidence. Soon as he recollected himself, he begged that no violence might be offered to his person, and entreated the husband to favour him with a conference, in which the affair might be compromised, without prejudice to the reputation of either.

At first Trapwell breathed nothing but implacable revenge, but, by the persuasion of his friends, after he had sent home his wife in a chair, he was prevailed upon to hear the proposals of the delinquent, who having assured him, by way of apology, that he had always believed the lady was a widow, made him an offer of five hundred pounds, as an atonement for the injury he had sustained. This being a sum no ways adequate to the expectation of the citizen, who looked upon the Count as possessor of an immense estate, he rejected the terms with disdain, and made instant application to a judge, from whom he obtained a warrant for securing his person till the day of trial. Indeed, in this case, money was but a secondary consideration with Trapwell, whose chief aim was to be legally divorced from a woman he detested. Therefore there was no remedy for the unhappy Count, who in vain offered to double the sum. He found himself reduced to the bitter alternative of procuring immediate bail, or going directly to Newgate.

In this dilemma he sent a messenger to his friend Ratchcali, whose countenance fell when he understood the Count's condition; nor would he open his mouth in the style of consolation, until he had consulted a certain solicitor of his acquaintance, who assured him the law abounded with such resources as would infallibly screen the defendant, had the fact been still more palpable than it was. He said there was great presumption to believe the Count had fallen a sacrifice to a conspiracy, which by some means or other would be detected; and, in that case, the plaintiff might obtain one shilling in lieu of damages. If that dependence should fail, he hinted that, in all probability, the witnesses were not incorruptible; or, should they prove to be so, one man's oath was as good as another's; and, thank Heaven, there was no dearth of evidence, provided money could be found to answer the necessary occasions.

Ratchcali, comforted by these insinuations, and dreading the resentment of our adventurer, who, in his despair, might punish him severely for his want of friendship, by some precipitate explanation of the commerce they had carried on; moved, I say, by these considerations, and moreover tempted with the prospect of continuing to reap the advantages resulting from their conjunction, he and another person of credit with whom he largely dealt in jewels, condescended to become sureties for the appearance of Fathom, who was accordingly admitted to bail. Not but that the Tyrolese knew Ferdinand too well to confide in his parole. He depended chiefly upon his ideas of self-interest, which, he thought, would persuade him to risk the uncertain issue of a trial, rather than quit the field before the harvest was half over; and he was resolved to make his own retreat without ceremony, should our hero be unwise enough to abandon his bail.

Such an adventure could not long lie concealed from the notice of the public, even if both parties had been at pains to suppress the circumstances. But the plaintiff, far from seeking to cover, affected to complain loudly of his misfortune, that he might interest his neighbours in his behalf, and raise a spirit of rancour and animosity, to influence the jury against this insolent foreigner, who had come over into England to debauch our wives and deflower our daughters; while he employed a formidable band of lawyers to support the indictment, which he laid at ten thousand pounds damages.

Meanwhile, Fathom and his associate did not fail to take all proper measures for his defence; they retained a powerful bar of counsel, and the solicitor was supplied with one hundred pounds after another, to answer the expense of secret service; still assuring his clients that everything was in an excellent train, and that his adversary would gain nothing but shame and confusion of face. Nevertheless, there was a necessity for postponing the trial, on account of a material evidence, who, though he wavered, was not yet quite brought over; and the attorney found means to put off the decision from term to term, until there was no quibble left for further delay. While this suit was depending, our hero continued to move in his usual sphere; nor did the report of his situation at all operate to his disadvantage in the polite world; on the contrary, it added a fresh plume to his character, in the eyes of all those who were not before acquainted with the triumphs of his gallantry. Notwithstanding this countenance of his friends, he himself considered the affair in a very serious light; and perceiving that, at any rate, he must be a considerable loser, he resolved to double his assiduity in trade, that he might be the more able to afford the extraordinary expense to which he was subjected.

CHAPTER THIRTY-SEVEN.
FRESH CAUSE FOR EXERTING HIS EQUANIMITY AND FORTITUDE.

The reader may have observed, that Fathom, with all his circumspection, had a weak side, which exposed him to sundry mischances; this was his covetousness, which on some occasions became too hard for his discretion. At this period of time it was, by the circumstances of his situation, inflamed to a degree of rapacity. He was now prevailed upon to take a hand at whist or piquet, and even to wield the hazard-box; though he had hitherto declared himself an irreconcilable enemy to all sorts of play; and so uncommon was his success and dexterity at these exercises, as to surprise his acquaintance, and arouse the suspicion of some people, who repined at his prosperity.

But in nothing was his conduct more inexcusable than in giving way to the dangerous temerity of Ratchcali, which he had been always at pains to restrain, and permitting him to practise the same fraud upon an English nobleman, which had been executed upon himself at Frankfort. In other words, the Tyrolese, by the canal of Ferdinand's finger and recommendation, sold a pebble for a real brilliant, and in a few days the cheat was discovered, to the infinite confusion of our adventurer, who nevertheless assumed the guise of innocence with so much art, and expressed such indignation against the villain who had imposed upon his judgment and unsuspecting generosity, that his lordship acquitted him of any share in the deceit, and contented himself with the restitution, which he insisted upon making out of his own pocket, until he should be able to apprehend the rogue, who had thought proper to abscond for his own safety. In spite of all this exculpation, his character did not fail to retain a sort of stigma, which indeed the plainest proofs of innocence are hardly able to efface; and his connexion with such a palpable knave as the Tyrolese appeared to be, had an effect to his prejudice in the minds of all those who were privy to the occurrence.

When a man's reputation is once brought in question, every trifle is, by the malevolence of mankind, magnified into a strong presumption against the culprit. A few whispers communicated by the envious mouth of slander, which he can have no opportunity to answer and refute, shall, in the opinion of the world, convict him of the most horrid crimes; and for one hypocrite who is decked with the honours of virtue, there are twenty good men who suffer the ignominy of vice; so well disposed are individuals to trample upon the fame of their fellow-creatures. If the most unblemished merit is not protected from this injustice, it will not be wondered at that no quarter was given to the character of an adventurer like Fathom, who, among other unlucky occurrences, had the misfortune to be recognised about this time by his two Parisian friends, Sir Stentor Stile and Sir Giles Squirrel.

These worthy knights-errant had returned to their own country, after having made a very prosperous campaign in France, at the end of which, however, they very narrowly escaped the galleys; and seeing the Polish Count seated at the head of taste and politeness, they immediately circulated the story of his defeat at Paris, with many ludicrous circumstances of their own invention, and did not scruple to affirm that he was a rank impostor. When the laugh is raised upon a great man, he never fails to dwindle into contempt. Ferdinand began to perceive a change in the countenance of his friends. His company was no longer solicited with that eagerness which they had formerly expressed in his behalf. Even his entertainments were neglected; when he appeared at any private or public assembly, the ladies, instead of glowing with pleasure, as formerly, now tittered or regarded him with looks of disdain; and a certain pert, little, forward coquette, with a view to put him out of countenance, by raising the laugh at his expense, asked him one night, at a drum, when he had heard from his relations in Poland? She succeeded in her design upon the mirth of the audience, but was disappointed in the other part of her aim; for our hero replied, without the least mark of discomposure, "They are all in good health at your service, madam; I wish I knew in what part of the world your relations reside, that I might return the compliment." By this answer, which was the more severe, as the young lady was of very doubtful extraction, he retorted the laugh upon the aggressor, though he likewise failed in his attempt upon her temper; for she was perhaps the only person present who equalled himself in stability of countenance.

Notwithstanding this appearance of unconcern, he was deeply touched with these marks of alienation in the behaviour of his friends, and, foreseeing in his own disgrace the total shipwreck of his fortune, he entered into a melancholy deliberation with himself about the means of retrieving his importance in the beau monde, or of turning his address into some other channel, where he could stand upon a less slippery foundation. In this exercise of his thoughts, no scheme occurred more feasible than that of securing the booty he had made, and retiring with his associate, who was also blown, into some other country, where their names and characters being unknown, they might pursue their old plan of commerce without molestation. He imparted this suggestion to the Tyrolese, who approved the proposal of decamping, though he combated with all his might our hero's inclination to withdraw himself before the trial, by repeating the assurances of the solicitor, who told him he might depend upon being reimbursed by the sentence of the court for great part of the sums he had expended in the course of the prosecution.

Fathom suffered himself to be persuaded by these arguments, supported with the desire of making an honourable retreat, and, waiting patiently for the day of trouble, discharged his sureties, by a personal appearance in court. Yet this was not the only score he discharged that morning; the solicitor presented his own bill before they set out for Westminster Hall, and gave the Count to understand that it was the custom, from time immemorial, for the client to clear with his attorney before trial. Ferdinand had nothing to object against this established rule, though he looked upon it as a bad omen, in spite of all the solicitor's confidence and protestations; and he was not a little confounded, when, looking into the contents, he found himself charged with 350 attendances. He knew it was not his interest to disoblige his lawyer at such a juncture; nevertheless, he could not help expostulating with him on this article, which seemed to be so falsely stated with regard to the number; when his questions drew on an explanation, by which he found he had incurred the penalty of three shillings and fourpence for every time he chanced to meet the conscientious attorney, either in the park, the coffee-house, or the street, provided they had exchanged the common salutation; and he had good reason to believe the solicitor had often thrown himself in his way, with a view to swell this item of his account.

With this extortion our adventurer was fain to comply, because he lay at the mercy of the caitiff; accordingly, he with a good grace paid the demand, which, including his former disbursements, amounted to three hundred and sixty-five pounds eleven shillings and threepence three farthings, and then presenting himself before the judge, quietly submitted to the laws of the realm. His counsel behaved like men of consummate abilities in their profession; they exerted themselves with equal industry, eloquence, and erudition, in their endeavours to perplex the truth, browbeat the evidence, puzzle the judge, and mislead the jury; but the defendant found himself wofully disappointed in the deposition of Trapwell's journeyman, whom the solicitor pretended to have converted to his interest. This witness, as the attorney afterwards declared, played booty, and the facts came out so clear, that Ferdinand Count Fathom was convicted of criminal conversation with the plaintiff's wife, and cast in fifteen hundred pounds, under the denomination of damages.

He was not so much surprised as afflicted at this decision, because he saw it gradually approaching from the examination of the first evidence. His thoughts were now employed in casting about for some method of deliverance from the snare in which he found himself entangled. To escape, he foresaw it would be impracticable, as Trapwell would undoubtedly be prepared for arresting him before he could quit Westminster Hall; he was too well acquainted with

Ratchcali's principles, to expect any assistance from that quarter in money matters; and he was utterly averse to the payment of the sum awarded against him, which would have exhausted his whole fortune. He therefore resolved to try the friendship of some persons of fashion, with whom he had maintained an intimacy of correspondence. Should they fail him in the day of his necessity, he proposed to have recourse to his former sureties, one of whom he meant to bilk, while the other might accompany him in his retreat; or, should both these expedients miscarry, he determined, rather than part with his effects, to undergo the most disagreeable confinement, in hope of obtaining the jailor's connivance at his escape.

These resolutions being taken, he met his fate with great fortitude and equanimity, and calmly suffered himself to be conveyed to the house of a sheriff's officer, who, as he made his exit from the hall, according to his own expectation, executed a writ against him, at the suit of Trapwell, for a debt of two thousand pounds. To this place he was followed by his solicitor, who was allured by the prospect of another job, and who, with great demonstrations of satisfaction, congratulated him upon the happy issue of the trial; arrogating to himself the merit of having saved him eight thousand pounds in the article of damages, by the previous steps he had taken, and the noble defence that he and his friends the counsel had made for their client; he even hinted an expectation of receiving a gratuity for his extraordinary care and discretion.

Fathom, galled as he was with his misfortune, and enraged at the effrontery of this pettifogger, maintained a serenity of countenance, and sent the attorney with a message to the plaintiff, importing, that, as he was a foreigner, and could not be supposed to have so much cash about him, as to spare fifteen hundred pounds from the funds of his ordinary expense, he would grant him a bond payable in two months, during which period he should be able to procure a proper remittance from his own estate. While the solicitor was employed in this negotiation, he despatched his valet-de-chambre to one nobleman, and Maurice to another, with billets, signifying the nature of the verdict which his adversary had obtained, and desiring that each would lend him a thousand pounds upon his parole, until he could negotiate bills upon the Continent.

His three messengers returned almost at the same instant of time, and these were the answers they brought back.

Trapwell absolutely rejected his personal security; and threatened him with all the horrors of a jail, unless he would immediately discharge the debt, or procure sufficient bondsmen; and one of his quality friends favoured him with this reply to his request:—

"MY DEAR COUNT!

I am mortally chagrined at the triumph you have furnished to that rascally citizen. By the lard! the judge must have been in the terrors of cuckoldom, to influence the decision; and the jury a mere herd of horned beasts, to bring in such a barbarous verdict. Egad! at this rate, no gentleman will be able to lie with another man's wife, but at the risk of a cursed prosecution. But to waive this disagreeable circumstance, which you must strive to forget; I declare my mortification is still the greater, because I cannot at present supply you with the trifle your present exigency requires; for, to tell you a secret, my own finances are in damnable confusion. But a man of Count Fathom's figure and address can never be puzzled for the want of such a paltry sum. Adieu, my dear Count! we shall, I suppose, have the pleasure of seeing you to-morrow at White's: meanwhile, I have the honour to be, with the most perfect attachment,

yours, GRIZZLEGRIN."

The other noble peer, to whom he addressed himself on this occasion, cherished the same sentiments of virtue, friendship, and generosity; but his expression was so different, that we shall, for the edification of the reader, transcribe his letter in his own words:—

"SIR,

I was never more astonished than at the receipt of your very extraordinary billet, wherein you solicit the loan of a thousand pounds, which you desire may be sent with the bearer on the faith of your parole. Sir, I have no money to send you or lend you; and cannot help repeating my expressions of surprise at your confidence in making such a strange and unwarranted demand. 'Tis true, I may have made professions of friendship, while I looked upon you as a person of honour and good morals; but now that you are convicted of such a flagrant violation of the laws of that kingdom where you have been treated with such hospitality and respect, I think myself fully absolved from any such conditional promise, which indeed is never interpreted into any other than a bare compliment. I am sorry you have involved your character and fortune in such a disagreeable affair, and am,

Sir, yours, etc.
TROMPINGTON."

Ferdinand was not such a novice in the world as to be disappointed at these repulses; especially as he had laid very little stress upon the application, which was made by way of an experiment upon the gratitude or caprice of those two noblemen, whom he had actually more than once obliged with the same sort of assistance which he now solicited, though not to such a considerable amount.

Having nothing further to expect from the fashionable world, he sent the Tyrolese to the person who had been bail for his appearance, with full instructions to explain his present occasion in the most favourable light, and desire he would reinforce the credit of the Count with his security; but that gentleman, though he placed the most perfect confidence on the honour of our hero, and would have willingly entered into bonds again for his personal appearance, was not quite so well satisfied of his circumstances, as to become liable for the payment of two thousand pounds, an expense which, in his opinion, the finances of no foreign Count were able to defray. He therefore lent a deaf ear to the most pressing remonstrances of the ambassador, who had recourse to several other merchants, with the same bad success; so that the prisoner, despairing of bail, endeavoured to persuade Ratchcali, that it would be his interest to contribute a thousand pounds towards his discharge, that he might be enabled to quit England with a good grace, and execute his part of the plan they had projected.

So powerful was his eloquence on the occasion, and such strength of argument did he use, that even the Tyrolese seemed convinced, though reluctantly, and agreed to advance the necessary sum upon the bond and judgment of our adventurer, who, being disabled from transacting his own affairs in person, was obliged to intrust Ratchcali with his keys, papers, and power of attorney, under the check and inspection of his faithful Maurice and the solicitor, whose fidelity he bespoke with the promise of an ample recompense.

CHAPTER THIRTY-EIGHT.
THE BITER IS BIT.

Yet, he had no sooner committed his effects to the care of this triumvirate, than his fancy was visited with direful warnings, which produced cold sweats and palpitations, and threw him into such agonies of apprehension as he had never known before. He remembered the former desertion of the Tyrolese, the recent villany of the solicitor, and recollected the remarks he had made upon the disposition and character of his valet, which evinced him a fit companion for the other two.

Alarmed at these reflections, he entreated the bailiff to indulge him with a visit to his own lodgings, and even offered one hundred guineas as a gratification for his compliance. But the officer, who had formerly lost a considerable sum by the escape of a prisoner, would not run any risk in an affair of such consequence, and our hero was obliged to submit to the tortures of his own presaging fears. After he had waited five hours in the most racking impatience, he saw the attorney enter with all the marks of hurry, fatigue, and consternation, and heard him exclaim, "Good God, have you seen the gentleman?"

Fathom found his fears realised in this interrogation, to which he answered in a tone of horror and dismay, "What gentleman? I suppose I am robbed. Speak, and keep me no longer in suspense." "Robbed!" cried the attorney, "the Lord forbid! I hope you can depend upon the person you empowered to receive your jewels and cash? I must own his proceedings are a little extraordinary; for after he had rummaged your scrutoire, from which, in presence of me and your servant, he took one hundred and fifty guineas, a parcel of diamond rings and buckles, according to this here inventory, which I wrote with my own hand, and East India bonds to the tune of five hundred more, we adjourned to Garraway's, where he left me alone, under pretence of going to a broker of his acquaintance who lived in the neighbourhood, while the valet, as I imagined, waited for us in the alley. Well, sir, he stayed so long, that I began to be uneasy, and at length resolved to send the servant in quest of him, but when I went out for that purpose, deuce a servant was to be found; though I in person inquired for him at every alehouse within half a mile of the place. I then despatched no less than five ticket porters upon the scent after them, and I myself, by a direction from the bar-keeper, went to Signior Ratchcali's lodgings, where, as they told me, he had not been seen since nine o'clock in the morning. Upon this intimation, I came directly hither, to give you timely notice, that you may without delay take measures for your own security. The best thing you can do, is to take out writs for apprehending him, in the counties of Middlesex, Surrey, Kent, and Essex, and I shall put them in the hands of trusty and diligent officers, who will soon ferret him out of his lurking-place, provided he skulks within ten miles of the bills of mortality. To be sure, the job will be expensive; and all these runners must be paid beforehand. But what then? the defendant is worth powder, and if we can once secure him, I'll warrant the prosecution will quit cost."

Fathom was almost choked with concern and resentment at the news of this mischance, so that he could not utter one word until this narrative was finished. Nor was his suspicion confined to the Tyrolese and his own lacquey; he considered the solicitor as their accomplice and director, and was so much provoked at the latter part of his harangue, that his discretion seemed to vanish, and, collaring the attorney, "Villain!" said he, "you yourself have been a principal actor in this robbery." Then turning to the bystanders, "and I desire in the King's name that he may be secured, until I can make oath before a magistrate in support of the charge. If you refuse your assistance in detaining him, I will make immediate application to one of the secretaries of state, who is my particular friend, and he will see justice done to all parties."

At mention of this formidable name, the bailiff and his whole family were in commotion, to obstruct the retreat of the lawyer, who stood aghast and trembled under the grasp of our adventurer. But, soon as he found himself delivered from this embrace, by the interposition of the spectators, and collected his spirits, which had been suddenly dissipated by Fathom's unexpected assault, he began to display one art of his occupation, which he always reserved for extraordinary occasions. This was the talent of abuse, which he poured forth with such fluency of opprobrious language, that our hero, smarting as he was, and almost desperate with his loss, deviated from that temperance of behaviour which he had hitherto preserved, and snatching up the poker, with one stroke opened a deep trench upon the attorney's skull, that extended from the hind head almost to the upper part of the nose, upon each side of which it discharged a sanguine stream. Notwithstanding the pain of this application, the solicitor was transported with joy at the sense of the smart, and inwardly congratulated himself upon the appearance of his own blood, which he no sooner perceived, than he exclaimed, "I'm a dead man," and fell upon the floor at full length.

Immediate recourse was had to a surgeon in the neighbourhood, who, having examined the wound, declared there was a dangerous depression of the first table of the skull, and that, if he could save the patient's life without the application of the trepan, it would be one of the greatest cures that ever were performed. By this time, Fathom's first transport being overblown, he summoned up his whole resolution, and reflected upon his own ruin with that fortitude which had never failed him in the emergencies of his fate. Little disturbed at the prognostic of the surgeon, which he considered in the right point of view; "Sir," said he, "I am not so unacquainted with the resistance of an attorney's skull, as to believe the chastisement I have bestowed on him will at all endanger his life, which is in much greater jeopardy from the hands of the common executioner. For, notwithstanding this accident, I am determined to prosecute the rascal for robbery with the utmost severity of the law; and, that I may have a sufficient fund left for that prosecution, I shall not at present throw away one farthing in unnecessary expense, but insist upon being conveyed to prison without farther delay."

This declaration was equally unwelcome to the bailiff, surgeon, and solicitor, who, upon the supposition that the Count was a person of fortune, and would rather part with an immense sum than incur the ignominy of a jail, or involve himself in another disgraceful lawsuit, had resolved to fleece him to the utmost of their power. But, now the attorney finding him determined to set his fate at defiance, and to retort upon him a prosecution, which he had no design to undergo, began to repent heartily of the provocation he had given, and to think seriously on some method to overcome the obstinacy of the incensed foreigner. With this view, while the bailiff conducted him to bed in another apartment, he desired the catchpole to act the part of mediator between him and the Count, and furnished him with proper instructions for that purpose. Accordingly the landlord, on his return, told Fathom that he was sure the solicitor was not a man for this world; for that he had left him deprived of his senses, and praying to God with great devotion for mercy to his murderer. He then exhorted him, with many protestations of friendship, to compromise the unhappy affair by exchanging releases with the attorney before his delirium should be known, otherwise he would bring himself into a most dangerous premunire, whether the plaintiff should die of his wound, or live to prosecute him for assault. "And with regard to your charge of robbery against him," said he, "as it is no more than a base suspicion, unsupported by the least shadow of evidence, the bill would be thrown out, and then he might sue you for damages. I therefore, out of pure friendship and good-nature, advise you to compromise the affair, and, if you think proper, will endeavour to bring about a mutual release."

Our hero, whose passion was by this time pretty well cooled, saw reason for assenting to the proposal; upon which the deed was immediately executed, the mediator's bill was discharged, and Ferdinand conveyed in an hackney-coach to prison, after he had empowered his own landlord to discharge his servants, and convert his effects into ready money. Thus, he saw himself, in the course of a few hours, deprived of his reputation, rank, liberty, and friends; and his fortune reduced from two thousand pounds to something less than two hundred, fifty of which he had carried to jail in his pocket.

END OF VOL. I.

BY TOBIAS SMOLLETT

PART II.

With the Author's Preface, and an Introduction by G. H. Maynadier, Ph.D. Department of English, Harvard University.

CHAPTER THIRTY-NINE.
OUR ADVENTURER IS MADE ACQUAINTED WITH A NEW SCENE OF LIFE.

Just as he entered these mansions of misery, his ears were invaded with a hoarse and dreadful voice, exclaiming, "You, Bess Beetle, score a couple of fresh eggs, a pennyworth of butter, and half a pint of mountain to the king; and stop credit till the bill is paid:—He is now debtor for fifteen shillings and sixpence, and d—n me if I trust him one farthing more, if he was the best king in Christendom. And, d'ye hear, send Ragged-head with five pounds of potatoes for Major Macleaver's supper, and let him have what drink he wants; the fat widow gentlewoman from Pimlico has promised to quit his score. Sir Mungo Barebones may have some hasty pudding and small beer, though I don't expect to see his coin, no more than to receive the eighteen pence I laid out for a pair of breeches to his backside—what then? he's a quiet sort of a body, and a great scholar, and it was a scandal to the place to see him going about in that naked condition. As for the mad Frenchman with the beard, if you give him so much as a cheese-paring, you b—ch, I'll send you back to the hole, among your old companions; an impudent dog! I'll teach him to draw his sword upon the governor of an English county jail. What! I suppose he thought he had to do with a French hang-tang-dang, rabbit him! he shall eat his white feather, before I give him credit for a morsel of bread."

Although our adventurer was very little disposed, at this juncture, to make observations foreign to his own affairs, he could not help taking notice of these extraordinary injunctions; especially those concerning the person who was entitled king, whom, however, he supposed to be some prisoner elected as the magistrate by the joint suffrage of his fellows. Having taken possession of his chamber, which he rented at five shillings a week, and being ill at ease in his own thoughts, he forthwith secured his door, undressed, and went to bed, in which, though it was none of the most elegant or inviting couches, he enjoyed profound repose after the accumulated fatigues and mortifications of the day. Next morning, after breakfast, the keeper entered his apartment, and gave him to understand, that the gentlemen under his care, having heard of the Count's arrival, had deputed one of their number to wait upon him with the compliments of condolence suitable to the occasion, and invite him to become a member of their society. Our hero could not politely dispense with this instance of civility, and their ambassador being instantly introduced by the name of Captain Minikin, saluted him with great solemnity.

This was a person equally remarkable for his extraordinary figure and address; his age seemed to border upon forty, his stature amounted to five feet, his visage was long, meagre, and weather-beaten, and his aspect, though not quite rueful, exhibited a certain formality, which was the result of care and conscious importance. He was very little encumbered with flesh and blood; yet what body he had was well proportioned, his limbs were elegantly turned, and by his carriage he was well entitled to that compliment which we pay to any person when we say he has very much the air of a gentleman. There was also an evident singularity in his dress, which, though intended as an improvement, appeared to be an extravagant exaggeration of the mode, and at once evinced him an original to the discerning eyes of our adventurer, who received him with his usual complaisance, and made a very eloquent acknowledgment of the honour and satisfaction he received from the visit of the representative, and the hospitality of his constituents. The captain's peculiarities were not confined to his external appearance; for his voice resembled the sound of a bassoon, or the aggregate hum of a whole bee-hive, and his discourse was almost nothing else than a series of quotations from the English poets, interlarded with French phrases, which he retained for their significance, on the recommendation of his friends, being himself unacquainted with that or any other outlandish tongue.

Fathom, finding this gentleman of a very communicative disposition, thought he could not have a fairer opportunity of learning the history of his fellow-prisoners; and, turning the conversation on that subject, was not disappointed in his expectation. "I don't doubt, sir," said he, with the utmost solemnity of declamation, "but you look with horror upon every object that surrounds you in this uncomfortable place; but, nevertheless, here are some, who, as my friend Shakespeare has it, have seen better days, and have with holy bell been knolled to church; and sat at good men's feasts, and wiped their eyes of drops that sacred pity hath engendered. You must know, sir, that, exclusive of the canaille, or the profanum vulgus, as they are styled by Horace, there are several small communities in the jail, consisting of people who are attracted by the manners and dispositions of each other; for this place, sir, is quite a microcosm, and as the great world, so is this, a stage, and all the men and women merely players. For my own part, sir, I have always made it a maxim to associate with the best of company I can find. Not that I pretend to boast of my family or extraction; because, you know, as the poet says, Vix ea nostra voco. My father, 'tis true, was a man that piqued himself upon his pedigree, as well as upon his politesse and personal merit; for he had been a very old officer in the army, and I myself may say I was born with a spontoon in my hand. Sir, I have had the honour to serve his Majesty these twenty years, and have been bandied about in the course of duty through all the British plantations, and you see the recompense of all my service. But this is a disagreeable subject, and therefore I shall waive it; however, as Butler observes:

> My only comfort is, that now
> My dubbolt fortune is so low,
> That either it must quickly end,
> Or turn about again and mend.

"And now, to return from this digression, you will perhaps be surprised to hear that the head or chairman of our club is really a sovereign prince; no less, I'll assure you, than the celebrated Theodore king of Corsica, who lies in prison for a debt of a few hundred pounds. Heu! quantum mutatus ab illo. It is not my business to censure the conduct of my superiors; but I always speak my mind in a cavalier manner, and as, according to the Spectator, talking to a friend is no more than thinking aloud, entre nous, his Corsican majesty has been scurvily treated by a certain administration. Be that as it will, he is a personage of a very portly appearance, and is quite master of the bienseance. Besides, they will find it their interest to have recourse again to his alliance; and in that case some of us may expect to profit by his restoration. But few words are best.

"He that maintains the second rank in our assembly is one Major Macleaver, an Irish gentleman, who has served abroad; a soldier of fortune, sir, a man of unquestionable honour and courage, but a little overbearing, in consequence of his knowledge and experience. He is a person of good address,—to be sure, and quite free of the mauvaise honte, and he may have seen a good deal of service. But what then? other people may be as good as he, though they have not had such opportunities; if he speaks five or six languages, he does not pretend to any taste in the liberal arts, which are the criterion of an accomplished gentleman.

"The next is Sir Mungo Barebones, the representative of a very ancient family in the north; his affairs are very much deranged, but he is a gentleman of great probity and learning, and at present engaged in a very grand scheme, which, if he can bring it to bear, will render him famous to all posterity; no less than the conversion of the Jews and the Gentiles. The project, I own, looks chimerical to one who has not conversed with the author; but, in my opinion, he has clearly demonstrated, from an anagrammatical analysis of a certain Hebrew word, that his present Majesty, whom God preserve, is the person pointed at in Scripture as the temporal Messiah of the Jews; and, if he could once raise by subscription such a trifling sum as twelve hundred thousand pounds, I make no doubt but he would accomplish his aim, vast and romantic as it seems to be.

"Besides these, we have another messmate, who is a French chevalier, an odd sort of a man, a kind of Lazarillo de Tormes, a caricatura; he wears a long beard, pretends to be a great poet, and makes a d—-ed fracas with his verses.

The king has been obliged to exert his authority over him more than once, by ordering him into close confinement, for which he was so rash as to send his majesty a challenge; but he afterwards made his submission, and was again taken into favour. The truth is, I believe his brain is a little disordered, and, he being a stranger, we overlook his extravagancies.

"Sir, we shall think ourselves happy in your accession to our society. You will be under no sort of restraint; for, though we dine at one table, every individual calls and pays for his own mess. Our conversation, such as it is, will not, I hope, be disagreeable; and though we have not opportunities of breathing the pure Arcadian air, and cannot, 'under the shade of melancholy boughs, lose and neglect the creeping hours of time,' we may enjoy ourselves over a glass of punch or a dish of tea. Nor are we destitute of friends, who visit us in these shades of distress. The major has a numerous acquaintance of both sexes; among others, a first cousin of good fortune, who, with her daughters, often cheer our solitude; she is a very sensible ladylike gentlewoman, and the young ladies have a certain degagee air, that plainly shows they have seen the best company. Besides, I will venture to recommend Mrs. Minikin as a woman of tolerable breeding and capacity, who, I hope, will not be found altogether deficient in the accomplishments of the sex. So that we find means to make little parties, in which the time glides away insensibly. Then I have a small collection of books which are at your service. You may amuse yourself with Shakespeare, or Milton, or Don Quixote, or any of our modern authors that are worth reading, such as the Adventures of Loveill, Lady Frail, George Edwards, Joe Thompson, Bampfylde Moore Carew, Young Scarron, and Miss Betsy Thoughtless; and if you have a taste for drawing, I can entertain you with a parcel of prints by the best masters."

A man of our hero's politeness could not help expressing himself in the warmest terms of gratitude for this courteous declaration. He thanked the captain in particular for his obliging offers, and begged he would be so good as to present his respects to the society, of which he longed to be a member. It was determined, therefore, that Minikin should return in an hour, when the Count would be dressed, in order to conduct him into the presence of his majesty; and he had already taken his leave for the present, when all of a sudden he came back, and taking hold of a waistcoat that lay upon a chair, "Sir," said he, "give me leave to look at that fringe; I think it is the most elegant knitting I ever saw. But pray, sir, are not these quite out of fashion? I thought plain silk, such as this that I wear, had been the mode, with the pockets very low." Before Fathom had time to make any sort of reply, he took notice of his hat and pumps; the first of which, he said, was too narrow in the brims, and the last an inch too low in the heels. Indeed, they formed a remarkable contrast with his own; for, exclusive of the fashion of the cock, which resembled the form of a Roman galley, the brim of his hat, if properly spread, would have projected a shade sufficient to shelter a whole file of musketeers from the heat of a summer's sun; and the heels of his shoes were so high as to raise his feet three inches at least from the surface of the earth.

Having made these observations, for the credit of his taste, he retired, and returning at the time appointed, accompanied Ferdinand to the apartment of the king, at the doors of which their ears were invaded with a strange sound, being that of a human voice imitating the noise of a drum. The captain, hearing this alarm, made a full stop, and, giving the Count to understand that his majesty was busy, begged he would not take it amiss, if the introduction should be delayed for a few moments. Fathom, curious to know the meaning of what he had heard, applied to his guide for information, and learned that the king and the major, whom he had nominated to the post of his general-in-chief, were employed in landing troops upon the Genoese territory; that is, that they were settling beforehand the manner of their disembarkation.

He then, by the direction of his conductor, reconnoitred them through the keyhole, and perceived the sovereign and his minister sitting on opposite sides of a deal board table, covered with a large chart or map, upon which he saw a great number of mussel and oyster shells ranged in a certain order, and, at a little distance, several regular squares and columns made of cards cut in small pieces. The prince himself, whose eyes were reinforced by spectacles, surveyed this armament with great attention, while the general put the whole in action, and conducted their motions by beat of drum. The mussel-shells, according to Minikin's explanation, represented the transports, the oyster-shells were considered as the men-of-war that covered the troops in landing, and the pieces of card exhibited the different bodies into which the army was formed upon its disembarkation.

As an affair of such consequence could not be transacted without opposition, they had provided divers ambuscades, consisting of the enemy, whom they represented by grey peas; and accordingly General Macleaver, perceiving the said grey peas marching along shore to attack his forces before they could be drawn up in battalia, thus addressed himself to the oyster-shells, in an audible voice:—"You men-of-war, don't you see the front of the enemy advancing, and the rest of the detachment following out of sight? Arrah! the devil burn you, why don't you come ashore and open your batteries?" So saying, he pushed the shells towards the breach, performed the cannonading with his voice, the grey peas were soon put in confusion, the general was beat, the cards marched forwards in order of battle, and the enemy having retreated with great precipitation, they took possession of their ground without farther difficulty.

CHAPTER FORTY.
HE CONTEMPLATES MAJESTY AND ITS SATELLITES IN ECLIPSE.

This expedition being happily finished, General Macleaver put the whole army, navy, transports, and scene of action into a canvas bag, the prince unsaddled his nose, and Captain Minikin being admitted, our hero was introduced in form. Very gracious was the reception he met with from his majesty, who, with a most princely demeanour, welcomed him to court, and even seated him on his right hand, in token of particular regard. True it is, this presence-chamber was not so superb, nor the appearance of the king so magnificent, as to render such an honour intoxicating to any person of our hero's coolness and discretion. In lieu of tapestry, the apartment was hung with halfpenny ballads, a trucklebed without curtains supplied the place of a canopy, and instead of a crown his majesty wore a woollen night-cap. Yet, in spite of these disadvantages, there was an air of dignity in his deportment, and a nice physiognomist would have perceived something majestic in the features of his countenance.

He was certainly a personage of very prepossessing mien; his manners were engaging, his conversation agreeable, and any man whose heart was subject to the meltings of humanity would have deplored his distress, and looked upon him as a most pathetic instance of that miserable reverse to which all human grandeur is exposed. His fall was even greater than that of Belisarius, who, after having obtained many glorious victories over the enemies of his country, is said to have been reduced to such extremity of indigence, that, in his old age, when he was deprived of his eyesight, he sat upon the highway like a common mendicant, imploring the charity of passengers in the piteous exclamation of Date obolum Belisario; that is, "Spare a farthing to your poor old soldier Belisarius." I say, this general's disgrace was not so remarkable as that of Theodore, because he was the servant of Justinian, consequently his fortune depended upon the nod of that emperor; whereas the other actually possessed the throne of sovereignty by the best of all titles, namely, the unanimous election of the people over whom he reigned; and attracted the eyes of all Europe, by the efforts he made in breaking the bands of oppression, and vindicating that liberty which is the birthright of man.

The English of former days, alike renowned for generosity and valour, treated those hostile princes, whose fate it was to wear their chains, with such delicacy of benevolence, as even dispelled the horrors of captivity; but their posterity of this refined age feel no compunction at seeing an unfortunate monarch, their former friend, ally, and partisan, languish amidst the miseries of a loathsome jail, for a paltry debt contracted in their own service. But, moralising apart, our hero had not long conversed with this extraordinary debtor, who in his present condition assumed no other title than that of Baron, than he perceived in him a spirit of Quixotism, which all his experience, together with the vicissitudes of his fortune, had not been able to overcome. Not that his ideas soared to such a pitch of extravagant hope as that which took possession of his messmates, who frequently quarrelled one with another about the degrees of favour to which they should be entitled after the king's restoration; but he firmly believed that affairs would speedily take such a turn in Italy, as would point out to the English court the expediency of employing him again; and his persuasion seemed to support him against every species of poverty and mortification.

While they were busy in trimming the balance of power on the other side of the Alps, their deliberations were interrupted by the arrival of a scullion, who came to receive their orders touching the bill of fare for dinner, and his majesty found much more difficulty in settling this important concern, than in compromising all the differences between the Emperor and the Queen of Spain. At length, however, General Macleaver undertook the office of purveyor for his prince; Captain Minikin insisted upon treating the Count; and in a little time the table was covered with a cloth, which, for the sake of my delicate readers, I will not attempt to describe.

At this period they were joined by Sir Mungo Barebones, who, having found means to purchase a couple of mutton chops, had cooked a mess of broth, which he now brought in a saucepan to the general rendezvous. This was the most remarkable object which had hitherto presented itself to the eyes of Fathom. Being naturally of a meagre habit, he was, by indigence and hard study, wore almost to the bone, and so bended towards the earth, that in walking his body described at least 150 degrees of a circle. The want of stockings and shoes he supplied with a jockey straight boot and an half jack. His thighs and middle were cased in a monstrous pair of brown trunk breeches, which the keeper bought for his use from the executor of a Dutch seaman who had lately died in the jail. His shirt retained no signs of its original colour, his body was shrouded in an old greasy tattered plaid nightgown; a blue and white handkerchief surrounded his head, and his looks betokened that immense load of care which he had voluntarily incurred for the eternal salvation of sinners. Yet this figure, uncouth as it was, made his compliments to our adventurer in terms of the most elegant address, and, in the course of conversation, disclosed a great fund of valuable knowledge. He had appeared in the great world, and borne divers offices of dignity and trust with universal applause. His courage was undoubted, his morals were unimpeached, and his person held in great veneration and esteem; when his evil genius engaged him in the study of Hebrew, and the mysteries of the Jewish religion, which fairly disordered his brain, and rendered him incapable of managing his temporal affairs. When he ought to have been employed in the functions of his post, he was always wrapt in visionary conferences with Moses on the Mount; rather than regulate the economy of his household, he chose to exert his endeavours in settling the precise meaning of the word Elohim; and having discovered that now the period was come, when the Jews and Gentiles would be converted, he postponed every other consideration, in order to facilitate that great and glorious event.

By this time Ferdinand had seen every member of the club, except the French chevalier, who seemed to be quite neglected by the society; for his name was not once mentioned during this communication, and they sat down to dinner, without asking whether he was dead or alive. The king regaled himself with a plate of ox-cheek; the major, who complained that his appetite had forsaken him, amused himself with some forty hard eggs, malaxed with salt butter; the knight indulged upon his soup and bouilli, and the captain entertained our adventurer with a neck of veal roasted with potatoes; but before Fathom could make use of his knife and fork, he was summoned to the door, where he found the chevalier in great agitation, his eyes sparkling like coals of fire.

Our hero was not a little surprised at this apparition, who, having asked pardon for the freedom he had used, observed, that, understanding the Count was a foreigner, he could not dispense with appealing to him concerning an outrage he had suffered from the keeper, who, without any regard to his rank or misfortunes, had been base enough to refuse him credit for a few necessaries, until he could have a remittance from his steward in France; he therefore conjured Count Fathom, as a stranger and nobleman like himself, to be the messenger of defiance, which he resolved to send to that brutal jailor, that, for the future, he might learn to make proper distinctions in the exercise of his function.

Fathom, who had no inclination to offend this choleric Frenchman, assured him that he might depend upon his friendship; and, in the meantime, prevailed upon him to accept of a small supply, in consequence of which he procured a pound of sausages, and joined the rest of the company without delay; making a very suitable addition to such an assemblage of rarities. Though his age did not exceed thirty years, his beard, which was of a brindled hue, flowed down, like Aaron's, to his middle. Upon his legs he wore red stockings rolled up over the joint of the knee, his breeches were of blue drab, with vellum button-holes, and garters of gold lace, his waistcoat of scarlet, his coat of rusty black cloth, his hair, twisted into a ramilie, hung down to his rump, of the colour of jet, and his hat was adorned with a white feather.

This original had formed many ingenious schemes to increase the glory and grandeur of France, but was discouraged by Cardinal Fleury, who, in all appearance, jealous of his great talents, not only rejected his projects, but even sent him to prison, on pretence of being offended at his impertinence. Perceiving that, like the prophet, he had no honour in his own country, he no sooner obtained his release, than he retired to England, where he was prompted by his philanthropy to propose an expedient to our ministry, which would have saved a vast effusion of blood and treasure; this was an agreement between the Queen of Hungary and the late Emperor, to decide their pretensions by a single combat; in which case he offered himself as the Bavarian champion; but in this endeavour he also proved unsuccessful. Then turning his attention to the delights of poetry, he became so enamoured of the muse, that he neglected every other consideration, and she as usual gradually conducted him to the author's never-failing goal—a place of rest appointed for all those sinners whom the profane love of poesy hath led astray.

CHAPTER FORTY-ONE.
ONE QUARREL IS COMPROMISED, AND ANOTHER DECIDED BY UNUSUAL ARMS.

Among other topics of conversation that were discussed at this genial meeting, Sir Mungo's scheme was brought upon the carpet by his majesty, who was graciously pleased to ask how his subscription filled? To this interrogation the knight answered, that he met with great opposition from a spirit of levity and self-conceit, which seemed to prevail in this generation, but that no difficulties should discourage him from persevering in his duty; and he trusted in God, that, in a very little time, he should be able to confute and overthrow the false philosophy of the moderns, and to restore the writings of Moses to that pre-eminence and veneration which is due to an inspired author. He spoke of the immortal Newton with infinite contempt, and undertook to extract from the Pentateuch a system of chronology which would ascertain the progress of time since the fourth day of the creation to the present hour, with such exactness, that not one vibration of a pendulum should be lost; nay, he affirmed that the perfection of all arts and sciences might be attained by studying these secret memoirs, and that he himself did not despair of learning from them the art of transmuting baser metals into gold.

The chevalier, though he did not pretend to contradict these assertions, was too much attached to his own religion to acquiesce in the knight's project of converting the Jews and the Gentiles to the Protestant heresy, which, he said, God Almighty would never suffer to triumph over the interests of his own Holy Catholic Church. This objection produced abundance of altercation between two very unequal disputants; and the Frenchman, finding himself puzzled by the learning of his antagonist, had recourse to the argumentum ad hominem, by laying his hand upon his sword, and declaring that he was ready to lose the last drop of his blood in opposition to such a damnable scheme.

Sir Mungo, though in all appearance reduced to the last stage of animal existence, no sooner heard this epithet applied to his plan, than his eyes gleamed like lightning, he sprung from his seat with the agility of a grasshopper, and, darting himself out at the door like an arrow from a bow, reappeared in a moment with a long rusty weapon, which might have been shown among a collection of rarities as the sword of Guy Earl of Warwick. This implement he brandished over the chevalier's head with the dexterity of an old prize-fighter, exclaiming, in the French language, "Thou art a profane wretch marked out for the vengeance of Heaven, whose unworthy minister I am, and here thou shalt fall by the sword of the Lord and of Gideon."

The chevalier, unterrified by this dreadful salutation, desired he would accompany him to a more convenient place; and the world might have been deprived of one or both these knights-errant, had not General Macleaver, at the desire of his majesty, interposed, and found means to bring matters to an accommodation.

In the afternoon the society was visited by the major's cousin and her daughters, who no sooner appeared than they were recognised by our adventurer, and his acquaintance with them renewed in such a manner as alarmed the delicacy of Captain Minikin, who in the evening repaired to the Count's apartment, and with a formal physiognomy, accosted him in these words: "Sir, I beg pardon for this intrusion, but I come to consult you about an affair in which my honour is concerned; and a soldier without honour, you know, is no better than a body without a soul. I have always admired that speech of Hotspur in the first part of Henry the Fourth:

> By Heaven, methinks it were an easy leap,
> To pluck bright honour from the pale-fac'd moon;
> Or dive into the bottom of the deep,
> Where fathom-line could never touch the ground,
> And pluck up drowned honour by the locks—

"There is a boldness and ease in the expression, and the images are very picturesque. But, without any further preamble, pray, sir, give me leave to ask how long you have been acquainted with those ladies who drank tea with us this afternoon. You'll forgive the question, sir, when I tell you that Major Macleaver introduced Mrs. Minikin to them as to ladies of character, and, I don't know how, sir, I have a sort of presentiment that my wife has been imposed upon. Perhaps I may be mistaken, and God grant I may. But there was a je ne sais quoi in their behaviour to-day, which begins to alarm my suspicion. Sir, I have nothing but my reputation to depend upon, and I hope you will excuse me, when I earnestly beg to know what rank they maintain in life."

Fathom, without minding the consequence, told him, with a simper, that he knew them to be very good-natured ladies, who devoted themselves to the happiness of mankind. This explanation had no sooner escaped from his lips, than the captain's face began to glow with indignation, his eyes seemed bursting from their spheres, he swelled to twice his natural dimensions, and, raising himself on his tiptoes, pronounced, in a strain that emulated thunder, "Blood! sir, you seem to make very light of the matter, but it is no joke to me, I'll assure you, and Macleaver shall see that I am not to be affronted with impunity.

Sir, I shall take it as a singular favour if you will be the bearer of a billet to him, which I shall write in three words; nay, sir, you must give me leave to insist upon it, as you are the only gentleman of our mess whom I can intrust with an affair of this nature."

Fathom, rather than run the risk of disobliging such a punctilious warrior, after having in vain attempted to dissuade him from his purpose, undertook to carry the challenge, which was immediately penned in these words:

"SIR,

You have violated my honour in imposing upon Mrs. Minikin your pretended cousins as ladies of virtue and reputation. I therefore demand such satisfaction as a soldier ought to receive, and expect you will adjust with my friend Count Fathom the terms upon which you shall be met by the much injured

GOLIAH MINIKIN."

This morceau being sealed and directed, was forthwith carried by our adventurer to the lodgings of the major, who had by this time retired to rest, but hearing the Count's voice, he got up and opened the door in cuerpo, to the astonishment of Ferdinand, who had never before seen such an Herculean figure. He made an apology for receiving the Count in his birthday suit, to which he said he was reduced by the heat of his constitution, though he might have assigned a more adequate cause, by owning that his shirt was in the hands of his washerwoman; then shrouding himself in a blanket, desired to know what had procured him the honour of such an extraordinary visit. He read the letter with great composure, like a man accustomed to such intercourse; then addressing himself to the bearer, "I will be after diverting the gentleman," said he, "in any manner he shall think proper; but, by Jesus, this is no place for such amusements, because, as you well know, my dear Count, if both should be killed by the chance of war, neither of us will be able to escape, and after the breath is out of his body, he will make but a sorry excuse to his family and friends. But that is no concern of mine, and therefore I am ready to please him in his own way."

Fathom approved of his remarks, which he reinforced with sundry considerations, to the same purpose, and begged the assistance of the major's advice, in finding some expedient to terminate the affair without bloodshed, that no troublesome consequences might ensue either to him or to his antagonist, who, in spite of this overstraining formality, seemed to be a person of worth and good-nature. "With all my heart," said the generous Hibernian, "I have a great regard for the little man, and my own character is not to seek at this time of day. I have served a long apprenticeship to fighting, as this same carcase can testify, and if he compels me to run him through the body, by my shoul, I shall do it in a friendly manner."

So saying, he threw aside the blanket, and displayed scars and seams innumerable upon his body, which appeared like an old patched leathern doublet. "I remember," proceeded this champion, "when I was a slave at Algiers, Murphy Macmorris and I happened to have some difference in the bagnio, upon which he bade me turn out. 'Arra, for what?' said I; 'here are no weapons that a gentleman can use, and you would not be such a negro as to box like an English carman.' After he had puzzled himself for some time, he proposed that we should retire into a corner, and funk one another with brimstone, till one of us should give out. Accordingly we crammed half a dozen tobacco pipes with sulphur, and, setting foot to foot, began to smoke, and kept a constant fire, until Macmorris dropped down; then I threw away my pipe, and taking poor Murphy in my arms, 'What, are you dead?' said I; 'if you are dead, speak.' 'No, by Jesus!' cried he, 'I an't dead, but I'm speechless.' So he owned I had obtained the victory, and we were as good friends as ever. Now, if Mr. Minikin thinks proper to put the affair upon the same issue, I will smoke a pipe of brimstone with him to-morrow morning, and if I cry out first, I will be after asking pardon for this supposed affront."

Fathom could not help laughing at the proposal, to which, however, he objected on account of Minikin's delicate constitution, which might suffer more detriment from breathing in an atmosphere of sulphur than from the discharge of a pistol, or the thrust of a small sword. He therefore suggested another expedient in lieu of the sulphur, namely, the gum called assafatida, which, though abundantly nauseous, could have no effect upon the infirm texture of the lieutenant's lungs. This hint being relished by the major, our adventurer returned to his principal, and having repeated the other's arguments against the use of mortal instruments, described the succedaneum which he had concerted with Macleaver. The captain at first believed the scheme was calculated for subjecting him to the ridicule of his fellow-prisoners, and began to storm with great violence; but, by the assurances and address of Fathom, he was at length reconciled to the plan, and preparations were made on each side for this duel, which was actually smoked next day, about noon, in a small closet, detached from the challenger's apartment, and within hearing of his majesty, and all his court, assembled as witnesses and umpires of the contest.

The combatants, being locked up together, began to ply their engines with great fury, and it was not long before Captain Minikin perceived he had a manifest advantage over his antagonist. For his organs were familiarised to the effluvia of this drug, which he had frequently used in the course of an hypochondriac disorder; whereas Macleaver, who was a stranger to all sorts of medicine, by his wry faces and attempts to puke, expressed the utmost abhorrence of the smell that invaded his nostrils. Nevertheless, resolved to hold out to the last extremity, he continued in action until the closet was filled with such an intolerable vapour as discomposed the whole economy of his entrails, and compelled him to disgorge his breakfast in the face of his opponent, whose nerves were so disconcerted by this disagreeable and unforeseen discharge, that he fell back into his chair in a swoon, and the major bellowed aloud for assistance. The door being opened, he ran directly to the window, to inhale the fresh air, while the captain, recovering from his fit, complained of Macleaver's unfair proceeding, and demanded justice of the arbitrators, who decided in his favour; and the major being prevailed upon to ask pardon for having introduced Mrs. Minikin to women of rotten reputation, the parties were reconciled to each other, and peace and concord re-established in the mess.

Fathom acquired universal applause for his discreet and humane conduct upon this occasion; and that same afternoon had an opportunity of seeing the lady in whose cause he had exerted himself. He was presented to her as the husband's particular friend, and when she understood how much she was indebted to his care and concern for the captain's safety, she treated him with uncommon marks of distinction; and he found her a genteel, well-bred woman, not without a good deal of personal charms, and a well-cultivated understanding.

CHAPTER FORTY-TWO.
AN UNEXPECTED RENCONTRE, AND A HAPPY REVOLUTION IN THE AFFAIRS OF OUR ADVENTURER.

As she did not lodge within the precincts of this garrison, she was one day, after tea, conducted to the gate by the captain and the Count, and just as they approached the turnkey's lodge, our hero's eyes were struck with the apparition of his old companion Renaldo, son of his benefactor and patron, the Count de Melvil. What were the emotions of his soul, when he saw that young gentleman enter the prison, and advance towards him, after having spoke to the jailor! He never doubted that, being informed of his confinement, he was come to upbraid him with his villany and ingratitude, and he in vain endeavoured to recollect himself from that terror and guilty confusion which his appearance had inspired; when the stranger, lifting up his eyes, started back with signs of extreme amazement, and, after a considerable pause, exclaimed, "Heaven and earth! Sure my eyes do not deceive me! is not your name Fathom? It is, it must be my old friend and companion, the loss of whom I have so long regretted!" With these words he ran towards our adventurer, and, while he clasped him in his arms with all the eagerness of affection, protested that this was one of the happiest days he had ever seen.

Ferdinand, who, from this salutation, concluded himself still in possession of Renaldo's good opinion, was not deficient in expressions of tenderness and joy; he returned his embraces with equal ardour, the tears trickled down his cheeks, and that perturbation which proceeded from conscious perfidy and fear, was mistaken by the unsuspecting Hungarian for the sheer effects of love, gratitude, and surprise. These first transports having subsided, they adjourned to the lodgings of Fathom, who soon recollected his spirits and invention so well as to amuse the other with a feigned tale of his having been taken by the French, sent prisoner into Champagne, from whence he had written many letters to Count Melvil and his son, of whom he could hear no tidings; of his having contracted an intimacy with a young nobleman of France, who died in the flower of his age, after having, in token of his friendship, bequeathed to him a considerable legacy; by this he had been enabled to visit the land of his forefathers in the character of a gentleman, which he had supported with some figure, until he was betrayed into a misfortune that exhausted his funds, and drove him to the spot where he was now found. And he solemnly declared, that, far from forgetting the obligation he owed to Count Melvil, or renouncing the friendship of Renaldo, he had actually resolved to set out for Germany on his return to the house of his patron in the beginning of the week posterior to that in which he had been arrested.

Young Melvil, whose own heart had never known the instigations of fraud, implicitly believed the story and protestations of Fathom; and though he would not justify that part of his conduct by which the term of his good fortune was abridged, he could not help excusing an indiscretion into which he had been hurried by the precipitancy of youth, and the allurements of an artful woman. Nay, with the utmost warmth of friendship, he undertook to wait upon Trapwell, and endeavour to soften him into some reasonable terms of composition.

Fathom seemed to be quite overwhelmed with a deep sense of all this goodness, and affected the most eager impatience to know the particulars of Renaldo's fate, since their unhappy separation, more especially his errand to this uncomfortable place, which he should henceforth revere as the providential scene of their reunion. Nor did he forget to inquire, in the most affectionate and dutiful manner, about the situation of his noble parents and amiable sister.

At mention of these names, Renaldo, fetching a deep sigh, "Alas! my friend," said he, "the Count is no more; and, what aggravates my affliction for the loss of such a father, it was my misfortune to be under his displeasure at the time of his death. Had I been present on that melancholy occasion, so well I knew his generosity and paternal tenderness, that, sure I am, he would in his last moments have forgiven an only son, whose life had been a continual effort to render himself worthy of such a parent, and whose crime was no other than an honourable passion for the most meritorious of her sex. But I was removed at a fatal distance from him, and doubtless my conduct must have been invidiously misrepresented. Be that as it will, my mother has again given her hand in wedlock to Count Trebasi; by whom I have the mortification to be informed that I am totally excluded from my father's succession; and I learn from other quarters, that my sister is barbarously treated by this inhuman father-in-law. Grant, Heaven, I may soon have an opportunity of expostulating with the tyrant upon that subject."

So saying, his cheeks glowed, and his eyes lightened with resentment. Then he thus proceeded: "My coming hither to-day was with a view to visit a poor female relation, from whom I yesterday received a letter, describing her most deplorable situation, and soliciting my assistance; but the turnkey affirms that there is no such person in the jail, and I was on my way to consult the keeper, when I was agreeably surprised with the sight of my dear Fathom."

Our adventurer having wiped from his eyes the tears which were produced by the news of his worthy patron's death, desired to know the name of that afflicted prisoner, in whose behalf he interested himself so much, and Renaldo produced the letter, subscribed, "Your unfortunate cousin, Helen Melvil." This pretended relation, after having explained the degree of consanguinity which she and the Count stood in to each other, and occasionally mentioned some anecdotes of the family in Scotland, gave him to understand that she had married a merchant of London, who, by repeated losses in trade, had been reduced to indigence, and afterwards confined to prison, where he then lay a breathless corpse, having left her in the utmost extremity of wretchedness and want, with two young children in the smallpox, and an incurable cancer in one of her own breasts. Indeed, the picture she drew was so moving, and her expressions so sensibly pathetic, that no person, whose heart was not altogether callous, could peruse it without emotion. Renaldo had sent two guineas by the messenger, whom she had represented as a trusty servant, whose fidelity had been proof against all the distress of her mistress; and he was now arrived in order to reinforce his bounty.

Fathom, in the consciousness of his own practices, immediately comprehended the scheme of this letter, and confidently assured him that no such person resided in the prison or in any other place. And when his friend applied for information to the keeper, these assurances were confirmed; and that stern janitor told him he had been imposed upon by a stale trick, which was often practised upon strangers by a set of sharpers, who make it their business to pick up hints of intelligence relating to private families, upon which they build such superstructures of fraud and imposition.

However piqued the young Hungarian might be to find himself duped in this manner, he rejoiced at the occasion which had thrown Fathom in his way; and, after having made him a tender of his purse, took his leave, on purpose to wait upon Trapwell, who was not quite so untractable as an enraged cuckold commonly is; for, by this time, he had accomplished the best part of his aim, which was to be divorced from his wife, and was fully convinced that the defendant was no more than a needy adventurer, who, in all probability, would be released by an act of parliament for the benefit of insolvent debtors; in which case, he, the plaintiff, would reap no solid advantage from his imprisonment.

He, therefore, listened to the remonstrances of the mediator, and, after much canvassing, agreed to discharge the defendant, in consideration of two hundred pounds, which were immediately paid by Count Melvil, who, by this deduction, was reduced to somewhat less than thirty.

Nevertheless, he cheerfully beggared himself in behalf of his friend, for whose release he forthwith obtained an order; and, next day, our adventurer, having bid a formal adieu to his fellows in distress, and, in particular, to his majesty, for whose restoration his prayers were preferred, he quitted the jail, and accompanied his deliverer, with all the outward marks of unutterable gratitude and esteem.

Surely, if his heart had been made of penetrable stuff, it would have been touched by the circumstances of this redemption; but had not his soul been invincible to all such attacks, these memoirs would possibly never have seen the light.

When they arrived at Renaldo's lodgings, that young gentleman honoured him with other proofs of confidence and friendship, by giving him a circumstantial detail of all the adventures in which he had been engaged after Fathom's desertion from the imperial camp. He told him, that, immediately after the war was finished, his father had pressed him to a very advantageous match, with which he would have complied, though his heart was not at all concerned, had not he been inflamed with the desire of seeing the world before he could take any step towards a settlement for life. That he had signified his sentiments on this head to the Count, who opposed them with unusual obstinacy, as productive of a delay which might be fatal to his proposal; for which reason he had retired incognito from his family, and travelled through sundry states and countries, in a disguise by which he eluded the inquiries of his parents.

That, in the course of these peregrinations, he was captivated by the irresistible charms of a young lady, on whose heart he had the good fortune to make a tender impression. That their mutual love had subjected both to many dangers and difficulties, during which they suffered a cruel separation; after the torments of which, he had happily found her in England, where she now lived entirely cut off from her native country and connexions, and destitute of every other resource but his honour, love, and protection. And, finally, that he was determined to combat his own desires, how violent soever they might be, until he should have made some suitable provision for the consequences of a stricter union with the mistress of his soul, that he might not, by a precipitate marriage, ruin the person whom he adored.

This end he proposed to attain, by an application to the court of Vienna, which he did not doubt would have some regard to his own service, and that of his father; and thither he resolved to repair, with the first opportunity, now that he had found a friend with whom he could intrust the inestimable jewel of his heart.

He likewise gave our hero to understand, that he had been eight months in England, during which he had lived in a frugal manner, that he might not unnecessarily exhaust the money he had been able to raise upon his own credit; that, hitherto, he had been obliged to defer his departure for Germany on account of his attendance upon the mother of his mistress, who was lately dead of sorrow and chagrin; and that, since he resided in London, he had often heard of the celebrated Count Fathom, though he never imagined that his friend Ferdinand could be distinguished by that appellation.

CHAPTER FORTY-THREE.
FATHOM JUSTIFIES THE PROVERB, "WHAT'S BRED IN THE BONE WILL NEVER COME OUT OF THE FLESH."

Some circumstances of this conversation made a deep impression upon the mind of our adventurer, who nevertheless concealed his emotions from the knowledge of his friend, and was next day introduced to that hidden treasure of which Renaldo had spoken with such rapture and adoration. It was not without reason he had expatiated upon the personal attractions of this young lady, whom, for the present, we shall call Monimia, a name that implies her orphan situation. When she entered the room, even Fathom, whose eyes had been sated with beauty, was struck dumb with admiration, and could scarce recollect himself so far as to perform the ceremony of his introduction.

She seemed to be about the age of eighteen. Her stature was tall; her motion graceful. A knot of artificial flowers restrained the luxuriancy of her fine black hair, that flowed in shining ringlets adown her snowy neck. The contour of her face was oval; her forehead remarkably high; her complexion clean and delicate, though not florid; and her eyes were so piercing, as to strike the soul of every beholder. Yet, upon this occasion, one half of their vivacity was eclipsed by a languishing air of melancholy concern; which, while it in a manner sheathed the edge of her beauty, added a most engaging sweetness to her looks. In short, every feature was elegantly perfect; and the harmony of the whole ravishing and delightful.

It was easy to perceive the mutual sentiments of the two lovers at meeting, by the pleasure that sensibly diffused itself in the countenances of both. Fathom was received by her as the intimate friend of her admirer, whom she had often heard of in terms of the most sincere affection; and the conversation was carried on in the Italian language, because she was a foreigner who had not as yet made great proficiency in the knowledge of the English tongue. Her understanding was such as, instead of diminishing, reinforced the prepossession which was inspired by her appearance; and if the sum-total of her charms could not melt the heart, it at least excited the appetite of Fathom to such a degree, that he gazed upon her with such violence of desire, as had never transported him before; and he instantly began to harbour thoughts, not only destructive to the peace of his generous patron, but also to the prudential maxims he had adopted on his first entrance into life.

We have already recorded divers instances of his conduct to prove that there was an intemperance in his blood, which often interfered with his caution; and although he had found means to render this heat sometimes subservient to his interest, yet, in all probability, Heaven mingled the ingredient in his constitution, on purpose to counteract his consummate craft, defeat the villany of his intention, and at least expose him to the justice of the law, and the contempt of his fellow-creatures.

Stimulated as he was by the beauty of the incomparable Monimia, he foresaw that the conquest of her heart would cost him a thousand times more labour and address than all the victories he had ever achieved; for, besides her superior understanding, her sentiments of honour, virtue, gratitude, religion, and pride of birth, her heart was already engaged by the tenderest ties of love and obligation, to a man whose person and acquired accomplishments at least equalled his own; and whose connexion with him was of such a nature as raised an almost insurmountable bar to his design; because, with what face could he commence rival to the person whose family had raised him from want and servility, and whose own generosity had rescued him from the miseries of a dreary gaol?

Notwithstanding these reflections, he would not lay aside an idea which so agreeably flattered his imagination. He, like every other projector in the same circumstances, was so partial to his own qualifications, as to think the lady would soon perceive a difference between him and Renaldo that could not fail to turn to his advantage in her opinion. He depended a good deal on the levity and inconstancy of the sex; and did not doubt that, in the course of their acquaintance, he should profit by that languor which often creeps upon and flattens the intercourse of lovers cloyed with the sight and conversation of each other.

This way of arguing was very natural to a man who had never known other motives than those of sensuality and convenience; and perhaps, upon these maxims, he might have succeeded with nine-tenths of the fair sex. But, for once, he erred in his calculation; Monimia's soul was perfect, her virtue impregnable. His first approaches were, as usual, performed by the method of insinuation, which succeeded so well, that in a few days he actually acquired a very distinguished share of her favour and esteem. To this he had been recommended, in the warmest strain of exaggerating friendship, by her dear Renaldo; so that, placing the most unreserved confidence in his honour and integrity, and being almost quite destitute of acquaintance, she made no scruple of owning herself pleased with his company and conversation; and therefore he was never abridged in point of opportunity. She had too much discernment to overlook his uncommon talents and agreeable address, and too much susceptibility to observe them with indifference. She not only regarded him as the confidant of her lover, but admired him as a person whose attachment did honour to Count Melvil's choice. She found his discourse remarkably entertaining, his politeness dignified with an air of uncommon sincerity, and she was ravished with his skill in music, an art of which she was deeply enamoured.

While he thus ingratiated himself with the fair Monimia, Renaldo rejoiced at their intimacy, being extremely happy in the thought of having found a friend who could amuse and protect the dear creature in his absence. That she might be the better prepared for the temporary separation which he meditated, he began to be less frequent in his visits, or rather to interrupt, by gradual intermissions, the constant attendance he had bestowed upon her since her mother's death. This alteration she was enabled to bear by the assiduities of Fathom, when she understood that her lover was indispensably employed in negotiating a sum of money for the purposes of his intended voyage. This was really the case; for, as the reader hath been already informed, the provision he had made for that emergency was expended in behalf of our adventurer; and the persons of whom he had borrowed it, far from approving of the use to which it was put, and accommodating him with a fresh supply, reproached him with his benevolence as an act of dishonesty to them; and, instead of favouring this second application, threatened to distress him for what he had already received. While he endeavoured to surmount these difficulties, his small reversion was quite exhausted, and he saw himself on the brink of wanting the common necessaries of life.

There was no difficulty which he could not have encountered with fortitude, had he alone been concerned. But his affection and regard for Monimia were of such a delicate nature, that, far from being able to bear the prospect of her wanting the least convenience, he could not endure that she should suspect her situation cost him a moment's perplexity; because he foresaw it would wring her gentle heart with unspeakable anguish and vexation. This, therefore, he endeavoured to anticipate by expressions of confidence in the Emperor's equity, and frequent declarations touching the goodness and security of that credit from which he derived his present subsistence.

CHAPTER FORTY-FOUR.
ANECDOTES OF POVERTY, AND EXPERIMENTS FOR THE BENEFIT OF THOSE WHOM IT MAY CONCERN.

His affairs being thus circumstanced, it is not to be supposed that he passed his time in tranquillity. Every day ushered in new demands and fresh anxiety; for though his economy was frugal, it could not be supported without money; and now not only his funds were drained, but also his private friends tired of relieving his domestic necessities; nay, they began to relinquish his company, which formerly they had coveted; and those who still favoured him with their company embittered that favour with disagreeable advice, mingled with impertinent reproof. They loudly exclaimed against the last instance of his friendship for Fathom, as a piece of wrong-headed extravagance, which neither his fortune could afford nor his conscience excuse; and alleged that such specimens of generosity are vicious in any man, let his finances be never so opulent, if he has any relations of his own who need his assistance; but altogether scandalous, not to say unjust, in a person who depends for his own support on the favour of his friends.

These expostulations did not even respect the beauteous, the accomplished, the gentle-hearted, the orphan Monimia. Although they owned her perfections, and did not deny that it would be highly meritorious in any man of fortune to make her happy, they disapproved of Renaldo's attachment to the fair beggar, made light of that intimate union of hearts which subsisted between the two lovers, and which no human consideration could dissolve; and some among them, in the consummation of their prudence, ventured to hint a proposal of providing for her in the service of some lady of fashion.

Any reader of sensibility will easily conceive how these admonitions were relished by a young gentleman whose pride was indomitable, whose notions of honour were scrupulously rigid and romantic, whose temper was warm, and whose love was intense. Every such suggestion was as a dagger to his soul; and what rendered the torture more exquisite, he lay under obligations to those very persons whose selfish and sordid sentiments he disdained; so that he was restricted by gratitude from giving vent to his indignation, and his forlorn circumstances would not permit him to renounce their acquaintance. While he struggled with these mortifications, his wants grew more and more importunate, and his creditors became clamorous.

Fathom, to whom all his grievances were disclosed, lamented his hard hap with all the demonstrations of sympathy which he could expect to find in such a zealous adherent. He upbraided himself incessantly as the cause of his patron's distress; took God to witness that he would rather have perished in gaol than have enjoyed his liberty, had he known it would have cost his dearest friend and benefactor one-tenth part of the anguish he now saw him suffer; and, in conclusion, the fervency of his affection glowed to such a degree, that he offered to beg, steal, or plunder on the highway, for Renaldo's assistance.

Certain it is, he might have recollected a less disagreeable expedient than any of these to alleviate the pangs of this unhappy lover; for, at that very period he was possessed of money and moveables to the amount of a much greater sum than that which was necessary to remove the severest pangs of the Count's misfortune. But, whether he did not reflect upon this resource, or was willing to let Melvil be better acquainted with adversity, which is the great school of life, I shall leave the reader to determine. Yet, so far was he from supplying the wants of the young Hungarian, that he did not scruple to receive a share of the miserable pittance which that gentleman made shift to extort from the complaisance of a few companions, whose countenance he still enjoyed.

Renaldo's life was now become a sacrifice to the most poignant distress. Almost his whole time was engrossed by a double scheme, comprehending his efforts to render his departure practicable, and his expedients for raising the means of daily bread. With regard to the first, he exerted himself among a set of merchants, some of whom knew his family and expectations; and, for the last, he was fain to depend upon the assistance of a few intimates, who were not in a condition to furnish him with sums of consequence. These, however, gradually dropped off, on pretence of friendly resentment for his indiscreet conduct; so that he found himself naked and deserted by all his former companions, except one gentleman, with whom he had lived in the most unreserved correspondence, as with a person of the warmest friendship, and the most unbounded benevolence; nay, he had actually experienced repeated proofs of his generosity; and such were the Count's sentiments of the gratitude, love, and esteem, which were due to the author of these obligations, that he would have willingly laid down his own life for his interest or advantage. He had already been at different times accommodated by this benefactor with occasional supplies, amounting in the whole to about forty or fifty pounds; and so fearful was he of taking any step by which he might forfeit the goodwill of this gentleman, that he struggled with unparelleled difficulty and vexation, before he could prevail upon himself to put his liberality to another proof.

What maxims of delicacy will not the dire calls of necessity infringe! Reduced to the alternative of applying once more to that beneficence which had never failed him, or of seeing Monimia starve, he chose the first, as of two evils the least, and intrusted Fathom with a letter explaining the bitterness of his case. It was not without trepidation that he received in the evening from his messenger an answer to this billet; but what were his pangs when he learned the contents! The gentleman, after having professed himself Melvil's sincere well-wisher, gave him to understand, that he was resolved for the future to detach himself from every correspondence which would be inconvenient for him to maintain; that he considered his intimacy with the Count in that light; yet, nevertheless, if his distress was really as great as he had described it, he would still contribute something towards his relief; and accordingly had sent by the bearer five guineas for that purpose; but desired him to take notice, that, in so doing, he laid himself under some difficulty.

Renaldo's grief and mortification at this disappointment were unspeakable. He now saw demolished the last screen betwixt him and the extremity of indigence and woe; he beheld the mistress of his soul abandoned to the bleakest scenes of poverty and want; and he deeply resented the lofty strain of the letter, by which he conceived himself treated as a worthless spendthrift and importunate beggar. Though his purse was exhausted to the last shilling; though he was surrounded with necessities and demands, and knew not how to provide another meal for his fair dependent, he, in opposition to all the suggestions and eloquence of Fathom, despatched him with the money and another billet, intimating, in the most respectful terms, that he approved of his friend's new-adopted maxim, which, for the future, he should always take care to remember; and that he had sent back the last instance of his bounty, as a proof how little he was disposed to incommode his benefactor.

This letter, though sincerely meant, and written in a very serious mood, the gentleman considered as an ungrateful piece of irony, and in that opinion complained to several persons of the Count's acquaintance, who unanimously exclaimed against him as a sordid, unthankful, and profligate knave, that abused and reviled those very people who had generously befriended him, whenever they found it inconvenient to nourish his extravagance with further supplies. Notwithstanding these accumulated oppressions, he still persevered with fortitude in his endeavours to disentangle himself from this maze of misery. To these he was encouraged by a letter which about this time he received from his sister, importing, that she had good reason to believe the real will of her father had been suppressed for certain sinister views; and desiring him to hasten his departure for Hungary, where he would still find some friends who were both able and willing to support his cause. He had some trinkets left; the pawnbroker's shop was still open; and hitherto he made shift to conceal from Monimia the extent of his affliction.

The money-broker whom he employed, after having amused him with a variety of schemes, which served no other purpose than that of protracting his own job, at length undertook to make him acquainted with a set of monied men who had been very venturous in lending sums upon personal security; he was therefore introduced to their club in the most favourable manner, after the broker had endeavoured to prepossess them separately, with magnificent ideas of his family and fortune. — By means of this anticipation he was received with a manifest relaxation of that severity which people of this class mingle in their aspects to the world in general; and they even vied with each other in their demonstrations of hospitality and respect; for every one in particular looked upon him as a young heir, who would bleed freely, and mortgage at cent. per cent.

Renaldo, buoyed up with these exterior civilities, began to flatter himself with hopes of success, which, however, were soon checked by the nature of the conversation; during which the chairman upbraided one of the members in open club for having once lent forty pounds upon slight security. The person accused alleged, in his own defence, that the borrower was his own kinsman, whose funds he knew to be sufficient; that he had granted his bond, and been at the expense of insuring his life for the money; and, in conclusion, had discharged it to the day with great punctuality. These allegations were not deemed exculpatory by the rest of the assembly, who with one voice pronounced him guilty of unwarrantable rashness and indiscretion, which, in time coming, must undoubtedly operate to the prejudice of his character and credit.

This was a bitter declaration to the young Count, who nevertheless endeavoured to improve the footing he had gained among them, by courting their company, conforming to their manners, and attentively listening to their discourse. When he had cultivated them with great assiduity for the space of some weeks, dined at their houses upon pressing invitations, and received repeated offers of service and friendship, believing that things were now ripe for the purpose, he, one day, at a tavern to which he had invited him to dinner, ventured to disclose his situation to him whose countenance was the least unpromising; and as he introduced the business with a proposal of borrowing money, he perceived his eyes sparkle with a visible alacrity, from which he drew a happy presage. But, alas! this was no more than a transient gleam of sunshine, which was suddenly obumbrated by the sequel of his explanation; insomuch, that, when the merchant understood the nature of the security, his visage was involved in a most disagreeable gloom, and his eyes distorted into a most hideous obliquity of vision; indeed, he squinted so horribly, that Renaldo was amazed and almost affrighted at his looks, until he perceived that this distortion proceeded from concern for a silver tobacco box which he had laid down by him on the table, after having filled his pipe. As the youth proceeded to unfold his necessities, the other became gradually alarmed for this utensil, to which he darted his eyes askance in this preternatural direction, until he had slyly secured it in his pocket.

Having made this successful conveyance, he shifted his eyes alternately from the young gentleman to the broker for a considerable pause, during which he in silence reproached the last for introducing such a beggarly varlet to his acquaintance; then taking the pipe from his mouth, "Sir," said he, addressing himself to the Count, "if I had all the inclination in the world to comply with your proposal, it is really not in my power. My correspondents abroad have remitted such a number of bad bills of late, that all my running cash hath been exhausted in supporting their credit. Mr. Ferret, sure I am, you was not ignorant of my situation; and I'm not a little surprised that you should bring the gentleman to me on business of this kind; but, as the wise man observes, Bray a fool in a mortar, and he'll never be wise." So saying, with a most emphatic glance directed to the broker, he rung the bell, and called for the reckoning; when, finding that he was to be the guest of Renaldo, he thanked him drily for his good cheer, and in an abrupt manner took himself away.

Though baffled in this quarter, the young gentleman would not despair; but forthwith employed Mr. Ferret in an application to another of the society; who, after having heard the terms of his commission, desired him to tell his principal, that he could do nothing without the concurrence of his partner, who happened to be at that time in one of our American plantations. A third being solicited, excused himself on account of an oath which he had lately taken on the back of a considerable loss. A fourth being tried, made answer, that it was not in his way. And a fifth candidly owned, that he never lent money without proper security.

Thus the forlorn Renaldo tried every experiment without success, and now saw the last ray of hope extinguished. Well-nigh destitute of present support, and encompassed with unrelenting duns, he was obliged to keep within doors, and seek some comfort in the conversation of his charming mistress, and his faithful friend; yet, even there, he experienced the extremest rigour of adverse fate. Every rap at the door alarmed him with the expectation of some noisy tradesman demanding payment. When he endeavoured to amuse himself with drawing, some unlucky feature of the occasional portrait recalled the image of an obdurate creditor, and made him tremble at the work of his own hands. When he fled for shelter to the flattering creation of fancy, some abhorred idea always started up amidst the gay vision, and dissolved the pleasing enchantment.— Even the seraphic voice of Monimia had no longer power to compose the anxious tumults of his mind. Every song she warbled, every tune she played, recalled to his remembrance some scene of love and happiness elapsed; and overwhelmed his soul with the woful comparison of past and present fate. He saw all that was amiable and perfect in woman, all that he held most dear and sacred upon earth, tottering on the brink of misery, without knowing the danger of her situation, and found himself unable to prevent her fall, or even to forewarn her of the peril; for as we have already observed, his soul could not brook the thought of communicating the tidings of distress to the tender-hearted Monimia.

CHAPTER FORTY-FIVE.
RENALDO'S DISTRESS DEEPENS, AND FATHOM'S PLOT THICKENS.

Such aggravated misfortune could not fail to affect his temper and deportment. The continual efforts he made to conceal his vexation produced a manifest distraction in his behaviour and discourse. He began to be seized with horror at the sight of poor Monimia, whom he therefore shunned as much as the circumstances of their correspondence would allow; and every evening he went forth alone to some solitary place, where he could, unperceived, give a loose to the transports of his sorrow, and in silence meditate some means to lighten the burden of his woe. His heart was sometimes so savaged with despair, which represented mankind as his inveterate enemies, that he entertained thoughts of denouncing war against the whole community, and supplying his own wants with the spoils he should win. At other times he was tempted with the desire of putting an end to his miseries and life together. Yet these were but the transitory suggestions of temporary madness, that soon yielded to the dictates of reason. From the execution of the first he was restrained by his own notions of honour and morality; and, from using the other expedient, he was deterred by his love for Monimia, together with the motives of philosophy and religion.

While in this manner he secretly nursed the worm of grief that preyed upon his vitals, the alteration in his countenance and conduct did not escape the eyes of that discerning young lady. She was alarmed at the change, yet afraid to inquire into the source of it; for, being ignorant of his distress, she could impute it to no cause in which her happiness was not deeply interested. She had observed his strained complaisance and extraordinary emotion. She had detected him in repeated attempts to avoid her company, and taken notice of his regular excursions in the dark. These were alarming symptoms to a lover of her delicacy and pride. She strove in vain to put the most favourable construction on what she saw; and, finally, imputed the effects of his despondence to the alienation of his heart. Made miserable beyond expression by these suspicions, she imparted them to Fathom, who, by this time, was in full possession of her confidence and esteem, and implored his advice touching her conduct in such a nice conjuncture.

This artful politician, who rejoiced at the effect of her penetration, no sooner heard himself questioned on the subject, than he gave tokens of surprise and confusion, signifying his concern to find she had discovered what, for the honour of his friend, he wished had never come to light. His behaviour on this occasion confirmed her fatal conjecture; and she conjured him, in the most pathetic manner, to tell her if he thought Renaldo's heart had contracted any new engagement. At this question, he started with signs of extreme agitation, and stifling an artificial sigh, "Sure, madam," said he, "you cannot doubt the Count's constancy—I am confident—he is certainly—I protest, madam, I am so shocked."

Here he made a full pause, as if the conflict between his integrity and his friendship would not allow him to proceed, and summoned the moisture into either eye—"Then are my doubts removed," cried the afflicted Monimia; "I see your candour in the midst of your attachment to Renaldo; and will no longer torment you with impertinent interrogations and vain complaints." With these words, a flood of tears gushed from her enchanting eyes, and she instantly withdrew into her own apartment, where she indulged her sorrow to excess. Nor was her grief unanimated with resentment. She was by birth, nature, and education inspired with that dignity of pride which ennobles the human heart; and this, by the circumstance of her present dependence, was rendered extremely jealous and susceptible; insomuch that she could not brook the least shadow of indifference, much less an injury of such a nature, from the man whom she had honoured with her affections, and for whom she had disobliged and deserted her family and friends.

Though her love was so unalterably fixed on this unhappy youth, that, without the continuation of reciprocal regard, her life would have become an unsupportable burden, even amidst all the splendour of affluence and pomp; and although she foresaw, that, when his protection should cease, she must be left a wretched orphan in a foreign land, exposed to all the miseries of want; yet, such was the loftiness of her displeasure, that she disdained to complain, or even demand an explanation from the supposed author of her wrongs.

While she continued undetermined in her purpose, and fluctuating on this sea of torture, Fathom, believing that now was the season for working upon her passions, while they were all in commotion, became, if possible, more assiduous than ever about the fair mourner, modelled his features into a melancholy cast, pretended to share her distress with the most emphatic sympathy, and endeavoured to keep her resentment glowing by cunning insinuations, which, though apparently designed to apologise for his friend, served only to aggravate the guilt of his perfidy and dishonour. This pretext of friendly concern is the most effectual vehicle for the conveyance of malice and slander; and a man's reputation is never so mortally stabbed, as when the assassin begins with the preamble of, "For my own part, I can safely say that no man upon earth has a greater regard for him than I have; and it is with the utmost anguish and concern that I see him misbehave in such a manner." Then he proceeds to mangle his character, and the good-natured hearers, concluding he is even blacker than he is represented, on the supposition that the most atrocious circumstances are softened or suppressed by the tenderness or friendship of the accuser, exclaim, "Good lack! what a wretch he must be, when his best friends will no longer attempt to defend him!" Nay, sometimes these well-wishers undertake his defence, and treacherously betray the cause they have espoused, by omitting the reasons that may be urged in his vindication.

Both these methods were practised by the wily Ferdinand, according to the predominant passion of Monimia. When her indignation prevailed, he expatiated upon his love and sincere regard for Renaldo, which, he said, had grown up from the cradle, to such a degree of fervour, that he would willingly part with life for his advantage. He shed tears for his apostasy; but every drop made an indelible stain upon his character; and, in the bitterness of his grief, swore, notwithstanding his fondness for Renaldo, which had become a part of his constitution, that the young Hungarian deserved the most infamous destiny for having injured such perfection. At other times, when he found her melted into silent sorrow, he affected to excuse the conduct of his friend. He informed her, that the young gentleman's temper had been uneven from his infancy; that frailty was natural to man; that he might in time be reclaimed by self-conviction; he even hinted, that she might have probably ascribed to inconstancy, what was really the effect of some chagrin which he industriously concealed from his participation. But, when he found her disposed to listen to this last suggestion, he destroyed the force of it, by recollecting the circumstances of his nocturnal rambles, which, he owned, would admit of no favourable construction.

By these means he blew the coals of her jealousy, and enhanced the value of his own character at the same time; for she looked upon him as a mirror of faith and integrity, and the mind being overcharged with woe, naturally seeks some confidant, upon whose sympathy it can repose itself. Indeed, his great aim was to make himself necessary to her affliction, and settle a gossiping correspondence, in the familiarity of which he hoped his purpose would certainly be answered.

Yet the exertion of these talents was not limited to her alone. While he laid these trains for the hapless young lady, he was preparing snares of another kind for her unsuspecting lover, who, for the completion of his misery, about this time began to perceive marks of disquiet and displeasure in the countenance and deportment of his adored Monimia. For that young lady, in the midst of her grief, remembered her origin, and over her vexation affected to throw a veil of tranquillity, which served only to give an air of disgust to her internal disturbance.

Renaldo, whose patience and philosophy were barely sufficient to bear the load of his other evils, would have been quite overwhelmed with the additional burden of Monimia's woe, if it had not assumed this appearance of disesteem, which, as he knew he had not deserved it, brought his resentment to his assistance. Yet this was but a wretched cordial to support him against the baleful reflections that assaulted him from every quarter; it operated like those desperate remedies, which, while they stimulate exhausted nature, help to destroy the very fundamentals of the constitution. He reviewed his own conduct with the utmost severity, and could not recollect one circumstance which could justly offend the idol of his soul. The more blameless he appeared to himself in this examination, the less excusable did her behaviour appear. He tasked his penetration to discover the cause of this alteration; he burned with impatience to know it; his discernment failed him, and he was afraid, though he knew not why, to demand an explanation. His thoughts were so circumstanced, that he durst not even unbosom himself to Fathom, though his own virtue and friendship resisted those sentiments that began to intrude upon his mind, with suggestions to the prejudice of our adventurer's fidelity.

Nevertheless, unable to endure the torments of such interesting suspense, he at length made an effort to expostulate with the fair orphan; and in an abrupt address, the effect of his fear and confusion, begged to know if he had inadvertently done anything to incur her displeasure. Monimia, hearing herself bluntly accosted in this unusual strain, after repeated instances of his reserve and supposed inconstancy, considered the question as a fresh insult, and, summoning her whole pride to her assistance, replied, with affected tranquillity, or rather with an air of scorn, that she had no title to judge, neither did she pretend to condemn his conduct. This answer, so wide of that tenderness and concern which had hitherto manifested itself in the disposition of his amiable mistress, deprived him of all power to carry on the conversation, and he retired with a low bow, fully convinced of his having irretrievably lost the place he had possessed in her affection; for, to his imagination, warped and blinded by his misfortunes, her demeanour seemed fraught, not with a transient gleam of anger, which a respectful lover would soon have appeased, but with that contempt and indifference which denote a total absence of affection and esteem. She, on the other hand, misconstrued his sudden retreat; and now they beheld the actions of each other through the false medium of prejudice and resentment. To such fatal misunderstandings the peace and happiness of whole families often fall a sacrifice.

CHAPTER FORTY-SIX.
OUR ADVENTURER BECOMES ABSOLUTE IN HIS POWER OVER THE PASSIONS OF HIS FRIEND, AND EFFECTS ONE HALF OF HIS AIM.

Influenced by this dire mistake, the breast of those unhappy lovers began to be invaded with the horrors of jealousy. The tender-hearted Monimia endeavoured to devour her griefs in silence; she in secret bemoaned her forlorn fate without ceasing; her tears flowed without intermission from night to morn, and from morn to night. She sought not to know the object for which she was forsaken; she meant not to upbraid her undoer; her aim was to find a sequestered corner, in which she could indulge her sorrow; where she could brood over the melancholy remembrance of her former felicity; where she could recollect those happy scenes she had enjoyed under the wings of her indulgent parents, when her whole life was a revolution of pleasures, and she was surrounded with affluence, pomp, and admiration; where she could, unmolested, dwell upon the wretched comparison between her past and present condition, and paint every circumstance of her misery in the most aggravating colours, that they might make the deeper impression upon her mind, and the more speedily contribute to that dissolution for which she ardently wished, as a total release from woe.

Amidst these pinings, she began to loathe all sustenance; her cheeks grew wan, her bright eyes lost their splendour, the roses vanished from her lips, and her delicate limbs could hardly support their burden; in a word, her sole consolation was limited to the prospect of depositing her sorrows in the grave; and her only wish was to procure a retreat in which she might wait with resignation for that happy period. Yet this melancholy comfort she could not obtain without the advice and mediation of Fathom, whom she therefore still continued to see and consult. While these consultations were held, Renaldo's bosom was ravaged with tempests of rage and distraction. He believed himself superseded in the affection of his mistress, by some favoured rival, whose success rankled at his soul; and though he scarce durst communicate the suspicion to his own heart, his observation continually whispered to him that he was supplanted by his friend Fathom; for Monimia was totally detached from the conversation of every other man, and he had of late noted their intercourse with distempered eyes.

These considerations sometimes transported him to such a degree of frenzy, that he was tempted to sacrifice them both as traitors to gratitude, friendship, and love; but such deliriums soon vanished before his honour and humanity. He would not allow himself to think amiss of Ferdinand, until some undoubted mark of his guilt should appear; and this was so far from being the case, that hitherto there was scarce a presumption. "On the contrary," said he to himself, "I am hourly receiving proofs of his sympathy and attachment. Not but that he may be the innocent cause of my mishap. His superior qualifications may have attracted the eye, and engaged the heart of that inconstant fair, without his being sensible of the victory he has won; or, perhaps, shocked at the conquest he hath unwillingly made, he discourages her advances, tries to reason down her unjustifiable passion, and in the meantime conceals from me the particulars, out of regard to my happiness and quiet."

Under cover of these favourable conjectures, our adventurer securely prosecuted his scheme upon the unfortunate Monimia. He dedicated himself wholly to her service and conversation, except at those times when his company was requested by Renaldo, who now very seldom exacted his attendance. In his ministry about the person of the beauteous orphan, this cunning incendiary mingled such awful regard, such melting compassion, as effectually screened him from the suspicion of treachery, while he widened the fatal breach between her and her lover by the most diabolical insinuations. He represented his friend as a voluptuary, who gratified his own appetite without the least regard to honour or conscience; and, with a show of infinite reluctance, imparted some anecdotes of his sensuality, which he had feigned for the purpose; then he would exclaim in an affected transport, "Gracious Heaven! is it possible for any man who has the least title to perception or humanity to injure such innocence and perfection! for my own part, had I been so undeservedly happy—Heaven and earth! forgive my transports, madam, I cannot help seeing and admiring such divine attractions. I cannot help resenting your wrongs; it is the cause of virtue I espouse; it ought to be the cause of every honest man."

He had often repeated such apostrophes as these, which she ascribed to nothing else than sheer benevolence and virtuous indignation, and actually began to think he had made some impression upon her heart, not that he now entertained the hope of an immediate triumph over her chastity. The more he contemplated her character, the more difficult the conquest seemed to be: he therefore altered his plan, and resolved to carry on his operations under the shelter of honourable proposals, foreseeing that a wife of her qualifications, if properly managed, would turn greatly to the account of the husband, or, if her virtue should prove refractory, that he could at any time rid himself of the encumbrance, by decamping without beat of drum, after he should be cloyed with possession.

Elevated by these expectations, he one day, in the midst of a preconcerted rhapsody, importing that he could no longer conceal the fire that preyed upon his heart, threw himself on his knees before the lovely mourner, and imprinted a kiss on her fair hand. Though he did not presume to take this liberty till after such preparation as he thought had altogether extinguished her regard for Melvil, and paved the way for his own reception in room of that discarded lover, he had so far overshot his mark, that Monimia, instead of favouring his declaration, started up, and retired in silence, her cheeks glowing with shame, and her eyes gleaming with indignation.

Ferdinand no sooner recovered from the confusion produced by this unexpected repulse, than he saw the necessity of coming to a speedy determination, lest the offended fair one should appeal to Renaldo, in which case they might be mutually undeceived, to his utter shame and confusion; he therefore resolved to deprecate her anger by humble supplications, and by protesting, that, whatever tortures he might suffer by suppressing his sentiments, she should never again be offended with a declaration of his passion.

Having thus appeased the gentle Monimia, and discovered that, in spite of her resentment, his friend still kept possession of her heart, he determined to work an effectual separation, so as that the young lady, being utterly deserted by Melvil, should be left altogether in his power. With this Christian intention, he began to sadden his visage with a double shade of pensive melancholy, in the presence of Renaldo, to stifle a succession of involuntary sighs, to answer from the purpose, to be incoherent in his discourse, and, in a word, to act the part of a person wrapt up in sorrowful cogitation.

Count Melvil, soon as he perceived these symptoms, very kindly inquired into the cause of them, and was not a little alarmed to hear the artful and evasive answers of Ferdinand, who, without disclosing the source of his disquiet, earnestly begged leave to retire into some other corner of the world. Roused by this entreaty, the Hungarian's jealousy awoke, and with violent agitation, he exclaimed, "Then are my fears too true, my dear Fathom: I comprehend the meaning of your request. I have for some time perceived an host of horrors approaching from that quarter. I know your worth and honour. I depend upon your friendship, and conjure you, by all the ties of it, to free me at once from the most miserable suspense, by owning you have involuntarily captivated the heart of that unhappy maiden."

To this solemn interrogation he made no reply, but shedding a flood of tears, of which he had always a magazine at command, he repeated his desire of withdrawing, and took God to witness, that what he proposed was solely for the quiet of his honoured patron and beloved friend. "Enough," cried the unfortunate Renaldo, "the measure of my woes is now filled up." So saying, he fell backwards in a swoon, from which he was with difficulty recovered to the sensation of the most exquisite torments. During this paroxysm, our adventurer nursed him with infinite care and tenderness, he exhorted him to summon all his fortitude to his assistance, to remember his forefathers, and exert himself in the imitation of their virtues, to fly from those bewitching charms which had enslaved his better part, to retrieve his peace of mind by reflecting on the inconstancy and ingratitude of woman, and amuse his imagination in the pursuit of honour and glory.

After these admonitions he abused his ears with a forged detail of the gradual advances made to him by Monimia, and the steps he had taken to discourage her addresses, and re-establish her virtue, poisoning the mind of that credulous youth to such a degree, that, in all probability, he would have put a fatal period to his own existence, had not Fathom found means to allay the rage of his ecstasy, by the cunning arrangement of opposite considerations. He set his pride against his love, he opposed his resentment to his sorrow, and his ambition to his despair. Notwithstanding the balance of power so settled among these antagonists, so violent were the shocks of their successive conflicts, that his bosom fared like a wretched province, harassed, depopulated, and laid waste, by two fierce contending armies. From this moment his life was nothing but an alternation of starts and reveries; he wept and raved by turns, according to the prevailing gust of passion; food became a stranger to his lips, and sleep to his eyelids; he could not support the presence of Monimia, her absence increased the torture of his pangs; and, when he met her by accident, he started back with horror, like a traveller who chances to tread upon a snake.

The poor afflicted orphan, worn to a shadow with self-consuming anguish, eager to find some lowly retreat, where she could breath out her soul in peace, and terrified at the frantic behaviour of Renaldo, communicated to Fathom her desire of removing, and begged that he would take a small picture of her father, decorated with diamonds, and convert them into money, for the expense of her subsistence. This was the last pledge of her family, which she had received from her mother, who had preserved it in the midst of numberless distresses, and no other species of misery but that which she groaned under could have prevailed upon the daughter to part with it; but, exclusive of other motives, the very image itself, by recalling to her mind the honours of her name, upbraided her with living in dependence upon a man who had treated her with such indignity and ingratitude; besides, she flattered herself with the hope that she should not long survive the loss of this testimonial.

Our adventurer, with many professions of sorrow and mortification at his own want of capacity to prevent such an alienation, undertook to dispose of it to the best advantage, and to provide her with a cheap and retired apartment, to which he would conduct her in safety, though at the hazard of his life. In the meantime, however, he repaired to his friend Renaldo, and, after having admonished him to arm his soul with patience and philosophy, declared that Monimia's guilty passion for himself could no longer be kept within bounds, that she had conjured him, in the most pressing manner, to assist her in escaping from an house which she considered as the worst of dungeons, because she was in it daily exposed to the sight and company of a man whom she detested, and that she had bribed him to compliance with her request, not only with repeated promises of eternal love and submission, but also with the picture of her father set with diamonds, which she had hitherto reserved as the last and greatest testimony of her affection and esteem.

With these words he presented the fatal pledge to the eyes of the astonished youth, upon whom it operated like the poisonous sight of the basilisk, for in an instant, the whole passions of his soul were in the most violent agitation. "What!" cried he, in an ecstasy of rage, "is she so abandoned to perfidy, so lost to shame, so damned to constancy, to gratitude, and virtuous love, as to meditate the means of leaving me without decency, without remorse! to forsake me in my adversity, when my hapless fortune can no longer flatter the pride and vanity of her expectation! O woman! woman! woman! what simile shall I find to illustrate the character of the sex? But I will not have recourse to vain complaints and feeble exclamations. By Heaven! she shall not 'scape, she shall not triumph in her levity, she shall not exult in my distress; no! I will rather sacrifice her to my just resentment, to the injured powers of love and friendship. I will act the avenging minister of Heaven! I will mangle that fair bosom, which contains so false a heart! I will tear her to pieces, and scatter those beauteous limbs as a prey to the beasts of the field, and the fowls of the air!"

Fathom, who expected this storm, far from attempting to oppose its progress, waited with patience until its first violence was overblown; then, assuming an air of condolence, animated with that resolution which a friend ought to maintain on such occasions, "My dear Count," said he, "I am not at all surprised at your emotion, because I know what an heart, susceptible as yours, must feel from the apostasy of one who has reigned so long the object of your love, admiration, and esteem. Your endeavours to drive her from your thoughts must create an agony much more severe than that which divorces the soul from the body. Nevertheless, I am so confident of your virtue and your manhood, as to foresee, that you will allow the fair Monimia to execute that resolution which she hath so unwisely taken, to withdraw herself from your love and protection. Believe me, my best friend and benefactor, this is a step, in consequence of which you will infallibly retrieve your peace of mind. It may cost you many bitter pangs, it may probe your wounds to the quick; but those pangs will be soothed by the gentle and salutary wing of time, and that probing will rouse you to a due sense of your own dignity and importance, which will enable you to convert your attention to objects far more worthy of your contemplation. All the hopes of happiness you had cherished in the possession of Monimia are now irrecoverably blasted; her heart is now debased beneath your consideration; her love is, without all doubt, extinguished, and her honour irretrievably lost; insomuch, that, were she to profess sorrow for her indiscretion, and implore your forgiveness, with the most solemn promises of regarding you for the future with unalterable fidelity and affection, you ought not to restore her to that place in your heart which she hath so meanly forfeited, because you could not at the same time reinstate her in the possession of that delicate esteem without which there is no harmony, no rapture, no true enjoyment in love.

"No, my dear Renaldo, expel the unworthy tenant from your bosom; allow her to fill up the measure of her ingratitude, by deserting her lover, friend, and benefactor. Your glory demands her dismission; the world will applaud your generosity, and your own heart approve of your conduct. So disencumbered, let us exert ourselves once more in promoting your departure from this island, that you may revisit your father's house, do justice to yourself and amiable sister, and take vengeance on the author of your wrongs; then dedicate yourself to glory, in imitation of your renowned ancestors, and flourish in the favour of your imperial patron."

These remonstrances had such an effect upon the Hungarian, that his face was lighted up with a transient gleam of satisfaction. He embraced Ferdinand with great ardour, calling him his pride, his Mentor, his good genius, and entreated him to gratify the inclination of that fickle creature so far as to convey her to another lodging, without loss of time, while he would, by absenting himself, favour their retreat.

Our hero having obtained this permission, went immediately to the skirts of the town, where he had previously bespoke a small, though neat apartment, at the house of an old woman, widow of a French refugee. He had already reconnoitred the ground, by sounding his landlady, from whose poverty and complaisance he found reason to expect all sorts of freedom and opportunity for the accomplishment of his aim upon Monimia's person. The room being prepared for her reception, he returned to that disconsolate beauty, to whom he presented ten guineas, which he pretended to have raised by pledging the picture, though he himself acted as the pawnbroker on this occasion, for a very plain and obvious reason.

The fair orphan was overjoyed to find her wish so speedily accomplished. She forthwith packed up her necessaries in a trunk; and a hackney-coach was called in the dusk of the evening, in which she embarked with her baggage and conductor.

Yet she did not leave the habitation of Renaldo without regret. In the instant of parting, the idea of that unfortunate youth was associated with every well-known object that presented itself to her eyes; not as an inconstant, ungenerous, and perjured swain, but as the accomplished, the virtuous, the melting lover, who had captivated her virgin heart. As Fathom led her to the door, she was met by Renaldo's dog, which had long been her favourite; and the poor animal fawning upon her as she passed, her heart was overwhelmed with such a gush of tenderness, that a flood of tears streamed down her cheeks, and she had well-nigh sunk upon the floor.

Ferdinand, considering this emotion as the last tribute she would pay to Renaldo, hurried her into the coach, where she soon recovered her composure; and in a little time he ushered her into the house of Madam la Mer, by whom she was received with great cordiality, and conducted to her apartment, with which she found no other fault than that of its being too good for one in her forlorn situation. Here, while the tear of gratitude started in either eye, she thanked our adventurer for his benevolence and kind concern, assuring him, that she would not fail duly to beseech the Most High to shower down blessings upon him, as the orphan's friend and protector.

Fathom was not deficient in those expressions that were best adapted to her present turn of mind. He observed, that what he had done was in obedience to the dictates of common humanity, which would have prompted him to assist any fellow-creature in distress; but that her peculiar virtue and qualifications were such as challenged the utmost exertion of his faculties in her service. He said, that surely Heaven had not created such perfection in vain; that she was destined to receive as well as to communicate happiness; and that the Providence, which she so piously adored, would not fail, in due season, to raise her from distress and affliction, to that honour and felicity for which she was certainly ordained. In the meantime, he entreated her to depend upon his service and fidelity, and the article of her board being settled, he left her to the company and consolation of her discreet hostess, who soon insinuated herself into the good opinion of her beauteous lodger.

While our hero was employed in this transaction, Renaldo sallied forth in a sort of intoxication, which Fathom's admonitions had inspired; and, repairing to a certain noted coffee-house, engaged at chess with an old French refugee, that his attention, by being otherwise employed, might not stray towards that fatal object which he ardently wished to forget. But, unluckily for him, he had scarce performed three moves of the game, when his ears were exposed to a dialogue between two young gentlemen, one of whom asked the other if he would go and see the "Orphan" acted at one of the theatres; observing, as a farther inducement, that the part of Monimia would be performed by a young gentlewoman who had never appeared on the stage. At mention of that name, Renaldo started; for though it did not properly belong to his orphan, it was the appellation by which she had been distinguished ever since her separation from her father's house, and therefore it recalled her to his imagination in the most interesting point of view. Though he endeavoured to expel the image, by a closer application to his play, every now and then it intruded upon his fancy, and at each return made a stronger impression; so that he found himself in the situation of an unfortunate bark stranded upon some hidden rock, which, when the wind begins to blow, feels every succeeding wave more boisterous than the former, until, with irresistible fury, they surmount her deck, sweep everything before them, and dash her all to pieces.

The refugee had observed his first emotion, which he attributed to an unforeseen advantage he himself had gained over the Hungarian; but seeing him, in the sequel, bite his lip, roll his eyes, groan, writhe his body, ejaculate incoherent curses, and neglect his game, the Huguenot concluded that he was mad, and being seized with terror and dismay, got up and scampered off, without ceremony or hesitation.

Melvil, thus left to the horrors of his own thought, which tortured him with the apprehension of losing Monimia for ever, could no longer combat that suggestion, but ran homewards with all the speed he could exert, in order to prevent her retreat. When he crossed the threshold, he was struck with such a damp of presaging fear, that he durst not in person approach her apartment, nor even, by questioning the servant, inform himself of the particulars he wanted to know. Yet his suspense becoming more insupportable than his fear, he rushed from room to room in quest of that which was not to be found; and, seeing Monimia's chamber door open, entered the deserted temple in a state of distraction, calling aloud upon her name. All was silent, solitary, and woful. "She is gone," he cried, shedding a flood of tears, "she is for ever lost; and all my hopes of happiness are fled!"

So saying, he sunk upon that couch on which Monimia had oft reposed, and abandoned himself to all the excess of grief and despondence. In this deplorable condition he was found by our adventurer, who gently chid him for his want of resolution, and again repelled his sorrow, by arousing his resentment against the innocent cause of his disquiet, having beforehand forged the particulars of provocation.

"Is it possible," said he, "that Renaldo can still retain the least sentiment of regard for a fickle woman, by whom he has been so ungratefully forsaken and so unjustly scorned? Is it possible he can be so disturbed by the loss of a creature who is herself lost to all virtue and decorum?—Time and reflection, my worthy friend, will cure you of that inglorious malady. And the future misconduct of that imprudent damsel will, doubtless, contribute to the recovery of your peace. Her behaviour, at leaving the house where she had received so many marks of the most delicate affection, was in all respects so opposite to honour and decency, that I could scarce refrain from telling her I was shocked at her deportment, even while she loaded me with protestations of love. When a woman's heart is once depraved, she bids adieu to all restraint;—she preserves no measures. It was not simply contempt which she expressed for Renaldo; she seems to resent his being able to live under her disdain; and that resentment stoops to objects unworthy of indignation. Even your dog was not exempted from the effects of her displeasure. For, in her passage to the door, she kicked the poor animal as one of your dependents; and, in our way to the apartment I had provided for her, she entertained me with a ludicrous comment upon the manner in which you first made her acquainted with your passion. All that modesty of carriage, all that chastity of conversation, all that dignity of grief, which she knew so well how to affect, is now entirely laid aside, and, when I quitted her, she seemed the most gay, giddy, and impertinent of her sex."

"Gracious powers!" exclaimed Renaldo, starting from the couch, "am I under the delusion of a dream; or are these things really so, as my friend has represented them? Such a total and sudden degeneracy is amazing! is monstrous and unnatural!"

"Such, my dear Count," replied our hero, "is the caprice of a female heart, fickle as the wind, uncertain as a calm at sea, fixed to no principle, but swayed by every fantastic gust of passion, or of whim. Congratulate yourself, therefore, my friend, upon your happy deliverance from such a domestic plague—upon the voluntary exile of a traitor from your bosom.—Recollect the dictates of your duty, your discretion, and your glory, and think upon the honours and elevated enjoyment for which you are certainly ordained. To-night let us over a cheerful bottle anticipate your success; and to-morrow I will accompany you to the house of an usurer, who, I am informed, fears no risk, provided twenty per cent be given, and the borrower's life insured."

CHAPTER FORTY-SEVEN.
THE ART OF BORROWING FURTHER EXPLAINED, AND AN ACCOUNT OF A STRANGE PHENOMENON.

In this manner did the artful incendiary work upon the passions of the credulous unsuspecting Hungarian, who pressed him to his breast with the most cordial expressions of friendship, calling him his guardian, his saviour, his second father, and gave himself up wholly to his advice.

Next morning, according to the plan they had laid overnight, they repaired to a tavern in the neighbourhood of the person to whom our adventurer had been directed, and were fortunate enough to find him in the house, transacting a money affair with a young gentleman who treated him with his morning's whet.

That affair being negotiated, he adjourned into another room with Renaldo and his companion, who were not a little surprised to see this minister of Plutus in the shape of a young sprightly beau, trimmed up in all the foppery of the fashion; for they had hitherto always associated with the idea of an usurer old age and rusty apparel. After divers modish congees, he begged to know to what he should attribute the honour of their message; when Ferdinand, who acted the orator, told him, that his friend Count Melvil, having occasion for a sum of money, had been directed to a gentleman of his name, "and, I suppose," added he, "you are the son of the person with whom the affair is to be negotiated."

"Sir," said this petit-maitre, with a smile, "I perceive you are surprised to see one of my profession in the appearance of a gentleman; and perhaps your wonder will not cease, when I tell you, that my education was liberal, and that I once had the honour to bear a commission in the British army. I was indeed a first lieutenant of marines, and will venture to say, that no officer in the service was more delicate than myself in observing all the punctilios of honour. I entertained the utmost contempt for all the trading part of the nation, and suffered myself to be run through the body in a duel, rather than roll with a brother-lieutenant, who was a broker's son. But, thank Heaven! I have long ago conquered all those ridiculous prejudices. I soon observed, that without money there was no respect, honour, or convenience to be acquired in life; that wealth amply supplied the want of wit, merit, and pedigree, having influence and pleasure ever at command; and that the world never failed to worship the flood of affluence, without examining the dirty channels through which it commonly flowed.

"At the end of the war, finding my appointments reduced to two shillings and fourpence per day, and being addicted to pleasures which I could not possibly purchase from such a fund, I sold my half-pay for two hundred pounds, which I lent upon bond to a young officer of the same regiment, on condition that he should insure his life, and restore one-fourth part of the sum by way of premium. I happened to be lucky in this first essay; for the borrower, having in six weeks expended the money, made an excursion on the highway, was apprehended, tried, convicted of felony, and cut his own throat, to prevent the shame of a public execution; so that his bond was discharged by the insurers.

"In short, gentlemen, when I engaged in this business, I determined to carry it on with such spirit, as would either make my fortune, or entirely ruin me in a little time; and hitherto my endeavours have been tolerably successful. Nor do I think my proceedings a whit more criminal or unjust than those of other merchants, who strive to turn their money to the best account. The commodity I deal in is cash; and it is my business to sell it to the best advantage. A London factor sends a cargo of goods to market, and if he gets two hundred per cent upon the sale, he is commended for industry and address. If I sell money for one-fourth part of that profit, certain persons will be so unjust as to cry, Shame upon me, for taking such advantage of my neighbour's distress; not considering, that the trader took four times the same advantage of those people who bought his cargo, though his risk was not half so great as mine, and although the money I sold perhaps retrieved the borrower from the very jaws of destruction. For example, it was but yesterday I saved a worthy man from being arrested for a sum of money, for which he had bailed a friend who treacherously left him in the lurch. As he did not foresee what would happen, he had made no provision for the demand, and his sphere of life secluding him from all sorts of monied intercourse, he could not raise the cash by his credit in the usual way of borrowing; so that, without my assistance, he must have gone to jail; a disgrace which would have proved fatal to the peace of his family, and utterly ruined his reputation.—Nay, that very young gentleman, from whom I am just now parted, will, in all probability, be indebted to me for a very genteel livelihood. He had obtained the absolute promise of being provided for by a great man, who sits at the helm of affairs in a neighbouring kingdom; but, being destitute of all other resources, he could not have equipped himself for the voyage, in order to profit by his lordship's intention, unless I had enabled him to pursue his good fortune."

Renaldo was not a little pleased to hear this harangue, to which Fathom replied with many florid encomiums upon the usurer's good sense and humane disposition; then he explained the errand of his friend, which was to borrow three hundred pounds, in order to retrieve his inheritance, of which he had been defrauded in his absence.

"Sir," said the lender, addressing himself to Count Melvil, "I pretend to have acquired by experience some skill in physiognomy; and though there are some faces so deeply disguised as to baffle all the penetration of our art, there are others, in which the heart appears with such nakedness of integrity, as at once to recommend it to our goodwill. I own your countenance prepossesses me in your favour; and you shall be accommodated, upon those terms from which I never deviate, provided you can find proper security, that you shall not quit the British dominions; for that, with me, is a condition sine qua non."

This was a very disagreeable declaration to Renaldo, who candidly owned, that, as his concerns lay upon the Continent, his purpose was to leave England without delay. The usurer professed himself sorry that it was not in his power to oblige him; and, in order to prevent any further importunity, assured them, he had laid it down as a maxim, from which he would never swerve, to avoid all dealings with people whom, if need should be, he could not sue by the laws of this realm.

Thus the intervention of one unlucky and unforeseen circumstance blasted in an instant the budding hopes of Melvil, who, while his visage exhibited the most sorrowful disappointment, begged to know, if there was any person of his acquaintance who might be less scrupulous in that particular.

The young gentleman directed them to another member of his profession, and wishing them success, took his leave with great form and complaisance. This instance of politeness was, however, no more than a shift to disengage himself the more easily from their entreaties; for, when the case was opened to the second usurer, he blessed himself from such customers, and dismissed them with the most mortifying and boorish refusal. Notwithstanding these repulses, Renaldo resolved to make one desperate push; and, without allowing himself the least respite, solicited, one by one, not fewer than fifteen persons who dealt in this kind of traffic, and his proposals were rejected by each. At last, fatigued by the toil, and exasperated at the ill success of his expedition, and half mad with the recollection of his finances, which were now drained to half-a-crown, "Since we have nothing to expect," cried he, "from the favour of Christians, let us have recourse to the descendants of Judah. Though they lie under the general reproach of nations, as a people dead to virtue and benevolence, and wholly devoted to avarice, fraud, and extortion, the most savage of their tribe cannot treat me with more barbarity of indifference, than I have experienced among those who are the authors of their reproach."

Although Fathom looked upon this proposal as an extravagant symptom of despair, he affected to approve of the scheme, and encouraged Renaldo with the hope of succeeding in another quarter, even if this expedition should fail; for, by this time, our adventurer was half resolved to export him at his own charge, rather than he should be much longer restricted in his designs upon Monimia.

Meanwhile, being resolved to try the experiment upon the children of Israel, they betook themselves to the house of a rich Jew, whose wealth they considered as a proof of his rapaciousness; and, being admitted into his counting-house, they found him in the midst of half a dozen clerks, when Renaldo, in his imagination, likened him unto a minister of darkness surrounded by his familiars, and planning schemes of misery to be executed upon the hapless sons of men. In spite of these suggestions, which were not at all mitigated by the forbidding aspect of the Hebrew, he demanded a private audience; and, being ushered into another apartment, he explained his business with manifest marks of disorder and affliction. Indeed, his confusion was in some measure owing to the looks of the Jew, who, in the midst of this exordium, pulled down his eyebrows, which were surprisingly black and bushy, so as, in appearance, totally to extinguish his visage, though he was all the time observing our youth from behind those almost impenetrable thickets.

Melvil, having signified his request, "Young gentleman," said the Israelite, with a most discordant voice, "what in the name of goodness could induce you to come to me upon such an errand? Did you ever hear that I lent money to strangers without security?" "No," replied Renaldo, "nor did I believe I should profit by my application; but my affairs are desperate; and my proposals having been rejected by every Christian to whom they were offered, I was resolved to try my fate among the Jews, who are reckoned another species of men."

Fathom, alarmed at this abrupt reply, which he supposed could not fail to disgust the merchant, interposed in the conversation, by making an apology for the plain dealing of his friend, who, he said, was soured and ruffled by his misfortunes; then exerting that power of eloquence which he had at command, he expostulated upon Renaldo's claim and expectations, described the wrongs he had suffered, extolled his virtue, and drew a most pathetic picture of his distress.

The Jew listened attentively for some time; then his eyebrows began to rise and fall alternately; he coughed, sneezed, and winking hard, "I'm plagued," said he, "with a salt rheum that trickles from my eyes without intermission." So saying, he wiped the moisture from his face, and proceeded in these words: "Sir, your story is plausible; and your friend is a good advocate; but before I give an answer to your demand, I must beg leave to ask if you can produce undeniable evidence of your being the identical person you really assume? If you are really the Count de Melvil, you will excuse my caution. We cannot be too much on our guard against fraud; though I must own you have not the air of an impostor."

Renaldo's eyes began to sparkle at this preliminary question; to which he replied, that he could procure the testimony of the Emperor's minister, to whom he had occasionally paid his respects since his first arrival in England.

"If that be the case," said the Jew, "take the trouble to call here to-morrow morning, at eight o'clock, and I will carry you in my own coach to the house of his excellency, with whom I have the honour to be acquainted; and, if he has nothing to object against your character or pretensions, I will contribute my assistance towards your obtaining justice at the Imperial court."

The Hungarian was so much confounded at this unexpected reception, that he had not power to thank the merchant for his promised favour, but stood motionless and silent, while the streams of emotion of the heart was of more weight with the Jew, than the eloquent acknowledgment which Ferdinand took the opportunity of making for his friend; and he was fain to dismiss them a little abruptly, in order to prevent a second discharge of that same rheum of which he had already complained.

Melvil recollected all that had happened as a dream, which had no foundation in truth, and was all day long in a sort of delirium, produced by the alternate gusts of hope and fear that still agitated his bosom; for he was not yet without apprehension of being again disappointed by some unlucky occurrence.

He did not, however, fail to be punctual to the hour of his appointment, when the Jew told him, there would be no occasion for visiting the ambassador, because Renaldo had been, the preceding day, recognised by one of the clerks who had been employed as a purveyor in the Imperial army; and who, knowing his family, confirmed everything he had alleged. "After breakfast," continued this benevolent Israelite, "I will give you an order upon my banker for five hundred pounds, that you may be enabled to appear at Vienna as the son and representative of Count Melvil; and you shall also be furnished with a letter of recommendation to a person of some influence at that court, whose friendship and countenance may be of some service to your suit; for I am now heartily engaged in your interest, in consequence of the fair and unblemished character which I find you have hitherto maintained."

The reader must appeal to his own heart, to acquire a just idea of Renaldo's feelings, when every tittle of these promises was fulfilled, and the merchant refused to take one farthing by way of premium, contenting himself with the slender security of a personal bond. He was, in truth, overwhelmed with the obligation, and certainly disposed to believe that his benefactor was something more than human. As for Fathom, his sentiments took a different turn; and he scrupled not to impute all this kindness to some deep-laid interested scheme, the scope of which he could not at present comprehend.

After the tumults of the young gentleman's joy had subsided, and he found himself eased of that burdensome poverty under which he had groaned so long, his thoughts, which before were dissipated upon the various circumstances of distress, began to collect themselves in a body, and to resume their deliberations upon a subject which they had been long accustomed to consider; this was no other than the forlorn Monimia, whose idea now emerged in his bosom, being disencumbered of one part of the load by which it had been depressed. He mentioned her name to Fathom with marks of the most melting compassion, deplored her apostasy, and, while he protested that he had divorced her for ever from his heart, expressed an inclination to see her once more before his departure, that he might in person exhort her to penitence and reformation.

Our adventurer, who dreaded such an interview as the infallible means of his own ruin, resisted the proposal with the whole power of his elocution. He affirmed, that Renaldo's desire was a manifest proof that he still retained part of the fatal poison which that enchantress had spread within his veins; and that the sight of her, softened by his reproaches into tears and affected contrition, would dispel his resentment, disable his manhood, and blow the embers of his former passion to such a rage, as would hurry him on to a reconciliation, which would debase his honour, and ruin his future peace. In a word, Ferdinand described the danger that would attend the meeting in such emphatic terms, that the Hungarian started with horror at the picture which he drew, and in this particular conformed with the admonition of his friend.

One hundred pounds of the Jew's money was immediately appropriated for the payment of his most urgent debts; the like sum he presented to his friend Fathom, with a solemn promise of sharing with him whatever good fortune might await him in Germany. And though Monimia had forfeited all title to his regard, so ill could he bear the prospect of her distress, that he entrusted his dear companion with the half of what remained, to be expended for her use, fully resolving to screen her from the shocks and temptations of want, as the circumstances of his future fate would allow.

Fathom, far from opposing, applauded his generosity with marks of extreme wonder and admiration, assuring him, that she should be put in possession of his bounty immediately after his departure, he being unwilling to make her acquainted with her good fortune before that period, lest, finding his affairs in a fair way of being retrieved, she should be base enough to worship his returning prosperity, and, by false professions, and artful blandishments, seek to ensnare his heart anew.

CHAPTER FORTY-EIGHT.
COUNT FATHOM UNMASKS HIS BATTERY; IS REPULSED; AND VARIES HIS OPERATIONS WITHOUT EFFECT.

Every necessary preparation being made, Renaldo, accompanied by our adventurer, took the road to Dover, where he embarked in a packet-boat for Calais, after having settled a correspondence with his dear Ferdinand, from whom he did not part without tears. He had before solicited him to be his fellow-traveller, that he might personally enjoy the benefit of his conversation and superior sagacity; but these entreaties he strenuously opposed, on pretence of his being determined to push his fortune in England, which he considered as his native country, and as the land in which, of all others, a man of merit has the best encouragement. Such were the reasons he alleged for refusing to attend his benefactor, who was himself eagerly desirous of attaining a settlement in the island of Great Britain. But our hero's real motives for staying were of a very different complexion.—The reader is already informed of his aim upon the fair orphan, which, at present, was the chief spring of his conduct. He may also recollect such passages of his life, as were sufficient to deter him from reappearing at Presburg or Vienna. But, besides these reflections, he was detained by a full persuasion that Renaldo would sink under the power and influence of his antagonist, consequently be rendered incapable to provide for his friends; and that he himself, fraught with wiles and experience as he was, could not fail to make himself amends for what he had suffered among a people equally rich and unthinking.

Melvil, having embraced our adventurer, and with a deep sigh bid him take care of the unfortunate Monimia, committed himself to the sea, and, by the assistance of a favourable gale, was in four hours safely landed on the French shore; while Fathom took post-horses for London, where he arrived that same night, and next day, in the forenoon, went to visit the beauteous mourner, who had as yet received no intimation of Renaldo's departure or design. He found her in the attitude of writing a letter to her inconstant lover, the contents of which the reader will be acquainted with in due time. Her countenance, notwithstanding the veil of melancholy by which it was overcast, seemed altogether serene and composed; she was the picture of pious resignation, and sat like PATIENCE on a monument, smiling at grief. After having paid the compliment of the morning, Fathom begged pardon for having omitted to visit her during three days, in which, he said, his time had been wholly engrossed in procuring a proper equipage for Count Melvil, who had at last bid an eternal adieu to the island of Great Britain.

At this information the hapless Monimia fell back in her chair, and continued some minutes in a swoon; from which being recovered, "Excuse me, Mr. Fathom," cried she with a deep sigh; "this, I hope, is the last agony I shall feel from my unhappy passion."—Then wiping the tears from her lovely eyes, she retrieved her tranquillity, and desired to know by what means Renaldo had been enabled to undertake his journey into the empire. Our hero, upon this occasion, assumed the whole merit of having promoted the interest of his friend, by giving her to understand, that he, in consequence of an unforeseen windfall, had defrayed the expense of the Count's equipment; though he observed, that it was not without reluctance he saw Renaldo make a wrong use of his friendship.

"Although I was happy," proceeded this artful traitor, "in being able to discharge my obligations to the house of Melvil, I could not help feeling the most sensible chagrin, when I saw my assistance rendered subservient to the triumphs of the youth's baseness and infidelity; for he chose, as the companion of his travels, the abandoned woman for whom he had forsaken the all-perfect Monimia, whose virtue and accomplishments did not preserve her sacred from his ungrateful sarcasms and unmannerly ridicule. Believe me, madam, I was so shocked at his conversation on that subject, and so much incensed at his want of delicacy, that my temper was scarce sufficient for the ceremony of parting. And, now that my debt to his family is over-paid, I have solemnly renounced his correspondence."

When she heard that, instead of betraying the least symptom of regret or compassion for her unhappy fate, the perfidious youth had exulted over her fall, and even made her a subject for his mirth, the blood revisited her faded cheeks, and resentment restored to her eyes that poignancy which sorrow had before overcome. Yet she scorned to give speech to her indignation; but, forcing a smile, "Why should I repine," said she, "at the mortifications of a life which I despise, and from which, I hope, Heaven speedily will set me free!"

Fathom, fired by her emotion, which had recalled all the graces of her beauty, exclaimed in a rapture, "Talk not so contemptuously of this life, which hath still a fund of happiness in store for the amiable, the divine Monimia. Though one admirer hath proved an apostate to his vows, your candour will not suffer you to condemn the whole sex. Some there are, whose bosoms glow with passion equally pure, unalterable, and intense. For my own part, I have sacrificed to a rigid punctilio of honour the dearest ideas of my heart. I beheld your unrivalled charms, and deeply felt their power. Yet, while a possibility of Melvil's reformation remained, and while I was restrained by my niggard fortune from making a tender worthy of your acceptance, I combated with my inclinations, and bore without repining the pangs of hopeless love. But, now that my honour is disengaged, and my fortune rendered independent, by the last will of a worthy nobleman, whose friendship I was favoured with in France, I presume to lay myself at the feet of the adorable Monimia, as the most faithful of admirers, whose happiness or misery wholly depends upon her nod. Believe me, madam, these are not the professions of idle gallantry—I speak the genuine, though imperfect, language of my heart. Words, even the most pathetic, cannot do justice to my love. I gaze upon your beauty with ravishment; but I contemplate the graces of your soul with such awful veneration, that I tremble while I approach you, as if my vows were addressed to some superior being."

During this declaration, which was pronounced in the most emphatic manner, Monimia was successively agitated with shame, anger, and grief; nevertheless, she summoned her whole philosophy to her aid, and, with a tranquil, though determined air, begged he would not diminish the obligations he had already conferred, by disturbing with such unseasonable addresses a poor unhappy maid, who had detached all her thoughts from earthly objects, and waited impatiently for that dissolution which alone could put a period to her misfortunes.

Fathom, imagining that these were no other than the suggestions of a temporary disappointment and despondence, which it was his business to oppose with all his eloquence and art, renewed his theme with redoubled ardour, and, at last, became so importunate in his desires, that Monimia, provoked beyond the power of concealing her resentment, said, she was heartily sorry to find herself under the necessity of telling him, that, in the midst of her misfortunes, she could not help remembering what she had been. Then, rising from her seat, with all the dignity of displeasure, "Perhaps," added she, "you have forgot who was the father of the once happy Monimia."

With these words she retired into another chamber, leaving our adventurer confounded by the repulse he had sustained. Not that he was discouraged from prosecuting his aim—on the contrary, this rebuff seemed to add fresh vigour to his operations. He now thought it high time to bring over Madam la Mer to his interest; and, to facilitate her conversion, took an opportunity of bribing her with some inconsiderable presents, after having amused her with a plausible tale of his passion for Monimia, with whom she undertook the office of his mediatrix, on the supposition that his intentions were honourable, and highly advantageous to her lodger.

She was, first of all, invested with the office of obtaining pardon for the offence he had given; and, in this negotiation she succeeded so well, as to become an advocate for his suit; accordingly, she took all occasions of magnifying his praise. His agreeable person was often the subject of her discourse to the fair mourner. Her admiration dwelt upon his politeness, good sense, and winning deportment; and she every day retailed little stories of his benevolence and greatness of soul. The defect in his birth she represented as a circumstance altogether foreign from the consideration of his merit; especially in a nation where such distinctions are as little respected as they will be in a future state. She mentioned several persons of note, who basked in the sunshine of power and fortune, without having enjoyed the least hereditary assistance from their forefathers. One, she said, sprung from the loins of an obscure attorney; another was the grandson of a valet-de-chambre; a third was the issue of an accountant; and a fourth the offspring of a woollen draper. All these were the children of their own good works, and had raised themselves upon their personal virtues and address; a foundation certainly more solid and honourable than a vague inheritance derived from ancestors, in whose deserts they could not be supposed to have borne the least share.

Monimia listened to all these arguments with great patience and affability, though she at once dived into the source from which all such insinuations flowed. She joined in the commendations of Fathom, and owned herself a particular instance of that benevolence which the old lady had so justly extolled; but, once for all, to prevent the supplication which Madam la Mer was about to make, she solemnly protested that her heart was altogether shut against any other earthly engagement, and that her thoughts were altogether employed upon her eternal salvation.

The assiduous landlady, perceiving the steadiness of her disposition, thought proper to alter her method of proceeding, and, for the present, suspended that theme by which she found her fair lodger disobliged. Resolved to reconcile Monimia to life, before she would again recommend Ferdinand to her love, she endeavoured to amuse her imagination, by recounting the occasional incidents of the day, hoping gradually to decoy her attention to those sublunary objects from which it had been industriously weaned. She seasoned her conversation with agreeable sallies; enlarged upon the different scenes of pleasure and diversion appertaining to this great metropolis; practised upon her palate with the delicacies of eating; endeavoured to shake her temperance with repeated proffers and recommendations of certain cordials and restoratives, which she alleged were necessary for the recovery of her health; and pressed her to make little excursions into the fields that skirt the town, for the benefit of air and exercise.

While this auxiliary plied the disconsolate Monimia on one hand, Fathom was not remiss on the other. He now seemed to have sacrificed his passion to her quiet; his discourse turned upon more indifferent subjects. He endeavoured to dispel her melancholy with arguments drawn from philosophy and religion. On some occasions, he displayed all his fund of good humour, with a view to beguile her sorrow; he importuned her to give him the pleasure of squiring her to some place of innocent entertainment; and, finally, insisted upon her accepting a pecuniary reinforcement to her finances, which he knew to be in a most consumptive condition.

CHAPTER FORTY-NINE.
MONIMIA'S HONOUR IS PROTECTED BY
THE INTERPOSITION OF HEAVEN.

With that complacency and fortitude which were peculiar to herself, this hapless stranger resisted all those artful temptations. Her sustenance was barely such as exempted her from the guilt of being accessory to her own death; her drink was the simple element. She encouraged no discourse but that which turned upon the concerns of her immortal part. She never went abroad, except in visits to a French chapel in the neighbourhood; she refused the proffered assistance of our adventurer with equal obstinacy and politeness, and with pleasure saw herself wasting towards that period of mortality which was the consummation of her wish. Yet her charms, far from melting away with her constitution, seemed to triumph over the decays of nature. Her shape and features still retained that harmony for which they had always been distinguished. A mixture of majesty and sweetness diffused itself in her looks, and her feebleness added to that soft and feminine grace which attracts the sympathy, and engages the protection of every humane beholder. The associates thus baffled in their attempts to excite her ideas of pleasure, again shifted their plan, and resolved to attack this forlorn beauty on the side of fear and mortification.

Our adventurer became less frequent in his visits, and more indifferent in his language and deportment; while Madam la Mer gradually relaxed in that complacency and respect with which she had hitherto behaved towards her fair lodger. She even began to drop hints of disapprobation and reproach against this pattern of innocence and beauty, and at length grew bold enough to tell her, that her misfortunes could be attributed to nothing but her own obstinacy and pride; that she had been at great pains to disoblige the only person who was able and willing to raise her above dependence; and that, if his protection should be withdrawn, she must be exposed to the utmost extremity of distress.

These insinuations, instead of producing the desired effect, inflamed the indignation of Monimia, who, in a most dignified style of rebuke, chid her for her indelicacy and presumption, observing, that she could have no title to take such freedoms with lodgers, whose punctuality and regular deportment left her no room to complain. Notwithstanding this animated reply, she underwent the most deplorable anguish, when she reflected upon the insolence of this woman, from whose barbarity she had no resource; and, seeing no other possibility of redress than that of appealing to the good offices of Fathom, she conquered her reluctance so far, as to complain to him of Madam la Mer's incivility.

Pleased with this application, he gave her to understand, with very little ceremony or preamble, that it wholly depended upon herself whether she should continue to be wretched, or be delivered at once from all her cares and perplexity; that, notwithstanding the disdain with which she had treated his addresses, he was still ready to lay himself and his fortune at her feet; and that, if she should again reject the disinterested proposal, the whole world and her own conscience would charge upon herself whatever calamities she might be subjected to in the sequel. Interpreting into a favourable hesitation her silence, which was the result of wrath and amazement, he proceeded to throw himself at her feet, and utter a romantic rhapsody, in the course of which, laying aside all that restraint which he had hitherto preserved, he seized her delicate hand, and pressed it to his lips; nay, so far did he forget himself on this occasion, that he caught the fair creature in his arms, and rudely ravished a kiss from those lips which he had before contemplated with the most distant reverence of desire.

Having thus broken down the fences of decorum, and being heated with transport, he, in all probability, would have acted the part of young Tarquin, and violated by force that sacred shrine of honour, beauty, and unblemished truth, had not the wrath kindled by such an unexpected outrage inspired her with strength and spirits sufficient to protect her virtue, and intimidate the ruffian who could offer violence to such perfection. She broke from his detested embrace with surprising agility, and called aloud to her landlady for assistance; but that discreet matron was resolved to hear nothing, and Fathom's appetite being whetted to a most brutal degree of eagerness, "Madam," said he, "all opposition is vain. What you have refused to my entreaties, you shall yield to my power; and I am determined to force you to your own advantage."

So saying, he sprung towards her, with the most savage and impious intent, when this amiable heroine snatching up his sword, which lay upon a by-table, and unsheathing it instantaneously, presented the point to his breast, and, while her eyes glanced with intolerable keenness, "Villain!" cried she, "the spirit of my father animates my bosom, and the vengeance of Heaven shall not be frustrated." He was not so much affected by his bodily danger, as awestruck at the manner of her address, and the appearance of her aspect, which seemed to shine with something supernatural, and actually disordered his whole faculties, insomuch that he retreated without attempting to make the least reply; and she, having secured the door after his departure, sat down to ponder upon this shocking event.

Words are wanting to describe the accumulated horrors that took possession of her mind, when she thus beheld all her presaging fears realised, and found herself at the mercy of two wretches, who had now pulled off the mask, after having lost all sentiments of humanity. Common affliction was an agreeable reverie to what she suffered, deprived of her parents, exiled from her friends and country, reduced to the brink of wanting the most indispensable necessaries of life, in a foreign land, where she knew not one person to whose protection she could have recourse, from the inexpressible woes that environed her. She complained to Heaven that her life was protracted, for the augmentation of that misery which was already too severe to be endured; for she shuddered at the prospect of being utterly abandoned in the last stage of mortality, without one friend to close her eyes, or do the last offices of humanity to her breathless corse. These were dreadful reflections to a young lady who had been born to affluence and splendour, trained up in all the elegance of education, by nature fraught with that sensibility which refines the sentiment and taste, and so tenderly cherished by her indulgent parents, that they suffered not the winds of Heaven to visit her face too roughly.

Having passed the night in such agony, she rose at daybreak, and, hearing the chapel bell toll for morning prayers, resolved to go to this place of worship, in order to implore the assistance of Heaven. She no sooner opened her chamber door, with this intent, than she was met by Madam la Mer, who, after having professed her concern for what had happened overnight, and imputed Mr. Fathom's rudeness to the spirit of intoxication, by which she had never before seen him possessed, she endeavoured to dissuade Monimia from her purpose, by observing, that her health would be prejudiced by the cold morning air; but finding her determined, she insisted upon accompanying her to chapel, on pretence of respect, though, in reality, with a view to prevent the escape of her beauteous lodger. Thus attended, the hapless mourner entered the place, and, according to the laudable hospitality of England, which is the only country in Christendom where a stranger is not made welcome to the house of God, this amiable creature, emaciated and enfeebled as she was, must have stood in a common passage during the whole service, had not she been perceived by a humane gentlewoman, who, struck with her beauty and dignified air, and melted with sympathy at the ineffable sorrow which was visible in her countenance, opened the pew in which she sat, and accommodated Monimia and her attendant. If she was captivated by her first appearance, she was not less affected by the deportment of her fair guest, which was the pattern of genuine devotion.

In a word, this good lady, who was a merchant's widow in opulent circumstances, was inflamed with a longing desire to know and befriend the amiable stranger, who, after service, turning about to thank her for her civility, Madam Clement, with that frankness which is the result of true benevolence, told her, she was too much prepossessed in her favour to let slip this opportunity of craving her acquaintance, and of expressing her inclination to alleviate, if possible, that affliction which was manifest in her looks.

Monimia, overwhelmed with gratitude and surprise at this unexpected address, gazed upon the lady in silence, and when she repeated her tenders of service, could make no other reply to her goodness, than by bursting into a flood of tears. This was a species of eloquence which did not pass unregarded by Madam Clement, who, while her own eyes were bedewed with the drops of sympathy and compassion, took the lovely orphan by the hand, and led her, without further ceremony, to her own coach, that stood waiting at the door, whither they were followed by Mrs. la Mer, who was so much confounded at the adventure, that she made no objections to the proposal of the lady, who handed her lodger into the carriage; but retired, with all possible despatch, to make Fathom acquainted with this unforeseen event.

Meanwhile the agitation of Monimia, at this providential deliverance, was such as had well-nigh destroyed her tender frame. The blood flushed and forsook her cheeks by turns; she trembled from head to foot, notwithstanding the consolatory assurances of Madam Clement, and, without being able to utter one word, was conducted to the house of that kind benefactress, where the violence of her transports overpowered her constitution, and she sunk down upon a couch in a swoon, from which she was not easily recovered. This affecting circumstance augmented the pity, and interested the curiosity of Madam Clement, who concluded there was something very extraordinary in the case of the stranger, to produce these agonies; and grew impatient to hear the particulars of her story.

Monimia no sooner retrieved the use of her faculties, than looking around, and observing with what humane concern her new hostess was employed in effecting her recovery, "Is this," said she, "a flattering illusion of the brain? or am I really under the protection of some beneficent being, whom Heaven hath inspired with generosity to rescue an hapless stranger from the most forlorn state of misery and woe?" Her voice was at all times ravishingly sweet; and this exclamation was pronounced with such pathetic fervour, that Madam Clement clasped her in her arms, and kissing her with all the eagerness of maternal affection, "Yes," cried she, "fair creature, Heaven hath bestowed upon me an heart to compassionate, and power, I hope, to lighten the burden of your sorrows."

She then prevailed upon her to take some nourishment, and afterwards to recount the particulars of her fate; a task she performed with such accuracy and candour, that Madam Clement, far from suspecting her sincerity, saw truth and conviction in every circumstance of her tale; and, having condoled her misfortunes, entreated her to forget them, or at least look upon herself as one sheltered under the care and tuition of a person whose study it would be to supply her want of natural parents. This would have been an happy vicissitude of fortune, had it not arrived too late; but such a sudden and unlooked-for transition not only disordered the faculties of poor Monimia's mind, but also overpowered the organs of her body, already fatigued and enfeebled by the distresses she had undergone; so that she was taken ill of a fever that same night, and became delirious before morning, when a physician was called to her assistance.

While this gentleman was in the house, Madam Clement was visited by Fathom, who, after having complained, in the most insinuating manner that she had encouraged his wife to abandon her duty, told her a plausible story of his first acquaintance with Monimia, and his marriage at the Fleet, which, he said, he was ready to prove by the evidence of the clergyman who joined them, and that of Mrs. la Mer, who was present at the ceremony. The good lady, although a little staggered at the genteel appearance and engaging address of this stranger, could not prevail upon herself to believe that she had been imposed upon by her fair lodger, who by this time had given too convincing a proof of her sincerity; nevertheless, in order to prevent any dispute that might be prejudicial to the health or recovery of Monimia, she gave him to understand, that she would not at present enter upon the merits of the cause, but only assure him, that the young lady was actually bereft of her senses, and in imminent danger of her life; for the truth of which assertions she would appeal to his own observation, and the opinion of the physician, who was then employed in writing a prescription for the cure of her disease.

So saying, she conducted him into the chamber, where he beheld the hapless virgin stretched upon a sick-bed, panting under the violence of a distemper too mighty for her weakly frame, her hair dishevelled, and discomposure in her looks; all the roses of her youth were faded, yet all the graces of her beauty were not fled. She retained that sweetness and symmetry, which death itself could not destroy; and though her discourse was incoherent, her voice was still musical, resembling those feathered songsters who warble their native woodnotes wild.

Fathom, as upon all other occasions, so on this, did behave like an inimitable actor; he ran to the bedside, with all the trepidation of a distracted lover; he fell upon his knees, and, while the tears rolled down his cheeks, imprinted a thousand kisses on the soft hand of Monimia, who regarding him with a lack-lustre and undistinguishing eye, "Alas! Renaldo," said she, "we were born to be unhappy." "Would to Heaven," cried Ferdinand, in a transport of grief, "the wretch Renaldo had never been born! that is the villain who seduced the affection of this unfortunate woman. I admitted the traitor into my friendship and confidence, relieved him in his necessities; and, like the ungrateful viper, he hath stung the very bosom that cherished him in his distress." Then he proceeded to inform Madam Clement how he had delivered that same Renaldo from prison, maintained him afterwards at a great expense, and at length furnished him with a sum of money and proper credentials to support his interest at the Court of Vienna.

Having finished this detail, he asked the physician's sentiments of his wife's distemper, and being told that her life was in extreme jeopardy, begged he would use his utmost endeavours in her behalf, and even made him a tender of an extraordinary fee, which was refused. He also thanked Madam Clement for her charity and benevolence towards a stranger, and took his leave with many polite professions of gratitude and esteem. He had no sooner quitted the house, than the physician, who was a humane man, and a foreigner, began to caution the lady against his insinuations, observing, that some circumstances of the story concerning Renaldo were, to his particular knowledge, contrary to truth; for that he himself had been applied to for letters of recommendation in behalf of Count Melvil, by a Jew merchant of his acquaintance, who had supplied the young gentleman with money sufficient for his occasions, in consequence of a minute inquiry he had made into the character of Renaldo, who was, by all reports, a youth of strict honour and untainted morals.

Madam Clement, thus cautioned, entered into deliberation with her own thoughts, and, comparing the particulars of this account with those of Monimia's own story, she concluded that Fathom was the very traitor he himself had described; and that he had, by abusing the confidence of both, effected a fatal breach between two innocent and deserving lovers. She accordingly looked upon him with horror and detestation; but nevertheless resolved to treat him with civility in the meantime, that the poor young lady might not be disturbed in her last moments; for she had now lost all hopes of her recovery. Yet the fever abated, and in two days she retrieved the use of her reason; though the distemper had affected her lungs, and she was in all appearance doomed to linger a few weeks longer in a consumption.

Fathom was punctual in his visitation, though never admitted into her presence after the delirium vanished; and he had the opportunity of seeing her conveyed in a chariot to Kensington Gravel Pits, a place which may be termed the last stage of many a mortal peregrination. He now implicitly believed that death would in a few days baffle all his designs upon the unfortunate Monimia; and foreseeing that, as he had owned himself her husband, he might be obliged to defray the expenses incurred by her sickness and burial, he very prudently intermitted in his visits, and had recourse to the intelligence of his auxiliary.

As for Monimia, she approached the goal of life, not simply with resignation, but with rapture. She enjoyed in tranquillity the conversation of her kind benefactress, who never stirred from her apartment; she was blessed with the spiritual consolation of a worthy clergyman, who removed all her religious scruples; and she congratulated herself on the near prospect of that land of peace where sorrow is not known.

At length Mrs. la Mer gave notice to our adventurer of this amiable young lady's decease, and the time fixed for the interment. Upon which these two virtuous associates took possession of a place from whence they could, unperceived, behold the funeral. He must have a hard heart, who, without an emotion of pity, can see the last offices performed to a young creature cut off in the flower of youth and beauty, even though he knows not her name, and is an utter stranger to her virtues. How callous then must the soul of that wretch have been, who, without a symptom of remorse or concern, saw the sable hearse adorned with white plumes, as emblems of Monimia's purity, pass before him, while her incomparable merit stood full in his remembrance, and he knew himself the wicked cause of her untimely fate!

Perfidious wretch! thy crimes turn out so atrocious, that I half repent me of having undertaken to record thy memoirs; yet such monsters ought to be exhibited to public view, that mankind may be upon their guard against imposture; that the world may see how fraud is apt to overshoot itself; and that, as virtue, though it may suffer for a while, will triumph in the end; so iniquity, though it may prosper for a season, will at last be overtaken by that punishment and disgrace which are its due.

CHAPTER FIFTY.
FATHOM SHIFTS THE SCENE, AND APPEARS IN A NEW CHARACTER.

Fathom's expectations with respect to the fair orphan having thus proved abortive, he lost no time in bewailing his miscarriage, but had immediate recourse to other means of improving his small fortune, which, at this period, amounted to near two hundred pounds. Whatever inclination he had to resume the character he had formerly borne in the polite world, he durst not venture to launch out again into the expense necessary to maintain that station, because his former resources were now stopped, and all the people of fashion by this time convinced of his being a needy adventurer. Nevertheless, he resolved to sound the sentiments of his old friends at a distance, and judge, from the reception he should meet with, how far he might presume upon their countenance and favour. For he rightly supposed, that if he could in any shape contribute to their interest or amusement, they would easily forgive his former pretensions to quality, arrogant as they were, and still entertain him on the footing of a necessary acquaintance.

With this view, he one day presented himself at court in a very gay suit of clothes, and bowed, at a distance, to many of his old fashionable friends of both sexes, not one of whom favoured him with any other notice, than that of a quarter curtsey, or slight inclination of the head. For, by this time, the few that remembered him knew from what retirement he now emerged, and avoided him accordingly as the jail infection. But the greater part of those who had cultivated him in the zenith of his fortune were now utter strangers to his person, which they had actually forgot, amidst the succession of novelties that surrounded them; or, if they did recollect his name, it was remembered as an old fashion which had been many months out of date.

Notwithstanding these mortifying discouragements, our hero, that same evening, effected a lodgment in a certain gaming-house not far from St. James's; and, as he played pretty high, and made a parade of his ready money, he was soon recognised by divers persons of consequence, who cordially welcomed him to England, on pretence of believing he had been abroad, and with great complacency repeated their former professions of friendship. Though this was a certain way of retaining the favour of those worthies, while his finances continued to flourish, and his payments were prompt, he knew the weakness of his funds too well, to think they could bear the vicissitudes of play; and the remembrance of the two British knights who had spoiled him at Paris, hung over his imagination with the most frightful presages. Besides, he perceived that gaming was now managed in such a manner, as rendered skill and dexterity of no advantage. For the spirit of play having overspread the land, like a pestilence, raged to such a degree of madness and desperation, that the unhappy people who were infected, laid aside all thoughts of amusement, economy, or caution, and risked their fortunes upon issues equally extravagant, childish, and absurd.

The whole mystery of the art was reduced to the simple exercise of tossing up a guinea, and the lust of laying wagers, which they indulged to a surprising pitch of ridiculous intemperance. In one corner of the room might be heard a pair of lordlings running their grandmothers against each other, that is, betting sums on the longest liver; in another the success of the wager depended upon the sex of the landlady's next child; and one of the waiters happening to drop down in an apoplectic fit, a certain noble peer exclaimed, "Dead for a thousand pounds." The challenge was immediately accepted; and when the master of the house sent for a surgeon to attempt the cure, the nobleman, who set the price upon the patient's head, insisted upon his being left to the efforts of nature alone, otherwise the wager should be void. Nay, when the landlord harped upon the loss he should sustain by the death of a trusty servant, his lordship obviated the objection, by desiring that the fellow might be charged in the bill.

In short, the rage of gaming seemed to have devoured all their other faculties, and to have equalled the rash enthusiasm of the inhabitants of Malacca in the East Indies, who are so possessed with that pernicious spirit, that they sacrifice to it not only their fortunes, but also their wives and children; and then letting their hair down upon their shoulders, in imitation of the ancient Lacedaemonians when they devoted themselves to death, those wretches unsheathe their daggers, and murder every living creature in their way. In this, however, they differ from the gamesters of our country, who never find their senses, until they have lost their fortunes, and beggared their families; whereas the Malays never run amuck, but in consequence of misery and despair.

Such are the amusements, or rather such is the continual employment of those hopeful youths who are destined by birth to be the judges of our property, and pillars of our constitution. Such are the heirs and representatives of those patriots who planned, and those heroes who maintained, the laws and freedom of their country; who were the patrons of merit, the fathers of the poor, the terror of vice and immorality, and at once the ornaments and support of a happy nation.

Our adventurer considered all these circumstances with his wonted sagacity, and, seeing upon what precarious footing he must stand, should he rank himself with such society, he wisely came to the resolution of descending one step in the degrees of life, and of taking upon him the title of physician, under which he did not despair of insinuating himself into the pockets of his patients, and into the secrets of private families, so as to acquire a comfortable share of practice, or captivate the heart of some heiress or rich widow, whose fortune would at once render him independent and happy.

After this determination, his next care was to concert measures for his first appearance in this new character; well knowing, that the success of a physician, in a great measure, depends upon the external equipage in which he first declares himself an adept in the healing art. He first of all procured a few books on the subject of medicine, which he studied with great attention during the remaining part of the winter and spring, and repaired to Tunbridge with the first of the season, where he appeared in the uniform of Aesculapius, namely, a plain suit, full trimmed, with a voluminous tie-periwig; believing that in this place he might glide, as it were, imperceptibly into the functions of his new employment, and gradually accustom himself to the method and form of prescription.

A man so well known in the gay world could not be supposed to effect such a transformation without being observed; and therefore, in order to anticipate the censure and ridicule of those who might be tempted to make themselves merry at his expense, he, on his arrival at the wells, repaired to the shop of an apothecary, and calling for pen, ink, and paper, wrote a prescription, which he desired might be immediately made up. While this was doing by the servant, he was invited into a parlour by the master, with whom he entered into conversation touching the properties of the Tunbridge water, which seemed to have been his particular study; and indeed he had perused Rouzee's treatise on that subject with indefatigable assiduity. From this theme, he made digressions into other parts of medicine, upon which he spoke with such plausible elocution, that the apothecary, whose knowledge in that art was not very profound, looked upon him as a physician of great learning and experience, and hinted a desire of knowing his name and situation.

Fathom accordingly gave him to understand, that he had studied physic, and taken his degrees at Padua, rather for his amusement, than with any view of exercising medicine, as he then could not possibly foresee the misfortunes which had since happened to his family, and by which he was now compelled to have recourse to a profession that was very much beneath the expectations of his birth. Yet he bore his disappointments with resignation, and even good-humour, and blessed his stars for having inclined him to the study of any branch of knowledge by which he might be enabled to laugh at the vicissitudes of fortune. He then observed, that he had practised with some applause at the hot well near Bristol, before he thought he should be ever reduced to the necessity of taking a fee, and that, in all probability, his metamorphosis, when known, would furnish matter of surprise and merriment to some of his old acquaintance.

The apothecary was equally struck with his polite address, and pleased with his agreeable discourse. He consoled him for the misfortunes of his family, by assuring him, that in England nothing could be more honourable, or indeed profitable, than the character of a physician, provided he could once wriggle himself into practice; and insinuated, that, although he was restricted by certain engagements with other persons of the faculty, he should be glad of an opportunity to show his regard for Doctor Fathom. This was a very effectual method which our hero took to intimate his new character to the public. By the industry and communicative disposition of the apothecary, it was circulated in half a day through every family in the place; and, next morning, when Ferdinand appeared, the company forthwith assembled in separate groups, and from each knot he heard his name reverberated in a whisper.

Having thus announced himself to all whom it might concern, and allowed the ladies two days to discuss the merit of his transfiguration, together with the novelty of the case, he ventured to salute, at a distance, a lady and her daughter, who had been his patients at the hot well; and, although they honoured his bow with the return of a slight curtsey, they gave him not the least encouragement to make a nearer approach. Notwithstanding this rebuff, he concluded, that, should the health of either come in question, they would renew their application to his skill, and what was refused by their pride would be granted by their apprehension. Here, however, he happened to be mistaken in his conjecture.

The young lady being seized with a violent headache and palpitation, her mother desired the apothecary to recommend a physician; and the person with whom he was contracted being at that time absent, he proposed Doctor Fathom as a man of great ability and discretion. But the good lady rejected the proposal with disdain, because she had formerly known him in the character of a Count—though that very character was the chief reason that had then induced her to crave his advice.

Such is the caprice of the world in general, that whatever bears the face of novelty captivates, or rather bewitches, the imagination, and confounds the ideas of reason and common sense. If, for example, a scullion, from the clinking of pewter, shall conceive a taste for the clinking of rhyme, and make shift to bring together twenty syllables, so as that the tenth and last shall have the like ending, the composition is immediately extolled as a miracle; and what appeals to the admiration is not the wit, the elegance, or poetry of the work, but the uncultivated talent and humble station of the author. A reader does not exclaim, "What a delicate sentiment! what a beautiful simile! what easy and musical versification!"—but cries in rapture, "Heavens! what a prodigy a poet from the scullery! a muse in livery! or, Apollo with a trowel!"—The public is astonished into liberality—the scullion eats from those trenchers he scoured before—the footman is admitted into the coach behind which he was wont to stand—and the bricklayer, instead of plastering walls, bedaubs his illustrious partner with the mortar of his praise. Thus, lifted into a higher sphere, their talents receive cultivation; they become professed bards, and though their subsequent works bear evident marks of improvement, they are neglected among the rest of their brethren, because that novelty, which recommended them in the beginning, no longer remains.

So it fared with our adventurer in his new occupation. There was something so extraordinary in a nobleman's understanding medicine, and so uncommon in a physician's prescribing gratis, that the curiosity and admiration of the company at Bristol were engaged, and they followed his advice, as the direction of some supernatural intelligence. But, now that he professed himself one of the faculty, and might be supposed to have refreshed his memory, and reinforced his knowledge for the occasion, he was as much overlooked as any other physician unsupported by interest or cabal; or, at least, the notice he attracted was not at all to the advantage of his character, because it wholly regarded the decline of his fortune, which is a never-failing fund of disgrace.

These mortifications did not overcome the patience and perseverance of Fathom, who foresaw, that the soothing hand of time would cast a veil of oblivion over those scenes which were remembered to his prejudice; and that, in the meantime, though he was excluded from the private parties of the fair sex, in which his main hope of success was placed, he should be able to insinuate himself into some degree of favour and practice among the male patients; and some lucky cure, properly displayed, might be the means of propagating his fame, and banishing that reserve which at present interfered with his purpose. Accordingly, it was not long before he found means to break that spell of universal prejudice that hedged him in. At the ordinary which he frequented, his polite carriage, facetious remarks, and agreeable stories soon conciliated the regard of his fellow-guests, among whom he sometimes rallied his own transformation with singular good-humour and success. He was even witty upon his want of employment, and used to observe, that a physician without practice had one comfort to which his brethren were strangers, namely, that the seldomer he had occasion to prescribe, the less he had upon his conscience on account of being accessory to the death of his fellow-creatures.

Nothing so effectually blunts the shafts of ridicule, and defeats the aims of slander, as this method of anticipation. In spite of the arrows that were levelled against his reputation from every tea-table at Tunbridge, he made his party good among almost all the gay young gentlemen that frequented the place. Far from avoiding his company, they began to court his conversation, and he was commonly seen in the walks surrounded with a group of admirers.

Having thus paved the way for a total removal of the invidious prepossession that obstructed his views, he, one night, while every person was lulled in the arms of repose, and universal silence prevailed, tuned his violin, and began to play some masterly airs, in a tone so uncommonly expressive, and with such ravishing dexterity of execution, that a certain lady, who lodged in the same house, being waked by the music, and ignorant of the source from which it flowed, listened with rapture, as to the harp of an angel, and, wrapping herself in a loose gown, rose and opened her chamber door, in order to discover in what apartment the musician resided. She no sooner entered the passage, than she found her fellow-lodgers already assembled on the same occasion; and there they remained during the best part of the night, transported by the harmony which our hero produced.

Doctor Fathom was immediately known to be the author of this entertainment; and thus retrieved the benefit of that admiration which he had forfeited by appearing in the shape of a physician. For, as people had formerly wondered to see a count skilled in medicine, they were now amazed to find a physician such a master in music.

The good effects of this stratagem were almost instantaneous. His performance became the topic of discourse among all the fashionable company. His male friends complimented him from the information of the other sex; and that lady whom he had regaled, instead of that shyness and disdain with which she used to receive his salutation, at their very next meeting in the thoroughfare, returned his bow with marks of profound respect. Nay, at midnight, she, with the rest, took post in the same place where they had been stationed before; and, by frequent tittering, and repeated whispers, gave intimation to Fathom, that they would be glad of a second serenade. But he was too well acquainted with the human passions to indulge this their desire. It was his interest to inflame their impatience, rather than to gratify their expectation; and therefore he tantalised them for some hours, by tuning his violin, and playing some flourishes, which, however, produced nothing to fulfil their wishes.

At the ordinary, he was accosted by a gentleman, a lodger in the same house, who assured him, that the ladies would take it as a great favour if he would let them know when he intended to amuse himself again with his instrument, that they might not, by falling asleep beforehand, deprive themselves of the pleasure of hearing his music. To this message he replied, with an air of consequence and reserve, that, though music was not the art he professed, he should be always complaisant enough to entertain the ladies to the utmost of his power, when their commands were signified to him in a manner suited to his character; but that he would never put himself on the footing of an itinerate harper, whose music is tolerated through the medium of a board partition. The gentleman having reported this answer to his constituents, they empowered him to invite Doctor Fathom to breakfast, and he was next morning introduced with the usual ceremony, and treated with uncommon regard by all the females of the house, assembled for his reception.

Having thus broken the ice of their aversion in one part, so as that the beams of his personal accomplishments had room to operate, he soon effected a general thaw in his favour, and found himself growing once more into request amongst the most amiable part of the creation. His company was coveted, and his taste consulted in their balls, concerts, and private assemblies; and he recompensed the regard they paid to him with an incessant exertion of his agreeable talents, politeness, and good-humour.

CHAPTER FIFTY-ONE.
TRIUMPHS OVER A MEDICAL RIVAL.

Yet, in the midst of all this attention, his medical capacity seemed to be quite forgot. They respected his good breeding, were charmed with his voice, and admired the fine touches of his hand upon the violin; but in cultivating the fiddler, they utterly neglected the physician; and in vain did he attempt to divide their regard, by taking all opportunities to turn the conversation into a more interesting channel. It was to little purpose he endeavoured to arouse the wonder of his audience with frequent descriptions of portentous maladies and amazing cures he had seen and performed in the course of his study and practice abroad; and to no effect did he publicly busy himself in making experiments on the mineral water, in which he pretended to have made several new and important discoveries. These efforts did not make a lasting impression upon the minds of the company; because they saw nothing surprising in a physician's being acquainted with all the mysteries of his art; and, as their custom was already bespoke for others of the profession, whom it was their interest to employ, our adventurer might have starved amidst the caresses of his acquaintance, had not he derived considerable advantage from a lucky accident in the course of his expectancy.

A gentlewoman's daughter, of a weakly constitution, by drinking the waters, had so far recovered her health and complexion, as to allure the affection of a young squire in the neighbourhood, who amused her for some time with his addresses, until his heart was seduced by the charms of another young lady lately arrived at the wells. The forsaken nymph, shocked at this disgrace and mortification, relapsed into her former languishing disorder; and was by her mother put under the management and prescription of a physician, who had been an industrious enemy of Fathom from his first appearance at Tunbridge. The patient, though violently chagrined at the levity of her quondam admirer, was not altogether without hope, that the very same inconstancy which had prompted him to leave her, might in time induce him to return, after the novelty of his new passion should be wore off; and this hope served to support her under the sorrow and disgrace of her disappointment. At length, however, the squire and his new mistress disappeared; and some busybody was officious enough to communicate this piece of news to the forlorn shepherdess, with this additional circumstance, that they were gone to a neighbouring parish to be joined in the bands of wedlock.

These fatal tidings were no sooner imparted to the abandoned Phillis, than she was seized with an hysteric fit; and, what rendered the accident more unfortunate, her physician had been called to the country, and was not expected at Tunbridge till next day. The apothecary was immediately summoned; and, being either puzzled by the symptoms, or afraid of encroaching upon the province of his superiors, advised the old lady to send for Doctor Fathom without delay. She had no other objection to this expedient, but the enmity which she knew subsisted between the two leeches; yet, hearing that her own doctor would not consult with Fathom upon his return but, perhaps renounce the patient, by which means her daughter's health might be endangered, she would not solicit our hero's assistance, until the young lady had remained seven hours speechless and insensible; when, her fear prevailing over every other consideration, she implored the advice of our adventurer, who, having made the necessary interrogations, and felt the patient's pulse, which was regular and distinct, found reason to conclude that the fit would not last much longer, and, after having observed that she was in a very dangerous way, prescribed some medicines for external application; and, to enhance their opinion of his diligence and humanity, resolved to stay in the room and observe their effect.

His judgment did not fail him on this occasion. In less than half an hour after his embrocations had been applied, she recovered the use of her tongue, opened her eyes, and having, in delirious exclamations, upbraided her perfidious lover, became quite sensible and composed, though she continued extremely low and dejected. To remedy these sinkings, certain cordials were immediately administered, according to the prescription of Doctor Fathom, upon whom extraordinary encomiums were bestowed by all present, who believed he had actually rescued her from the jaws of death; and as he was by this time let into the secrets of the family, he found himself in a fair way of being an egregious favourite of the old gentlewoman; when, unluckily, his brother, having dismissed his country patient with uncommon despatch, entered the apartment, and eyed his rival with looks of inexpressible rage; then, surveying the patient, and the phials that stood upon the table, by turns, "What, in the name of God!" cried he, "is the meaning of all this trash!"

"Really, doctor," replied the mother, a little confounded at being thus taken by surprise, "Biddy has been taken dangerously ill, and lain seven or eight hours in a severe fit, from which I am confident she would never have recovered without the help of a physician; and as you were absent, we had recourse to this gentleman, whose prescription hath had a happy and surprising effect." "Effect!" cried this offended member of the faculty, "pshaw!—stuff!—who made you judge of effects or causes?" Then advancing to the patient, "What has been the matter, Miss Biddy, that you could not wait till my return?"

Here Fathom interposing, "Sir," said he, "if you will step into the next room, I will communicate my sentiments of the case, together with the method upon which I have proceeded, that we may deliberate upon the next step that is to be taken." Instead of complying with this proposal, he seated himself in a chair, with his back to our adventurer, and, while he examined Miss Biddy's pulse, gave him to understand, that he should not consult with him about the matter.

Fathom, not in the least disconcerted at this uncivil answer, walked round his antagonist, and, placing himself in his front, desired to know his reason for treating him with such supercilious contempt. "I am resolved," said the other, "never to consult with any physician who has not taken his degrees at either of the English universities." "Upon the supposition," replied our adventurer, "that no person can be properly educated for the profession at any other school." "You are in the right," answered Doctor Looby; "that is one of many reasons I have to decline the consultation."

"How far you are in the right," retorted Fathom, "I leave the world to judge, after I have observed, that, in your English universities, there is no opportunity of studying the art; no, not so much as a lecture given on the subject. Nor is there one physician of note in this kingdom who has not derived the greatest part of his medical knowledge from the instructions of foreigners."

Looby, incensed at this asseveration, which he was not prepared to refute, exclaimed, in a most infuriate accent, "Who are you?—whence came you?—where was you bred? You are one of those, I believe, who graduate themselves, and commence doctors, the Lord knows how; an interloper, who, without licence or authority, comes hither to take the bread out of the mouths of gentlemen who have been trained to the business in a regular manner, and bestowed great pains and expense to qualify themselves for the profession. For my own part, my education cost me fifteen hundred pounds."

"Never was money laid out to less purpose," said Ferdinand; "for it does not appear that you have learned so much as the basis of medical requirements, namely, that decorum and urbanity which ought to distinguish the deportment of every physician. You have even debased the noblest and most beneficial art that ever engaged the study of mankind, which cannot be too much cultivated, and too little restrained, in seeking to limit the practice of it to a set of narrow-minded, illiberal wretches, who, like the lowest handicraftsmen, claim the exclusive privileges of a corporation. Had you doubted my ability, you ought to have satisfied yourself in a manner consistent with decency and candour; but your behaviour on this occasion is such a malicious outrage upon good manners and humanity, that, were it not for my regard to these ladies, I would chastise you for your insolence on the spot. Meanwhile, madam," addressing himself to the mother, "you must give me leave to insist upon your dismissing either that gentleman, or me, without hesitation."

This peremptory language had an instantaneous effect upon the hearers. Looby's face grew pale, and his nether lip began to tremble. The patient was dismayed, and the old gentlewoman concerned and perplexed. She earnestly besought the gentlemen to be reconciled to each other, and enter into a friendly consultation upon her daughter's distemper; but, finding both equally averse to accommodation, and Fathom becoming more and more importunate in his demand, she presented him with a double fee; and giving him to understand that Doctor Looby had long attended the family, and was intimately acquainted with her own and Biddy's constitution, said, she hoped he would not take it amiss if she retained her old physician.

Though our hero was much mortified at this triumph of his rival, he made a virtue of necessity, and retired with great complaisance, wishing that Miss Biddy might never again be the subject of such a disagreeable dispute. Whether the patient was frighted at this altercation, or displeased with her mother's decision against an agreeable young fellow, who had, as it were, recalled her from the grave, and made himself master of the secret that rankled at her heart, or the disease had wound up her nerves for another paroxysm, certain it is, she all of a sudden broke forth into a violent peal of laughter, which was succeeded by the most doleful cries, and other expressions of grief; then she relapsed into a fit, attended with strong convulsions, to the unspeakable terror of the old gentlewoman, who entreated Doctor Looby to be expeditious in his prescription. Accordingly he seized the pen with great confidence, and a whole magazine of antihysteric medicines were, in different forms, externally and internally applied.

Nevertheless, either nature was disturbed in her own efforts by these applications, or the patient was resolved to disgrace the doctor. For the more remedies that were administered, her convulsions became the more violent; and in spite of all his endeavours, he could not overcome the obstinacy of the distemper. Such a miscarriage, upon the back of his rival's success, could not fail to overwhelm him with confusion; especially as the mother baited him with repeated entreaties to do something for the recovery of her daughter. At length, after having exercised her patience in vain for several hours, this affectionate parent could no longer suppress the suggestions of her concern, but, in an incoherent strain, told him that her duty would not suffer her to be longer silent in an affair on which depended the life of her dear child. That she had seen enough to believe he had mistaken the case of poor Biddy, and he could not justly blame her for recalling Doctor Fathom, whose prescription had operated in a miraculous manner.

Looby, shocked at this proposal, protested against it with great vehemence, as an expedient highly injurious to himself. "My remedies," said he, "are just beginning to take effect, and, in all probability, the fit will not last much longer; so that, by calling in another person at this juncture, you will defraud me of that credit which is my due, and deck my adversary with trophies to which he has no pretension." She was prevailed upon, by this remonstrance, to wait another half hour, when perceiving, as yet, no alteration for the better, and being distracted with her fears, which reproached her with want of natural affection, she sent a message to Doctor Fathom, desiring to see him with all possible despatch.

He was not slow in obeying the call, but hastening to the scene of action, was not a little surprised to find Looby still in the apartment. This gentleman, since better might not be, resolved to sacrifice his pride to his interest, and, rather than lose his patient altogether, and run the risk of forfeiting his reputation at the same time, stayed with intention to compromise his difference with Fathom, that he might not be wholly excluded from the honour of the cure, in case it could be effected. But he had reckoned without his host in his calculation of the Count's placability; for, when he put on his capitulating face, and, after a slight apology for his late behaviour, proposed that all animosity should subside in favour of the young lady, whose life was at stake, our hero rejected his advances with infinite disdain, and assured the mother, in a very solemn tone, that, far from consulting with a man who had treated him so unworthily, he would not stay another minute in the house, unless he should see him discarded; a satisfaction barely sufficient to atone for the affront he himself had suffered by the unjust preference she had before given to his rival.

There was no remedy. Looby was obliged to retreat in his turn; then our adventurer, approaching the bedside, reconnoitred the patient, examined the medicines which had been administered, and lifting up his eyes in expressive silence, detached the footman with a new order to the apothecary. It was well the messenger used expedition, otherwise Doctor Fathom would have been anticipated by the operation of nature; for, the fit having almost run its career, Miss Biddy was on the point of retrieving her senses, when the frontal prescribed by Fathom was applied; to the efficacy of this, therefore, was ascribed her recovery, when she opened her eyes, and began to pour forth unconnected ejaculations; and in a few moments after, she was persuaded to swallow a draught prepared for the purpose, her perception returned, and Ferdinand gained the reputation of having performed a second miracle.

But he was furnished with a piece of intelligence, of much more energy than all she had taken, and so soon as he concluded she was capable to bear the news without any dangerous emotion, he, among other articles of chit-chat culled for her amusement, took the opportunity of telling the company, that Squire Stub (the cause of Miss Biddy's disorder) had, in his way to matrimony, been robbed of his bride, by a gentleman to whom she had been formerly engaged. He had waited for her on purpose at an inn on the road, where he found means to appease her displeasure, which he had, it seems, incurred, and to supersede her new lover, whom she quitted without ceremony; upon which the squire had returned to Tunbridge, cursing her levity, yet blessing his good stars for having so seasonably prevented his ruin, which would have infallibly been the consequence of his marrying such an adventurer.

It would be superfluous to observe, that these tidings operated like an admirable specific on the spirits of the young lady, who, while she affected to pity the squire, was so much overjoyed at his disappointment, that her eyes began to sparkle with uncommon vivacity, and in less than two hours after the last of those terrible attacks, she was restored to a better state of health than she had enjoyed for many weeks. Fathom was not forgot amidst the rejoicings of the family. Besides an handsome gratuity for the effects of his extraordinary skill, the old lady favoured him with a general invitation to her house, and the daughter not only considered him as the restorer of her health, and angel of her good fortune, but also began to discover an uncommon relish for his conversation; so that he was struck with the prospect of succeeding Squire Stub in her affection. A conquest which, if sanctioned by the approbation of the mother, would console him for all the disappointments he had sustained; for Miss Biddy was entitled to a fortune of ten thousand pounds, provided she should marry with the consent of her parent, who was the sole executrix of the father's will.

Animated with the hope of such an advantageous match, our adventurer missed no opportunity of improving the lodgment he had made, while the two ladies failed not to extol his medical capacity among all their female acquaintances. By means of this circulation, his advice was demanded in several other cases, which he managed with such an imposing air of sagacity and importance, that his fame began to spread, and before the end of the season, he had ravished more than one half of the business from his competitor. Notwithstanding these fortunate events, he foresaw, that he should find great difficulty in transplanting his reputation, so as to take root in London, which was the only soil in which he could propose to rise to any degree of prosperity and independence; and this reflection was grounded upon a maxim which universally prevails among the English people, namely, to overlook and wholly neglect, on their return to the metropolis, all the connexions they may have chanced to acquire during their residence at any of the medical wells. And this social disposition is so scrupulously maintained, that two persons who lived in the most intimate correspondence at Bath or Tunbridge, shall in four-and-twenty hours so totally forget their friendship, as to meet in St. James's Park, without betraying the least token of recognition; so that one would imagine these mineral waters were so many streams issuing from the river Lethe, so famed of old for washing away all traces of memory and recollection.

Aware of this oblivious principle, Doctor Fathom collected all his qualifications, in order to make such an impression upon the heart of Miss Biddy, as would resist all her endeavours to shake him from her remembrance; and his efforts succeeded so well, that Squire Stub's advances to a reconciliation were treated with manifest indifference. In all probability our hero would have made a very advantageous campaign, had not his good fortune been retarded by an obstruction, which, as he did not perceive it, he could not possibly surmount. In displaying his accomplishments to captivate the daughter, he had unwittingly made an absolute conquest of the mother, who superintended the conduct of Miss Biddy with such jealous vigilance, that he could find no opportunity of profiting by the progress he had made in her heart; for the careful matron would never lose sight of her, no, not for one moment.

Had the old lady given the least intimation to our adventurer, of the sentiments she entertained in his behalf, his complaisance was of such a pliable texture, that he would have quitted his other pursuit, and made her the sole object of his attention. But she either depended upon the effect of his own good taste and discernment, or was too proud to disclose a passion which he had hitherto overlooked.

CHAPTER FIFTY-TWO.
REPAIRS TO THE METROPOLIS, AND ENROLS HIMSELF AMONG THE SONS OF PAEAN.

Before this affair could be brought to a proper explanation, the season being almost ended, the ladies departed from Tunbridge, and in a little time Doctor Fathom followed them to London, having previously obtained permission to visit them in that metropolis. He had solicited the same favour of some other families, in which he hoped to take root, though he knew they were pre-engaged to different physicians; and resolving to make his first medical appearance in London with some eclat, he not only purchased an old chariot, which was new painted for the purpose, but likewise hired a footman, whom he clothed in laced livery, in order to distinguish himself from the common run of his brethren.

This equipage, though much more expensive than his finances could bear, he found absolutely necessary to give him a chance for employment; as every shabby retainer to physic, in this capital, had provided himself with a vehicle, which was altogether used by way of a travelling sign-post, to draw in customers; so that a walking physician was considered as an obscure pedlar, trudging from street to street, with his pack of knowledge on his shoulders, and selling his remnants of advice by retail. A chariot was not now set up for the convenience of a man sinking under the fatigue of extensive practice, but as a piece of furniture every way as necessary as a large periwig with three tails; and a physician, let his merit, in other respects, be never so conspicuous, can no more expect to become considerable in business, without the assistance of this implement, than he can hope to live without food, or breathe without a windpipe.

This requisite is so well understood, that, exclusive of those who profess themselves doctors, every raw surgeon, every idle apothecary, who can make interest with some foolhardy coachmaker, may be seen dancing the bays in all places of public resort, and grinning to one another from their respective carriages. Hence proceed many of those cruel accidents which are recorded in the daily papers. An apothecary's horses take fright, and run away with his chariot, which is heard of no more. An eminent surgeon being overturned, is so terrified at the thoughts of mutilation, that he resolves to walk on foot all the days of his life; and the coachman of a physician of great practice, having the misfortune to be disabled by a fall from the box, his master can never find another to supply his place.

None of these observations escaped the penetrating eye of Fathom, who, before he pretended to seat himself in this machine, had made proper inquiry into all the other methods practised, with a view to keep the wheels in motion. In his researches, he found that the great world was wholly engrossed by a few practitioners who had arrived at the summit of reputation, consequently were no longer obliged to cultivate those arts by which they rose; and that the rest of the business was parcelled out into small enclosures, occupied by different groups of personages, male and female, who stood in rings, and tossed the ball from one to another, there being in each department two sets, the individuals of which relieved one another occasionally. Every knot was composed of a waiting-woman, nurse, apothecary, surgeon, and physician, and sometimes a midwife was admitted into the party; and in this manner the farce was commonly performed.

A fine lady, fatigued with idleness, complains of the vapours, is deprived of her rest, though not so sick as to have recourse to medicine. Her favourite maid, tired with giving her attendance in the night, thinks proper, for the benefit of her own repose, to complain of a violent headache, and recommends to her mistress a nurse of approved tenderness and discretion; at whose house, in all likelihood, the said chambermaid hath oft given the rendezvous to a male friend. The nurse, well skilled in the mysteries of her occupation, persuades the patient, that her malady, far from being slight or chimerical, may proceed to a very dangerous degree of the hysterical affection, unless it be nipt in the bud by some very effectual remedy. Then she recounts a surprising cure performed by a certain apothecary, and appeals to the testimony of the waiting-woman, who being the gossip of his wife, confirms the evidence, and corroborates the proposal. The apothecary being summoned, finds her ladyship in such a delicate situation, that he declines prescribing, and advises her to send for a physician without delay. The nomination of course falls to him, and the doctor being called, declares the necessity of immediate venesection, which is accordingly performed by a surgeon of the association.

This is one way of beginning the game. Though the commencement often varies, and sometimes the apothecary and sometimes the physician opens the scene; but, be that as it will, they always appear in a string, like a flight of wild geese, and each confederacy maintains a correspondence with one particular undertaker. Fathom, upon these considerations, set up his rest in the first floor of an apothecary in the neighbourhood of Charing Cross, to whom he was introduced by a letter from a friend at Tunbridge, and who being made acquainted with his ability and scheme, promised to let slip no opportunity of serving him; and, indeed, seemed to espouse his interest with great alacrity. He introduced him to some of his patients, on the strength of a gratis visit, sounded forth his praise among all the good women of his acquaintance; and even prevailed upon him to publish advertisements, importing that he would every day, at a certain time and place, give his advice to the poor for nothing; hoping that, by means of some lucky cure, his fame might be extended, and his practice grow into request.

In the meantime his chariot rolled along through all the most frequented streets, during the whole forenoon, and, at the usual hour, he never failed to make his appearance at the medical coffee-house, with all that solemnity of feature and address, by which the modern sons of Paean are distinguished; not but that he was often puzzled about the decision of his diurnal route. For the method of driving up one street and down another, without halting, was become such a stale expedient, that the very 'prentices used to stand at the shop doors, and ridicule the vain parade. At length, however, he perused the map of London with great diligence, and, having acquired a distinct idea of its topography, used to alight at the end of long narrow thoroughfares and paved courts, where the chariot was ordered to wait till his return; and, walking with great gravity through the different turnings of these alleys, regain his carriage by another passage, and resume his seat with an air of vast importance. With a view to protract the time of his supposed visits, he would, at one place, turn aside to a wall; at another, cheapen an urinal; at a third corner, read a quack advertisement, or lounge a few minutes in some bookseller's shop; and, lastly, glide into some obscure coffee-house, and treat himself with a dram of usquebaugh.

The other means used to force a trade, such as ordering himself to be called from church, alarming the neighbourhood with knocking at his door in the night, receiving sudden messages in places of resort, and inserting his cures by way of news in the daily papers, had been so injudiciously hackneyed by every desperate sculler in physic, that they had lost their effect upon the public, and therefore were excluded from the plan of our adventurer, whose scheme, for the present, was to exert himself in winning the favour of those sage Sibyls, who keep, as it were, the temple of medicine, and admit the young priest to the service of the altar; but this he considered as a temporary project only, until he should have acquired interest enough to erect an hospital, lock, or infirmary, by the voluntary subscription of his friends, a scheme which had succeeded to a miracle with many of the profession, who had raised themselves into notice upon the carcases of the poor.

Yet even this branch was already overstocked, insomuch that almost every street was furnished with one of these charitable receptacles, which, instead of diminishing the taxes for the maintenance of the poor, encouraged the vulgar to be idle and dissolute, by opening an asylum to them and their families, from the diseases of poverty and intemperance. For it remains to be proved, that the parish rates are decreased, the bills of mortality lessened, the people more numerous, or the streets less infested with beggars, notwithstanding the immense sums yearly granted by individuals for the relief of the indigent.

But, waiving these reflections, Doctor Fathom hoped, that his landlord would be a most useful implement for extending his influence, and, for that reason, admitted him into a degree of partnership, after being fully convinced that he was not under articles to any other physician. Nevertheless, he was very much mistaken in reckoning on the importance of his new ally, who was, like himself, a needy adventurer, settled upon credit, and altogether unemployed, except among the very refuse of the people, whom no other person would take the trouble to attend. So that our hero got little else than experience and trouble, excepting a few guineas which he made shift to glean among sojourners, with whom he became occasionally acquainted, or young people, who had been unfortunate in their amours.

In the midst of these endeavours, he did not omit his duty to the old gentlewoman, whose daughter he had cured at Tunbridge; and was always received with particular complacency, which, perhaps, he, in some measure, owed to his genteel equipage, that gave credit to every door before which it was seen; yet, Miss Biddy was as inaccessible as ever, while the mother became more and more warm in her civilities, till at length, after having prepared him with some extraordinary compliments, she gave him to understand, that Biddy was no better than a giddy-headed girl, far from being unexceptionable in her moral character, and particularly deficient in duty and gratitude to her, who had been always a tender and indulgent parent; she was therefore determined to punish the young minx for her levity and want of natural affection, by altering her own condition, could she find a worthy and agreeable man, on whom she could bestow her hand and fortune without a blush.

The film was instantly removed from Fathom's eyes by this declaration, which she uttered with such a significancy of look, as thrilled to his soul with joyful presage, while he replied, it would, indeed, be a difficult task to find a man who merited such happiness and honour; but, surely, some there were, who would task their faculties to the uttermost, in manifesting their gratitude, and desire of rendering themselves worthy of such distinction. Though this answer was pronounced in such a manner as gave her to understand he had taken the hint, she would not cheapen her condescension so much as to explain herself further at that juncture, and he was very well contented to woo her on her own terms; accordingly he began to season his behaviour with a spice of gallantry, when he had opportunities of being particular with this new inamorata, and, in proportion to the returns she made, he gradually detached himself from Miss Biddy, by intermitting, and, at last, discontinuing those ardent expressions of love and admiration, which he had made shift to convey in private looks and stolen whispers, during the rancorous inspection of her mother.

Such alteration could not long escape the jealous eyes of the young lady, no more than the cause of this alienation, which, in a moment, converted all her love into irreconcilable hate, and filled her whole soul with the most eager desire of vengeance. For she now not only considered him as a mercenary wretch, who had slighted her attractions for the sordid gratifications of avarice, but also as an interloper, who wanted to intercept her fortune, in the odious character of a father-in-law. But, before she could bring her aim to any ripeness of contrivance, her mother, having caught cold at church, was seized with a rheumatic fever, became delirious in less than three days, and, notwithstanding all the prescriptions and care of her admirer, gave up the ghost, without having retrieved the use of her senses, or been able to manifest, by will, the sentiments she entertained in favour of her physician, who, as the reader will easily perceive, had more reasons than one to be mortally chagrined at this event.

Miss Biddy being thus put in possession of the whole inheritance, not only renounced all correspondence with Doctor Fathom, by forbidding him the house, but likewise took all opportunities of prejudicing his character, by hinting, that her dear mamma had fallen a sacrifice to his ignorance and presumption.

CHAPTER FIFTY-THREE.
ACQUIRES EMPLOYMENT IN CONSEQUENCE OF A LUCKY MISCARRIAGE.

These ill offices, however, far from answering her purpose, had a quite contrary effect. For, in consequence of her invectives, he was, in a few days, called to the wife of a merchant, who piously hoped, that his practice would not give Miss Biddy the lie. The patient had long lingered under a complication of distempers, and being in no immediate danger of her life, Doctor Fathom was in no hurry to strike a decisive stroke; till the husband growing impatient of delay, and so explicit in his hints, that it was impossible to misapprehend his meaning, our adventurer resolved to do something effectual for his satisfaction, and prescribed a medicine of such rough operation, as he thought must either oblige his employer, or produce a change in the lady's constitution, that would make a noise in the world, and bring a new accession to his fame.

Proceeding upon these maxims, he could not be disappointed. The remedy played its part with such violence, as reduced the patient to extremity, and the merchant had actually bespoke an undertaker; when, after a series of swoonings and convulsions, nature so far prevailed, as to expel, at once, the prescription and the disease; yet the good-natured husband was so much affected with the agonies to which he saw the wife of his bosom exposed by this specific, that, although the effect of it was her perfect recovery, he could never bear the sight of Fathom for the future, nor even hear his name mentioned, without giving signs of horror and indignation. Nay, he did not scruple to affirm, that, had our adventurer been endowed with the least tincture of humanity, he would have suffered the poor woman to depart in peace, rather than restore her to health, at the expense of such anxiety and torture.

On the other hand, this extraordinary cure was blazoned abroad by the good lady and her gossips, with such exaggerations as roused the astonishment of the public, and concurred with the report of his last miscarriage to bring him upon the carpet, as the universal subject of discourse. When a physician becomes the town talk, he generally concludes his business more than half done, even though his fame should wholly turn upon his malpractice; insomuch that some members of the faculty have been heard to complain, that they never had the good fortune to be publicly accused of homicide; and it is well known, that a certain famous empiric, of our day, never flourished to any degree of wealth and reputation till after he had been attacked in print, and fairly convicted of having destroyed a good number of the human species. Success raised upon such a foundation would, by a disciple of Plato, and some modern moralists, be ascribed to the innate virtue and generosity of the human heart, which naturally espouses the cause that needs protection. But I, whose notions of human excellence are not quite so sublime, am apt to believe it is owing to that spirit of self-conceit and contradiction, which is, at least, as universal, if not as natural, as the moral sense so warmly contended for by those ideal philosophers.

The most infamous wretch often finds his account in these principles of malevolence and self-love. For wheresoever his character falls under discussion there is generally some person present, who, either from an affectation of singularity, or envy to the accusers, undertakes his defence, and endeavours to invalidate the articles of his impeachment, until he is heated by altercation, and hurried into more effectual measures for his advantage. If such benefits accrue to those who have no real merit to depend upon, surely our hero could not but reap something extraordinary from the debates to which he now gave rise; as, by the miraculous cure he had affected, all his patient's friends, all the enemies of her husband, all those who envied his other adversary, were interested in his behalf, exclusive of such admirers as surprise and curiosity might engage in his cause.

Thus wafted upon the wings of applause, his fame soon diffused itself into all the corners of this great capital. The newspapers teemed with his praise; and in order to keep up the attention of the public, his emissaries, male and female, separated into different coffee-houses, companies, and clubs, where they did not fail to comment upon these articles of intelligence. Such a favourable incident is, of itself, sufficient to float the bark of a man's fortune. He was, in a few days, called to another lady, labouring under the same disorder he had so successfully dispelled, and she thought herself benefited by his advice. His acquaintance naturally extended itself among the visitants and allies of his patients; he was recommended from family to family; the fees began to multiply; a variety of footmen appeared every day at his door; he discontinued his sham circuit, and looking upon the present conjuncture, as that tide in his affairs, which, according to Shakespeare, when taken at the full, leads on to fortune, he resolved that the opportunity should not be lost, and applied himself with such assiduity to his practice, that, in all likelihood, he would have carried the palm from all his contemporaries, had he not split upon the same rock which had shipwrecked his hopes before.

We have formerly descanted upon that venereal appetite which glowed in the constitution of our adventurer, and with all his philosophy and caution could hardly keep within bounds. The reader, therefore, will not be much surprised to learn, that, in the exercise of his profession, he contracted an intimacy with a clergyman's wife, whom he attended as a physician, and whose conjugal virtue he subdued by a long and diligent exertion of his delusive arts, while her mind was enervated by sickness, and her husband abroad upon his necessary occasions. This unhappy patient, who was a woman of an agreeable person and lively conversation, fell a sacrifice to her own security and self-conceit; her want of health had confined her to a sedentary life, and her imagination being active and restless, she had spent those hours in reading which other young women devote to company and diversion, but, as her studies were not superintended by any person of taste, she had indulged her own fancy without method or propriety. The Spectator taught her to be a critic and philosopher; from plays she learned poetry and wit, and derived her knowledge of life from books of history and adventures. Fraught with these acquisitions, and furnished by nature with uncommon vivacity, she despised her own sex, and courted the society of men, among whom she thought her talents might be more honourably displayed, fully confident of her own virtue and sagacity, which enabled her to set all their arts at defiance.

Thus qualified, she, in an evil hour, had recourse to the advice of our adventurer, for some ailment under which she had long laboured, and found such relief from his skill as very much prepossessed her in his favour. She was no less pleased with his obliging manners than with his physic, and found much entertainment in his conversation, so that the acquaintance proceeded to a degree of intimacy, during which he perceived her weak side, and being enamoured of her person, flattered her out of all her caution. The privilege of his character furnished him with opportunities to lay snares for her virtue, and, taking advantage of that listlessness, languor, and indolence of the spirits, by which all the vigilance of the soul is relaxed, he, after a long course of attention and perseverance, found means to make shipwreck of her peace.

Though he mastered her chastity, he could not quiet her conscience, which incessantly upbraided her with breach of the marriage vow; nor did her undoer escape without a share of the reproaches suggested by her penitence and remorse. This internal anxiety co-operating with her disease, and perhaps with the medicines he prescribed, reduced her to the brink of the grave; when her husband returned from a neighbouring kingdom, in consequence of her earnest request, joined to the information of her friends, who had written to him an account of the extremity in which she was. The good man was afflicted beyond measure when he saw himself upon the verge of losing a wife whom he had always tenderly loved; but what were his emotions, when she, taking the first opportunity of his being alone with her, accosted him to this effect:

"I am now hastening towards that dissolution from which no mortal is exempted, and though the prospect of futurity is altogether clouded and uncertain, my conscience will not allow me to plunge into eternity without unburdening my mind, and, by an ingenuous confession, making all the atonement in my power for the ingratitude I have been guilty of, and the wrongs I have committed against a virtuous husband, who never gave me cause of complaint. You stand amazed at this preamble, but alas! how will you be shocked when I own that I have betrayed you in your absence, that I have trespassed against God and my marriage vow, and fallen from the pride and confidence of virtue to the most abject state of vice; yes, I have been unfaithful to your bed, having fallen a victim to the infernal insinuations of a villain, who took advantage of my weak and unguarded moments. Fathom is the wretch who hath thus injured your honour, and ruined my unsuspecting innocence. I have nothing to plead in alleviation of my crime but the most sincere contrition of heart, and though, at any other juncture, I could not expect your forgiveness, yet, as I now touch the goal of life, I trust in your humanity and benevolence for that pardon which will lighten the sorrows of my soul, and those prayers which I hope will entitle me to favour at the throne of grace."

The poor husband was so much overwhelmed with grief and confusion at this unexpected address that he could not recollect himself till after a pause of several minutes, when uttering a hollow groan, "I will not," said he, "aggravate your sufferings, by reproaching you with my wrongs, though your conduct hath been but an ill return for all my tenderness and esteem. I look upon it as a trial of my Christian patience, and bear my misfortune with resignation; meanwhile, I forgive you from my heart, and fervently pray that your repentance may be acceptable to the Father of Mercy." So saying, he approached her bedside, and embraced her in token of his sincerity. Whether this generous condescension diffused such a composure upon her spirits as tended to the ease and refreshment of nature, which had been almost exhausted by disease and vexation, certain it is, that from this day she began to struggle with her malady in surprising efforts, and hourly gained ground, until her health was pretty well re-established.

This recovery was so far beyond the husband's expectation, that he began to make very serious reflections on the event, and even to wish he had not been quite so precipitate in pardoning the backslidings of his wife; for, though he could not withhold his compassion from a dying penitent, he did not at all relish the thoughts of cohabiting, as usual, with a wife self-convicted of the violation of the matrimonial contract; he therefore considered his declaration as no more than a provisional pardon, to take place on condition of her immediate death, and, in a little time, not only communicated to her his sentiments on this subject, but also separated himself from her company, secured the evidence of her maid, who had been confidant in her amour with Fathom, and immediately set on foot a prosecution against our adventurer, whose behaviour to his wife he did not fail to promulgate, with all its aggravating circumstances. By these means the doctor's name became so notorious that every man was afraid of admitting him into his house, and every woman ashamed of soliciting his advice.

CHAPTER FIFTY-FOUR.
HIS ECLIPSE, AND GRADUAL DECLINATION.

Misfortunes seldom come single; upon the back of this hue and cry he unluckily prescribed phlebotomy to a gentleman of some rank, who chanced to expire during the operation, and quarrelled with his landlord the apothecary, who charged him with having forgot the good offices he had done him in the beginning of his career, and desired he would provide himself with another lodging.

All these mishaps, treading upon the heels of one another, had a very mortifying effect upon his practice. At every tea-table his name was occasionally put to the torture, with that of the vile creature whom he had seduced, though it was generally taken for granted by all those female casuists, that she must have made the first advances, for it could not be supposed that any man would take much trouble in laying schemes for the ruin of a person whose attractions were so slender, especially considering the ill state of her health, a circumstance that seldom adds to a woman's beauty or good-humour; besides, she was always a pert minx, that affected singularity, and a masculine manner of speaking, and many of them had foreseen that she would, some time or other, bring herself into such a premunire. At all gossipings, where the apothecary or his wife assisted, Fathom's pride, ingratitude, and malpractice were canvassed; in all clubs of married men he was mentioned with marks of abhorrence and detestation, and every medical coffee-house rung with his reproach. Instances of his ignorance and presumption were quoted, and many particulars feigned for the purpose of defamation, so that our hero was exactly in the situation of a horseman, who, in riding at full speed for the plate, is thrown from the saddle in the middle of the race, and left without sense or motion upon the plain.

His progress, though rapid, had been so short, that he could not be supposed to have laid up store against such a day of trouble, and as he still cherished hopes of surmounting those obstacles which had so suddenly started up in his way, he would not resign his equipage nor retrench his expenses, but appeared as usual in all public places with that serenity and confidence of feature which he had never deposited, and maintained his external pomp upon the little he had reserved in the days of his prosperity, and the credit he had acquired by the punctuality of his former payments. Both these funds, however, failed in a very little time, his lawsuit was a gulf that swallowed up all his ready money, and the gleanings of his practice were scarce sufficient to answer his pocket expenses, which now increased in proportion to the decrease of business, for, as he had more idle time, and was less admitted into private families, so he thought he had more occasion to enlarge his acquaintance among his own sex, who alone were able to support him in his disgrace with the other. He accordingly listed himself in several clubs, and endeavoured to monopolise the venereal branch of trade, though this was but an indifferent resource, for almost all his patients of this class were such as either could not, or would not, properly recompense the physician.

For some time he lingered in this situation, without going upwards or downwards, floating like a wisp of straw at the turning of the tide, until he could no longer amuse the person of whom he had hired his coach-horses, or postpone the other demands, which multiplied upon him every day. Then was his chariot overturned with a hideous crash, and his face so much wounded with the shivers of the glass, which went to pieces in the fall, that he appeared in the coffee-house with half a dozen black patches upon his countenance, gave a most circumstantial detail of the risk he had run, and declared, that he did not believe he should ever hazard himself again in any sort of wheel carriage.

Soon after this accident, he took an opportunity of telling his friends, in the same public place, that he had turned away his footman on account of his drunkenness, and was resolved, for the future, to keep none but maids in his service, because the menservants are generally impudent, lazy, debauched, or dishonest; and after all, neither so neat, handy, or agreeable as the other sex. In the rear of this resolution, he shifted his lodgings into a private court, being distracted with the din of carriages, that disturb the inhabitants who live towards the open street; and gave his acquaintance to understand, that he had a medical work upon the anvil, which he could not finish without being indulged in silence and tranquillity. In effect, he gradually put on the exteriors of an author. His watch, with an horizontal movement by Graham, which he had often mentioned, and shown as a very curious piece of workmanship, began, about this time, to be very much out of order, and was committed to the care of a mender, who was in no hurry to restore it. His tie-wig degenerated into a major; he sometimes appeared without a sword, and was even observed in public with a second day's shirt. At last, his clothes became rusty; and when he walked about the streets, his head turned round in a surprising manner, by an involuntary motion in his neck, which he had contracted by a habit of reconnoitring the ground, that he might avoid all dangerous or disagreeable encounters.

Fathom, finding himself descending the hill of fortune with an acquired gravitation, strove to catch at every twig, in order to stop or retard his descent. He now regretted the opportunities he had neglected, of marrying one of several women of moderate fortune, who had made advances to him in the zenith of his reputation; and endeavoured, by forcing himself into a lower path of life than any he had hitherto trod, to keep himself afloat, with the portion of some tradesman's daughter, whom he meant to espouse. While he exerted himself in this pursuit, he happened, in returning from a place about thirty miles from London, to become acquainted, in the stage-coach, with a young woman of a very homely appearance, whom, from the driver's information, he understood to be the niece of a country justice, and daughter of a soap-boiler, who had lived and died in London, and left her, in her infancy, sole heiress of his effects, which amounted to four thousand pounds. The uncle, who was her guardian, had kept her sacred from the knowledge of the world, resolving to effect a match betwixt her and his own son; and it was with much difficulty he had consented to this journey, which she had undertaken as a visit to her own mother, who had married a second husband in town.

Fraught with these anecdotes, Fathom began to put forth his gallantry and good-humour, and, in a word, was admitted by the lady to the privilege of an acquaintance, in which capacity he visited her during the term of her residence in London; and, as there was no time to be lost, declared his honourable intentions. He had such a manifest advantage, in point of personal accomplishments, over the young gentleman who was destined for her husband, that she did not disdain his proposals; and, before she set out for the country, he had made such progress in her heart, that the day was actually fixed for their nuptials, on which he faithfully promised to carry her off in a coach and six. How to raise money for this expedition was all the difficulty that remained; for, by this time, his finances were utterly dried up, and his credit altogether exhausted. Upon a very pressing occasion, he had formerly applied himself to a certain wealthy quack, who had relieved his necessities by lending him a small sum of money, in return for having communicated to him a secret medicine, which he affirmed to be the most admirable specific that ever was invented. The nostrum had been used, and, luckily for him, succeeded in the trial; so that the empiric, in the midst of his satisfaction, began to reflect, that this same Fathom, who pretended to be in possession of a great many remedies, equally efficacious, would certainly become a formidable rival to him in his business, should he ever be able to extricate himself from his present difficulties.

In consequence of these suggestions, he resolved to keep our adventurer's head under water, by maintaining him in the most abject dependence.

Accordingly he had, from time to time, accommodated him with small trifles, which barely served to support his existence, and even for these had taken notes of hand, that he might have a scourge over his head, in case he should prove insolent or refractory. To this benefactor Fathom applied for a reinforcement of twenty guineas, which he solicited with the more confidence, as that sum would certainly enable him to repay all other obligations. The quack would advance the money upon no other condition, than that of knowing the scheme, which being explained, he complied with Ferdinand's request; but, at the same time, privately despatched an express to the young lady's uncle, with a full account of the whole conspiracy; so that, when the doctor arrived at the inn, according to appointment, he was received by his worship in person, who gave him to understand, that his niece had changed her mind, and gone fifty miles farther into the country to visit a relation. This was a grievous disappointment to Fathom, who really believed his mistress had forsaken him through mere levity and caprice, and was not undeceived till several months after her marriage with her cousin, when, at an accidental meeting in London, she explained the story of the secret intelligence, and excused her marriage, as the effect of rigorous usage and compulsion.

Had our hero been really enamoured of her person, he might have probably accomplished his wishes, notwithstanding the steps she had taken. But this was not the case. His passion was of a different nature, and the object of it effectually without his reach. With regard to his appetite for women, as it was an infirmity of his constitution, which he could not overcome, and as he was in no condition to gratify it at a great expense, he had of late chosen a housekeeper from the hundreds of Drury, and, to avoid scandal, allowed her to assume his name. As to the intimation which had been sent to the country justice, he immediately imputed it to the true author, whom he marked for his vengeance accordingly; but, in the meantime, suppressed his resentment, because he in some measure depended upon him for subsistence. On the other hand, the quack, dreading the forwardness and plausibility of our hero, which might, one time or other, render him independent, put a stop to those supplies, on pretence of finding them inconvenient; but, out of his friendship and goodwill to Fathom, undertook to procure for him such letters of recommendation as would infallibly make his fortune in the West Indies, and even to set him out in a genteel manner for the voyage. Ferdinand perceived his drift, and thanked him for his generous offer, which he would not fail to consider with all due deliberation; though he was determined against the proposal, but obliged to temporise, that he might not incur the displeasure of this man, at whose mercy he lay. Meanwhile the prosecution against him in Doctors' Commons drew near a period, and the lawyers were clamorous for money, without which, he foresaw he should lose the advantage which his cause had lately acquired by the death of his antagonist's chief evidence; he therefore, seeing every other channel shut up, began to doubt, whether the risk of being apprehended or slain in the character of a highwayman, was not overbalanced by the prospect of being acquitted of a charge which had ruined his reputation and fortune, and actually entertained thoughts of taking the air on Hounslow Heath, when he was diverted from this expedient by a very singular adventure.

CHAPTER FIFTY-FIVE.
AFTER DIVERS UNSUCCESSFUL EFFORTS, HE HAS RECOURSE TO THE MATRIMONIAL NOOSE.

Chancing to meet with one of his acquaintance at a certain coffee-house, the discourse turned upon the characters of mankind, when, among other oddities, his friend brought upon the carpet a certain old gentlewoman of such a rapacious disposition, that, like a jackdaw, she never beheld any metalline substance, without an inclination, and even an effort to secrete it for her own use and contemplation. Nor was this infirmity originally produced from indigence, inasmuch as her circumstances had been always affluent, and she was now possessed of a considerable sum of money in the funds; notwithstanding which, the avarice of her nature tempted her to let lodgings, though few people could live under the same roof with such an original, who, rather than be idle, had often filched pieces of her own plate, and charged her servants with the theft, or hinted suspicion of her lodgers. Fathom, struck with the description, soon perceived how this woman's disease might be converted to his advantage; and after having obtained sufficient intelligence, on pretence of satisfying his curiosity, he visited the widow, in consequence of a bill at her door, and actually hired an apartment in her house, whither he forthwith repaired with his inamorata.

It was not long before he perceived that his landlady's character had not been misrepresented. He fed her distemper with divers inconsiderable trinkets, such as copper medals, corkscrews, odd buckles, and a paltry seal set in silver, which were, at different times, laid as baits for her infirmity, and always conveyed away with remarkable eagerness, which he and his Dulcinea took pleasure in observing from an unsuspected place. Thus confirmed in his opinion, he, at length, took an opportunity of exposing a metal watch that belonged to his mistress, and saw it seized with great satisfaction, in the absence of his helpmate, who had gone abroad on purpose. According to instruction, she soon returned, and began to raise a terrible clamour about the loss of her watch; upon which she was condoled by her landlady, who seemed to doubt the integrity of the maid, and even proposed that Mrs. Fathom should apply to some justice of the peace for a warrant to search the servant's trunk. The lady thanked her for the good advice, in compliance with which she had immediate recourse to a magistrate, who granted a search warrant, not against the maid, but the mistress; and she, in a little time, returned with the constable at her back.

These precautions being taken, Doctor Fathom desired a private conference with the old gentlewoman, in which he gave her to understand, that he had undoubted proofs of her having secreted, not only the watch, but also several other odd things of less consequence, which he lost since his residence in her house. He then showed the warrant he had obtained against her, and asked if she had anything to offer why the constable should not do his duty? Inexpressible were the anguish and confusion of the defendant, when she found herself thus entrapped, and reflected, that she was on the point of being detected of felony; for she at once concluded, that the snare was laid for her, and knew that the officer of justice would certainly find the unlucky watch in one of the drawers of her scrutoire.

Tortured with these suggestions, afraid of public disgrace, and dreading the consequence of legal conviction, she fell on her knees before the injured Fathom, and, after having imputed her crime to the temptations of necessity, implored his compassion, promised to restore the watch, and everything she had taken, and begged he would dismiss the constable, that her reputation might not suffer in the eye of the world.

Ferdinand, with a severity of countenance purposely assumed, observed that, were she really indigent, he had charity enough to forgive what she had done; but, as he knew her circumstances were opulent, he looked upon this excuse as an aggravation of her guilt, which was certainly the effect of a vicious inclination; and he was therefore determined to prosecute her with the utmost severity of the law, as an example and terror to others, who might be infected with the same evil disposition. Finding him deaf to all her tears and entreaties, she changed her note, and offered him one hundred guineas, if he would compromise the affair, and drop the prosecution, so as that her character should sustain no damage. After much argumentation, he consented to accept of double the sum, which being instantly paid in East India bonds, Doctor Fathom told the constable, that the watch was found; and for once her reputation was patched up. This seasonable supply enabled our hero to stand trial with his adversary, who was nonsuited, and also to mend his external appearance, which of late had not been extremely magnificent.

Soon after this gleam of good fortune, a tradesman, to whom he was considerably indebted, seeing no other probable means to recover his money, introduced Fathom to the acquaintance of a young widow who lodged at his house, and was said to be in possession of a considerable fortune. Considering the steps that were taken, it would have been almost impossible for him to miscarry in his addresses. The lady had been bred in the country, was unacquainted with the world, and of a very sanguine disposition, which her short trial of matrimony had not served to cool. Our adventurer was instructed to call at the tradesman's house, as if by accident, at an appointed time, when the widow was drinking tea with her landlady. On these occasions he always behaved to admiration. She liked his person, and praised his politeness, good-humour, and good sense; his confederates extolled him as a prodigy of learning, taste, and good-nature; they likewise represented him as a person on the eve of eclipsing all his competitors in physic. An acquaintance and intimacy soon ensued, nor was he restricted in point of opportunity. In a word, he succeeded in his endeavours, and, one evening, on pretence of attending her to the play, he accompanied her to the Fleet, where they were married, in presence of the tradesman and his wife, who were of the party.

This grand affair being accomplished to his satisfaction, he, next day, visited her brother, who was a counsellor of the Temple, to make him acquainted with the step his sister had taken; and though the lawyer was not a little mortified to find that she had made such a clandestine match, he behaved civilly to his new brother-in-law, and gave him to understand, that his wife's fortune consisted of a jointure of one hundred and fifty pounds a year, and fifteen hundred pounds bequeathed to her during her widowhood, by her own father, who had taken the precaution of settling it in the hands of trustees, in such a manner as that any husband she might afterwards espouse should be restricted from encroaching upon the capital, which was reserved for the benefit of her heirs. This intimation was far from being agreeable to our hero, who had been informed, that this sum was absolutely at the lady's disposal, and had actually destined the greatest part of it for the payment of his debts, for defraying the expense of furnishing an elegant house, and setting up a new equipage.

Notwithstanding this disappointment, he resolved to carry on his plan upon the credit of his marriage, which was published in a very pompous article of the newspapers; a chariot was bespoke, a ready furnished house immediately taken, and Doctor Fathom began to reappear in all his former splendour.

His good friend the empiric, alarmed at this event, which not only raised our adventurer into the sphere of a dangerous rival, but also furnished him with means to revenge the ill office he had sustained at his hands on the adventure of the former match—for, by this time, Fathom had given him some hints, importing, that he was not ignorant of his treacherous behaviour—roused, I say, by these considerations, he employed one of his emissaries, who had some knowledge of Fathom's brother-in-law, to prejudice him against our adventurer, whom he represented as a needy sharper, not only overwhelmed with debt and disgrace, but likewise previously married to a poor woman, who was prevented by nothing but want from seeking redress at law. To confirm these assertions, he gave him a detail of Fathom's encumbrances, which he had learned for the purpose, and even brought the counsellor into company with the person who had lived with our hero before marriage, and who was so much incensed at her abrupt dismission, that she did not scruple to corroborate these allegations of the informer.

The lawyer, startled at this intelligence, set on foot a minute inquiry into the life and conversation of the doctor, which turned out so little to the advantage of his character and circumstances, that he resolved, if possible, to disunite him from his family; and, as a previous step, repeated to his sister all that he had heard to the prejudice of her husband, not forgetting to produce the evidence of his mistress, who laid claim to him by a prior title, which, she pretended, could be proved by the testimony of the clergyman who joined them. Such an explanation could not fail to inflame the resentment of the injured wife, who, at the very first opportunity, giving a loose to the impetuosity of her temper, upbraided our hero with the most bitter invectives for his perfidious dealing.

Ferdinand, conscious of his own innocence, which he had not always to plead, far from attempting to soothe her indignation, assumed the authority and prerogative of a husband, and sharply reprehended her for her credulity and indecent warmth. This rebuke, instead of silencing, gave new spirit and volubility to her reproaches, in the course of which she plainly taxed him with want of honesty and affection, and said that, though his pretence was love, his aim was no other than a base design upon her fortune.

Fathom, stung with these accusations, which he really did not deserve, replied with uncommon heat, and charged her in his turn with want of sincerity and candour, in the false account she had given of that same fortune before marriage. He even magnified his own condescension, in surrendering his liberty to a woman who had so little to recommend her to the addresses of the other sex; a reflection which provoked this mild creature to such a degree of animosity, that, forgetting her duty and allegiance, she lent him a box on the ear with such energy as made his eyes water; and he, for the honour of manhood and sovereignty, having washed her face with a dish of tea, withdrew abruptly to a coffee-house in the neighbourhood, where he had not long remained, when his passion subsided, and he then saw the expediency of an immediate reconciliation, which he resolved to purchase, even at the expense of a submission.

It was pity that such a salutary resolution had not been sooner taken. For, when he returned to his own house, he understood, that Mrs. Fathom had gone abroad in a hackney-coach; and, upon examining her apartment, in lieu of her clothes and trinkets, which she had removed with admirable dexterity and despatch, he found this billet in one of the drawers of her bureau:—"Sir, being convinced that you are a cheat and an impostor, I have withdrawn myself from your cruelty and machinations, with a view to solicit the protection of the law; and I doubt not but I shall soon be able to prove, that you have no just title to, or demand upon, the person or effects of the unfortunate Sarah Muddy."

The time had been when Mr. Fathom would have allowed Mrs. Muddy to refine at her leisure, and blessed God for his happy deliverance; but at present the case was quite altered. Smarting as he was from the expense of lawsuits, he dreaded a prosecution for bigamy, which, though he had justice on his side, he knew he could not of himself support. Besides, all his other schemes of life were frustrated by this unlucky elopement. He therefore speedily determined to anticipate, as much as in him lay, the malice of his enemies, and to obtain, without delay, authentic documents of his marriage. With this view, he hastened to the house of the tradesman, who, with his wife, had been witness to the ceremony and consummation; and, in order to interest them the more warmly in his cause, made a pathetic recital of this unhappy breach, in which he had suffered such injury and insult. But all his rhetoric would not avail. Mrs. Muddy had been beforehand with him, and had proved the better orator of the two; for she had assailed this honest couple with such tropes and figures of eloquence, as were altogether irresistible.

Nevertheless, they heard our hero to an end, with great patience. Then the wife, who was the common mouth upon all such occasions, contracting her features into a very formal disposition, "I'll assure you," said she, "Doctor Fathom, my husband and I have been in a very great terrification and numplush, to hear such bad things of a person, whom, as one may say, we thought a worthy gentleman, and were ready to serve at all times, by day and by night, as the saying is. And besides, for all that, you know, and God knows, as we are dustrious people, and work hard for what we get, and we have served gentlemen to our own harm, whereby my husband was last Tuesday served with a siserary, being that he was bound for an officer that ran away. And I said to my husband, Timothy, says I, 'tis a very hard thing for one to ruin one's self for stranger people—There's Doctor Fathom, says I, his account comes to nine-and-forty pounds seven shillings and fourpence halfpenny; and you know, doctor, that was before your last bill began. But, howsomever, little did I think, as how a gentleman of your learning would go to deceive a poor gentlewoman, when you had another wife alive."

In vain did our adventurer endeavour to vindicate himself from this aspersion; the good woman, like a great many modern disputants, proceeded with her declamation, without seeming to hear what was said on the other side of the question; and the husband was altogether neutral. At length, Ferdinand, finding all his protestations ineffectual, "Well," said he, "though you are resolved, I see, to discredit all that I can say in opposition to that scandalous slander, of which I can easily acquit myself in a court of justice, surely you will not refuse to grant me a certificate, signifying that you were present at the ceremony of my marriage with this unhappy woman." "You shall excuse us," replied the female orator; "people cannot be too wary in signing their names in this wicked world; many a one has been brought to ruination by signing his name, and my husband shall not, with my goodwill, draw himself into such a primmineery."

Fathom, alarmed at this refusal, earnestly argued against the inhumanity and injustice of it, appealing to their own consciences for the reasonableness of his proposal; but, from the evasive answers of the wife, he had reason to believe, that, long before the time of trial, they would take care to have forgotten the whole transaction.

Though he was equally confounded and incensed at this instance of their perfidy, he durst not manifest his indignation, conscious of the advantage they had over him in divers respects; but repaired, without loss of time, to the lodging of the clergyman who had noosed him, resolved to consult his register, and secure his evidence. Here too his evil genius had got the start of him; for the worthy ecclesiastic not only could not recollect his features, or find his name in the register, but, when importuned by his pressing remonstrances, took umbrage at the freedom of his behaviour, and threatened, if he would not immediately take himself away, to raise the posse of the Fleet, for the safety of his own person.

Rather than put the pastor to the trouble of alarming his flock, he retreated with a heavy heart, and went in quest of his mistress, whom he had dismissed at his marriage, in hopes of effecting a reconciliation, and preventing her from joining in the conspiracy against him. But, alas! he met with such a reception as he had reason to expect from a slighted woman, who had never felt any real attachment for his person. She did not upbraid him with his cruelty in leaving her as a mistress, but, with a species of effrontery never enough to be admired, reproached him with his villany, in abandoning her, who was his true and lawful wife, to go and ruin a poor gentlewoman, by whose fortune he had been allured.

When he attempted to expostulate with this virago, upon the barbarity of this assertion, she very prudently declined engaging in private conversation with such an artful and wicked man; and, calling up the people of the house, insisted upon his being conducted to the door.

CHAPTER FIFTY-SIX.
IN WHICH HIS FORTUNE IS EFFECTUALLY STRANGLED.

The last resource, and that upon which he least depended, was the advice and assistance of his old friend the empiric, with whom he still maintained a slight correspondence; and to whose house he steered his course, in great perplexity and tribulation. That gentleman, instead of consoling him with assurances of friendship and protection, faithfully recapitulated all the instances of his indiscretion and misconduct, taxed him with want of sincerity in the West India affair, as well as with want of honesty in this last marriage, while his former wife was alive; and, finally, reminded him of his notes, which he desired might be immediately taken up, as he (the quack) had present occasion for a sum of money.

Ferdinand, seeing it would be impracticable to derive any succour from this quarter, sneaked homewards, in order to hold a consultation with his own thoughts; and the first object that presented itself to his eyes when he entered his apartment, was a letter from the tradesman, with his account inclosed, amounting to forty-five pounds, which the writer desired might be paid without delay. Before he had time to peruse the articles, he received a summons, in consequence of a bill of indictment for bigamy, found against him in Hicks' Hall, by Sarah Muddy, widow; and, while he was revolving measures to avert these storms, another billet arrived from a certain attorney, giving him to understand, that he had orders from Doctor Buffalo, the quack, to sue him for the payment of several notes, unless he would take them up in three days from the date of this letter.

Such a concurrence of sinister events made a deep impression upon the mind of our adventurer. All his fortitude was insufficient to bear him up against this torrent of misfortunes; his resources were all dried up, his invention failed, and his reflection began to take a new turn. "To what purpose," said he to himself, "have I deserted the paths of integrity and truth, and exhausted a fruitful imagination, in contriving schemes to betray my fellow-creatures, if, instead of acquiring a splendid fortune, which was my aim, I have suffered such a series of mortifications, and at last brought myself to the brink of inevitable destruction? By a virtuous exertion of those talents I inherit from nature and education, I might, long before this time, have rendered myself independent, and, perhaps, conspicuous in life. I might have grown up like a young oak, which, being firmly rooted in its kindred soil, gradually raises up its lofty head, expands its leafy arms, projects a noble shade, and towers the glory of the plain. I should have paid the debt of gratitude to my benefactors, and made their hearts sing with joy for the happy effects of their benevolence. I should have been a bulwark to my friends, a shelter to my neighbours in distress. I should have run the race of honour, seen my fame diffused like a sweet-smelling odour, and felt the ineffable pleasure of doing good. Whereas I am, after a vicissitude of disappointments, dangers, and fatigues, reduced to misery and shame, aggravated by a conscience loaded with treachery and guilt. I have abused the confidence and generosity of my patron; I have defrauded his family, under the mask of sincerity and attachment; I have taken the most cruel and base advantages of virtue in distress; I have seduced unsuspecting innocence to ruin and despair; I have violated the most sacred trust reposed in me by my friend and benefactor; I have betrayed his love, torn his noble heart asunder, by means of the most perfidious slander and false insinuations; and, finally, brought to an untimely grave the fairest pattern of human beauty and perfection. Shall the author of these crimes pass with impunity? Shall he hope to prosper in the midst of such enormous guilt? It were an imputation upon Providence to suppose it! Ah, no! I begin to feel myself overtaken by the eternal justice of Heaven! I totter on the edge of wretchedness and woe, without one friendly hand to save me from the terrible abyss!"

These reflections, which, perhaps, the misery of his fellow-creatures would never have inspired, had he himself remained without the verge of misfortune, were now produced from the sensation of his own calamities; and, for the first time, his cheeks were bedewed with the drops of penitence and sorrow. "Contraries," saith Plato, "are productive of each other." Reformation is oftentimes generated from unsuccessful vice; and our adventurer was, at this juncture, very well disposed to turn over a new leaf in consequence of those salutary suggestions; though he was far from being cured beyond the possibility of a relapse. On the contrary, all the faculties of his soul were so well adapted, and had been so long habituated to deceit, that, in order to extricate himself from the evils that environed him, he would not, in all probability, have scrupled to practise it upon his own father, had a convenient opportunity occurred.

Be that as it may, he certainly, after a tedious and fruitless exercise of his invention, resolved to effect a clandestine retreat from that confederacy of enemies which he could not withstand, and once more join his fortune to that of Renaldo, whom he proposed to serve, for the future, with fidelity and affection, thereby endeavouring to atone for the treachery of his former conduct. Thus determined, he packed up his necessaries in a portmanteau, attempted to amuse his creditors with promises of speedy payment, and, venturing to come forth in the dark, took a place in the Canterbury stage-coach, after having converted his superfluities into ready money. These steps were not taken with such privacy as to elude the vigilance of his adversaries; for, although he had been cautious enough to transport himself and his baggage to the inn on Sunday evening, and never doubted that the vehicle, which set out at four o'clock on Monday morning, would convey him out of the reach of his creditors, before they could possibly obtain a writ for securing his person, they had actually taken such precautions as frustrated all his finesse; and the coach being stopped in the borough of Southwark, Doctor Fathom was seized by virtue of a warrant obtained on a criminal indictment, and was forthwith conducted to the prison of the King's Bench; yet, not before he had, by his pathetic remonstrances, excited the compassion, and even drawn tears from the eyes of his fellow-passengers.

He no sooner recollected himself from the shock which must have been occasioned by this sinister incident, than he despatched a letter to his brother-in-law, the counsellor, requesting an immediate conference, in which he promised to make such a proposal as would save him all the expense of a lawsuit and trial, and, at the same time, effectually answer all the purposes of both. He was accordingly favoured with a visit from the lawyer, to whom, after the most solemn protestations of his own innocence, he declared, that, finding himself unable to wage war against such powerful antagonists, he had resolved even to abandon his indubitable right, and retire into another country, in order to screen himself from persecution, and remove all cause of disquiet from the prosecutrix, when he was, unfortunately, prevented by the warrant which had been executed against him. He said he was still willing, for the sake of his liberty, to sign a formal renunciation of his pretensions to Mrs. Fathom and her fortune, provided the deeds could be executed, and the warrant withdrawn, before he should be detained by his other creditors; and, lastly, he conjured the barrister to spare himself the guilt and the charge of suborning evidence for the destruction of an unhappy man, whose misfortune was his only fault.

The lawyer felt the force of his expostulations; and though he would by no means suppose him innocent of the charge of bigamy, yet, under the pretext of humanity and commiseration, he undertook to persuade his sister to accept of a proper release, which, he observed, would not be binding, if executed during the confinement of Fathom; he therefore took his leave, in order to prepare the papers, withdraw the action, and take such other measures as would hinder the prisoner from giving him the slip. Next day, he returned with an order to release our hero, who, being formally discharged, was conducted by the lawyer to a tavern in the neighbourhood, where the releases were exchanged, and everything concluded with amity and concord. This business being happily transacted, Fathom stept into a hackney-coach, with his baggage, and was followed by a bailiff, who told him, with great composure, that he was again a prisoner, at the suit of Doctor Buffalo, and desired the coachman to reconduct him to the lodging he had so lately discharged.

Fathom, whose fortitude had been hitherto of the pagan temper, was now fain to reinforce it with the philosophy of Christian resignation, though he had not as yet arrived to such a pitch of self-denial as to forgive the counsellor, to whose double dealing he imputed this new calamity. After having received the compliments of the jailer on his recommitment, he took pen, ink, and paper, and composed an artful and affecting epistle to the empiric, imploring his mercy, flattering his weakness, and demonstrating the bad policy of cooping up an unhappy man in a jail, where he could never have an opportunity of doing justice to his creditors; nor did he forget to declare his intention of retiring into another country, where he might have some chance of earning a subsistence, which he had so long toiled for to no purpose in England. This last declaration he made in consequence of the jealous disposition of the quack, who he knew had long looked upon him in the odious light of an interloping rival. However, he reaped no benefit from this supplication, which served only to gratify the pride of Buffalo, who produced the extravagant encomiums which Fathom had bestowed upon him, as so many testimonials of his foe's bearing witness to his virtue.

CHAPTER FIFTY-SEVEN.
FATHOM BEING SAFELY HOUSED, THE READER IS ENTERTAINED WITH A RETROSPECT.

But now it is high time to leave our adventurer to chew the cud of reflection and remorse in this solitary mansion, that we may trace Renaldo in the several steps he took to assert his right, and do justice to his family. Never man indulged a more melancholy train of ideas than that which accompanied him in his journey to the Imperial court. For, notwithstanding the manifold reasons he had to expect a happy issue to his aim, his imagination was incessantly infected with something that chilled his nerves and saddened his heart, recurring, with quick succession, like the unwearied wave that beats upon the bleak, inhospitable Greenland shore. This, the reader will easily suppose, was no other than the remembrance of the forlorn Monimia, whose image appeared to his fancy in different attitudes, according to the prevalence of the passions which raged in his bosom. Sometimes he viewed her in the light of apostasy, and then his soul was maddened with indignation and despair. But these transitory blasts were not able to efface the impressions she had formerly made upon his heart; impressions which he had so often and so long contemplated with inconceivable rapture. These pictures still remained, representing her fair as the most perfect idea of beauty, soft and tender as an angel of mercy and compassion, warmed with every virtue of the heart, and adorned with every accomplishment of human nature. Yet the alarming contrast came still in the rear of this recollection; so that his soul was by turns agitated by the tempests of horror, and overwhelmed by the floods of grief.

He recalled the moment on which he first beheld her, with that pleasing regret which attends the memory of a dear deceased friend. Then he bitterly cursed it, as the source of all his misfortunes and affliction. He thanked Heaven for having blessed him with a friend to detect her perfidy and ingratitude; and then ardently wished he had still continued under the influence of her delusion. In a word, the loneliness of his situation aggravated every horror of his reflection; for, as he found himself without company, his imagination was never solicited, or his attention diverted from these subjects of woe; and he travelled to Brussels in a reverie, fraught with such torments as must have entirely wrecked his reason, had not Providence interposed in his behalf. He was, by his postillion, conducted to one of the best inns of the place, where he understood the cloth was already laid for supper; and as the ordinary is open to strangers in all these houses of entertainment, he introduced himself into the company, with a view to alleviate, in some measure, his sorrow and chagrin, by the conversation of his fellow-guests. Yet he was so ill prepared to obtain the relief which he courted, that he entered the apartment, and sat down to table, without distinguishing either the number or countenances of those who were present, though he himself did not long remain so unregarded. His mien and deportment produced a prepossession in his favour; and the air of affliction, so remarkable in his visage, did not fail to attract their sympathy and observation.

Among the rest, was an Irish officer in the Austrian service, who having eyed Renaldo attentively, "Sir," said he, rising, "if my eyes and memory do not deceive me, you are the Count de Melvil, with whom I had the honour to serve upon the Rhine during the last war." The youth, hearing his own name mentioned, lifted up his eyes, and at once recognising the other to be a gentleman who had been a captain in his father's regiment, ran forwards, and embraced him with great affection.

This was, in divers respects, a fortunate rencontre for young Melvil; as the officer was not only perfectly well acquainted with the situation of the Count's family, but also resolved, in a few days, to set out for Vienna, whither he promised to accompany Renaldo, as soon as he understood his route lay the same way. Before the day fixed for their departure arrived, this gentleman found means to insinuate himself so far into the confidence of the Count, as to learn the cause of that distress which he had observed in his features at their first meeting; and being a gentleman of uncommon vivacity, as well as sincerely attached to the family of Melvil, to which he had owed his promotion, he exerted all his good-humour and good sense in amusing the fancy, and reasoning down the mortification of the afflicted Hungarian. He in particular endeavoured to wean his attention from the lost Monimia, by engaging it upon his domestic affairs, and upon the wrongs of his mother and sister, who, he gave him to understand, were languishing under the tyranny of his father-in-law.

This was a note that effectually roused him from the lethargy of his sorrow; and the desire of taking vengeance on the oppressor, who had ruined his fortune, and made his nearest relations miserable, so entirely engrossed his thoughts, as to leave no room for other considerations. During their journey to Austria, Major Farrel, (that was the name of his fellow-traveller,) informed him of many circumstances touching his father's house, to which himself was an utter stranger.

"The conduct of your mother," said he, "in marrying Count Trebasi, was not at all agreeable either to the friends of the Count de Melvil, or to her own relations, who knew her second husband to be a man of a violent temper, and rapacious disposition, which the nature of his education and employment had served rather to inflame than allay; for you well know he was a partisan during the whole course of the late war. They were, moreover, equally surprised and chagrined, when they found she took no step to prevent his seizing upon that inheritance which of right belonged to you, and which, by the laws of Hungary, is unalienable from the heir of blood. Nevertheless, they are now fully convinced, that she hath more than sufficiently atoned for her indiscretion, by the barbarity of her husband, who hath not only secluded her from all communication with her friends and acquaintance, but even confined her to the west tower of your father's house, where she is said to be kept close prisoner, and subjected to all sorts of inconvenience and mortification. This severity she is believed to have incurred in consequence of having expostulated to him upon his unjust behaviour to you and Mademoiselle, whom he hath actually shut up in some convent in Vienna, which your relations have not as yet been able to discover. But the memory of your noble father is so dear to all those who were favoured with his friendship, and the sufferings of the Countess and Mademoiselle have raised such a spirit of resentment against her cruel jailor, that nothing is wanted but your presence to begin the prosecution, and give a sanction to the measures of your friends, which will in a little time restore your family to the fruition of its rights and fortune. For my own part, my dear Count, I consider myself as one wholly indebted to your house for the rank and expectation I now enjoy; and my finances, interest, and person, such as they are, I dedicate to your service."

Renaldo was not slow in making his acknowledgments to this generous Hibernian, whom he informed of his scheme, recounting to him his uncommon transaction with the benevolent Jew, and communicating the letters of recommendation he had received by his means to some of the first noblemen at the Imperial court. Meanwhile, he burned with impatience to chastise Count Trebasi for his perfidious conduct to the widow and the fatherless, and would have taken the road to Presburg, without touching at Vienna, in order to call him to a severe account, had not he been strenuously opposed by Major Farrel, who represented the imprudence of taking such a step before he had secured a proper protection from the consequences with which it might be attended.

"It is not," said he, "your own life and fortune only which depend upon your behaviour in this emergency, but also the quiet and happiness of those who are most dear to your affection. Not you alone, but likewise your mother and sister, would infallibly suffer by your temerity and precipitation. First of all, deliver your credentials at court, and let us join our endeavours to raise an interest strong enough to counterbalance that of Trebasi. If we succeed, there will be no necessity for having recourse to personal measures. He will be compelled to yield up your inheritance which he unjustly detains, and to restore your sister to your arms; and if he afterwards refuses to do justice to the Countess, you will always have it in your power to evince yourself the son of the brave Count de Melvil."

These just and salutary representations had a due effect upon Renaldo, who no sooner arrived at the capital of Austria, than he waited upon a certain prince of distinction, to whose patronage he was commended; and from whom he met with a very cordial reception, not only on account of his credentials, but also for the sake of his father, who was well known to his highness. He heard his complaints with great patience and affability, assured him of his assistance and protection, and even undertook to introduce him to the empress-queen, who would not suffer the weakest of her subjects to be oppressed, much less disregard the cause of an injured young nobleman, who, by his own services, and those of his family, was peculiarly entitled to her favour.

Nor was he the only person whose countenance and patronage Melvil solicited upon this occasion; he visited all the friends of his father, and all his mother's relations, who were easily interested in his behalf; while Major Farrel contributed all his efforts in strengthening the association. So that a lawsuit was immediately commenced against Count Trebasi, who on his side was not idle, but prepared with incredible industry for the assault, resolving to maintain with his whole power the acquisition he had made.

The laws of Hungary, like those of some other countries I could name, afford so many subterfuges for the purposes of perfidy and fraud, that it is no wonder our youth began to complain of the slow progress of his affair; especially as he glowed with the most eager desire of redressing the grievances of his parent and sister, whose sufferings he did not doubt were doubled since the institution of his process against their tormentor. He imparted his sentiments on this head to his friend; and, as his apprehensions every moment increased, plainly told him he could no longer live without making some effort to see those with whom he was so nearly connected in point of blood and affection. He therefore resolved to repair immediately to Presburg; and, according to the intelligence he should procure, essay to see and converse with his mother, though at the hazard of his life.

CHAPTER FIFTY-EIGHT.
RENALDO ABRIDGES THE PROCEEDINGS AT LAW, AND APPROVES HIMSELF THE SON OF HIS FATHER.

The Major, finding him determined, insisted upon attending him in this expedition, and they set out together for Presburg, where they privately arrived in the dark, resolving to keep themselves concealed at the house of a friend, until they should have formed some plan for their future operations. Here they were informed that Count Trebasi's castle was altogether inaccessible; that all the servants who were supposed to have the least veneration or compassion for the Countess were dismissed; and that, since Renaldo was known to be in Germany, the vigilance and caution of that cruel husband was redoubled to such a degree, that nobody knew whether his unfortunate lady was actually alive or dead.

Farrel perceiving Melvil exceedingly affected with this intimation, and hearing him declare that he would never quit Presburg until he should have entered the house, and removed his doubts on that interesting subject, not only argued with great vehemence against such an attempt, as equally dangerous and indiscreet, but solemnly swore he would prevent his purpose, by discovering his design to the family, unless he would promise to listen to a more moderate and feasible expedient. He then proposed that he himself should appear in the equipage of one of the travelling Savoyards who stroll about Europe, amusing ignorant people with the effects of a magic lanthorn, and in that disguise endeavour to obtain admittance from the servants of Trebasi, among whom he might make such inquiries as would deliver Melvil from his present uneasy suspense.

This proposal was embraced, though reluctantly, by Renaldo, who was unwilling to expose his friend to the least danger or disgrace; and the Major being next day provided with the habit and implements of his new profession, together with a ragged attendant who preceded him, extorting music from a paltry viol, approached the castle gate, and proclaimed his show so naturally in a yell, partaking of the scream of Savoy and the howl of Ireland, that one would have imagined he had been conductor to Madam Catherina from his cradle. So far his stratagem succeeded; he had not long stood in waiting before he was invited into the court-yard, where the servants formed a ring, and danced to the efforts of his companion's skill; then he was conducted into the buttery, where he exhibited his figures on the wall, and his princess on the floor; and while they regaled him in this manner with scraps and sour wine, he took occasion to inquire about the old lady and her daughter, before whom he said he had performed in his last peregrination. Though this question was asked with all that air of simplicity which is peculiar to these people, one of the domestics took the alarm, being infected with the suspicions of his master, and plainly taxed the Major with being a spy, threatening at the same time that he should be stripped and searched.

This would have been a very dangerous experiment for the Hibernian, who had actually in his pocket a letter to the Countess from her son, which he hoped fortune might have furnished him with an opportunity to deliver. When he therefore found himself in this dilemma, he was not at all easy in his own mind. However, instead of protesting his innocence in an humble and beseeching strain, in order to acquit himself of the charge, he resolved to elude the suspicion by provoking the wrath of his accuser, and, putting on the air of vulgar integrity affronted, began to reproach the servant in very insolent terms for his unfair supposition, and undressed himself in a moment to the skin, threw his tattered garments in the face of his adversary, telling him he would find nothing there which he would not be very glad to part with; at the same time raising his voice, he, in the gibberish of the clan he represented, scolded and cursed with great fluency, so that the whole house resounded with the noise. The valet's jealousy, like a smaller fire, was in a trice swallowed up in the greater flame of his rage enkindled by this abrupt address. In consequence of which, Farrel was kicked out at the gate, naked as he was to the waist, after his lanthorn had been broke to pieces on his head; and there he was joined by his domestic, who had not been able to recover his apparel and effect a retreat, without incurring marks of the same sort of distinction.

The Major, considering the risk he must have run in being detected, thought himself cheaply quit for this moderate discipline, though he was really concerned for his friend Renaldo, who, understanding the particulars of the adventure, determined, as the last effort, to ride round the castle in the open day, on pretence of taking the air, when, peradventure, the Countess would see him from the place of her confinement, and favour him with some mark or token of her being alive.

Though his companion did not much relish this plan, which he foresaw would expose him to the insults of Trebasi, yet, as he could not contrive a better, he acquiesced in Renaldo's invention, with the proviso that he would defer the execution of it until his father-in-law should be absent in the chase, which was a diversion he every day enjoyed.

Accordingly they set a proper watch, and lay concealed until they were informed of Trebasi's having gone forth; when they mounted their horses, and rode into the neighbourhood of the castle. Having made a small excursion in the adjoining fields, they drew nearer the walls, and at an easy pace had twice circled them, when Farrel descried, at the top of a tower, a white handkerchief waved by a woman's hand through the iron bars that secured the window. This signal being pointed out to Renaldo, his heart began to throb with great violence; he made a respectful obeisance towards the part in which it appeared, and perceiving the hand beckoning him to approach, advanced to the very buttress of the turret; upon which, seeing something drop, he alighted with great expedition, and took up a picture of his father in miniature, the features of which he no sooner distinguished, than the tears ran down his cheeks; he pressed the little image to his lips with the most filial fervour; then conveying it to his bosom, looked up to the hand, which waved in such a manner as gave him to understand it was high time to retire. Being by this time highly persuaded that his kind monitor was no other than the Countess herself, he pointed to his heart, in token of his filial affection, and laying his hand on his sword, to denote his resolution of doing her justice, he took his leave with another profound bow, and suffered himself to be reconducted to his lodging.

Every circumstance of this transaction was observed by the servants of Count Trebasi, who immediately despatched a messenger to their lord, with an account of what had happened. Alarmed at this information, from which he immediately concluded that the stranger was young Melvil, he forthwith quitted the chase, and returning to the castle by a private postern, ordered his horse to be kept ready saddled, in hope that his son-in-law would repeat the visit to his mother. This precaution would have been to no purpose, had Renaldo followed the advice of Farrel, who represented the danger of returning to a place where the alarm was undoubtedly given by his first appearance; and exhorted him to return to Vienna for the prosecution of his suit, now that he was satisfied of his mother's being alive. In order to strengthen this admonition, he bade him recollect the signal for withdrawing, which was doubtless the effect of maternal concern, inspired by the knowledge of the Count's vigilance and vindictive disposition.

Notwithstanding these suggestions, Melvil persisted in his resolution of appearing once more below the tower, on the supposition that his mother, in expectation of his return, had prepared a billet for his acceptance, from which he might obtain important intelligence. The Major, seeing him lend a deaf ear to his remonstrances, was contented to attend him in his second expedition, which he pressed him to undertake that same afternoon, as Trebasi had taken care to circulate a report of his having gone to dine at the seat of a nobleman in the neighbourhood. Our knight-errant and his squire, deceived by this finesse, presented themselves again under the prison of the Countess, who no sooner beheld her son return, than she earnestly entreated him to be gone, by the same sign which she had before used; and he, taking it for granted that she was debarred the use of pen, ink, and paper, and that she had nothing more to expect, consented to retire, and had already moved to some distance from the house, when, in crossing a small plantation that belonged to the castle, they were met by Count Trebasi and another person on horseback.

At sight of this apparition, the blood mounted into Renaldo's cheeks, and his eyes began to lighten with eagerness and indignation; which was not at all diminished by the ferocious address of the Count, who advancing to Melvil, with a menacing air. "Before you proceed," said he, "I must know with what view you have been twice to-day patroling round my enclosures, and reconnoitring the different avenues of my house. You likewise carry on a clandestine correspondence with some person in the family, of which my honour obliges me to demand an explanation."

"Had your actions been always regulated by the dictates of honour," replied Renaldo, "I should never have been questioned for riding round that castle, which you know is my rightful inheritance; or excluded from the sight of a parent who suffers under your tyranny and oppression. It is my part, therefore, to expostulate; and, since fortune hath favoured me with an opportunity of revenging our wrongs in person, we shall not part until you have learned that the family of the Count de Melvil is not to be injured with impunity. Here is no advantage on either side, in point of arms or number; you are better mounted than I am, and shall have the choice of the ground on which our difference ought to be brought to a speedy determination."

Trebasi, whose courage was not of the sentimental kind, but purely owing to his natural insensibility of danger, instead of concerting measures coolly for the engagement, or making any verbal reply to this defiance, drew a pistol, without the least hesitation, and fired it at the face of Renaldo, part of whose left eyebrow was carried off by the ball. Melvil was not slow in returning the compliment, which, as it was deliberate, proved the more decisive. For the shot entering the Count's right breast, made its way to the backbone with such a shock, as struck him to the ground; upon which the other alighted, in order to improve the advantage he had gained.

During this transaction, Farrel had well-nigh lost his life by the savage behaviour of Trebasi's attendant, who had been a hussar officer, and who, thinking it was his duty to imitate the example of his patron on this occasion, discharged a pistol at the Major, before he had the least intimation of his design. The Hibernian's horse being a common hireling, and unaccustomed to stand fire, no sooner saw the flash of Trebasi's pistol, than, starting aside, he happened to plunge into a hole, and was overturned at the very instant when the hussar's piece went off, so that no damage ensued to his rider, who, pitching on his feet, flew with great nimbleness to his adversary, then, laying hold on one leg, dismounted him in a twinkling, and, seizing his throat as he lay, would have soon despatched him without the use of firearms, had he not been prevented by his friend Renaldo, who desired him to desist, observing that his vengeance was already satisfied, as the Count seemed to be in the agonies of death. The Major was loth to quit his prey, as he thought his aggressor had acted in a treacherous manner; but recollecting that there was no time to lose, because, in all probability, the firing had alarmed the castle, he took his leave of the vanquished hussar, with a couple of hearty kicks, and, mounting his horse, followed Melvil to the house of a gentleman in the neighbourhood, who was kinsman to the Countess, and very well disposed to grant him a secure retreat, until the troublesome consequences of this rencontre should be overblown.

Trebasi, though to the young gentleman he seemed speechless and insensible, had neither lost the use of his reason nor of his tongue, but affected that extremity, in order to avoid any further conversation with the victor. He was one of those people who never think of death until he knocks at the door, and then earnestly entreat him to excuse them for the present, and be so good as to call another time. The Count had so often escaped unhurt, in the course of his campaigns, that he looked upon himself as invulnerable, and set all danger at defiance. Though he had hitherto taken no care of the concerns of his soul, he had a large fund of superstition at bottom; and, when the surgeon, who examined his wound, declared it was mortal, all the terrors of futurity took hold on his imagination, all the misdemeanours of his life presented themselves in aggravated colours to his recollection.

He implored the spiritual assistance of a good priest in the neighbourhood, who, in the discharge of his own conscience, gave him to understand that he had little mercy to expect, unless he would, as much as lay in his power, redress the injuries he had done to his fellow-creatures. As nothing lay heavier upon his soul than the cruelty and fraud he had practised upon the family of Count Melvil, he earnestly besought this charitable clergyman to mediate his pardon with the Countess, and at the same time desired to see Renaldo before his death, that he might put him in possession of his paternal estate, and solicit his forgiveness for the offence he had given.

His lady, far from waiting for the priest's intercession, no sooner understood the lamentable situation of her husband, and found herself at liberty, than she hastened to his apartment, expressed the utmost concern for his misfortune, and tended him with truly conjugal tenderness and fidelity. Her son gladly obeyed the summons, and was received with great civility and satisfaction by his father-in-law, who, in presence of the judge and divers gentlemen assembled for that purpose, renounced all right and title to the fortune he had so unjustly usurped; disclosed the name of the convent to which Mademoiselle de Melvil had been conveyed, dismissed all the agents of his iniquity, and being reconciled to his son-in-law, began to prepare himself in tranquillity for his latter end.

The Countess was overwhelmed with an excess of joy, while she embraced her long-lost son, who had proved himself so worthy of his father. Yet this joy was embittered, by reflecting that she was made a widow by the hands of that darling son. For, though she knew his honour demanded the sacrifice, she could not lay aside that regard and veneration which is attached to the name of husband; and therefore resolved to retire into a monastery, where she could spend the remainder of her life in devotion, without being exposed to any intercourse which might interfere with the delicacy of her sentiments on that subject.

CHAPTER FIFTY-NINE.
HE IS THE MESSENGER OF HAPPINESS TO HIS SISTER, WHO REMOVES THE FILM WHICH HAD LONG OBSTRUCTED HIS PENETRATION, WITH REGARD TO COUNT FATHOM.

As the most endearing affection had always subsisted between Renaldo and his sister, he would not one moment deny himself the pleasure of flying to her embrace, and of being the glad messenger of her deliverance. Soon, therefore, as he understood the place of her retreat, and had obtained a proper order to the abbess, signed by Count Trebasi, he set out post for Vienna, still accompanied by his faithful Hibernian, and, arriving at the convent, found the abbess and the whole house so engrossed in making preparations for the ceremony of giving the veil next day to a young woman who had fulfilled the term of her probation, that he could not possibly see his sister with that leisure and satisfaction which he had flattered himself with enjoying at this meeting; and therefore he was fain to bridle his impatience for two days, and keep his credentials until the hurry should be over, that Mademoiselle might have no intimation of her good fortune, except from his own mouth.

In order to fill up this tedious interval, he visited his friends at court, who were rejoiced to hear the happy issue of his excursion to Presburg; the prince, who was his particular patron, desired he would make himself perfectly easy with regard to the death of Count Trebasi, for he would take care to represent him in such a light to the empress-queen, as would screen him from any danger or prosecution on that account. His highness, moreover, appointed the following day for performing the promise he had made of presenting him to that august princess, and in the meantime prepossessed her so much in his favour, that when he approached her presence, and was announced by his noble introductor, she eyed him with a look of peculiar complacency, saying, "I am glad to see you returned to my dominions. Your father was a gallant officer, who served our house with equal courage and fidelity; and as I understand you tread in his footsteps, you may depend upon my favour and protection."

He was so much overwhelmed with this gracious reception, that, while he bowed in silence, the drops of gratitude trickled from his eyes; and her imperial majesty was so well pleased with this manifestation of his heart, that she immediately gave directions for promoting him to the command of a troop of horse. Thus fortune seemed willing, and indeed eager to discharge the debt she owed him for the different calamities he had undergone. And as he looked upon the generous Hebrew to be the sole source of his success, he did not fail to make him acquainted with the happy effects of his recommendation and friendship, and to express, in the warmest terms, the deep sense he had of his uncommon benevolence, which, by the bye, was still greater, with regard to Renaldo, than the reader as yet imagines; for he not only furnished him with money for his present occasions, but also gave him an unlimited credit on a banker in Vienna, to whom one of his letters was directed.

The ceremony of the nun's admission being now performed, and the convent restored to its former quiet, Melvil hastened thither on the wings of brotherly affection, and presented his letter to the abbess, who having perused the contents, by which she learned that the family disquiets of Count Trebasi no longer subsisted, and that the bearer was the brother of Mademoiselle, she received him with great politeness, congratulated him on this happy event, and, begging he would excuse her staying with him in the parlour, on pretence of business, withdrew, saying, she would immediately send in a young lady who would console him for her absence. In a few minutes he was joined by his sister, who, expecting nothing less than to see Renaldo, no sooner distinguished his features, than she shrieked aloud with surprise, and would have sunk upon the floor, had not he supported her in his embrace.

Such a sudden apparition of her brother at any time, or in any place, after their long separation, would have strongly affected this sensible young lady; but to find him so abruptly in a place where she thought herself buried from the knowledge of all her relations, occasioned such commotions in her spirits as had well-nigh endangered her reason. For it was not till after a considerable pause, that she could talk to him with connexion or coherence. However, as those transports subsided, they entered into a more deliberate and agreeable conversation; in the course of which, he gradually informed her of what had passed at the castle; and inexpressible was the pleasure she felt in learning that her mother was released from captivity, herself restored to freedom, and her brother to the possession of his inheritance, by the only means to which she had always prayed these blessings might be owing.

As she had been treated with uncommon humanity by the abbess, she would not consent to leave the convent until he should be ready to set out for Presburg; so that they dined together with that good lady, and passed the afternoon in that mutual communication with which a brother and sister may be supposed to entertain themselves on such an occasion. She gave him a detail of the insults and mortifications she had suffered from the brutality of her father-in-law, and told him, that her confinement in this monastery was owing to Trebasi having intercepted a letter to her from Renaldo, signifying his intention to return to the empire, in order to assert his own right, and redress his grievances. Then turning the discourse upon the incidents of his peregrinations, she in a particular manner inquired about that exquisite beauty who had been the innocent source of all his distresses, and upon whose perfections he had often, in his letters to his sister, expatiated with indications of rapture and delight.

This inquiry in a moment blew up that scorching flame which had been well-nigh stifled by other necessary avocations. His eyes gleamed, his cheeks glowed and grew pale alternately, and his whole frame underwent an immediate agitation; which being perceived by Mademoiselle, she concluded that some new calamity was annexed to the name of Monimia, and, dreading to rip up a wound which she saw was so ineffectually closed, she for the present suppressed her curiosity and concern, and industriously endeavoured to introduce some less affecting subject of conversation. He saw her aim, approved of her discretion, and, joining her endeavours, expressed his surprise at her having omitted to signify the least remembrance of her old favourite, Fathom, whom he had left in England. He had no sooner pronounced this name, than she suffered some confusion in her turn; from which, however, recollecting herself, "Brother," said she, "you must endeavour to forget that wretch, who is altogether unworthy of retaining the smallest share of your regard."

Astonished, and indeed angry, at this expression, which he considered as the effect of malicious misrepresentation, he gently chid her for her credulity in believing the envious aspersion of some person, who repined at the superior virtue of Fathom, whom he affirmed to be an honour to the human species.

"Nothing is more easy," replied the young lady, "than to impose upon a person, who, being himself unconscious of guile, suspects no deceit. You have been a dupe, dear brother, not to the finesse of Fathom, but to the sincerity of your own heart. For my own part, I assume no honour to my own penetration in having comprehended the villany of that impostor, which was discovered, in more than one instance, by accidents I could not possibly foresee.

"You must know, that Teresa, who attended me from my childhood, and in whose honesty I reposed such confidence, having disobliged some of the inferior servants, was so narrowly watched in all her transactions, as to be at last detected in the very act of conveying a piece of plate, which was actually found concealed among her clothes.

"You may guess how much I was astonished when I understood this circumstance. I could not trust to the evidence of my own senses, and should have still believed her innocent, in spite of ocular demonstration, had not she, in the terrors of being tried for felony, promised to make a very material discovery to the Countess, provided she would take such measures as would save her life.

"This request being complied with, she, in my hearing, opened up such an amazing scene of iniquity, baseness, and ingratitude, which had been acted by her and Fathom, in order to defraud the family to which they were so much indebted, that I could not have believed the human mind capable of such degeneracy, or that traitor endowed with such pernicious cunning and dissimulation, had not her tale been congruous, consistent, and distinct, and fraught with circumstances that left no room to doubt the least article of her confession; on consideration of which she was permitted to go into voluntary exile."

She then explained their combination in all the particulars, as we have already recounted them in their proper place, and finally observed, that the opinion she had hence conceived of Fathom's character, was confirmed by what she had since learned of his perfidious conduct towards that very nun who had lately taken the veil.

Perceiving her brother struck dumb with astonishment, and gaping with the most eager attention, she proceeded to relate the incidents of his double intrigue with the jeweller's wife and daughter, as they were communicated to her by the nun, who was no other than the individual Wilhelmina. After those rivals had been forsaken by their gallant, their mutual animosities and chagrin served to whet the attention and invention of each; so that in a little time the whole mystery stood disclosed to both. The mother had discovered the daughter's correspondence with Fathom, as we have formerly observed, by means of that unfortunate letter which he unwittingly committed to the charge of the old beldame; and, as soon as she understood he was without the reach of all solicitation or prosecution, imparted this billet to her husband, whose fury was so ungovernable, that he had almost sacrificed Wilhelmina with his own hands, especially when, terrified by his threats and imprecations, she owned that she had bestowed the chain on this perfidious lover. However, this dreadful purpose was prevented, partly by the interposition of his wife, whose aim was not the death but immurement of his daughter, and partly by the tears and supplication of the young gentlewoman herself, who protested, that, although the ceremony of the church had not been performed, she was contracted to Fathom by the most solemn vows, to witness which he invoked all the saints in heaven.

The jeweller, upon cooler consideration, was unwilling to lose the last spark of hope that glittered among the ruins of his despair, and resisted all the importunities of his wife, who pressed him to consult the welfare of his daughter's soul, in the fond expectation of finding some expedient to lure back the chain and its possessor. In the meantime Wilhelmina was daily and hourly exposed to the mortifying animadversions of her mamma, who, with all the insolence of virtue, incessantly upbraided her with the backslidings of her vicious life, and exhorted her to reformation and repentance. This continual triumph lasted for many months, till at length, a quarrel happening between the mother and the gossip at whose house she used to give the rendezvous to her admirers, that incensed confidante, in the precipitation of her anger, promulgated the history of those secret meetings; and, among the rest, her interviews with Fathom were brought to light.

The first people who hear news of this sort are generally those to whom they are most unwelcome. The German was soon apprised of his wife's frailty, and considered the two females of his house as a couple of devils incarnate, sent from hell to exercise his patience. Yet, in the midst of his displeasure, he found matter of consolation, in being furnished with a sufficient reason for parting with his helpmate, who had for many years kept his family in disquiet. He therefore, without hazarding a personal conference, sent proposals to her by a friend, which she did not think proper to reject; and seeing himself restored to the dominion of his own house, exerted his sway so tyrannically, that Wilhelmina became weary of her life, and had recourse to the comforts of religion, of which she soon became enamoured, and begged her father's permission to dedicate the rest of her life to the duties of devotion. She was accordingly received in this convent, the regulations of which were so much to her liking, that she performed the task of probation with pleasure, and voluntarily excluded herself from the vanities of this life. It was here she had contracted an acquaintance with Mademoiselle de Melvil, to whom she communicated her complaints of Fathom, on the supposition that he was related to the Count, as he himself had often declared.

While the young lady rehearsed the particulars of this detail, Renaldo sustained a strange vicissitude of different passions. Surprise, sorrow, fear, hope, and indignation raised a most tumultuous conflict in his bosom. Monimia rushed upon his imagination in the character of innocence betrayed by the insinuations of treachery. He with horror viewed her at the mercy of a villain, who had broken all the ties of gratitude and honour.

Affrighted at the prospect, he started from his seat, exclaiming, in the most unconnected strain of distraction and despair, "Have I then nourished a serpent in my bosom! Have I listened to the voice of a traitor, who hath murdered my peace! who hath torn my heart-strings asunder, and perhaps ruined the pattern of all earthly perfection. It cannot be. Heaven would not suffer such infernal artifice to take effect. The thunder would be levelled against the head of the accursed projector."

From this transport, compared with his agitation when he mentioned Monimia, his sister judged that Fathom had been the occasion of a breach between the two lovers; and this conjecture being confirmed by the disjointed answers he made to her interrogations upon the affair, she endeavoured to calm his apprehensions, by representing that he would soon have an opportunity of returning to England, where the misunderstanding might be easily cleared up; and that, in the meantime, he had nothing to fear on account of the person of his mistress, in a country where individuals were so well protected by the laws and constitution of the realm. At length he suffered himself to be flattered with the fond hope of seeing Monimia's character triumph in the inquiry, of retrieving that lost jewel, and of renewing that ravishing intercourse and exalted expectation which had been so cruelly cut off. He now wished to find Fathom as black as he had been exhibited, that Monimia's apostasy might be numbered among the misrepresentations of his treachery and fraud.

His love, which was alike generous and ardent, espoused the cause, and he no longer doubted her constancy and virtue. But when he reflected how her tender heart must have been wrung with anguish at his unkindness and cruelty, in leaving her destitute in a foreign land; how her sensibility must have been tortured in finding herself altogether dependent upon a ruffian, who certainly harboured the most baleful designs upon her honour; how her life must be endangered both by his barbarity and her own despair—I say, when he reflected on these circumstances, he shuddered with horror and dismay; and that very night despatched a letter to his friend the Jew, entreating him, in the most pressing manner, to employ all his intelligence in learning the situation of the fair orphan, that she might be protected from the villany of Fathom, until his return to England.

CHAPTER SIXTY.
HE RECOMPENSES THE ATTACHMENT OF HIS FRIEND; AND RECEIVES A LETTER THAT REDUCES HIM TO THE VERGE OF DEATH AND DISTRACTION.

This step being taken, his mind in some measure retrieved its former tranquillity. He soothed himself with the prospect of a happy reconciliation with the divine Monimia, and his fancy was decoyed from every disagreeable presage by the entertaining conversation of his sister, with whom in two days he set out for Presburg, attended by his friend the Major, who had never quitted him since their meeting at Brussels. Here they found Count Trebasi entirely rid of the fever which had been occasioned by his wound, and in a fair way of doing well; a circumstance that afforded unspeakable pleasure to Melvil, whose manner of thinking was such, as would have made him unhappy, could he have charged himself with the death of his mother's husband, howsoever criminal he might have been.

The Count's ferocity did not return with his health. His eyes were opened by the danger he had incurred, and his sentiments turned in a new channel. He heartily asked pardon of Mademoiselle for the rigorous usage she had suffered from the violence of his temper; thanked Renaldo for the seasonable lesson he had administered to him; and not only insisted upon being removed from the castle to a house of his own in Presburg, but proffered to make immediate restitution of all the rents which he had unjustly converted to his own use.

These things being settled in the most amicable manner, to the entire satisfaction of the parties concerned, as well as of the neighbouring noblesse, among whom the house of Melvil was in universal esteem, Renaldo resolved to solicit leave at the Imperial court to return to England, in order to investigate that affair of Monimia, which was more interesting than all the points he had hitherto adjusted. But, before he quitted Presburg, his friend Farrel taking him aside one day, "Count," said he, "will you give me leave to ask, if, by my zeal and attachment for you, I have had the good fortune to acquire your esteem?" "To doubt that esteem," replied Renaldo, "were to suspect my gratitude and honour, of which I must be utterly destitute before I lose the sense of those obligations I owe to your gallantry and friendship—obligations which I long for a proper occasion to repay."

"Well then," resumed the Major, "I will deal with you like a downright Swiss, and point out a method by which you may shift the load of obligation from your own shoulders to mine. You know my birth, rank, and expectations in the service; but perhaps you do not know, that, as my expense has always unavoidably exceeded my income, I find myself a little out at elbows in my circumstances, and want to piece them up by matrimony. Of those ladies with whom I think I have any chance of succeeding, Mademoiselle de Melvil seems the best qualified to render my situation happy in all respects. Her fortune is more than sufficient to disembarrass my affairs; her good sense will be a seasonable check upon my vivacity; her agreeable accomplishments will engage a continuation of affection and regard. I know my own disposition well enough to think I shall become a most dutiful and tractable husband; and shall deem myself highly honoured in being more closely united to my dear Count de Melvil, the son and representative of that worthy officer under whom my youth was formed. If you will therefore sanction my claim, I will forthwith begin my approaches, and doubt not, under your auspices, to bring the place to a capitulation."

Renaldo was pleased with the frankness of this declaration, approved of his demand, and desired him to depend upon his good offices with his sister, whom he sounded that same evening upon the subject, recommending the Major to her favour, as a gentleman well worthy of her choice. Mademoiselle, who had never been exercised in the coquetries of her sex, and was now arrived at those years when the vanity of youth ought to yield to discretion, considered the proposal as a philosopher, and after due deliberation candidly owned she had no objection to the match. Farrel was accordingly introduced in the character of a lover, after the permission of the Countess had been obtained; and he carried on his addresses in the usual form, so much to the satisfaction of all concerned in the event, that a day was appointed for the celebration of his nuptials, when he entered into peaceable possession of his prize.

A few days after this joyful occasion, while Renaldo was at Vienna, where he had been indulged with leave of absence for six months, and employed in making preparations for his journey to Britain, he was one evening presented by his servant with a package from London, which he no sooner opened, than he found enclosed a letter directed to him, in the handwriting of Monimia. He was so much affected at sight of those well-known characters, that he stood motionless as a statue, eager to know the contents, yet afraid to peruse the billet. While he hesitated in this suspense, he chanced to cast his eye on the inside of the cover, and perceived the name of his Jewish friend at the bottom of a few lines, importing, that the enclosed was delivered to him by a physician of his acquaintance, who had recommended it in a particular manner to his care. This intimation served only to increase the mystery, and whet his impatience; and as he had the explanation in his hand, he summoned all his resolution to his aid, and, breaking the seal, began to read these words: "Renaldo will not suppose that this address proceeds from interested motives, when he learns, that, before it can be presented to his view, the unfortunate Monimia will be no more."

Here the light forsook Renaldo's eyes, his knees knocked together, and he fell at full length insensible on the floor. His valet, hearing the noise, ran into the apartment, lifted him upon a couch, and despatched a messenger for proper assistance, while he himself endeavoured to recall his spirits by such applications as chance afforded. But before the Count exhibited any signs of life, his brother-in-law entered his chamber by accident, and as soon as he recollected himself from the extreme confusion and concern produced by this melancholy spectacle, he perceived the fatal epistle, which Melvil, though insensible, still kept within his grasp; justly suspecting this to be the cause of that severe paroxysm, he drew near the couch, and with difficulty read what is above rehearsed, and the sequel, to this effect:—

"Yes, I have taken such measures as will prevent it from falling into your hands, until after I shall have been released from a being embittered with inexpressible misery and anguish. It is not my intention, once loved, and ah! still too fondly remembered youth, to upbraid you as the source of that unceasing woe which hath been so long the sole inhabitant of my lonely bosom. I will not call you inconstant or unkind. I dare not think you base or dishonourable; yet I was abruptly sacrificed to a triumphant rival, before I had learned to bear such mortification; before I had overcome the prejudices which I had imbibed in my father's house. I was all at once abandoned to despair, to indigence, and distress, to the vile practices of a villain, who, I fear, hath betrayed us both. What have not I suffered from the insults and vicious designs of that wretch, whom you cherished in your bosom! Yet to these I owe this near approach to that goal of peace, where the canker-worm of sorrow will expire. Beware of that artful traitor; and, oh! endeavour to overcome that levity of disposition, which, if indulged, will not only stain your reputation, but also debauch the good qualities of your heart. I release you, in the sight of Heaven, from all obligations. If I have been injured, let not my wrongs be visited on the head of Renaldo, for whom shall be offered up the last fervent prayers of the hapless Monimia."

This letter was a clue to the labyrinth of Melvil's distress. Though the Major had never heard him mention the name of this beauty, he had received such hints from his own wife, as enabled him to comprehend the whole of the Count's disaster. By the administration of stimulating medicines, Renaldo recovered his perception; but this was a cruel alternative, considering the situation of his thoughts. The first word he pronounced was Monimia, with all the emphasis of the most violent despair. He perused the letter, and poured forth incoherent execrations against Fathom and himself. He exclaimed, in a frantic tone, "She is lost for ever! murdered by my unkindness! We are both undone by the infernal arts of Fathom! execrable monster! Restore her to my arms. If thou art not a fiend in reality, I will tear out thy false heart."

So saying, he sprung upon his valet, who would have fallen a sacrifice to his undistinguishing fury, had not he been saved by the interposition of Farrel and the family, who disengaged him from his master's gripe by dint of force; yet, notwithstanding their joint endeavours, he broke from this restraint, leaped upon the floor, and seizing his sword, attempted to plunge it in his own breast. When he was once more overcome by numbers, he cursed himself, and all those who withheld him; swore he would not survive the fair victim who had perished by his credulity and indiscretion; and the agitation of his spirits increased to such a degree, that he was seized with strong convulsions, which nature was scarce able to sustain. Every medical expedient was used to quiet his perturbation, which at length yielded so far as to subside into a continual fever and confirmed delirium, during which he ceased not to pour forth the most pathetic complaints, touching his ruined love, and to rave about the ill-starred Monimia. The Major, half distracted by the calamity of his friend, would have concealed it from the knowledge of his family, had not the physician, by despairing of his life, laid him under the necessity of making them acquainted with his condition.

The Countess and Mrs. Farrel were no sooner informed of his case than they hastened to the melancholy scene, where they found Renaldo deprived of his senses, panting under the rage of an exasperated disease. They saw his face distorted, and his eyes glaring with frenzy; they heard him invoke the name of Monimia with a tenderness of accent which even the impulse of madness could not destroy. Then, with a sudden transition of tone and gesture, he denounced vengeance against her betrayer, and called upon the north wind to cool the fervour of his brain. His hair hung in dishevelled parcels, his cheeks were wan, his looks ghastly, his vigour was fled, and all the glory of his youth faded; the physician hung his head in silence, the attendants wrung their hands in despair, and the countenance of his friend was bathed in tears.

Such a picture would have moved the most obdurate heart; what impression then must it have made upon a parent and sister, melting with all the enthusiasm of affection! The mother was struck dumb, and stupefied with grief; the sister threw herself on the bed in a transport of sorrow, caught her loved Renaldo in her arms, and was, with great difficulty, torn from his embrace. Such was the dismal reverse that overtook the late so happy family of Melvil; such was the extremity to which the treachery of Fathom had reduced his best benefactor!

Three days did nature struggle with surprising efforts, and then the constitution seemed to sink under the victorious fever; yet, as his strength diminished, his delirium abated, and on the fifth morning he looked round, and recognised his weeping friends. Though now exhausted to the lowest ebb of life, he retained the perfect use of speech, and his reason being quite unclouded, spoke to each with equal kindness and composure; he congratulated himself upon the sight of shore after the horrors of such a tempest; called upon the Countess and his sister, who were not permitted to see him at such a conjuncture; and being apprised by the Major of his reason for excluding them from his presence, he applauded his concern, bequeathed them to his future care, and took leave of that gentleman with a cordial embrace. Then he desired to be left in private with a certain clergyman, who regulated the concerns of his soul, and he being dismissed, turned his face from the light, in expectation of his final discharge. In a few minutes all was still and dreary, he was no longer heard to breathe, no more the stream of life was perceived to circulate, he was supposed to be absolved from all his cares, and an universal groan from the bystanders announced the decease of the gallant, generous, and tender-hearted Renaldo.

"Come hither, ye whom the pride of youth and health, of birth and affluence inflames, who tread the flowery maze of pleasure, trusting to the fruition of ever-circling joys; ye who glory in your accomplishments, who indulge the views of ambition, and lay schemes for future happiness and grandeur, contemplate here the vanity of life! behold how low this excellent young man is laid! mowed down even in the blossom of his youth, when fortune seemed to open all her treasures to his worth!"

Such were the reflections of the generous Farrel, who, while he performed the last office of friendship, in closing the eyes of the much-lamented Melvil, perceived a warmth on the skin, which the hand of death seldom leaves unextinguished. This uncommon sensation he reported to the physician, who, though he could feel no pulsation of the heart or arteries, conjectured that life still lingered in some of its interior haunts, and immediately ordered such applications to the extremities and surface of the body, as might help to concentrate and reinforce the natural heat.

By these prescriptions, which for some time produced no sensible effect, the embers were, in all probability, kept glowing, and the vital power revived, for, after a considerable pause, respiration was gradually renewed at long intervals, a languid motion was perceived at the heart, a few feeble and irregular pulsations were felt at the wrist, the clay-coloured livery of death began to vanish from his face, the circulation acquired new force, and he opened his eyes with a sigh, which proclaimed his return from the shades of death.

When he recovered the faculty of swallowing, a cordial was administered, and whether the fever abated, in consequence of the blood's being cooled and condensed during the recess of action in the solids, or nature, in that agony, had prepared a proper channel for the expulsion of the disease, certain it is, he was from this moment rid of all bodily pain; he retrieved the animal functions, and nothing remained of his malady but an extreme weakness and languor, the effect of nature's being fatigued in the battle she had won.

Unutterable was the joy that took possession of his mother and sister when Farrel flew into her apartment to intimate this happy turn. Scarce could they be restrained from pouring forth their transports in the presence of Renaldo, who was still too feeble to endure such communication; indeed, he was extremely mortified and dejected at this event, which had diffused such pleasure and satisfaction among his friends, for though his distemper was mastered, the fatal cause of it still rankled at his heart, and he considered this respite from death as a protraction of his misery.

When he was congratulated by the Major on the triumph of his constitution, he replied, with a groan, "I would to heaven it had been otherwise, for I am reserved for all the horrors of the most poignant sorrow and remorse. O Monimia! Monimia! I hoped by this time to have convinced thy gentle shade, that I was, at least intentionally, innocent of that ruthless barbarity which hath brought thee to an untimely grave. Heaven and earth! do I still survive the consciousness of that dire catastrophe! and lives the atrocious villain who hath blasted all our hopes!"

With these last words the fire darted from his eyes, and his brother, snatching this occasional handle for reconciling him to life, joined in his exclamations against the treacherous Fathom, and observed, that he should not, in point of honour, wish to die, until he should have sacrificed that traitor to the manes of the beauteous Monimia. This incitement acted as a spur upon exhausted nature, causing the blood to circulate with fresh vigour, and encouraging him to take such sustenance as would recruit his strength, and repair the damage which his health had sustained.

His sister assiduously attended him in his recovery, flattering his appetite, and amusing his sorrow at the same time; the clergyman assailed his despondence with religious weapons, as well as with arguments drawn from philosophy; and the fury of his passions being already expended, he became so tractable as to listen to his remonstrances. But notwithstanding the joint endeavours of all his friends, a deep fixed melancholy remained after every consequence of his disease had vanished. In vain they essayed to elude his grief by gaiety and diversions, in vain they tried to decoy his heart into some new engagement.

These kind attempts served only to feed and nourish that melancholy which pined within his bosom. Monimia still haunted him in the midst of these amusements, while his reflection whispered to him, "Pleasures like these I might have relished with her participation." That darling idea mingled in all the female assemblies at which he was present, eclipsing their attractions, and enhancing the bitterness of his loss; for absence, enthusiasm, and even his despair had heightened the charms of the fair orphan into something supernatural and divine.

Time, that commonly weakens the traces of remembrance, seemed to deepen its impressions in his breast; nightly, in his dreams, did he converse with his dear Monimia, sometimes on the verdant bank of a delightful stream, where he breathed, in soft murmurs, the dictates of his love and admiration; sometimes reclined within the tufted grove, his arm encircled and sustained her snowy neck, whilst she, with looks of love ineffable, gazed on his face, invoking Heaven to bless her husband and her lord. Yet, even in these illusions was his fancy oft alarmed for the ill-fated fair. Sometimes he viewed her tottering on the brink of a steep precipice, far distant from his helping hand; at other times she seemed to sail along the boisterous tide, imploring his assistance, then would he start with horror from his sleep, and feel his sorrows more than realised; he deserted his couch, he avoided the society of mankind, he courted sequestered shades where he could indulge his melancholy; there his mind brooded over his calamity until his imagination became familiar with all the ravages of death; it contemplated the gradual decline of Monimia's health, her tears, her distress, her despair at his imagined cruelty; he saw, through that perspective, every blossom of her beauty wither, every sparkle vanish from her eyes; he beheld her faded lips, her pale cheek, and her inanimated features, the symmetry of which not death itself was able to destroy. His fancy conveyed her breathless corse to the cold grave, o'er which, perhaps, no tear humane was shed, where her delicate limbs were consigned to dust, where she was dished out a delicious banquet to the unsparing worm.

Over these pictures he dwelt with a sort of pleasing anguish, until he became so enamoured of her tomb, that he could no longer resist the desire that compelled him to make a pilgrimage to the dear hallowed spot, where all his once gay hopes lay buried; that he might nightly visit the silent habitation of his ruined love, embrace the sacred earth with which she was now compounded, moisten it with his tears, and bid the turf lie easy on her breast. Besides the prospect of this gloomy enjoyment, he was urged to return to England, by an eager desire of taking vengeance on the perfidious Fathom, as well as of acquitting himself of the obligations he owed in that kingdom, to those who had assisted him in his distress. He therefore communicated his intention to Farrel, who would have insisted upon attending him in the journey, had not he been conjured to stay and manage Renaldo's affairs in his absence. Every previous step being taken, he took leave of the Countess and his sister, who had, with all their interest and elocution, opposed his design, the execution of which, they justly feared, would, instead of dissipating, augment his chagrin; and now, seeing him determined, they shed a flood of tears at his departure, and he set out from Vienna in a post-chaise, accompanied by a trusty valet-de-chambre on horseback.

CHAPTER SIXTY-ONE.
RENALDO MEETS WITH A LIVING MONUMENT OF JUSTICE, AND ENCOUNTERS A PERSONAGE OF SOME NOTE IN THESE MEMOIRS.

As this domestic was very well qualified for making all the proper dispositions, and adjusting every necessary article on the road, Renaldo totally abstracted himself from earthly considerations, and mused without ceasing on that theme which was the constant subject of his contemplation. He was blind to the objects that surrounded him; he scarce ever felt the importunities of nature; and had not they been reinforced by the pressing entreaties of his attendant, he would have proceeded without refreshment or repose. In this absence of mind did he traverse a great part of Germany, in his way to the Austrian Netherlands, and arrived at the fortress of Luxemburg, where he was obliged to tarry a whole day on account of an accident which had happened to his chaise. Here he went to view the fortifications; and as he walked along the ramparts, his ears were saluted with these words: "Heaven bless the noble Count de Melvil! will not he turn the eyes of compassion on an old fellow-soldier reduced to misfortune and disgrace?"

Surprised at this address, which was attended with the clanking of chains, Renaldo lifted up his eyes, and perceived the person who spoke to be one of two malefactors shackled together, who had been sentenced for some crime to work as labourers on the fortifications. His face was so covered with hair, and his whole appearance so disguised by the squalid habit which he wore, that the Count could not recollect his features, until he gave him to understand that his name was Ratchcali. Melvil immediately recognised his fellow-student at Vienna, and his brother-volunteer upon the Rhine, and expressed equal surprise and concern at seeing him in such a deplorable situation.

Nothing renders the soul so callous and insensible as the searing brands of infamy and disgrace. Without betraying the least symptoms of shame or confusion, "Count," says he, "this is the fate of war, at least of the war in which I have been engaged, ever since I took leave of the Imperial army, and retreated with your old companion Fathom. Long life to that original genius! If he is not unhappily eclipsed by some unfortunate interposition, before his terrene parts

The Adventures of Ferdinand Count Fathom | 325

are purified, I foresee that he will shine a star of the first magnitude in the world of adventure."

At mention of this detested name, Renaldo's heart began to throb with indignation; yet he suppressed the emotion, and desired to know the meaning of that splendid encomium which he had bestowed upon his confederate. "It would be quite unnecessary," replied Ratchcali, "for a man in my present situation to equivocate or disguise the truth. The nature of my disgrace is perfectly well known. I am condemned to hard labour for life; and unless some lucky accident, which I cannot now foresee, shall intervene, all I can expect is some alleviation of my hard lot from the generosity of such gentlemen as you, who compassionate the sufferings of your fellow-creatures. In order to engage your benevolence the more in my behalf, I shall, if you will give me the hearing, faithfully inform you of some particulars, which it may import you to know, concerning my old acquaintance Ferdinand Count Fathom, whose real character hath perhaps hitherto escaped your notice."

Then he proceeded to give a regular detail of all the strokes of finesse which he, in conjunction with our adventurer, had practised upon Melvil and others, during their residence at Vienna, and the campaigns they had made upon the Rhine. He explained the nature of the robbery which was supposed to have been done by the Count's valet, together with the manner of their desertion. He described his separation from Fathom, their meeting at London, the traffic they carried on in copartnership; and the misfortune that reduced Ferdinand to the condition in which he was found by Melvil.

"After having gratified the honest lawyer," said he, "with a share of the unfortunate Fathom's spoils, and packed up all my own valuable effects, my new auxiliary Maurice and I posted to Harwich, embarked in the packet-boat, and next day arrived at Helvoetsluys; from thence we repaired to the Hague, in order to mingle in the gaieties of the place, and exercise our talents at play, which is there cultivated with universal eagerness. But, chancing to meet with an old acquaintance, whom I did not at all desire to see, I found it convenient to withdraw softly to Rotterdam; from whence we set out for Antwerp; and, having made a tour of the Austrian Netherlands, set up our rest at Brussels, and concerted a plan for laying the Flemings under contribution.

"From our appearance we procured admission into the most polite assemblies, and succeeded to a wonder in all our operations; until our career was unfortunately checked by the indiscretion of my ally, who, being detected in the very act of conveying a card, was immediately introduced to a magistrate. And this minister of justice was so curious, inquisitive, and clear-sighted, that Count Maurice, finding it impossible to elude his penetration, was fain to stipulate for his own safety, by giving up his friend to the cognisance of the law. I was accordingly apprehended, before I knew the cause of my arrest; and being unhappily known by some soldiers of the Prince's guard, my character turned out so little to the approbation of the inquisitors, that all my effects were confiscated for the benefit of the state, and I was by a formal sentence condemned to labour on the fortifications all the days of my life; while Maurice escaped at the expense of five hundred stripes, which he received in public from the hands of the common executioner.

"Thus have I, without evasion or mental reservation, given a faithful account of the steps by which I have arrived at this barrier, which is likely to be the ne plus ultra of my peregrinations, unless the generous Count de Melvil will deign to interpose his interest in behalf of an old fellow-soldier, who may yet live to justify his mediation."

Renaldo had no reason to doubt the truth of this story, every circumstance of which tended to corroborate the intelligence he had already received touching the character of Fathom, whom he now considered with a double portion of abhorrence, as the most abandoned miscreant that nature had ever produced. Though Ratchcali did not possess a much higher place in his opinion, he favoured him with marks of his bounty, and exhorted him, if possible, to reform his heart; but he would by no means promise to interpose his credit in favour of a wretch self-convicted of such enormous villany and fraud. He could not help moralising upon this rencontre, which inspired him with great contempt for human nature. And next day he proceeded on his journey with a heavy heart, ruminating on the perfidy of mankind, and, between whiles, transported with the prospect of revenging all his calamities upon the accursed author.

While he was wrapped up in these reveries, his carriage rolled along, and had already entered a wood between Mons and Tournay, when his dream was suddenly interrupted by the explosion of several pistols that were fired among the thickets at a little distance from the road. Roused at this alarm, he snatched his sword that stood by him, and springing from the chaise, ran directly towards the spot, being close followed by his valet, who had alighted and armed himself with a pistol in each hand. About forty yards from the highway, they arrived in a little glade or opening, where they saw a single man standing at bay against five banditti, after having killed one of their companions, and lost his own horse, that lay dead upon the ground.

Melvil seeing this odds, and immediately guessing their design, rushed among them without hesitation, and in an instant ran his sword through the heart of one whose hand was raised to smite the gentleman behind, while he was engaged with the rest in front. At the same time the valet disabled another by a shot in the shoulder; so that the number being now equal on both sides, a furious combat ensued, every man being paired with an antagonist, and each having recourse to swords, as all their pieces had been discharged. Renaldo's adversary, finding himself pressed with equal fury and skill, retreated gradually among the trees, until he vanished altogether into the thickest of the wood; and his two companions followed his example with great ease, the valet-de-chambre being hurt in the leg, and the stranger so much exhausted by the wounds he had received before Renaldo's interposition, that, when the young gentleman approached to congratulate him on the defeat of the robbers, he, in advancing to embrace his deliverer, dropped down motionless on the grass.

The Count, with that warmth of sympathy and benevolence which was natural to his heart, lifted up the wounded cavalier in his arms, and carried him to the chaise, in which he was deposited, while the valet-de-chambre reloaded his pistols, and prepared for a second attack, as they did not doubt that the banditti would return with a reinforcement. However, before they reappeared, Renaldo's driver disengaged him from the wood, and in less than a quarter of an hour they arrived at a village, where they halted for assistance to the stranger, who, though still alive, had not recovered the use of his senses.

After he was undressed, and laid in a warm bed, a surgeon examined his body, and found a wound in his neck by a sword, and another in his right side, occasioned by a pistol-shot; so that his prognostic was very dubious. Meanwhile, he applied proper dressings to both; and, in half an hour after this administration, the gentleman gave some tokens of perception. He looked around him with a wildness of fury in his aspect, as if he had thought himself in the hands of the robbers by whom he had been attacked. But, when he saw the assiduity with which the bystanders exerted themselves in his behalf, one raising his head from the pillow, while another exhorted him to swallow a little wine which was warmed for the purpose; when he beheld the sympathising looks of all present, and heard himself accosted in the most cordial terms by the person whom he recollected as his deliverer, all the severity vanished from his countenance; he took Renaldo's hand, and pressed it to his lips; and, while the tears gushed from his eyes, "Praised be God," said he, "that virtue and generosity are still to be found among the sons of men."

Everybody in the apartment was affected by this exclamation; and Melvil, above all the rest, felt such emotions as he could scarcely restrain. He entreated the gentleman to believe himself in the midst of such friends as would effectually secure him from all violence and mortification; he conjured him to compose the perturbation of his spirits, and quiet the apprehensions of his mind with that reflection; and protested, that he himself would not quit the house while his attendance should be deemed necessary for the stranger's cure, or his conversation conducive to his amusement.

These assurances, considered with the heroic part which the young Hungarian had already acted in his behalf, inspired the cavalier with such a sublime idea of Melvil, that he gazed upon him with silent astonishment, as an angel sent from heaven for his succour; and, in the transport of his gratitude, could not help exclaiming, "Sure Providence hath still something in reserve for this unfortunate wretch, in whose favour such a miracle of courage and generosity hath interposed!"

Being accommodated with proper care and attendance, his constitution in a little time overcame the fever; and, at the third dressing, the surgeon declared him out of all danger from his wounds. Then was Renaldo indulged with opportunities of conversing with the patient, and of inquiring into the particulars of his fortune and designs in life, with a view to manifest the inclination he felt to serve him in his future occasions.

The more this stranger contemplated the character of the Count, the more his amazement increased, on account of his extraordinary benevolence in favour of a person whose merit he could not possibly know; he even expressed his surprise on this subject to Renaldo, who at length told him, that, although his best offices should always be ready for the occasions of any gentleman in distress, his particular attachment and regard to him was improved by an additional consideration. "I am no stranger," said he, "to the virtues and honour of the gallant Don Diego de Zelos."

"Heaven and earth!" cried the stranger, starting from his seat with extreme emotion, "do I then live to hear myself addressed by that long-lost appellation! my heart glows at the expression! my spirits are kindled with a flame that thrills through every nerve! Say, young gentleman, if you are really an inhabitant of earth, by what means are you acquainted with the unhappy name of Zelos?"

In answer to this eager interrogation, Renaldo gave him to understand, that in the course of his travels, he had resided a short time at Seville, where he had frequently seen Don Diego, and often heard his character mentioned with uncommon esteem and veneration. "Alas!" replied the Castilian, "that justice is no longer done to the wretched Zelos; his honours are blasted, and his reputation canker-bitten by the venomous tooth of slander."

He then proceeded to unfold his misfortunes, as they have already been explained in the former part of these memoirs; at the recapitulation of which, the heart of Melvil, being intendered by his own calamities, was so deeply affected, that he re-echoed the groans of Don Diego, and wept over his sufferings with the most filial sympathy. When he repeated the story of that cruel fraud which was practised upon him by the faithless Fadini, Melvil, whose mind and imagination teemed with the villanies of Fathom, was immediately struck with the conjecture of his being the knave; because, indeed, he could not believe that any other person was so abandoned by principle and humanity as to take such a barbarous advantage of a gentleman in distress.

CHAPTER SIXTY-TWO.
HIS RETURN TO ENGLAND, AND MIDNIGHT PILGRIMAGE TO MONIMIA'S TOMB.

He considered the date of that unparalleled transaction, which agreed with his conjecture, and from the inquiries he made concerning the person of the traitor, gathered reasons sufficient to confirm his supposition. Thus certified, "That is the villain," cried the Count, "whose infernal arts have overwhelmed me with such misery as Heaven itself hath made no remedy to dispel! To revenge my wrongs on that perfidious miscreant, is one of the chief reasons for which I deign to drag about an hateful being. O Don Diego! what is life, when all its enjoyments are so easily poisoned by the machinations of such a worm!" So saying, he smote his breast in all the agony of woe, and besought the Spaniard to relate the steps he took in consequence of this disaster.

The Castilian's cheeks reddened at this information, which enforced his own resentment, and casting up his eyes to heaven, "Sacred powers!" cried he, "let him not perish, before you bring him within my reach. You ask me, noble cavalier, what measures I took in this abyss of misery? For the first day, I was tortured with apprehensions for the friendly Fadini, fearing that he had been robbed and murdered for the jewels which he had, perhaps, too unwarily exposed to sale. But this terror soon vanished before the true presages of my fate, when, on the morrow, I found the whole family in tears and confusion, and heard my landlord pour forth the most bitter imprecations against the fugitive, who had deflowered his daughter, and even robbed the house. You will ask, which of the passions of my heart were interested on this occasion? they were shame and indignation. All my grief flowed in another channel; I blushed to find my judgment deceived; I scorned to complain; but, in my heart, denounced vengeance against my base betrayer. I silently retired to my apartment, in order to commune with my own thoughts.

"I had borne greater calamities without being driven to despair; I summoned all my fortitude to my assistance, and resolved to live in spite of affliction. Thus determined, I betook myself to the house of a general officer, whose character was fair in the world; and having obtained admission in consequence of my

Oriental appearance, 'To a man of honour,' said I, 'the unfortunate need no introduction. My habit proclaims me a Persian; this passport from the States of Holland will confirm that supposition. I have been robbed of jewels to a considerable value, by a wretch whom I favoured with my confidence; and now, reduced to extreme indigence, I come to offer myself as a soldier in the armies of France. I have health and strength sufficient to discharge that duty. Nor am I unacquainted with a military life, which was once my glory and occupation. I therefore sue for your protection, that I may be received, though in the lowest order of them that serve the King; and that your future favour may depend upon my behaviour in that capacity.'

"The general, surprised at my declaration, surveyed me with uncommon attention; he perused my certificate; asked divers questions concerning the art of war, to which I returned such answers as convinced him that I was not wholly ignorant in that particular. In short, I was enlisted as a volunteer in his own regiment, and soon after promoted to the rank of a subaltern, and the office of equerry to his own son, who, at that time, had attained to the degree of colonel, though his age did not exceed eighteen years.

"This young man was naturally of a ferocious disposition, which had been rendered quite untractable by the pride of birth and fortune, together with the licence of his education. As he did not know the respect due to a gentleman, so he could not possibly pay it to those who were, unfortunately, under his command. Divers mortifications I sustained with that fortitude which became a Castilian who lay under obligations to the father; till, at length, laying aside all decorum, he smote me. Sacred Heaven! he smote Don Diego de Zelos, in presence of his whole household.

"Had my sword been endowed with sensation, it would of itself have started from its scabbard at this indignity offered to its master. I unsheathed it without deliberation, saying, 'Know, insolent boy, he is a gentleman whom thou hast outraged; and thou hast thus cancelled the ties which have hitherto restrained my indignation.' His servants would have interposed, but he commanded them to retire; and, flushed with that confidence which the impetuosity of his temper inspired, he drew, in his turn, and attacked me with redoubled rage; but his dexterity being very unequal to his courage, he was soon disarmed, and overthrown; when, pointing my sword to his breast, 'In consideration of thy youth and ignorance,' said I, 'I spare that life which thou hast forfeited by thy ungenerous presumption.'

"With these words, I put up my weapon, retired through the midst of his domestics, who, seeing their master safe, did not think proper to oppose my passage, and, mounting my horse, in less than two hours entered the Austrian dominions, resolving to proceed as far as Holland, that I might embark in the first ship for Spain, in order to wash away, with my own blood, or that of my enemies, the cruel stain which hath so long defiled my reputation.

"This was the grievance that still corroded my heart, and rendered ineffectual the inhuman sacrifice I had made to my injured honour. This was the consideration that incessantly prompted, and still importunes me to run every risk of life and fortune, rather than leave my fame under such an ignominious aspersion. I purpose to obey this internal call. I am apt to believe it is the voice of Heaven—of that Providence which manifested its care by sending such a generous auxiliary to my aid, when I was overpowered by banditti, on the very first day of my expedition."

Having in this manner gratified the curiosity of his deliverer, he expressed a desire of knowing the quality of him to whom he was so signally obliged; and Renaldo did not scruple to make the Castilian acquainted with his name and family. He likewise communicated the story of his unfortunate love, with all the symptoms of unutterable woe, which drew tears from the noble-hearted Spaniard, while, with a groan, that announced the load which overwhelmed his soul, "I had a daughter," said he, "such as you describe the peerless Monimia; had Heaven decreed her for the arms of such a lover, I, who am now the most wretched, should have been the most happy parent upon earth."

Thus did these new friends alternately indulge their mutual sorrow, and concert measures for their future operations. Melvil earnestly solicited the Castilian to favour him with his company to England, where, in all probability, both would enjoy the gloomy satisfaction of being revenged upon their common betrayer, Fathom; and, as a farther inducement, he assured him, that, as soon as he should have accomplished the melancholy purposes of his voyage, he would accompany Don Diego to Spain, and employ his whole interest and fortune in his service. The Spaniard, thunderstruck at the extravagant generosity of this proposal, could scarce believe the evidence of his own senses; and, after some pause, replied, "My duty would teach me to obey any command you should think proper to impose; but here my inclination and interest are so agreeably flattered, that I should be equally ungrateful and unwise, in pretending to comply with reluctance."

This point being settled, they moved forwards to Mons, as soon as Don Diego was in a condition to bear the shock of such a removal, and there remaining until his wounds were perfectly cured, they hired a post-chaise for Ostend, embarked in a vessel at that port, reached the opposite shore of England, after a short and easy passage, and arrived in London without having met with any sinister accident on the road.

As they approached this capital, Renaldo's grief seemed to regurgitate with redoubled violence. His memory was waked to the most minute and painful exertion of its faculties; his imagination teemed with the most afflicting images, and his impatience became so ardent, that never lover panted more eagerly for the consummation of his wishes, than Melvil, for an opportunity of stretching himself upon the grave of the lost Monimia. The Castilian was astonished, as well as affected, at the poignancy of his grief, which, as a proof of his susceptibility and virtue, endeared him still more to his affection; and though his own misfortunes had rendered him very unfit for the office of a comforter, he endeavoured, by soothing discourse, to moderate the excess of his friend's affliction.

Though it was dark when they alighted at the inn, Melvil ordered a coach to be called; and, being attended by the Spaniard, who would not be persuaded to quit him upon such an occasion, he repaired to the house of the generous Jew, whose rheum distilled very plentifully at his approach. The Count had already acquitted himself in point of pecuniary obligations to this benevolent Hebrew; and now, after having made such acknowledgments as might be expected from a youth of his disposition, he begged to know by what channel he had received that letter which he had been so kind as to forward to Vienna.

Joshua, who was ignorant of the contents of that epistle, and saw the young gentleman extremely moved, would have eluded his inquiry, by pretending he had forgot the circumstance; but when he understood the nature of the case which was not explained without the manifestation of the utmost inquietude, he heartily condoled the desponding lover, telling him he had in vain employed all his intelligence about that unfortunate beauty, in consequence of Melvil's letter to him on that subject; and then directed him to the house of the physician, who had brought the fatal billet which had made him miserable.

No sooner did he receive this information than he took his leave abruptly, with promise of returning next day, and hied him to the lodgings of that gentleman, whom he was lucky enough to find at home. Being favoured with a private audience, "When I tell you," said he, "that my name is Renaldo Count de Melvil, you will know me to be the most unfortunate of men. By that letter, which you committed to the charge of my worthy friend Joshua, the fatal veil was removed from my eyes, which had been so long darkened by the artifices of incredible deceit, and my own incurable misery fully presented to my view. If you were acquainted with the unhappy fair, who hath fallen a victim to my mistake, you will have some idea of the insufferable pangs which I now feel in recollecting her fate. If you have compassion for these pangs, you will not refuse to conduct me to the spot where the dear remains of Monimia are deposited; there let me enjoy a full banquet of woe; there let me feast that worm of sorrow that preys upon my heart. For such entertainment have I revisited this (to me) ill-omened isle; for this satisfaction I intrude upon your condescension at these unseasonable hours; for to such a degree of impatience is my affliction whetted, that no slumber shall assail mine eyelids, no peace reside within my bosom, until I shall have adored that earthly shrine where my Monimia lies! Yet would I know the circumstances of her fate. Did Heaven ordain no angel to minister to her distress? were her last moments comfortless? ha! was not she abandoned to indigence, to insults; left in the power of that inhuman villain who betrayed us both? Sacred Heaven! why did Providence wink at the triumph of such consummate perfidy?"

The physician, having listened with complacency to this effusion, replied, "It is my profession, it is my nature to sympathise with the afflicted. I am a judge of your feelings, because I know the value of your loss. I attended the incomparable Monimia in her last illness, and am well enough acquainted with her story to conclude that she fell a sacrifice to an unhappy misunderstanding, effected and fomented by that traitor who abused your mutual confidence."

He then proceeded to inform him of all the particulars which we have already recorded, touching the destiny of the beauteous orphan, and concluded with telling him he was ready to yield him any other satisfaction which it was in his power to grant. The circumstances of the tale had put Renaldo's spirits into such commotion, that he could utter nothing but interjections and unconnected words. When Fathom's behaviour was described, he trembled with fierce agitation, started from his chair, pronouncing, "Monster! fiend! but we shall one day meet."

When he was made acquainted with the benevolence of the French lady, he exclaimed, "O heaven-born charity and compassion! sure that must be some spirit of grace sent hither to mitigate the tortures of life! where shall I find her, to offer up my thanks and adoration?" Having heard the conclusion of the detail, he embraced the relater, as the kind benefactor of Monimia, shed a flood of tears in his bosom, and pressed him to crown the obligation, by conducting him to the solitary place where now she rested from all her cares.

The gentleman perceiving the transports of his grief were such as could not be opposed, complied with his request, attended him in the vehicle, and directed the coachman to drive to a sequestered field, at some distance from the city, where stood the church, within whose awful aisle this scene was to be acted. The sexton being summoned from his bed, produced the keys, in consequence of a gratification, after the physician had communed with him apart, and explained the intention of Renaldo's visit.

During this pause the soul of Melvil was wound up to the highest pitch of enthusiastic sorrow. The uncommon darkness of the night, the solemn silence, and lonely situation of the place, conspired with the occasion of his coming, and the dismal images of his fancy, to produce a real rapture of gloomy expectation, which the whole world would not have persuaded him to disappoint. The clock struck twelve, the owl screeched from the ruined battlement, the door was opened by the sexton, who, by the light of a glimmering taper, conducted the despairing lover to a dreary aisle, and stamped upon the ground with his foot, saying, "Here the young lady lies interred."

Melvil no sooner received this intimation, than falling on his knees, and pressing his lips to the hallowed earth, "Peace," cried he, "to the gentle tenant of this silent habitation." Then turning to the bystanders, with a bloodshot eye, said, "Leave me to the full enjoyment of this occasion; my grief is too delicate to admit the company even of my friends. The rites to be performed require privacy; adieu, then, here must I pass the night alone."

The doctor, alarmed at this declaration, which he was afraid imported some resolution fatal to his own life, began to repent of having been accessory to the visit, attempted to dissuade him from his purpose, and finding him obstinately determined, called in the assistance of the sexton and coachman, and solicited the aid of Don Diego, to force Renaldo from the execution of his design.

The Castilian knowing his friend was then very unfit for common altercation, interposed in the dispute, saying, "You need not be afraid that he will obey the dictates of despair; his religion, his honour will baffle such temptations; he hath promised to reserve his life for the occasions of his friend; and he shall not be disappointed in his present aim." In order to corroborate this peremptory address, which was delivered in the French language, he unsheathed his sword, and the others retreating at sight of his weapon, "Count," said he, "enjoy your grief in full transport; I will screen you from interruption, though at the hazard of my life; and while you give a loose to sorrow, within the ghastly vault, I will watch till morning in the porch, and meditate upon the ruin of my own family and peace."

He accordingly prevailed upon the physician to retire, after he had satisfied the sexton, and ordered the coachman to return by break of day.

Renaldo, thus left alone, prostrated himself upon the grave, and poured forth such lamentations as would have drawn tears from the most savage hearer. He called aloud upon Monimia's name, "Are these the nuptial joys to which our fate hath doomed us? Is this the fruit of those endearing hopes, that intercourse divine, that raptured admiration, in which so many hours insensibly elapsed? where now are those attractions to which I yielded up my captive heart? quenched are those genial eyes that gladdened each beholder, and shone the planets of my happiness and peace! cold! cold and withered are those lips that swelled with love, and far outblushed the damask rose! and ah! forever silenced is that tongue, whose eloquence had power to lull the pangs of misery and care! no more shall my attention be ravished with the music of that voice, which used to thrill in soft vibrations to my soul! O sainted spirit! O unspotted shade of her whom I adored; of her whose memory I shall still revere with ever-bleeding sorrow and regret; of her whose image will be the last idea that forsakes this hapless bosom! now art thou conscious of my integrity and love; now dost thou behold the anguish that I feel. If the pure essence of thy nature will permit, wilt thou, ah! wilt thou indulge this wretched youth with some kind signal of thy notice, with some token of thy approbation? wilt thou assume a medium of embodied air, in semblance of that lovely form which now lies mouldering in this dreary tomb, and speak the words of peace to my distempered soul! Return, Monimia, appear, though but for one short moment, to my longing eyes! vouchsafe one smile! Renaldo will be satisfied; Renaldo's heart will be at rest; his grief no more will overflow its banks, but glide with equal current to his latest hour! Alas! these are the raving of my delirious sorrow! Monimia hears not my complaints; her soul, sublimed far, far above all sublunary cares, enjoys that felicity of which she was debarred on earth. In vain I stretch these eyes, environed with darkness undistinguishing and void. No object meets my view; no sound salutes mine ear, except the noisy wind that whistles through these vaulted caves of death."

In this kind of exclamation did Renaldo pass the night, not without a certain species of woful enjoyment, which the soul is often able to conjure up from the depths of distress; insomuch that, when the morning intruded on his privacy, he could scarce believe it was the light of day, so fast had fleeted the minutes of his devotion.

His heart being thus disburdened, and his impatience gratified, he became so calm and composed, that Don Diego was equally pleased and astonished at the air of serenity with which he came forth, and embraced him with warm acknowledgments of his goodness and attachment. He frankly owned, that his mind was now more at ease than he had ever found it, since he first received the fatal intimation of his loss; that a few such feasts would entirely moderate the keen appetite of his sorrow, which he would afterwards feed with less precipitation.

He also imparted to the Castilian the plan of a monument, which he had designed for the incomparable Monimia; and Don Diego was so much struck with the description, that he solicited his advice in projecting another, of a different nature, to be erected to the memory of his own ill-fated wife and daughter, should he ever be able to re-establish himself in Spain.

CHAPTER SIXTY-THREE.
HE RENEWS THE RITES OF SORROW, AND IS ENTRANCED.

While they amused themselves with this sort of conversation, the physician returned with the coach, and accompanied them back to their inn, where he left them to their repose, after having promised to call again at noon, and conduct Renaldo to the house of Madam Clement, the benefactress of Monimia, to whom he eagerly desired to be introduced.

The appointment was observed with all imaginable punctuality on both sides. Melvil had arrayed himself in a suit of deep mourning, and he found the good lady in the like habit, assumed upon the same occasion. The goodness of her heart was manifest in her countenance; the sensibility of the youth discovered itself in a flood of tears, which he shed at her appearance. His sensations were too full for utterance; nor was she, for some time, able to give him welcome. While she led him by the hand to a seat, the drops of sympathy rushed into either eye; and at length she broke silence, saying, "Count, we must acquiesce in the dispensations of Providence; and quiet the transports of our grief, with a full assurance that Monimia is happy."

This name was the key that unlocked the faculty of his speech. "I must strive," said he, "to ease the anguish of my heart with that consolation. But say, humane, benevolent lady, to whose compassion and generosity that hapless orphan was indebted for the last peaceful moment she enjoyed upon earth; say, in all your acquaintance with human nature, in all your intercourse with the daughters of men, in all the exercise of your charity and beneficence, did you ever observe such sweetness, purity, and truth; such beauty, sense, and perfection, as that which was the inheritance of her whose fate I shall for ever deplore?"—"She was, indeed," replied the lady, "the best and fairest of our sex."

This was the beginning of a conversation touching that lovely victim, in the course of which he explained those wicked arts which Fathom practised to alienate his affections from the adorable Monimia; and she described the cunning hints and false insinuations by which that traitor had aspersed the unsuspecting lover, and soiled his character in the opinion of the virtuous orphan. The intelligence he obtained on this occasion added indignation to his grief. The whole mystery of Monimia's behaviour, which he could not before explain, now stood disclosed before him. He saw the gradual progress of that infernal plan which had been laid for their mutual ruin; and his soul was inflamed with such desire of vengeance, that he would have taken his leave abruptly, in order to set on foot an immediate inquiry about the perfidious author of his wrongs, that he might exterminate such a monster of iniquity from the face of the earth. But he was restrained by Madam Clement, who gave him to understand, that Fathom was already overtaken by the vengeance of Heaven; for she had traced him in all the course of his fortune, from his first appearance in the medical sphere to his total eclipse. She represented the villain as a wretch altogether unworthy of his attention. She said, he was so covered with infamy, that no person could enter the lists against him, without bearing away some stain of dishonour; that he was, at present, peculiarly protected by the law, and sheltered from the resentment of Renaldo, in the cavern of his disgrace.

Melvil, glowing with rage, replied, that he was a venomous serpent, which it was incumbent on every foot to crush; that it was the duty of every man to contribute his whole power in freeing society from such a pernicious hypocrite; and that, if such instances of perfidy and ingratitude were suffered to pass with impunity, virtue and plain-dealing would soon be expelled from the habitations of men. "Over and above these motives," said he, "I own myself so vitiated with the alloy of human passion and infirmity, that I desire—I eagerly pant for an occasion of meeting him hand to hand, where I may upbraid him with his treachery, and shower down vengeance and destruction on his perfidious head."

Then he recounted the anecdotes of our adventurer which he had learned in Germany and Flanders, and concluded with declaring his unalterable resolution of releasing him from jail, that he might have an opportunity of sacrificing him, with his own hand, to the manes of Monimia. The discreet lady, perceiving the perturbation of his mind, would not further combat the impetuosity of his passion; contenting herself with exacting a promise, that he would not execute his purpose, until he should have deliberated three days upon the consequences by which a step of that kind might be attended. Before the expiration of that term, she thought measures might be taken to prevent the young gentleman from exposing his life or reputation to unnecessary hazard.

Having complied with her request in this particular, he took his leave, after he had, by repeated entreaties, prevailed upon her to accept a jewel, in token of his veneration for the kind benefactress of the deceased Monimia; nor could his generous heart be satisfied, until he had forced a considerable present on the humane physician who had attended her in her last moments, and now discovered a particular sympathy and concern for her desponding lover. This gentleman attended him to the house of the benevolent Joshua, where they dined, and where Don Diego was recommended, in the most fervid terms of friendship, to the good offices of their host. Not that this duty was performed in presence of the stranger—Renaldo's delicacy would not expose his friend to such a situation. While the physician, before dinner, entertained that stranger in one apartment, Melvil withdrew into another, with the Jew, to whom he disclosed the affair of the Castilian, with certain circumstances, which shall, in due time, be revealed.

Joshua's curiosity being whetted by this information, he could not help eyeing the Spaniard at table with such a particular stare, that Don Diego perceived his attention, and took umbrage at the freedom of his regard. Being unable to conceal his displeasure, he addressed himself to the Hebrew, with great solemnity, in the Spanish tongue, saying, "Signior, is there any singularity in my appearance? or, do you recollect the features of Don Diego de Zelos?"

"Signior Don Diego," replied the other in pure Castilian, "I crave your pardon for the rudeness of my curiosity, which prompted me to survey a nobleman, whose character I revere, and to whose misfortunes I am no stranger. Indeed, were curiosity alone concerned, I should be without excuse; but as I am heartily inclined to serve you, as far as my weak abilities extend, I hope your generosity will not impute any little involuntary trespass of punctilio to my want of cordiality or esteem."

The Spaniard was not only appeased by this apology, but also affected with the compliment, and the language in which it was conveyed. He thanked the Jew for his kind declaration, entreated him to bear, with the peevishness of a disposition sore with the galling hand of affliction; and, turning up his eyes to Heaven, "Were it possible," cried he, "for fate to reconcile contradictions, and recall the irremediable current of events, I would now believe that there was happiness still in reserve for the forlorn Zelos, now that I tread the land of freedom and humanity, now that I find myself befriended by the most generous of men. Alas! I ask not happiness! If, by the kind endeavours of the gallant Count de Melvil, to whom I am already indebted for my life, and by the efforts of his friends, the honour of my name shall be purified and cleared from the poisonous stains of malice by which it is at present spotted, I shall then enjoy all that satisfaction which destiny can bestow upon a wretch whose woes are incurable."

Renaldo comforted him with the assurance of his being on the eve of triumphing over his adversaries; and Joshua confirmed the consolation, by giving him to understand, that he had correspondents in Spain of some influence in the state; that he had already written to them on the subject of Don Diego, in consequence of a letter which he had received from Melvil while he tarried at Mons, and that he, every post, expected a favourable answer on that subject.

After dinner, the physician took his leave, though not before he had promised to meet Renaldo at night, and accompany him in the repetition of his midnight visit to Monimia's tomb; for this pilgrimage the unfortunate youth resolved nightly to perform during the whole time of his residence in England. It was, indeed, a sort of pleasure, the prospect of which enabled him to bear the toil of living through the day, though his patience was almost quite exhausted before the hour of assignation arrived.

When the doctor appeared with the coach, he leaped into it with great eagerness, after he had, with much difficulty, prevailed with Don Diego to stay at home, on account of his health, which was not yet perfectly established. The Castilian, however, would not comply with his request, until he had obtained the Count's promise, that he should be permitted to accompany him next night, and take that duty alternately with the physician.

About midnight, they reached the place, where they found the sexton in waiting, according to the orders he had received. The door was opened, the mourner conducted to the tomb, and left, as before, to the gloom of his own meditations. Again he laid himself on the cold ground; again he renewed his lamentable strain; his imagination began to be heated into an ecstasy of enthusiasm, during which he again fervently invoked the spirit of his deceased Monimia.

In the midst of these invocations, his ear was suddenly invaded with the sound of some few solemn notes issuing from the organ, which seemed to feel the impulse of an invisible hand.

At this awful salutation, Melvil was roused to the keenest sense of surprise and attention. Reason shrunk before the thronging ideas of his fancy, which represented this music as the prelude to something strange and supernatural; and, while he waited for the sequel, the place was suddenly illuminated, and each surrounding object brought under the cognisance of his eye.

What passed within his mind on this occasion is not easy to be described. All his faculties were swallowed up by those of seeing and hearing. He had mechanically raised himself upon one knee, with his body advancing forwards; and in this attitude he gazed with a look through which his soul seemed eager to escape. To his view, thus strained upon vacant space, in a few minutes appeared the figure of a woman arrayed in white, with a veil that covered her face, and flowed down upon her back and shoulders. The phantom approached him with an easy step, and, lifting up her veil, discovered (believe it, O reader!) the individual countenance of Monimia.

At sight of these well-known features, seemingly improved with new celestial graces, the youth became a statue, expressing amazement, love, and awful adoration. He saw the apparition smile with meek benevolence, divine compassion, warm and intendered by that fond pure flame which death could not extinguish. He heard the voice of his Monimia call Renaldo! Thrice he essayed to answer; as oft his tongue denied its office. His hair stood upright, and a cold vapour seemed to thrill through every nerve. This was not fear, but the infirmity of human nature, oppressed by the presence of a superior being.

At length his agony was overcome. He recollected all his resolution, and, in a strain of awestruck rapture, thus addressed the heavenly visitant: "Hast thou then heard, pure spirit! the wailings of my grief? hast thou descended from the realms of bliss, in pity to my woe? and art thou come to speak the words of peace to my desponding soul? To bid the wretched smile, to lift the load of misery and care from the afflicted breast; to fill thy lover's heart with joy and pleasing hope, was still the darling task of my Monimia, ere yet refined to that perfection which mortality can never attain. No wonder then, blessed shade, that now, when reunited to thy native heaven, thou art still kind, propitious, and beneficent to us, who groan in this inhospitable vale of sorrow thou hast left. Tell me, ah! tell me, dost thou still remember those fond hours we passed together? Doth that enlightened bosom feel a pang of soft regret, when thou recallest our fatal separation? Sure that meekened glance bespeaks thy sympathy! Ah! how that tender look o'erpowers me! Sacred Heaven! the pearly drops of pity trickle down thy cheeks! Such are the tears that angels shed o'er man's distress!—Turn not away—Thou beckonest me to follow. Yes, I will follow thee, ethereal spirit, as far as these weak limbs, encumbered with mortality, will bear my weight; and, would to Heaven! I could, with ease, put off these vile corporeal shackles, and attend thy flight."

So saying, he started from the ground, and, in a transport of eager expectation, at awful distance, traced the footsteps of the apparition, which, entering a detached apartment, sunk down upon a chair, and with a sigh exclaimed, "Indeed, this is too much!" What was the disorder of Renaldo's mind, when he perceived this phenomenon! Before reflection could perform its office, moved by a sudden impulse, he sprung forwards, crying, "If it be death to touch thee, let me die!" and caught in his arms, not the shadow, but the warm substance of the all-accomplished Monimia. "Mysterious powers of Providence! this is no phantom! this is no shade! this is the life! the panting bosom of her whom I have so long, so bitterly deplored! I fold her in my arms! I press her glowing breast to mine! I see her blush with virtuous pleasure and ingenuous love! She smiles upon me with enchanting tenderness! O let me gaze on that transcendent beauty, which, the more I view it, ravishes the more! These charms are too intense; I sicken while I gaze! Merciful Heaven! is not this a mere illusion of the brain? Was she not fled for ever? Had not the cold hand of death divorced her from my hope? This must be some flattering vision of my distempered fancy! perhaps some soothing dream— If such it be, grant, O ye heavenly powers! that I may never wake."

"O gentle youth!" replied the beauteous orphan, still clasped in his embrace, "what joy now fills the bosom of Monimia, at this triumph of thy virtue and thy love? When I see these transports of thy affection, when I find thee restored to that place in my esteem and admiration, which thou hadst lost by the arts of calumny and malice—this is a meeting which my most sanguine hopes durst not presage!"

So entirely were the faculties of Renaldo engrossed in the contemplation of his restored Monimia, that he saw not the rest of the company, who wept with transport over this affecting scene. He was therefore amazed at the interposition of Madam Clement, who, while the shower of sympathetic pleasure bedewed her cheeks, congratulated the lovers upon this happy event, crying, "These are the joys which virtue calls her own." They also received the compliments of a reverend clergyman, who told Monimia, she had reaped, at last, the fruits of that pious resignation to the will of Heaven, which she had so devoutly practised during the term of her affliction. And, lastly, they were accosted by the physician, who was not quite so hackneyed in the ways of death, or so callous to the finer sensations of the soul, but that he blubbered plentifully, wile he petitioned Heaven in behalf of such an accomplished and deserving pair.

Monimia taking Madam Clement by the hand, "Whatever joy," said she, "Renaldo derives from this occasion, is owing to the bounty, the compassion, and maternal care of this incomparable lady, together with the kind admonitions and humanity of those two worthy gentlemen."

Melvil, whose passions were still in agitation, and whose mind could not yet digest the incidents that occurred, embraced them all by turns; but, like the faithful needle, which, though shaken for an instant from its poise, immediately regains its true direction, and points invariably to the pole, he soon returned to his Monimia; again he held her in his arms, again he drank enchantment from her eyes, and thus poured forth the effusions of his soul:—"Can I then trust the evidence of sense? And art thou really to my wish restored? Never, O never did thy beauty shine with such bewitching grace, as that which now confounds and captivates my view! Sure there is something more than mortal in thy looks!—Where hast thou lived?—where borrowed this perfection?—whence art thou now descended?—Oh! I am all amazement, joy, and fear!—Thou wilt not leave me!—No! we must not part again. By this warm kiss! a thousand times more sweet than all the fragrance of the East! we nevermore will part. O! this is rapture, ecstasy, and what no language can explain!"

In the midst of these ejaculations, he ravished a banquet from her glowing lips, that kindled in his heart a flame which rushed through every vein, and glided to his marrow. This was a privilege he had never claimed before, and now permitted as a recompense for all the penance he had suffered. Nevertheless, the cheeks of Monimia, who was altogether unaccustomed to such familiarities, underwent a total suffusion; and Madam Clement discreetly relieved her from the anxiety of her situation, by interfering in the discourse, and rallying the Count upon his endeavours to monopolise such a branch of happiness.

"O my dear lady!" replied Renaldo, who by this time had, in some measure, recovered his recollection, "forgive the wild transports of a fond lover, who hath so unexpectedly retrieved the jewel of his soul! Yet, far from wishing to hoard up his treasure, he means to communicate and diffuse his happiness to all his friends. O my Monimia! how will the pleasure of this hour be propagated! As yet thou knowest not all the bliss that is reserved for thy enjoyment!— Meanwhile, I long to learn by what contrivance this happy interview hath been effected. Still am I ignorant how I was transported into this apartment, from the lonely vault in which I mourned over my supposed misfortune!"

CHAPTER SIXTY-FOUR.
THE MYSTERY UNFOLDED—ANOTHER RECOGNITION, WHICH, IT IS TO BE HOPED, THE READER COULD NOT FORESEE.

The French lady then explained the whole mystery of Monimia's death, as a stratagem she had concerted with the clergyman and doctor, in order to defeat the pernicious designs of Fathom, who seemed determined to support his false pretensions by dint of perjury and fraud, which they would have found it very difficult to elude. She observed, that the physician had actually despaired of Monimia's life, and it was not till after she herself was made acquainted with the prognostic, that she wrote the letter to Renaldo, which she committed to the care of Madam Clement, with an earnest entreaty, that it should not be sent till after her decease. But that lady, believing the Count had been certainly abused by his treacherous confidant, despatched the billet without the knowledge of Monimia, whose health was restored by the indefatigable care of the physician, and the sage exhortations of the clergyman, by which she was reconciled to life. In a word, the villany of Fathom had inspired her with some faint hope that Renaldo might still be innocent; and that notion contributed not a little to her cure.

The letter having so effectually answered their warmest hopes, in bringing back Renaldo such a pattern of constancy and love, the confederates, in consequence of his enthusiastic sorrow, had planned this meeting, as the most interesting way of restoring two virtuous lovers to the arms of each other; for which purpose the good clergyman had pitched upon his own church, and indulged them with the use of the vestry, in which they now were presented with a small but elegant collation.

Melvil heard this succinct detail with equal joy and admiration. He poured forth the dictates of his gratitude to the preservers of his happiness.—"This church," said he, "shall henceforth possess a double share of my veneration; this holy man will, I hope, finish the charitable work he has begun, by tying those bands of our happiness, which nought but death shall have power to unbind." Then turning to that object which was the star of his regard, "Do I not overrate," said he, "my interest with the fair Monimia?" She made no verbal reply; but answered by an emphatic glance, more eloquent than all the power of rhetoric and speech. This language, which is universal in the world of love, he perfectly well understood, and, in token of that faculty, sealed the assent which she had smiled, with a kiss imprinted on her polished forehead.

In order to dissipate these interesting ideas, which, by being too long indulged, might have endangered his reason, Madam Clement entreated him to entertain the company with a detail of what had happened to him in his last journey to the empire, and Monimia expressed a desire of knowing, in particular, the issue of his contest with Count Trebasi, who, she knew, had usurped the succession of his father.

Thus solicited, he could not refuse to gratify their curiosity and concern. He explained his obligations to the benevolent Jew; related the steps he had taken at Vienna for the recovery of his inheritance; informed them of his happy rencontre with his father-in-law; of his sister's deliverance, and marriage; of the danger into which his life had been precipitated by the news of Monimia's death; and, lastly, of his adventure with the banditti, in favour of a gentleman, who, he afterwards understood, had been robbed in the most base and barbarous manner by Fathom. He likewise, to the astonishment of all present, and of his mistress in particular, communicated some circumstances, which shall appear in due season.

Monimia's tender frame being quite fatigued with the scene she had acted, and her mind overwhelmed with the prosperous tidings she had heard, after having joined the congratulations of the company, on the good fortune of her Renaldo, begged leave to retire, that she might by repose recruit her exhausted spirits; and the night being pretty far spent, she was conducted by her lover to Madam Clement's coach, that stood in waiting, in which also the rest of the company made shift to embark, and were carried to the house of that good lady, where, after they were invited to dine, and Melvil entreated to bring Don Diego and the Jew along with them, they took leave of one another, and retired to their respective lodgings in a transport of joy and satisfaction.

As for Renaldo, his rapture was still mixed with apprehension, that all he had seen and heard was no more than an unsubstantial vision, raised by some gay delirium of a disordered imagination. While his breast underwent those violent, though blissful emotions of joy and admiration, his friend the Castilian spent the night in ruminating over his own calamities, and in a serious and severe review of his own conduct. He compared his own behaviour with that of the young Hungarian, and found himself so light in the scale, that he smote his breast with violence, exclaiming in an agony of remorse:

"Count Melvil has reason to grieve; Don Diego to despair. His misfortunes flow from the villany of mankind; mine are the fruit of my own madness. He laments the loss of a mistress, who fell a sacrifice to the perfidious arts of a crafty traitor. She was beautiful, virtuous, accomplished, and affectionate; he was fraught with sensibility and love. Doubtless his heart must have deeply suffered; his behaviour denotes the keenness of his woe; his eyes are everflowing fountains of tears; his bosom the habitation of sighs; five hundred leagues hath he measured in a pilgrimage to her tomb; nightly he visits the dreary vault where she now lies at rest; her solitary grave is his couch; he converses with darkness and the dead, until each lonely aisle re-echoes his distress. What would be his penance, had he my cause! were he conscious of having murdered a beloved wife and darling daughter! Ah wretch!—ah cruel homicide!—what had those dear victims done to merit such a fate? Were they not ever gentle and obedient, ever aiming to give thee satisfaction and delight? Say, that Serafina was enamoured of a peasant; say, that she had degenerated from the honour of her race. The inclinations are involuntary; perhaps that stranger was her equal in pedigree and worth. Had they been fairly questioned, they might have justified, at least excused, that conduct which appeared so criminal; or had they owned the offence, and supplicated pardon—O barbarous monster that I am! was all the husband—was all the father extinguished in my heart? How shall my own errors be forgiven, if I refused to pardon the frailties of my own blood—of those who are most dear to my affection? Yet nature pleaded strongly in their behalf!—My heart was bursting while I dismissed them to the shades of death. I was maddened with revenge! I was guided by that savage principle which falsely we call honour.

"Accursed phantom! that assumes the specious title, and misleads our wretched nation! Is it then honourable to skulk like an assassin, and plunge the secret dagger in the heart of some unhappy man, who hath incurred my groundless jealousy or suspicion, without indulging him with that opportunity which the worst criminal enjoys? Or is it honourable to poison two defenceless women, a tender wife, an amiable daughter, whom even a frown would almost have destroyed?—O! this is cowardice, brutality, hell-born fury and revenge! Heaven hath not mercy to forgive such execrable guilt. Who gave thee power, abandoned ruffian! over the lives of those whom God hath stationed as thy fellows of probation;—over those whom he had sent to comfort and assist thee; to sweeten all thy cares, and smooth the rough uneven paths of life? O! I am doomed to never-ceasing horror and remorse! If misery can atone for such enormous guilt, I have felt it in the extreme. Like an undying vulture it preys upon my heart;—to sorrow I am wedded; I hug that teeming consort to my soul;—never, ah! never shall we part; for soon as my fame shall shine unclouded by the charge of treason that now hangs over it, I will devote myself to penitence and woe. A cold, damp pavement shall be my bed; my raiment shall be sackcloth; the fields shall furnish herbage for my food; the stream shall quench my thirst; the minutes shall be numbered by my groans; the night be privy to my strains of sorrow, till Heaven, in pity to my sufferings, release me from the penance I endure. Perhaps the saints whom I have murdered will intercede for my remission."

Such was the exercise of grief, in which the hapless Castilian consumed the night; he had not yet consigned himself to rest, when Renaldo entering his chamber, displayed such a gleam of wildness and rapture on his countenance, as overwhelmed him with amazement; for, till that moment, he had never seen his visage unobscured with woe. "Pardon this abrupt intrusion, my friend," cried Melvil, "I could no longer withhold from your participation, the great, the unexpected turn, which hath this night dispelled all my sorrows, and restored me to the fruition of ineffable joy. Monimia lives!—the fair, the tender, the virtuous Monimia lives, and smiles upon my vows! This night I retrieved her from the grave. I held her in these arms; I pressed her warm delicious lips to mine! Oh, I am giddy with intolerable pleasure!"

Don Diego was confounded at this declaration, which he considered as the effects of a disordered brain. He never doubted that Renaldo's grief had at length overpowered his reason, and that his words were the effects of mere frenzy. While he mused on this melancholy subject, the Count composed his features, and, in a succinct and well-connected detail, explained the whole mystery of his happiness, to the inexpressible astonishment of the Spaniard, who shed tears of satisfaction, and straining the Hungarian to his breast, "O my son," said he, "you see what recompense Heaven hath in store for those who pursue the paths of real virtue; those paths from which I myself have been fatally misled by a faithless vapour, which hath seduced my steps, and left me darkling in the abyss of wretchedness. Such as you describe this happy fair, was once my Serafina, rich in every grace of mind and body which nature could bestow. Had it pleased Heaven to bless her with a lover like Renaldo! but no more, the irrevocable shaft is fled. I will not taint your enjoyment with my unavailing sighs!"

Melvil assured this disconsolate father, that no pleasure, no avocation should ever so entirely engross his mind, but that he should still find an hour for sympathy and friendship. He communicated the invitation of Madam Clement, and insisted upon his compliance, that he might have an opportunity of seeing and approving the object of his passion. "I can refuse nothing to the request of Count de Melvil," replied the Spaniard, "and it were ungrateful in me to decline the honour you propose. I own myself inflamed with a desire of beholding a young lady, whose perfections I have seen reflected in your sorrow; my curiosity is, moreover, interested on account of that humane gentlewoman, whose uncommon generosity sheltered such virtue in distress; but my disposition is infectious, and will, I am afraid, hang like a damp upon the general festivity of your friends."

Melvil would take no denial, and having obtained his consent, repaired to the house of Joshua, whose countenance seemed to unbend gradually into a total expression of joy and surprise, as he learned the circumstances of this amazing event. He faithfully promised to attend the Count at the appointed hour, and, in the meantime, earnestly exhorted him to take some repose, in order to quiet the agitation of his spirits, which must have been violently hurried on this occasion. The advice was salutary, and Renaldo resolved to follow it.

He returned to his lodgings, and laid himself down; but, notwithstanding the fatigue he had undergone, sleep refused to visit his eyelids, all his faculties being kept in motion by the ideas that crowded so fast upon his imagination. Nevertheless, though his mind continued in agitation, his body was refreshed, and he arose in the forenoon with more serenity and vigour than he had enjoyed for many months. Every moment his heart throbbed with new rapture, when he found himself on the brink of possessing all that his soul held dear and amiable; he put on his gayest looks and apparel; insisted upon the Castilian's doing the same honour to the occasion; and the alteration of dress produced such an advantageous change in the appearance of Don Diego, that when Joshua arrived at the appointed hour, he could scarce recognise his features, and complimented him very politely on the improvement of his looks.

True it is, the Spaniard was a personage of a very prepossessing mien and noble deportment; and had not grief, by increasing his native gravity, in some measure discomposed the symmetry of his countenance, he would have passed for a man of a very amiable and engaging physiognomy. They set out in the Jew's coach for the house of Madam Clement, and were ushered into an apartment, where they found the clergyman and physician with that lady, to whom Don Diego and the Hebrew were by Melvil introduced.

Before they had seated themselves, Renaldo inquired about the health of Monimia, and was directed to the next room by Madam Clement, who permitted him to go thither, and conduct her to the company. He was not slow of availing himself of this permission. He disappeared in an instant, and, during his short absence, Don Diego was strangely disturbed The blood flushed and forsook his cheeks by turns; a cold vapour seemed to shiver through his nerves; and at his breast he felt uncommon palpitation. Madam Clement observed his discomposure, and kindly inquired into the cause; when he replied, "I have such an interest in what concerns the Count de Melvil, and my imagination is so much prepossessed with the perfections of Monimia, that I am, as it were, agonised with expectation; yet never did my curiosity before raise such tumults as those that now agitate my bosom."

He had scarce pronounced these words, when the door, reopening, Renaldo led in this mirror of elegance and beauty, at sight of whom the Israelite's countenance was distorted into a stare of admiration. But if such was the astonishment of Joshua, what were the emotions of the Castilian, when, in the beauteous orphan, he beheld the individual features of his long-lost Serafina!

His feelings are not to be described. The fond parent, whose affection shoots even to a sense of pain, feels not half such transport, when he unexpectedly retrieves a darling child from the engulfing billows or devouring flame. The hope of Zelos had been totally extinguished. His heart had been incessantly torn with anguish and remorse, upbraiding him as the murderer of Serafina. His, therefore, were the additional transports of a father disburdened of the guilt of such enormous homicide. His nerves were too much overpowered by this sudden recognition, to manifest the sensation of his soul by external signs. He started not, nor did he lift an hand in token of surprise; he moved not from the spot on which he stood; but, riveting his eyes to those of the lovely phantom, remained without motion, until she, approaching with her lover, fell at his feet, and clasping his knees, exclaimed, "May I yet call you father?"

This powerful shock aroused his faculties; a cold sweat bedewed his forehead; his knees began to totter; he dropped upon the floor, and throwing his arms around her, cried, "O nature! O Serafina! Merciful Providence! thy ways are past finding out." So saying, he fell upon her neck, and wept aloud. The tears of sympathetic joy trickled down her snowy bosom, that heaved with rapture inexpressible. Renaldo's eyes poured forth the briny stream. The cheeks of Madam Clement were not dry in this conjuncture; she kneeled by Serafina, kissed her with all the eagerness of maternal affection, and with uplifted hands adored the Power that preordained this blessed event. The clergyman and doctor intimately shared the general transport; and as for Joshua, the drops of true benevolence flowed from his eyes, like the oil on Aaron's beard, while he skipped about the room in an awkward ecstasy, and in a voice resembling the hoarse notes of the long-eared tribe, cried, "O father Abraham! such a moving scene hath not been acted since Joseph disclosed himself unto his brethren in Egypt."

Don Diego having found utterance to his passion, proceeded in this strain: "O my dear child! to find thee thus again, after our last unhappy parting, is wonderful! miraculous! Blessed be the all-good, my conscience. I am not then the dire assassin, who sacrificed his wife and daughter to an infernal motive, falsely titled honour? though I am more and more involved in a mystery, which I long to hear explained."

"That shall be my task," cried Renaldo, "but first permit me to implore your sanction to my passion for the incomparable Serafina. You already know our mutual sentiments; and though I own the possession of such inestimable worth and beauty would be a recompense that infinitely transcends the merit I can plead, yet, as it hath been my good fortune to inspire her with a mutual flame, I hope to reap from your indulgence here, what I could not expect from my own desert; and we present ourselves, in hope of your paternal assent and benediction."

"Were she more fair and good and gentle than she is," answered the Castilian, "and to my partial observation nought e'er appeared on earth more beauteous and engaging, I would approve your title to her heart, and recommend you to her smiles, with all a father's influence and power. Yes, my daughter! my joy on this occasion is infinitely augmented by the knowledge of those tender ties of love that bind thee to this amiable youth; a youth to whose uncommon courage and generosity I owe my life and my subsistence, together with the inexpressible delight that now revels in my bosom. Enjoy, my children, the happy fruits of your reciprocal attachment. May Heaven, which hath graciously conducted you through a labyrinth of perplexity and woe, to this transporting view of blissful days, indulge you with that uninterrupted stream of pure felicity, which is the hope, and ought to be the boon of virtue, such as yours!"

So saying, he joined their hands, and embraced them with the most cordial love and satisfaction, which diffused itself to every individual of the company, who fervently invoked the Almighty Power, in behalf of this enraptured pair. The tumult of these emotions having a little subsided, and the Castilian being seated betwixt Renaldo and his beauteous bride, he politely bespoke the indulgence of Madam Clement, begging she would permit him to demand the performance of the Count's promise, that he might be forthwith made acquainted with those circumstances of his own fate which he was so impatient to learn.

The lady having assured him, that she and all the company would take pleasure in hearing the recapitulation, the Spaniard, addressing himself to Melvil, "In the name of Heaven!" said he, "how could you supplant that rival, who fell a sacrifice to my resentment, after he had bewitched the heart of Serafina? for, sure, the affection he had kindled in her breast must have long survived his death," "That rival," replied the Count, "who incurred your displeasure, was no other than Renaldo." With these words, he applied to one eye a patch of black silk provided for the purpose, and turning his face towards Don Diego, that gentleman started with astonishment, crying, "Good Heaven! the very countenance of Orlando, whom I slew! this is still more amazing!"

CHAPTER SIXTY-FIVE.
A RETROSPECTIVE LINK, NECESSARY FOR THE CONCATENATION OF THESE MEMOIRS.

"Indulge me with a patient hearing," proceeded the Hungarian, "and all these riddles soon will be explained. Inflamed with the desire of seeing foreign countries, I disobeyed the will of an indulgent father, from whose house, withdrawing privately, I set out for Italy, in disguise, by the way of Tyrol, visited Venice, Rome, Florence, and, embarking at Naples, in an English ship, arrived at St. Lucar, from whence I repaired to Seville; there, in a few days, was my curiosity engaged by the fame of the fair Serafina, who was justly deemed the most accomplished beauty in that part of Spain. Nay, blush not, gentle creature! for by my hopes of heaven! thy charms were even injured by the cold applause of that report. Nevertheless, I was warmly interested by the uncommon character, and eagerly longed to see this pattern of perfection. As Don Diego did not train her up in that restraint to which the Spanish ladies are subjected, I soon found an opportunity of seeing her at church; and no person here present will, I presume, doubt but that I was instantly captivated by her beauty and deportment. Had I thought that Don Diego's favour was unengaged, perhaps I should have followed the dictates of vanity and inexperience, and presented myself in my own character, among the crowd of her professed admirers. I knew her father had been an officer of distinguished rank and reputation, and did not doubt that he would have regarded a young soldier of unexceptionable pedigree, and, I will even add, of untainted fame. Nor did I suppose my own father could have objected against such an advantageous match; but, by dint of industrious inquiry, I learned, that the divine Serafina was already betrothed to Don Manuel de Mendoza, and this information overwhelmed me with despair.

"After having revolved a thousand projects for retarding and preventing that detested union, I resolved to avail myself of my talent for drawing, and professed myself a master of that science, in hope of being employed by the father of Serafina, who, I knew, let slip no opportunity of improving his daughter's education. Accordingly I had the good fortune to attract his notice, was invited to his house, honoured with his approbation, and furnished with unrestricted opportunities of conversing with the dear object of my love. The passion which her beauty had kindled was by the perfections of her mind inflamed to such a degree of transport, as could not be concealed from her penetration. She chanced to relish my conversation; I gradually acquired her friendship; pity was the next passion that she entertained in my favour. I then ventured to disclose myself, and the dear charmer did not disapprove of my presumption. She and her mother had been perplexed with some religious scruples, concerning which they appealed to my opinion; and I was happy enough to set their minds at ease.

"This sort of intercourse naturally created a mutual confidence among us; and, in a word, I was blessed with the daughter's love and mother's approbation. Don Diego will pardon these clandestine measures, which we took, from a full persuasion that it was impossible to render him propitious to the views in which our hearts and hands were so deeply interested. I did not then know how little he was addicted to superstition.

"Without entering into a detail of the schemes we projected to delay the happiness of Mendoza, I shall only observe, that, knowing the fatal day was at length unalterably fixed, we determined to elude the purpose of Don Diego by flight; and everything was actually prepared for our escape. When the hour of appointment arrived, I repaired to the place at which I had proposed to enter the house, and stumbled, in the dark, over the body of a man still warm, and bleeding. Alarmed at this occurrence, I darted myself through the window, and rushing to the apartment of the ladies, (immortal powers!) beheld the peerless Serafina, and her virtuous mother, stretched on a couch, and, in all appearance, deprived of life.

"The company will easily conceive what agonies I felt at such a spectacle! I ran towards the spot in a transport of horror! I clasped my lovely mistress in my arms, and, finding her still breathing, endeavoured, but in vain, to wake her from the trance Antonia was overwhelmed with the same lethargic power. My fancy was immediately struck with the apprehension of their being poisoned. Regardless of my own situation, I alarmed the family, called for assistance, and requested the servants to summon Don Diego to the dismal scene. I was informed that their master had rode forth in manifest confusion; and while I pondered on this surprising excursion, an apothecary in the neighbourhood entered the chamber, and having examined the pulses of the ladies, declared that their lives were in no danger, and advised that they should be undressed, and conveyed to bed. While their women were busied in this employment, I went into the court-yard, attended by some of the servants with lights, in order to view the body of the man which I had found at my arrival. His apparel was mean, his countenance ferocious; a long spado was buckled to his thigh, and, in his belt, were stuck a brace of loaded pistols; so that we concluded he was some thief, who had waited for an opportunity, and seeing the casement open, intended to rob the house, but was prevented, and slain by Don Diego himself, whose retreat, however, did not a little confound our conjecture. For my own part, I remained all night in the house, tortured with fear, vexation, and suspense.

"My hope was altogether disappointed by this unhappy accident; and I shuddered at the prospect of losing Serafina for ever, either by this mysterious malady, or by her marriage with Mendoza, which I now despaired of being able to defeat. The major-domo having waited several hours for his lord's return, without seeing him appear, thought proper to despatch a messenger to Don Manuel, with an account of what had happened; and that nobleman arriving in the morning, took possession of the house. About four o'clock in the afternoon, Serafina began to stir, and, at five, she and her mother were perfectly awake.

"They no sooner recovered the use of reflection, than they gave signs of equal sorrow and amazement, and earnestly called for Isabella, who was privy to our design, and who, after a very minute inquiry, was found in a lone and solitary chamber, where she had been confined. Such was the confusion of the house, that no person ever dreamed of asking how I entered, each domestic, in all probability, supposing I had been introduced by his fellow; so that I tarried unquestioned, on pretence of concern for the distress of a family in which I had been so generously entertained, and, by Isabella, sent my respects and duty to her ladies. She was, therefore, not a little surprised, when, after every other servant had withdrawn, she heard the lovely Serafina exclaim, with all the violence of grief, 'Ah! Isabella, Orlando is no more!' But their astonishment was still greater, when she assured them of my being alive, and in the house. They recounted to her the adventure of last night, which she explained, by informing them of the letters which Don Diego had intercepted. And they immediately concluded, that he had, in the precipitation of his wrath, killed, by mistake, the person who was found dead in the court-yard. This conjecture alarmed them on my account; they, by the medium of Isabella, conjured me to leave the house, lest Don Diego should return, and accomplish his resentment; and I was persuaded to withdraw, after I had settled the channel of a correspondence with the confidant.

"Being now obliged to alter our measures, because our former intention was discovered by Don Diego, I secured a retreat for Serafina and her mother, at the house of the English consul in Seville, who was my particular friend; and, next day, understanding from Isabella that her lord had not yet reappeared, and that Don Manuel was very urgent in his addresses, we concerted an assignation in the garden, and that same evening I was fortunate enough to convey my prize to the asylum I had prepared for their reception. Inexpressible was the rage of Mendoza, when he heard of their elopement. He raved like one deprived of reason—swore he would put all the servants of the family to the rack—and, in consequence of the intelligence he obtained by threats and promises, set on foot a very strict inquiry, in order to apprehend the fugitives and Orlando, who had by some means or other incurred his suspicion.

"We eluded his search by the vigilance and caution of our kind host; and, while we remained in concealment, were extremely astonished to hear that the unfortunate Don Diego was proclaimed a traitor, and a price set upon his head. This information overwhelmed us all with the utmost affliction. Antonia lamented, without ceasing, the disgrace of her beloved lord, from whom she never would have withdrawn herself, but with the lively hope of a reconciliation, after the first transports of his ire should have subsided, and the real character of Orlando should have appeared. It was not long before we had reason to believe that Mendoza was the accuser of Don Diego—

"Nay, start not, Signior; Manuel was actually that traitor! This was the turn of his revenge! when he found himself disappointed in the hope of possessing the incomparable Serafina, he took a base advantage of your absence and retreat. He posted to Madrid, impeached you to the secretary of state of having maintained a criminal correspondence with the enemies of Spain, included me in his accusation, as a spy for the house of Austria, and framed such a plausible tale, from the circumstances of your distress, that Don Diego was outlawed, and Mendoza gratified with a grant of his estate.

"These melancholy incidents made a deep impression upon the mind of the virtuous Antonia, who waiving every other consideration, would have personally appeared for the vindication of her husband's honour, had not we dissuaded her from such a rash undertaking, by demonstrating her inability to contend with such a powerful antagonist; and representing that her appearance would be infallibly attended with the ruin of Serafina, who would certainly fall into the hands of the villain to whom she had been contracted. We exhorted her to wait patiently for some happy revolution of fortune, and encouraged her with the hope of Don Diego's exerting himself effectually in his own defence.

"Meanwhile our worthy landlord was suddenly cut off by death; and his widow being resolved to retire into her own country, we secretly embarked in the same ship, and arrived in England about eighteen months ago. Antonia still continued to pine over the ruin of her house; as she could hear no tidings of Don Diego, she concluded he was dead, and mourned with unabating sorrow. In vain I assured her, that, soon as my own affairs should be adjusted, I would exert my whole endeavours to find and succour him. She could not imagine that a man of his spirit and disposition would live so long in obscurity. And her affliction derived new force from the death of the consul's widow, with whom she had lived in the most unbounded intimacy and friendship. From that day, her health evidently declined. She foresaw her dissolution, and comforted herself with the hope of seeing her husband and her friend in a place where no treachery is felt, and no sorrow is known; confident of my integrity, and the purity of my love, she, in the most pathetic terms, recommended Serafina to my care.

"Ha! weepest thou, fair excellence, at the remembrance of that tender scene, when the good Antonia, on the bed of death, joined thy soft hand to mine, and said, 'Renaldo, I bequeath this orphan to your love; it is a sacred pledge, which, if you cherish with due honour and regard, internal peace and happiness will ever smile within your bosom; but if you treat it with indifference, dishonour, or neglect, just Heaven will punish your breach of trust with everlasting disappointments and disquiet.'

"Signior Don Diego, I see you are moved, and therefore will not dwell on such distressful circumstances. The excellent Antonia exchanged this life for a more happy state; and so exquisite was the sorrow of the tender-hearted Serafina, as to torture me with the apprehension that she would not long survive her pious mother. How I obeyed the injunctions of that departing saint, Monimia (for that name she now assumed) can testify, until that artful serpent Fathom glided into our mutual confidence, abused our ears, poisoned our unsuspected faith, and effected that fatal breach, productive of all the misery and vexation which we have suffered, and which is now so happily expelled."

"Heaven," said the Castilian, "hath visited me for the sins and errors of my youth; yet, such mercy hath been mingled with its chastisements, I dare not murmur or repine. The tears of penitence and sorrow shall water my Antonia's grave; as for Mendoza, I rejoice at his treachery, by which the obligation of my promise is cancelled, and my honour fully acquitted. He shall not triumph in his guilt. My services, my character, and innocence shall soon confront his perfidy, and, I hope, defeat his interest. The King is just and gracious, nor is my family and name unknown."

Here the Jew interposing, presented to him a letter from a person of consequence at Madrid, whom Joshua had interested in the cause of Don Diego; that nobleman had already found means to represent the case of Zelos to his Majesty, who had actually ordered Don Manuel to be confined, until the injured person should appear to justify himself, and prosecute his accuser according to the terms of law. At the same time Don Diego was summoned to present himself before the King within a limited time, to answer to the charge which Mendoza had brought against him.

The Spaniard's heart overflowed with gratitude and joy, when he read this intimation; he embraced the Jew, who, before Zelos could give utterance to his thoughts, told him that the Spanish Ambassador at London, having been prepossessed in his favour, craved the honour of seeing Don Diego; and that he, Joshua, was ready to conduct him to the house.

"Then is my heart at rest!" cried the Castilian; "the house of Zelos once more shall lift up its head. I shall again revisit my native country with honour, and abase the villain who hath soiled my fame! O my children! this day is replete with such joy and satisfaction, as I did not think had been in the power of Heaven to grant, without the interposition of a miracle! To you, Renaldo, to you illustrious lady, and to these worthy gentlemen, am I indebted for the restoration of that for which alone I wish to live; and when my heart ceases to retain the obligation, may I forfeit the name of a Castilian, and scorn and dishonour be my portion."

Perhaps all Europe could not produce another company so happy as that which now sat down to dinner in the house of Madam Clement, whose own benevolent heart was peculiarly adapted for such enjoyment. The lovers feasted their eyes more than their appetite, by a tender intercourse of glances, which needed not the slow interpretation of speech; while the Spaniard regarded them alternately with looks of wonder and paternal joy, and every individual surveyed the all-deserving pair with admiration and esteem.

Serafina taking the advantage of this general satisfaction, when the heart, softened into complacency, deposits every violent thought: "I must now," said she, "try my interest with Renaldo. The good company shall bear witness to my triumph or repulse. I do not ask you to forgive, but to withhold your vengeance from the wretched Fathom. His fraud, ingratitude, and villany are, I believe, unrivalled; yet his base designs have been defeated; and Heaven perhaps hath made him the involuntary instrument for bringing our constancy and virtue to the test; besides, his perfidy is already punished with the last degree of human misery and disgrace. The doctor, who has traced him in all his conduct and vicissitudes of fortune, will draw a picture of his present wretchedness, which, I doubt not, will move your compassion, as it hath already excited mine."

The generous hostess was ready to enforce this charitable proposal with all her eloquence, when Melvil, with a look that well expressed his magnanimity of love, replied, "Such a boon becomes the gentle Serafina! O! every moment furnishes me with fresh matter to admire the virtues of thy soul. If thou, whose tender heart hath been so rent with misery and anguish, canst intercede for thy tormentor, who now suffers in his turn, shall I refuse to pardon the miserable wretch! No, let me glory in imitating the great example, and solicit Don Diego in behalf of the same miscreant whose perfidious barbarity cost him such intolerable woe." "Enough," cried the Castilian, "I have disclaimed the vindictive principles of a Spaniard; and leave the miserable object to the sting of his own conscience, which, soon or late, will not fail to avenge the wrongs we have sustained from his deceit."

CHAPTER SIXTY-SIX.
THE HISTORY DRAWS NEAR A PERIOD.

Universal was the applause which they acquired by this noble sacrifice of their resentment. The afternoon was spent in the utmost harmony and good-humour; and at the earnest solicitation of Renaldo, whose fancy still harboured the apprehensions of another separation, Don Diego consented that the indissoluble knot should be tied between that young gentleman and Serafina in two days, and the place appointed for the ceremony was the very church where they had been restored to the arms of each other.

The lovely bride, with a silent blush that set her lover's heart on fire, submitted to this determination, in consequence of which the company was bespoke for that auspicious hour, and the evening being pretty far advanced, they took leave of the ladies, and retired to their respective homes; Don Diego and his future son-in-law being reconducted to their lodgings, in the coach of the Jew, who, taking an opportunity of being alone with Melvil, observed that it would be necessary on this occasion to supply the Castilian with a sum of money, in order to support his dignity and independence, in furnishing Serafina with everything suitable to her rank and merit; and that he would willingly accommodate him, provided he knew how to propose it so as to give no offence to his punctilious disposition.

Renaldo, thanking him for this generous anticipation, advised him to solicit the Spaniard's correspondence in the way of business, and to put the whole on the footing of his own interest; by which means Don Diego's delicacy could sustain no affront. Fraught with this instruction, the Israelite desired a private audience of the Castilian, in which, after an apology for the freedom of his demand, "Signior Don Diego," said he, "as your fortune hath been so long embezzled by your adversary in Spain, and your correspondence with that country entirely cut off, it is not to be supposed that your finances are at present in such a condition as to maintain the splendour of your family. Count de Melvil's whole fortune is at your command; and had not he been afraid of giving umbrage to the peculiar delicacy of your sentiments, he would have pressed you to use it for your convenience. For my own part, over and above the inclination I have to serve Don Diego, I consult my own private advantage in desiring you to accept my service on this occasion. Money is the chief commodity in which I deal, and, if you honour me with your commands, I shall be a gainer by my obedience."

Don Diego replied, with a smile that denoted how well he understood the meaning of this address, "Surely, Signior, I am bound by the strongest ties to exert my utmost endeavours for your advantage; and I pray God this your proposal may have that issue. I am well acquainted with the Count's generosity and refined notions of honour; and too much obliged by him already, to hesitate with punctilious reserve in accepting his future assistance. Nevertheless, since you have contrived a scheme for removing all scruples of that sort, I shall execute it with pleasure; and, in the form of business, you shall have all the security I can give for what shall be necessary to answer my present occasions."

The preliminaries being thus settled, Joshua advanced for his use a thousand pounds, for which he would take neither bond, note, nor receipt, desiring only that the Castilian would mark it in his own pocket-book, that the debt might appear, in case any accident should befall the borrower. Although the Spaniard had been accustomed to the uncommon generosity of Melvil, he could not help wondering at this nobleness of behaviour, so little to be expected from any merchant, much less from a Jewish broker.

While this affair was on the anvil, Renaldo, who could no longer withhold the communication of his happiness from his sister and relations in Germany, took up the pen, and, in a letter to his brother-in-law, recounted all the circumstances of the surprising turn of fate which he had experienced since his arrival in England. He likewise related the story of Don Diego, informed them of the day appointed for his nuptials, and entreated the Major to make a journey to London with his wife; or, if that should be impracticable, to come as far as Brussels, where they should be met by him and his Serafina. There was now but one day between him and the accomplishment of his dearest wish, and that was spent in procuring a licence, and adjusting the preparations for the grand festival. Don Diego in the forenoon visited Madam Clement, to whom he repeated his warm acknowledgments of her bounty and maternal affection to his daughter, and presented to Serafina bank notes to the amount of five hundred pounds, to defray the necessary expense for her wedding ornaments.

All the previous steps being taken for the solemnisation of this interesting event, and the hour of appointment arrived, the bridegroom, accompanied by his father-in-law, hastened to the place of rendezvous, which was the vestry-room of the church we have already described; where they were received by the good clergyman in his canonicals; and here they had not waited many minutes, when they were joined by Madam Clement and the amiable bride, escorted by the friendly physician, who had all along borne such a share in their concerns. Serafina was dressed in a sack of white satin, and the ornaments of her head were adjusted in the Spanish fashion, which gave a peculiar air to her appearance, and an additional spirit to those attractions which engaged the heart of each beholder. There was nothing remarkable in the habit of Renaldo, who had copied the plainness and elegance of his mistress; but, when she entered the place, his features were animated with a double proportion of vivacity, and their eyes meeting, seemed to kindle a blaze which diffused warmth and joy through the countenances of all present.

After a short pause, her father led her to the altar, and gave her away to the transported Renaldo, before the priest who performed the ceremony, and bestowed the nuptial benediction on this enraptured pair. The sanction of the church being thus obtained, they withdrew into the vestry, where Melvil sealed his title on her rosy lips, and presented his wife to the company, who embraced her in their turns, with fervent wishes for their mutual happiness.

Though the scene of this transaction was remote from any inhabited neighbourhood, the church was surrounded by a crowd of people, who, with uncommon demonstration of surprise and admiration, petitioned Heaven to bless so fair a couple. Such indeed was their eagerness to see them, that some lives were endangered by the pressure of the crowd, which attended them with loud acclamations to the coach, after the bridegroom had deposited in the hands of the minister one hundred pounds for the benefit of the poor of that parish, and thrown several handfuls of money among the multitude. Serafina re-embarked in Madam Clement's convenience, with that good lady and Don Diego, while Renaldo, with the clergyman and doctor, followed in Joshua's coach, to a pleasant country-house upon the Thames, at a distance of a few miles from London. This the Jew had borrowed from the owner for a few days, and there they were received by that honest Hebrew, who had provided a very elegant entertainment for the occasion. He had also bespoke a small but excellent band of music, which regaled their ears while they sat at dinner; and the afternoon being calm and serene, he prevailed on them to take the air on the river, in a barge which he had prepared for the purpose.

But, notwithstanding this diversity of amusement, Renaldo would have found it the longest day he had ever passed, had not his imagination been diverted by an incident which employed his attention during the remaining part of the evening. They had drunk tea, and engaged in a party at whist, when they were surprised with a noise of contention from a public-house, that fronted the windows of the apartment in which they sat. Alarmed at this uproar, they forsook their cards, and, throwing up the casement, beheld a hearse surrounded by four men on horseback, who had stopped the carriage, and violently pulled the driver from his seat. This uncommon arrest had engaged the curiosity of the publican's family, who stood at the door to observe the consequence, when all of a sudden appeared a person in canonicals, well mounted, who, riding up to those who maltreated the driver, bestowed upon one of them such a blow with the butt-end of his whip, as laid him sprawling on the ground; and, springing from his saddle upon the box, took the reins into his own hand, swearing with great vehemence, that he would murder every man who should attempt to obstruct the hearse.

The good priest who had married Renaldo was not a little scandalised at this ferocious behaviour in a clergyman, and could not help saying aloud, he was a disgrace to the cloth when the horseman looking up to the window, replied, "Sir, may I be d—n'd, if any man in England has a greater respect for the cloth than I have; but at present I am quite distracted." So saying, he whipped up the horses, and had actually disentangled the hearse from those who surrounded it, when he was opposed by another troop, one of whom alighted with great expedition, and cut the harness so as that he could not possibly proceed. Finding himself thus driven to bay, he leaped upon the ground, and exercised his weapon with such amazing strength and agility, that several of his antagonists were left motionless on the field, before he was overpowered and disarmed by dint of numbers, who assailed him on all sides.

The mad parson being thus taken prisoner, an elderly person, of a very prepossessing appearance, went up to the hearse, and, unbolting the door, a young lady sprung out, and shrieking, ran directly to the public-house, to the infinite astonishment and affright of the whole family, who believed it was the spirit of the deceased person, whose body lay in the carriage. Renaldo, who was with difficulty restrained from interposing in behalf of the clergyman against such odds, no sooner perceived this apparition, than, supposing her to be some distressed damsel, his Quixotism awoke, he descended in an instant, and rushed into the house, among those that pursued the fair phantom. Don Diego and the physician took the same road, while the real clergyman and Joshua tarried with the ladies, who were, by this time, very much interested in the event.

Melvil found the young lady in the hands of the old gentleman, who had released her from the hearse, and who now bitterly upbraided her for her folly and disobedience; while she protested with great vivacity, that whatever she might suffer from his severity, she would never submit to the hateful match he had proposed, nor break the promise she had already made to the gentleman who now attempted to rescue her from the tyranny of a cruel father. This declaration was followed by a plentiful shower of tears, which the father could not behold with unmoistened eyes, although he reviled her with marks of uncommon displeasure; and turning to the Count, "I appeal to you, sir," said he, "whether I have not reason to curse the undutiful obstinacy of that pert baggage, and renounce her for ever as an alien to my blood. She has, for some months, been solicited in marriage by an honest citizen, a thirty thousand pound man; and instead of listening to such an advantageous proposal, she hath bestowed her heart upon a young fellow not worth a groat. Ah! you degenerate hussy, this comes of your plays and romances. If thy mother were not a woman of an unexceptionable life and conversation, I should verily believe thou art no child of mine. Run away with a beggar! for shame!"

"I suppose," replied Renaldo, "the person to whom your daughter's affection inclines, is that clergyman who exerted himself so manfully at the door?" "Clergyman!" cried the other, "adad! he has more of the devil than the church about him. A ruffian! he has, for aught I know, murdered the worthy gentleman whom I intended for my son-in-law; and the rogue, if I had not kept out of his way, would, I suppose, have served me with the same sauce. Me! who have been his master for many years, and had resolved to make a man of him. Sir, he was my own clerk, and this is the return I have met with from the serpent which I cherished in my bosom."

Here he was interrupted by the arrival of the citizen for whom he had expressed such concern; that gentleman had received a contusion upon one eye, by which the sight was altogether obstructed, so that he concluded he should never retrieve the use of that organ, and with great clamour took all the spectators to witness the injury he had sustained; he entered the room with manifest perturbation, demanded satisfaction of the father, and peremptorily declared it should not be a lost eye to him if there was law in England. This unseasonable demand, and the boisterous manner in which it was made, did not at all suit the present humour of the old gentleman, who told him peevishly he owed him no eye, and bade him go and ask reparation of the person who had done him wrong.

The young lady snatching this favourable occasion, earnestly entreated Melvil and his company to intercede with her father in behalf of her lover, who, she assured them, was a young gentleman of a good family, and uncommon merit; and in compliance with her request they invited him and his daughter to the house in which they lodged, where they would be disencumbered of the crowd which this dispute had gathered together, and more at leisure to consult about the measures necessary to be taken. The old gentleman thanked them for their courtesy, which he did not think proper to refuse, and while he led, or rather hauled Mademoiselle over the way, under the auspices of the Castilian, Renaldo set the lover at liberty, made him a tender of his good offices, and advised him to wait at the public-house for an happy issue of their negotiation.

The pseudo-parson was very much affected by this generous proffer, for which he made suitable acknowledgments, and protested before God he would die a thousand deaths rather than part with his dear Charlotte. Her father no sooner entered the apartment, than he was known by Joshua to be a considerable trader in the city of London, and the merchant was glad to find himself among his acquaintance. He was so full of the story which had brought him thither, that he had scarce sat down when he began to complain of his hard fate, in having an only child who was so mean, stubborn, and contumacious; and every sentence was concluded with an apostrophe of reproaches to the delinquent.

The Jew having allowed him to ring out his alarm, condoled his misfortune, and gravely counselled the young lady to wean her affections from such an unworthy object, for he supposed her favourite was a man of no principle, or liberal endowments, otherwise her father would not exclaim so bitterly against her conduct. Charlotte, who wanted neither beauty nor understanding, assured him that her lover's character was, in all respects, unblemished, for the truth of which assertion she appealed to her papa, who owned, with reluctance, that the young man was a gentleman by birth, that he had served him with remarkable diligence and integrity, and that his accomplishments were far superior to his station in life. "But then," said he, "the fellow has not a shilling of his own, and would you have me give away my daughter to a beggar?"

"God forbid!" cried the Jew, "I always understood you possessed an ample fortune, and am sorry to find it otherwise." "Otherwise!" cried the citizen, with some acrimony, "take care what you say, sir; a merchant's credit is not to be tampered with." "I beg your pardon," answered the Hebrew, "I concluded that your circumstances were bad, because you objected to the poverty of the young man after you had owned he was possessed of every other qualification to make your daughter happy; for it is not to be imagined that you would thwart her inclinations, or seek to render an only child miserable on account of an obstacle which you yourself could easily remove. Let us suppose you can afford to give with your daughter ten thousand pounds, which would enable this young man to live with credit and reputation, and engage advantageously in trade, for which you say he is well qualified, the alternative then will be, whether you would rather see her in the arms of a deserving youth whom she loves, enjoying all the comforts of life with a moderate fortune, which it will always be in your own power to improve, or tied for life to a monied man whom she detests, cursing her hard fate, and despising that superfluity of wealth, in spite of which she finds herself so truly wretched."

The old gentleman seemed to be startled at this observation, which was reinforced by Renaldo's saying, that he would, moreover, enjoy the unutterable pleasure of giving happiness to a worthy man, whose gratitude would co-operate with his love, in approving himself a dutiful son, as well as an affectionate husband. He then represented the family disquiets and dismal tragedies produced from such mercenary and compulsive matches, and, in conclusion related the story of Don Diego and his daughter, which when the merchant heard, he started up with marks of terror in his countenance, and, throwing up the casement, called upon Valentine with great vociferation. This was the name of his daughter's admirer, who no sooner heard the summons than he flew to the spot from whence it came, and the merchant, without any further preamble, seizing his hand, joined it with that of Charlotte, saying, with great trepidation, "Here, take her, in the name of God, and thank this honourable company for your good fortune."

The lovers were transported with exquisite joy at this sudden determination in their favour. Valentine, having kissed the hand of his mistress with all the eagerness of rapture, and acknowledged the merchant's generosity, paid his respects to the ladies with a very polite address, and with demonstrations of uncommon gratitude and sensibility, thanked the gentlemen, and the Count in particular, for their good offices, to which he attributed the happiness he now enjoyed. While Serafina and Madam Clement caressed the amiable Charlotte, the rest of the company congratulated her admirer upon his choice and success, though the clergyman could not help reprehending him for profaning the sacerdotal habit.

Valentine heartily asked pardon for having given such cause of offence, and hoped he should be forgiven, as it was a disguise which he thought absolutely necessary for the execution of a scheme upon which his happiness depended. He then, at the request of Renaldo, unfolded the mystery of the hearse, by giving them to understand that Charlotte's father having got inkling of their mutual passion, had dismissed his clerk, and conveyed his daughter to a country-house in the neighbourhood of London, in order to cut off their correspondence; notwithstanding these precautions they had found means to communicate with each other by letters, which were managed by a third person; and his rival being very importunate in his solicitations, they had concerted the expedient of the hearse, which he provided and conducted through a road contiguous to the end of the merchant's garden, where Charlotte, being apprised of the design, waited for its approach, and embarked in it without hesitation. Valentine thought himself sufficiently screened from discovery by his disguise, but he was unfortunately met by a servant of the family, who recollected his features, and immediately gave the alarm, upon which the father and his friends took horse, and pursued them by two different roads, until they were overtaken at this place.

He had scarce finished this short relation, when his rival, bluntly entering the apartment, with an handkerchief tied round his eye, committed Valentine to the charge of a constable, who attended him, by a warrant from a justice of the peace in that neighbourhood, and threatened to prosecute the merchant on an action of damages for the loss of an eye, which he said he had sustained in his service. The company endeavoured to appease this citizen, by representing that his misfortune was no other than a common inflammation, nor was it owing to malice aforethought, but entirely to the precipitate passion of an incensed young man, who, by the bye, acted in his own defence. At the same time the merchant promised to make any reasonable satisfaction, upon which the other demanded an obligation, importing that he would, in ten days from the date, bestow upon him his daughter in marriage, with a portion of fifteen thousand pounds, or, in case of failure, pay him double the sum.

The merchant, exasperated at this extravagant demand, told him flatly he had already disposed of his daughter to Valentine, who, he believed, was a much more deserving man, and that he was ready to wait upon the magistrate who had granted the warrant, in order to give bail for his future son-in-law. This was a mortifying declaration to the plaintiff, though he condoled himself with the hope of being a gainer by the loss of his eye, and now the pain was over would have been very sorry to find his sight retrieved. The old gentleman, Joshua, and Renaldo accompanied the prisoner to the house of the justice, where he was immediately admitted to bail. Upon their return Valentine shifted his dress, and they supped together with great cordiality and mirth, maintained at the expense of the discarded lover.

After supper Don Diego walked a minuet with Madam Clement; for whom, by this time, he had contracted an extraordinary degree of affection. Valentine had the honour to dance with the incomparable Serafina, whose beauty and attractions dazzled the eyes of the new-comers, and struck her bashful partner with awe and confusion; and Melvil presented his hand to the agreeable Charlotte, who performed so much to the satisfaction of her father, that he could not help expressing his joy and pride. He praised God for throwing him in the way of our company, and engaged the clergyman to unite the young couple, after having appointed a day for the ceremony, and invited all present to the wedding. The evening having been insensibly consumed in these avocations, and the night pretty far advanced, the ladies withdrew without ceremony; and the retreat of Serafina filled Renaldo's breast with tumult and emotion; his blood began to flow in impetuous tides, his heart to beat with redoubled vigour and velocity, while his eyes seemed to flash with more than human splendour. Now his imagination began to anticipate with the enthusiastic rage of an inspired sibyl; he was instantaneously transported from the conversation, and every nerve was braced to such a degree of impatience, that human nature could not long endure the tension.

He, therefore, having withstood the impulse about a quarter of an hour, at length gave way to his impetuosity, and, springing from his friends, found himself in a dark passage, at the farther end of which he perceived Madam Clement coming out of a chamber with a light, which, at sight of him, she set down, and vanished in a moment. This was the star that pointed to his paradise; he hailed the signal, entered the apartment, and, like a lion, rushing on his prey, approached the nuptial bed, where Serafina, surrounded by all the graces of beauty, softness, sentiment, and truth, lay trembling as a victim at the altar, and strove to hide her blushes from his view—the door was shut, the light extinguished—he owned his lot was more than mortal man could claim.

Here let me draw the decent veil that ought to shade the secret mysteries of Hymen. Away, unhallowed scoffers, who profane, with idle pleasantry or immodest hint, these holy rites; and leave those happy lovers to enjoy, in one another's arms, unutterable bliss, the well-earned palm of virtue and of constancy, which had undergone the most severe refinement. A more deserving pair night's curtain shrouds not in its dark extent.

The thoughts of Renaldo's felicity threw a damp on the spirits of Valentine, who saw the term of his probation protracted a few days longer, and could not help wishing in his heart that he had achieved the adventure which would have abridged his expectation, though at the expense of the old gentleman's displeasure. He filled a bumper to the health of the bride and bridegroom, and throwing up his eyes with marks of admiration, exclaimed, "How happy is the Count! alas! five days longer must I rein my impatience!" "It is but reasonable, you rogue, that your betters should have the start of you," said the merchant, who did him justice in the glass, and counselled him to drown his impatience with good claret. The youth followed his advice, and it was late before the company retired to rest.

These citizens, however, resolved to seize an opportunity of rallying the new-married couple, according to custom, and with that view arose early in the morning, on the supposition of finding them still asleep; but they were not a little surprised, when they entered the breakfasting room, to see Renaldo, and his amiable bed-fellow, already dressed, and awaiting to do the honours of the house. The old gentleman would fain have cracked a joke upon their extraordinary despatch, but he was so much overawed by the dignity and tamed by the sweetness of Serafina's carriage, that he durst not give utterance to his conception; and Valentine stood silent and abashed, as in the presence of a superior being. After breakfast these gentlemen and Charlotte again expressed their sense of the obligations they owed to this happy family, repeated their invitation, and, taking leave, returned to London in a coach that was provided overnight.

Our friends being thus left to themselves, Don Diego turned towards Melvil: "Now," said he, "that I have yielded to the impatience of your love, as well as to the eagerness of my own desire to make you happy, I must beg leave to interrupt, for a little while, the stream of your mutual pleasure, and propose a melancholy excursion, which, however, will not be wholly void of enjoyment. I have too long delayed the performance of my duty at Antonia's grave—let us spend the forenoon in that pious pilgrimage—I will drop a few tears to the memory of that excellent woman, and never afterwards shall my friends be troubled with my grief."

The proposal being universally approved, they set out for the place, which had oft been visited by the gentle Serafina, who conducted her father to a black marble stone, which Renaldo had ordered to be laid over the grave; and, as he kneeled to kiss the monument, he perceived this plain inscription in the Spanish tongue:—Antonia de Zelos primera en todo lo que es ser bueno, y sin segundo en todo lo que fue ser desdichado, quedad con Dios! that is, Antonia de Zelos, unmatched in virtue, and unequalled in misfortune, adieu! "O faithful record!" cried the Castilian, smiting his breast, while his tears distilled upon the marble, "thy goodness was the gift of Heaven, but thy misfortunes were derived from the guilt of Don Diego; yet his sorrow shall expiate his offence, and his penitence find favour in the sight of Heaven! Rest, rest, ill-fated virtue!—eternal peace shall guard thy tomb, and angels minister to thy unspotted shade; nor shall thine ashes lie in dark obscurity here will I raise a monument, more suited to thy excellence and name." Serafina melted with filial tenderness; nor were the rest unmoved at this affecting scene, which Don Diego did not quit without reluctance.

CHAPTER SIXTY-SEVEN.
THE LONGEST AND THE LAST.

The nature of this visit had softened every heart, and saddened every countenance; and they walked in solemn silence to the other side of the church-yard, in order to regain their carriages; when, at the turning of the stile, they saw a young woman, in wretched attire, running out of a poor habitation, wringing her hands in all the agony of despair. Notwithstanding the distraction in her countenance, and the meanness of her apparel, she discovered a regularity of features, and a delicacy of air, which did not at all correspond with the misery of her equipage. These exhibitions of extreme distress soon attracted the notice and compassion of our company, and Melvil's beauteous help-mate, accosting this forlorn damsel with a pity-breathing aspect, asked the cause of her disorder.

"Alas! dear lady," cried the other, with all the emphasis of woe, "an unhappy gentleman now breathes his last within this inhospitable hovel, amidst such excess of misery as would melt the most flinty bosom. What then must I feel, who am connected with him by the strongest ties of love and conjugal affection?" "Who is the unfortunate object?" said the physician. "He was once well known in the gay world," replied the young woman; "his name is Fathom." Every individual of the company started at mention of that detested name. Serafina began to tremble with emotion; and Renaldo, after a short pause, declared he would go in, not with a view to exult over his misery, but in order to contemplate the catastrophe of such a wicked life, that the moral might be the more deeply engraved on his remembrance. The young Countess, whose tender heart could not bear the shock of such a spectacle, retired to the coach with Madam Clement and the Jew, while Renaldo, accompanied by the rest, entered a dismal apartment, altogether void of furniture and convenience, where they beheld the wretched hero of these memoirs stretched almost naked upon straw, insensible, convulsed, and seemingly in the grasp of death. He was worn to the bone either by famine or distemper; his face was overshadowed with hair and filth; his eyes were sunk, glazed, and distorted; his nostrils dilated; his lips covered with a black slough; and his complexion faded into a pale clay-colour, tending to a yellow hue. In a word, the extremity of indigence, squalor, and distress could not be more feelingly represented.

While Melvil perused this melancholy lesson, and groaning, cried, "Behold the fate of man!" he perceived a letter in the right hand of the unfortunate Fathom, which lay fast clenched across his breast. Curious to know the contents of this paper, which the young woman said he had kept in that position for several days, he drew nearer the wretched couch, and was not a little surprised to see it addressed to the Right Honourable Renaldo Count de Melvil, to the care of Mr. Joshua Manesseh, merchant in London. When he attempted to disengage this billet from the author's hand, the sorrowing female fell upon her knees, entreating him to desist, and telling him, she had promised, upon oath, to communicate the contents to no person upon earth, but to carry the letter, upon her husband's decease, to the gentleman to whose care it was directed.

Renaldo assured her, upon his honour, that he was the very Renaldo Count de Melvil, for whom it was intended; and the young creature was so much confounded at this information, that, before she could recollect herself, Melvil had opened the billet, and read these words: "If this paper should fall into the hands of the noble Renaldo, he will understand, that Fathom was the most execrable traitor that ever imposed upon unsuspecting benevolence, or attempted to betray a generous benefactor. His whole life was a series of fraud, perfidy, and the most abominable ingratitude. But, of all the crimes that lay heavy upon his soul, his being accessory to the death of the incomparable Serafina, whose father he had also robbed, was that for which he despaired of Heaven's forgiveness, notwithstanding the dreadful compunction and remorse which have long preyed upon his heart, together with the incredible misery and deplorable death which by this time he hath undergone. Though these sufferings and sorrows cannot atone for his enormous guilt, perhaps they will excite the compassion of the humane Count de Melvil; at least, this confession, which my conscience dictates under all the terrors of death and futurity, may be a warning for him to avoid henceforth a smiling villain, like the execrable Fathom, upon whose miserable soul Almighty God have mercy."

Renaldo was deeply affected with the contents of this scroll, which denoted such horror and despair. He saw there could be no dissimulation or sinister design in this profession of penitence. He beheld the condition of the writer, which put all his humane passions in commotion; so that he remembered nothing of Fathom but his present distress. He could scarce maintain those indications which might have been justly deemed the effect of weakness and infirmity; and having desired the physician and clergyman to contribute their assistance for the benefit of that wretch's soul and body, he ran to the coach, and communicated the letter to the ladies; at the same time drawing a picture of the object he had seen, which brought tears into the eyes of the gentle Serafina, who earnestly entreated her lord to use his endeavours for the relief and recovery of the unhappy man, that he might, if possible, live to enjoy the benefit of mature repentance, and not die in that dreadful despair which he manifested in the letter.

Renaldo, returning to the house, found the pious clergyman reading prayers with great fervency, while Don Diego stood with his right hand upon his breast, looking steadfastly upon the agonising Fathom, and the young woman kneeled, with her streaming eyes lifted up to heaven, in an ecstasy of grief and devotion. The physician had run to an apothecary's shop in the neighbourhood, from whence he soon returned with an assistant, who applied a large blister to the back of the miserable patient, while the female, by the doctor's direction, moistened his mouth with a cordial which he had prescribed.

These charitable steps being taken, Count de Melvil entreated the apothecary's servant to procure a tent-bed for the accommodation of the sick person with all imaginable despatch; and, in less than an hour, one was actually pitched, and Fathom lifted into it, after he had been shifted, and in some measure purified from the dregs of his indigence. During this transaction the ladies were conducted to a tavern not far off, where dinner was bespoke, that they might be at hand to see the effect of their charity, which was not confined to what we have already described, but extended so far, that, in a little time, the apartment was comfortably furnished, and the young creature provided with change of apparel, and money to procure the necessaries of subsistence.

Notwithstanding all their care, the wretched Fathom still remained insensible, and the doctor pronounced a very unfavourable prognostic, while he ordered a pair of additional vesicatories to be laid upon his arms, and other proper medicines to be administered. After dinner, the ladies ventured to visit the place, and when Serafina crossed the threshold, the weeping female fell at her feet, and, kissing her robe, exclaimed, "Sure you are an angel from heaven."

The alteration in her dress had made a very agreeable change in her appearance, so that the Countess could now look upon her without shuddering at her distress. And, as Fathom was not in a condition to be disturbed, she took this opportunity of inquiring by what steps that unfortunate wretch was conveyed from the prison, in which she knew he had been confined, to the place where he now lay in such extremity; and by what occurrence he had found a wife in such an abyss of misfortune. Here the other's tears began to flow afresh. "I am ashamed," said she, "to reveal my own folly; yet I dare not refuse a satisfaction of this kind to a person who has laid me under such signal obligations."

She then proceeded to relate her story, by which it appeared, she was no other than the fair and unhappy Elenor, whom the artful Fathom had debauched upon his first arrival in town, in the manner already described in these memoirs. "Heaven," continued she, "was pleased to restore the use of my reason, which I had lost when I found myself abandoned by the Count; but, all my connexion with my own family being entirely cut off, and every door shut against a poor creature who could procure no recommendation, except the certificate signed by the physician of Bedlam, which, instead of introducing me to service, was an insurmountable objection to my character, I found myself destitute of all means of subsisting, unless I would condescend to live the infamous and wretched life of a courtezan, an expedient rendered palatable by the terrors of want, cooperating with the reflection of the irretrievable loss I had already sustained. I ask pardon for offending your chaste ears with this impure confession of my guilt, which, Heaven knows, I then did, and now do look upon with abhorrence and detestation. I had already forfeited my innocence, and wanted resolution to encounter misery and death. Nevertheless, before I could determine to embrace the condition of a prostitute, I was one day accosted in the Park by an elderly gentleman who sat down by me upon a bench, and, taking notice of the despondence which was evident in my countenance, pressed me to make him acquainted with the nature of my misfortune. So much sympathy and good sense appeared in his deportment and conversation, that I gratified his request, and he, in return for my confidence, saved me from the most horrible part of my prospect, by taking me into his protection, and reserving me for his own appetite. In this situation I lived a whole year, until I was deprived of my keeper by an apoplectic fit, and turned out of doors by his relations, who did not, however, strip me of the clothes and moveables which I owed to his bounty. Far from being as yet reconciled to a vicious life, I resolved to renounce the paths of shame, and, converting my effects into ready money, hired a small shop, and furnished it with haberdashery ware, intending to earn an honest livelihood by the sale of these commodities, together with the plain work in which I hoped to be employed so soon as my talents should be known. But this scheme did not answer my expectation. The goods spoiled upon my hands, and, as I was a stranger in the neighbourhood, nobody would intrust me with any other business. So that, notwithstanding the most parsimonious economy, I ran in debt to my landlord, who seized my effects; and an hosier, from whom I had received some parcels upon credit, took out a writ against me, by virtue of which I was arrested and imprisoned in the Marshalsea, where I found my first seducer. Good Heaven! what did I feel at this unexpected meeting, overwhelmed as I was before with my own distress! I with a loud scream fainted away, and, when I recovered, found myself in the arms of Mr. Fathom, who wept over me with great affliction. All his prospects of gaiety had now vanished, and his heart was softened by his own misfortunes, to a feeling of another's woe, as well as to a due sense of his own guilt. He expressed the deepest sorrow for having been the occasion of my ruin, endeavoured to comfort me with a promise of assistance, and indeed, by practising medicine among the prisoners, made shift to keep us both from starving. But surely no sinner underwent such severe remorse as that which he suffered during his imprisonment. From the day of our meeting, I never once saw him smile; a melancholy cloud continually overhung his countenance. He numbered the minutes by his groans, he used to start with horror from his sleep, and, striking his breast, would exclaim, 'O Elenor! I am the worst of villains!' Sometimes he seemed disordered in his brain, and raved about Renaldo and Monimia. In a word, his mind was in a dreadful situation, and all his agonies were communicated to me, whom by this time he had married, in order to make some atonement for my wrongs. Wretched as he then was, I remembered the accomplished youth who had captivated my virgin heart, the old impressions still remained, I saw his penitence, pitied his misfortune, and his wife being dead, consented to join his fate, the ceremony having been performed by a fellow-prisoner, who was in orders. Though his hard-hearted creditor had no other chance of being paid, than that of setting him at liberty, he lent a deaf ear to all our supplications; and this cruelty conspiring with the anguish of my husband's own reflection, affected his health and spirits to such a degree, that he could no longer earn the miserable pittance which had hitherto supported our lives. Then our calamities began to multiply. Indigence and famine stared us in the face; and it was with the utmost difficulty that we resisted their attacks, by selling or pledging our wearing apparel, until we were left almost quite naked, when we found ourselves discharged by an act passed for the relief of insolvent debtors. This charitable law, which was intended for a consolation to the wretched, proved to us the most severe disaster; for we were turned out into the streets, utterly destitute of food, raiment, and lodging, at a time when Mr. Fathom was so weakened by his distemper, that he could not stand alone. I supported him from door to door, imploring the compassion of charitable Christians, and was at length permitted to shelter him in this miserable place, where his disease gaining ground, he lay three days in that deplorable condition, from which he hath now been rescued, though I fear too late, by your humanity and benevolence."

She shed a flood of tears at the conclusion of this mournful tale, which did not fail to affect the whole audience, especially Serafina, who assured her, that, whatever should happen to her husband, she might depend upon finding favour and protection, provided her conduct should correspond with her professions. While this grateful creature kissed the hand of her kind benefactress, Fathom uttered a groan, began to stir in the bed, and with a languid voice called upon Elenor, who, instantly withdrawing the curtain, presented the whole company to his view. He had now retrieved the use of his perception by the operation of the blisters, which began to torture him severely; he looked around him with amazement and affright, and distinguishing the three persons against whom the chief arrows of his fraud and treachery had been levelled, he concluded that he was now arrived at the land of departed souls, and that the shades of those whom he had so grievously injured were come to see him tormented according to his demerits.

Fraught with this notion, which was confirmed by the bodily pain which he felt, and the appearance of the clergyman and Joshua, whom he mistook for the ministers of vengeance, he cried in a tone replete with horror, "Is there no mercy then for penitence? Is there no pity due to the miseries I suffered upon earth? Save me, O bountiful Heaven! from the terrors of everlasting woe; hide me from these dreadful executioners, whose looks are torture. Forgive me, generous Castilian. O Renaldo! thou hadst once a tender heart. I dare not lift my eyes to Serafina! that pattern of human excellence, who fell a victim to my atrocious guilt; yet her aspect is all mildness and compassion. Hah! are not these the drops of pity? Yes, they are the tears of mercy. They fall like refreshing showers upon my drooping soul! Ah, murdered innocence! wilt thou not intercede for thy betrayer at the throne of grace!"

Here he was interrupted by Melvil, who with a grave and solemn air pronounced, "Great hath been thy guilt, unhappy Ferdinand, and great have been thy sufferings. Yet we come not to insult, but to alleviate thy distress. Providence hath kindly defeated thy dire intentions, which we therefore now forgive and transmit to oblivion, whether it be thy lot to yield up thy spirit immediately, or to survive the dangerous malady with which thou art at present overwhelmed. Suffer not thyself to despair; for the mercy of Heaven is infinite; and submit to the directions of this worthy gentleman, who will employ his skill for thy recovery, while we shall take care to furnish thee with necessary attendance. As too much speaking may be prejudicial to thy health, I dispense with thy reply, and exhort thee to compose thyself to rest." So saying, he drew the curtain, and the company retired, leaving Fathom entranced with wonder.

The next step which Renaldo took for the benefit of this wretched penitent, was to send for the apothecary, with whom he left a sum of money to be expended for the convenience of Fathom and his wife; then he laid injunctions upon the physician to repeat his visits; and that gentleman, together with the clergyman and Joshua, taking leave of the others till next day, the Count set out with the ladies and his father-in-law to the house where they had lodged the preceding night.

The reader may well imagine the conversation of the evening turned wholly upon the strange occurrence of the day, which seemed to have been concerted by supernatural prescience, in order to satisfy the vengeance, and afford matter of triumph to the generosity of those who had been so grievously injured by the guilty Fathom. Though not one of them would say that such a miscreant ought to live, yet all concurred in approving the offices of humanity which had been performed, and even endeavoured to find specious pretext for vindicating their compassion. Don Diego said, it would ill become a transgressor like him to withhold his forgiveness from a sinner who had wronged him. Madam Clement appealed to the approbation of Heaven, which had undoubtedly directed them that way, for the purpose they had fulfilled. Serafina observed, that the crimes of the delinquent were obliterated by his sorrow, misery, and repentance. Renaldo honestly owned, that, exclusive of other reasons, he could not deny himself the luxurious enjoyment of communicating happiness to his fellow-creatures in distress; and each fervently prayed, that their charity might not be disappointed by the death of the object.

While they amused themselves in these discussions, Fathom, after having lain some hours silent, in consequence of Renaldo's advice, could no longer suppress the astonishment of his mind, but, addressing himself to his wife, "O Elenor!" said he, "my delirium is now past; though I still remember the phantasies of my distempered brain. Among other reveries, my imagination was regaled with a vision so perfect and distinct, as to emulate truth and reality. Methought Count de Melvil, Don Diego de Zelos, and the divine Serafina, the very persons who are now crying before the throne of Heaven for vengeance against the guilty Fathom, stood by my bedside, with looks of pity and forgiveness; and that Renaldo spoke peace to my despairing soul. I heard the words distinctly. I retain them in my memory. I saw the tears trickle from Serafina's eyes. I heard her father utter a compassionate sigh; and should actually believe that they were personally present, had not I long ago seen with my own eyes the funeral procession of that young lady, whose wrongs God pardon; and were I not convinced that such a meeting could not be effected without the immediate and miraculous interposition of Heaven. Yet everything I now see corresponds with the words of Renaldo, which still sound in my ears. When my perception forsook me, I lay in the most abject misery, among straw; and thou, poor injured innocence, wast naked and forlorn. Now, I find myself reposed in a warm, easy, comfortable bed. I see around me the marks of human charity and care, and the favourable change in thy appearance glads my poor dejected heart. Say, whence this happy alteration? Do I really awake from that dream of misery in which we have continued so long? or do I still utter the extravagant ravings of a distempered brain?"

Elenor was afraid of imparting at once all the particulars of the happy change he had undergone, lest they might leave a dangerous impression upon his fancy, which was not yet duly composed. She contented herself, therefore, with telling him, that he had been obliged to the humanity of a gentleman and lady, who chanced to pass that way by accident, and who, understanding his deplorable case, had furnished him with the conveniences which he now enjoyed. She then presented to him what the doctor had directed her to administer, and, admonishing him to commit his head to the pillow, he was favoured with a breathing sweat, fell fast asleep, and in a few hours waked again altogether cool and undisturbed.

It was upon this occasion that his wife explained the circumstances of that visit which had redeemed him from extremity of wretchedness and the jaws of death; upon which he started up, and throwing himself upon his knees, exclaimed, "All-gracious Power! this was the work of thy own bounteous hand; the voice of my sorrow and repentance hath been heard. Thou hast inspired my benefactors with more than mortal goodness in my behalf; how shall I praise thy name! how shall I requite their generosity! Oh, I am bankrupt to both! yet let me not perish until I shall have convinced them of my reformation, and seen them enjoying that felicity which ought to be reserved for such consummate virtue."

Next day, in the forenoon, he was visited by the physician, whom he now recollected to have seen at the house of Madam Clement; and, after having thanked that gentleman for his humanity and care, he earnestly begged to know by what means Serafina had been preserved. When he was satisfied in this particular, and given to understand that she was now happy in the arms of Renaldo, "Blessed be God!" he cried, "for having defeated the villany of him who sought to part such lovers. Dear sir, will you add one circumstance to your charity, and bear to that happy couple, and the noble Don Diego, the respects and the remorse of a sincere penitent, whom their compassion hath raised to life? I have been such a traitor to them, that my words deserve no regard. I will not therefore use professions. I dare not hope to be admitted into their presence. I am indeed ashamed to see the light of the sun. How then could I bear the looks of that injured family? ah, no! let me hide myself in some obscure retreat, where I may work out my salvation with fear and trembling, and pray incessantly to Heaven for their prosperity."

The physician promised to represent his contrition to the Count and his lady, and accordingly proceeded to their habitation, where he repeated these expressions, and pronounced his patient out of danger. So that their thoughts were now employed in concerting a scheme for his future subsistence, that he might not be exposed by indigence to a relapse in point of morals. Renaldo being still averse to any personal intercourse with such a wretch, until he should give some undoubted proofs of amendment, and, as yet afraid of intrusting him with any office that required integrity, resolved, with the approbation of all present, to settle him in a cheap county in the north of England, where he and his wife could live comfortably on an annuity of sixty pounds, until his behaviour should entitle him to a better provision.

This resolution was just taken, when Joshua arrived with a gentleman whom he introduced to Don Diego as the secretary of the Spanish ambassador. After the first compliments, the stranger told the Castilian, that he waited upon him at the desire of his Excellency, who would have come in person, had he not been confined by the gout. Then he put into his hand a letter from the court of

Madrid, written by a nobleman of Diego's acquaintance, who informed him, that Don Manuel de Mendoza having made away with himself by poison, in order to avoid the disgrace of a legal conviction, his Catholic Majesty was now convinced of Don Diego's innocence, and granted him leave to return and take possession of his honours and estate. This information was confirmed by the secretary, who assured him that the ambassador had orders to make him acquainted with this favourable decision of the King. The Castilian having first acquitted himself in the most polite terms to the secretary and the Jew, who, he said, had always been a messenger of glad tidings, communicated his happiness to the company; and this evening concluded the third day of their rejoicing.

Next morning Don Diego went to visit the ambassador, accompanied by Joshua and the secretary; while the physician, repairing to the habitation of Fathom, signified, by Renaldo's direction, the resolution which had been taken in his behalf; and the patient no sooner heard his doom, than, lifting up his hands, he cried, "I am unworthy of such tenderness and benevolence." While Elenor shed a flood of tears in silence, unable to give utterance to her grateful thought; Melvil's bounty having so far transcended her most sanguine hope.

The Spaniard having paid his devoirs to his Excellency, returned before dinner; and, in the afternoon, desiring a private conference with Serafina, they retired into another apartment, and he expressed himself to this effect: "You have contracted, my dear child, an habit of calling Madam Clement your mother, and doubtless, by her maternal tenderness and regard, she hath acquired a just title to the appellation. Yet I own I would fain strengthen it by a legal claim. I no sooner retrieved my daughter than I gave her away to the most deserving youth that ever sighed with love.—I rejoice in the gift which secured your happiness. But I left myself in a solitary situation, which even the return of my good fortune cannot render easy and supportable. When I revisit the Castle of Zelos, every well-known object will recall the memory of my Antonia, and I shall want a companion to fill her place, and to sympathise with me in that sorrow which will be derived from my remembrance. Who is there so worthy to succeed your mother in the affection of Don Diego, as she who interests her love for Serafina, and resembles her so strongly in every virtue of the sex? Similar attractions will produce similar effects. My heart is already attached to that good lady; and, provided Serafina shall approve of my choice, I will lay myself and fortune at her feet."

The fair Countess replied, with an enchanting smile, that, before this declaration, she had with pleasure perceived the progress which Madam Clement had made in his heart; and that she did not believe there was a person upon earth better qualified to repair the loss he had sustained; though she foresaw one obstacle to his happiness, which she was afraid would not be easily surmounted. "You mean," answered the Castilian, "the difference of religion, which I am resolved to remove by adopting the Protestant faith; though I am fully satisfied that real goodness is of no particular persuasion, and that salvation cannot depend upon belief, over which the will has no influence. I invest you, therefore, with the charge of declaring my passion and proposal, and empower you to satisfy her scruples with regard to the religion which I now profess, and which I shall not openly relinquish, until I shall have secured, in this country, effects sufficient to screen me from the ill consequences of my King's displeasure."

Serafina undertook this office with pleasure, because she had reason to think his addresses would not be disagreeable to Madam Clement; and that same night made the Count acquainted with the nature of her commission. Nor was her expectation disappointed. The French lady, with that frankness which is peculiar to virtue and good breeding, confessed that Don Diego was not indifferent to her choice, and did not hesitate in receiving him upon the footing of a lover. — As we have already dwelt circumstantially on the passion of love, so as perhaps even to have tired our readers, we shall not repeat the dialogue that passed, when the Spaniard was indulged with an opportunity to explain his sentiments. Suffice it to observe, that the lady's days of coquetry were now over, and that she was too wise to trifle with the time, which every moment became more and more precious. It was agreed then, that Don Diego should settle his affairs in Spain, and return to England, in order to espouse Madam Clement, with a view to fix his residence in this island, where Renaldo likewise proposed to enjoy the sweets of his fortune, provided he could draw hither his interests and connexions.

Meanwhile, having for some days enjoyed his bliss with all the fulness of rapture amidst this small but agreeable society, he shifted the scene, and conducted his dear partner to a ready-furnished house in town, which, together with an occasional equipage, his friend Joshua had hired for the accommodation of him and his father-in-law, who, during his stay in England, failed not to cultivate the mistress of his heart with the most punctual assiduity. Hitherto Serafina had been as a precious jewel locked up in a casket, which the owner alone had an opportunity to contemplate. But now the Count, who was proud of such a prize, resolved to let her shine forth to the admiration of the whole world. With this view he bespoke such ornaments as befitted her quality, and, while the mantua-makers were employed in her service, made a tour among his former acquaintance, and discharged the obligations under which he lay to some who had assisted him in his distress. He did not, however, introduce them to his charming Serafina; because not one of them had formerly treated her with that delicacy of regard which he thought her due; and some of them were much mortified at their neglect, when they saw what a dazzling figure she made in the beau monde.

She was visited by the Spanish and Imperial ambassadors, and divers other foreigners of distinction, to whom Melvil had letters of recommendation. But her first public appearance was in a box at the opera, accompanied by Madam Clement, the Count, and Don Diego. The entertainment was already begun, so that her entrance had the greater effect upon the audience, whose attention was soon detached from the performance, and riveted upon this amiable apparition, which seemed to be some bright being of another world dropped from the clouds among them. Then did the spirit of curiosity play its part. A thousand whispers circulated; as many glasses were exalted to reconnoitre this box of foreigners; for such they concluded them to be from their appearance. Every male spectator acknowledged Serafina to be the paragon of beauty; and every female confessed, that Melvil was the model of a fine gentleman. The charms of the young Countess did not escape the eye and approbation of royalty itself; and when her rank was known, from the information of the ambassadors and other people of condition who were seen saluting her at a distance, that same evening a thousand bumpers were swallowed in honour of the Countess de Melvil. The fame of her beauty was immediately extended over this immense metropolis, and different schemes were concerted for bringing her into life. These, however, she resisted with unwearied obstinacy. Her happiness centred in Renaldo, and the cultivation of a few friends within the shade of domestic quiet. She did not even forget the concerns of the wretched Fathom and his faithful Elenor, who daily enjoyed fresh instances of her humanity and care. When his fever forsook him, he was supplied with nourishing food for the recovery of his health; and as soon as he found himself in a condition to travel, he gave notice to his benefactor, who desired Joshua to settle with him the manner in which he was to receive his allowance, and to pay the first half-year's salary per advance.

This affair being adjusted, and the place of his retreat signified, the Jew told Elenor, that she might wait upon the Countess before their departure; and she did not fail to make use of this permission. After they had made the necessary preparations for their journey, and taken places in the York stage-coach, Mrs. Fathom, clothing herself in decent apparel, went to the house of Count Melvil, and was immediately admitted to the presence of Serafina, who received her with her usual complacency, enriched her with salutary advice, comforted her with the hope of better things, provided her conduct and that of her husband should henceforth be found irreproachable; and, wishing her peace and happiness, presented her with a box of linen, and twenty guineas in a purse. Such excessive goodness overpowered this sensible young woman to such a degree, that she stood before her in speechless awe and veneration; and the Countess, in order to relieve her from the confusion under which she suffered, quitted the room, leaving her to the care of her woman. It was not long, however, before her gratitude broke out in loud exclamations and a violent passion of tears, which all her efforts could not, for a while, overcome. By this time the coach was brought up to the gate for the reception of Serafina, who took an airing every day at the same hour; when Renaldo, leading her to the vehicle, beheld a man plainly dressed standing within the court, with his head and body bent towards the earth, so that his countenance could not be perceived.

Melvil, who supposed him to be some unfortunate man come to implore his charity, turned towards him, and asked with a humane accent, if he wanted to speak with any person in the house? To this interrogation the stranger replied, without lifting up his head, "Overwhelmed as I am with Count Melvil's generosity, together with a consciousness of my own unworthiness, it ill becomes a wretch like me to importune him for further favour; yet I could not bear the thought of withdrawing, perhaps for ever, from the presence of my benefactor, without soliciting his permission to see his face in mercy, to acknowledge my atrocious crimes, to hear my pardon confirmed by his voice, and that of his accomplished Countess, whom I dare not even at a distance behold; and to express my fervent wish for their prosperity."

Melvil, whose heart was but too tender, could not hear this address without emotion. He recognised the companion of his infancy and youth; he remembered the happy scenes he had enjoyed with Fathom, whose voice had always such an effect upon his ear, as to excite the ideas of friendship and esteem; and he was disturbed by this unexpected meeting, which also discomposed the beauteous Serafina. Renaldo having paused a little, "It is with pain," said he, "I recollect anything to the prejudice of Fathom, whose future behaviour will, I hope, erase the memory of his offences, and justify what other steps I may take in his favour. Meanwhile, I heartily forgive what is past; and, in token of my sincerity, present my hand;" which our adventurer bathed with his tears. The Countess, whose mind was in unison with her husband, repeated her assurances of pardon and protection; at which the penitent rejoiced in silence, while he raised his head and took a parting view of those charms which had formerly enslaved his heart.

Having thus obeyed the dictates of his duty and inclination, he next morning embarked in the stage-coach, with his faithful Elenor, and in six days arrived at the place of his retreat, which he found extremely well adapted to the circumstances of his mind and fortune. For all his vice and ambition was now quite mortified within him, and his whole attention engrossed in atoning for his former crimes, by a sober and penitent life, by which alone he could deserve the uncommon generosity of his patrons.

While he thus accommodated himself to his new system, Renaldo received letters of congratulation from his sister, who with the Major had come to Brussels, in order to meet her brother and Serafina, according to his proposal.

This intimation being communicated to Don Diego, he resolved to accompany them to Flanders, on his way to Spain. Preparations were made for their departure; the clergyman and physician were honoured with valuable marks of friendship and esteem from the Countess, Renaldo, and the Castilian, who were convoyed to Deal by Madam Clement, to whom, at parting, Don Diego presented a diamond ring, as a pledge of his inviolable love.

Here the travellers hired a vessel for Ostend, which they reached in a few hours; in two days more they arrived at Brussels, where Mrs. Farrel and her husband were struck with admiration at the surprising beauty and accomplishment of their sister-in-law, whom they caressed with equal tenderness and joy.—In a word, all parties were as happy as good fortune could make them; and Don Diego set out for Spain, after they had agreed to reside in the Low Countries till his return.